BOLLINGEN SERIES XXX

PAPERS FROM THE ERANOS YEARBOOKS

Edited by Joseph Campbell

Selected and translated from the *Eranos-Jahrbücher*
edited by Olga Froebe-Kapteyn

VOLUME 3

Man and Time

PAPERS FROM THE ERANOS YEARBOOKS

Henry Corbin • Mircea Eliade • C. G. Jung • Max Knoll
G. van der Leeuw • Louis Massignon • Erich Neumann
Helmuth Plessner • Adolf Portmann • Henri-Charles Puech
Gilles Quispel • Hellmut Wilhelm

BOLLINGEN SERIES XXX • 3

PRINCETON UNIVERSITY PRESS

Published by Princeton University Press

Second Printing, 1973

First Princeton / Bollingen Paperback printing, 1983

THIS IS THE THIRD VOLUME
OF PAPERS SELECTED FROM THE ERANOS YEARBOOKS.
THESE VOLUMES OF SELECTIONS CONSTITUTE NUMBER XXX
IN BOLLINGEN SERIES, SPONSORED BY BOLLINGEN FOUNDATION

These papers were originally published in French or German in *Eranos-Jahrbücher* XVII (1949) and XX (1951) by Rhein-Verlag, Zurich, Switzerland

Library of Congress Catalog Card No. 72-1982

ISBN 0-691-09732-1
ISBN 0-691-01857-X pbk.

Manufactured in the United States of America

Translated by

Ralph Manheim

except for the paper by C. G. Jung

which was translated by

R. F. C. Hull

The papers by Max Knoll and Hellmut Wilhelm
have been revised by their authors in English
with the collaboration of Ximena de Angulo

NOTE OF ACKNOWLEDGMENT

Grateful acknowledgment is made to the following publishers for permission to quote as indicated: Mr. Tönnes Kleberg, President of the Ekmanska Fonden, Uppsala University Library, for a passage from *Studies in the Coptic Manichaean Psalm-Book,* edited by T. Säve-Söderbergh; Henry Holt, New York, for quotations from the Savill translation of Hesse's *Magister Ludi;* Alfred A. Knopf, Inc., New York, and Secker & Warburg, London, for passages from Thomas Mann's *The Magic Mountain* and *The Tales of Jacob;* W. W. Norton and Co., Inc., New York, and the Hogarth Press, London, for passages from Rilke's *Duino Elegies* in the Leishman and Spender translation; and Sheed and Ward for quotations from *The Confessions of St. Augustine* in the translation of F. J. Sheed, copyright 1943.

The advice and assistance of Mrs. Cary F. Baynes, Dr. L. d'Azambuja, Dr. Susan K. Deri, Dr. E. W. Eschmann, and Jackson Mathews are gratefully acknowledged.

Acknowledgment is gratefully made to Alice Dunn for reference to her translation of Jung's "On Synchronicity" published in *Spring.*

CONTENTS

CONTENTS

LIST OF PLATES

EDITOR'S FOREWORD

The Eranos Meeting of 1951 seemed to many of those who attended to mark a fresh stage in the development of this common enterprise, which, since its inception in 1933, has been continued every summer at the home of Frau Olga Froebe-Kapteyn, on the shore of Lake Maggiore, near Ascona, Switzerland. As in the old Indo-Āryan myth of the Churning of the Milky Ocean, where the gods and demons took the World Mountain for their churning rod and the World Serpent for their string, wrapped the serpent around the mountain, and—gods tugging at the head end, demons at the tail—churned for a thousand years to produce the Butter of Immortality from the inexhaustible depths, so here, the relentless work has brought up remarkable gifts. The points of view represented are too numerous, however, to permit of any simple classification of the participants according to what I presume are now the archaic categories of "gods" and "demons." Any mind sympathetically following the pell-mell of their arguments cannot but lose momentarily (and, in fortunate cases, forever) those old sureties that once enabled the learned to tell us precisely where hell is and where heaven. The meetings are festivals of emergent visions, and those who return from them with precisely and only the visions of the world that they brought with them must have hardy god's and devil's minds indeed.

The sureties were particularly well pulverized in the meeting of 1951, which was devoted to the mystery of Man and Time: a subject nicely calculated to make difficult the maintenance of any footing whatsoever. "What is time? When you do not ask me, I know; but when you ask me, I no longer know." The differing intuitions of man's relationship to this mystery, as rendered in the Chinese *Book of Changes* and the Indian concept of *māyā,* the Greek *aeon* and the Judeo-Christian notion of God's personal interest in the course of history, the Gnostic idea—so close to the Indian—of the mutual exclusion of Eternity and Space-Time, and the various inflections of all of these themes in the rich traditions of Islam, here appear in a fluctuating relationship to a number of points of view stemming from the laboratories of modern science; and in the end, one hardly knows how much of the old has been vaporized as dream and how much brought back to us again as dawning insight. Our minds at this meeting were prodigiously churned.

We have therefore taken as our base for the present volume of translated selections from the *Eranos-Jahrbücher* the bulk of the papers of that notable year; and have added only one contribution from an earlier meeting, namely that of the late Gerardus van der Leeuw, who, standing in his long and productive life as teacher and scholar perfectly balanced in this point of time between two eras, brought to Eranos the inspiration of his warm friendship as well as learning. His moving discourse on "Primordial Time and Final Time" was the opening paper of the meeting on Man and the Mythical World, held in the summer of 1949. It was his last contribution to the "shared feast" of Eranos and here supplies a fitting *envoi* to the meditations of his friends who in 1951 were still facing the mystery that he had already left behind.

For her selection and organization of the papers presented in the present volume, I am again grateful to Frau Olga Froebe-Kapteyn. It is an evocative representation of the spirit of that co-operative international enterprise of which she has been the guiding genius these many years. I must also thank Professor Henry Corbin for his generous contribution of a Preface, setting forth for those who have not had the privilege of attending any of the meetings a suggestion of the place that Eranos holds in the life and thought of one of its leading contributors. And once again I express to the members of the Bollingen Series editorial staff my sincere appreciation for their loyal and tireless attention to all the work of editorial detail.

JOSEPH CAMPBELL

THE TIME OF ERANOS

Possibly in a century or two, perhaps a little less or a little more, some historian of ideas, if any historians of ideas are still left, or some student with a thesis to write will find an ideal subject for a monograph in the phenomenon of Eranos in the twentieth century. And perhaps his monograph will turn out to be like so many others that, ever since the rise of historical criticism, have been devoted to the "schools," the "ideological currents" of the past, demonstrating their "causes," explaining their "influences," the "migrations of themes," and so on.

But it is to be feared that, if he in his turn is content to do no more than to apply a scientific method which will have had all the virtues, except the primary virtue that would have consisted in establishing its object by recognizing the way it gives its object to itself—it is to be feared that our future historian will completely miss the phenomenon of Eranos. He will perhaps believe that he has "explained" it by a profound and ingenious dialectic of causes. But he will not have divined that the real problem would have been to discover not *what* explains Eranos, but *what* Eranos *ex-plains* by virtue of what it *im-plies:* for example, the idea of a true community, bringing together speakers and listeners, a community so paradoxical that it displays none of the characteristics that are of concern to statistics and sociology.

This is why, if the eventuality of our future historian is forecast here, the forecast is made from no vanity of an expected fame, but rather in fear that the soul of Eranos may one day be lost in such a venture. Had he not felt this fear, he to whom it has fallen to play a soloist's role at the beginning of the present volume would have hesitated thus to step out from the chorus of his confrères. But he has become convinced of one thing. This whole volume is devoted to the question of Time, which each of us has envisaged from the angle of his habitual meditations. Now, if it is true that,

---

Translated from the French by Willard R. Trask.

while they explain things and beings by their time, historians as such are not in the habit of beginning by reflecting on the nature of historical time, the theme of this volume perhaps contains the best warning against the dubious formula that would try to explain Eranos "by its time."

It would be well to meditate on the possible meaning of these words: *the time of Eranos.* For it will be no explanation of Eranos to say that it was "very much of its time," that is, of everybody's time, in accordance with the formula that is so soothing to alarmed or hasty conformisms. Nothing indicates that Eranos ever tried to "be of its time." What, on the contrary, it will perhaps have succeeded in doing is to *be its time,* its own time. And it is by being its own time that it will have realized its own *meaning,* willingly accepting the appearance of being untimely. It is not certain things that give its meaning to Eranos; rather, it is Eranos that gives their meaning to these other things. How, then, are we to conceive the proposition that it is not by "being of our time," as so many well-meaning people say, but by ourselves being our own time, that each of us explains and fulfills his own meaning? Can this be suggested in a brief summary?

To return to our hypothetical future historian: why, undertaking to explain Eranos by the circumstances, the "currents" and "influences" of the period, would he miss its meaning and its essence, its "seminal reason"? For the same reason, for example, that the first and last explanation of the various gnostic families referred to in the present book is those gnostics themselves. The historian may suppose every kind of favorable circumstances, draw all possible conclusions, he would be merely reasoning *in vacuo* if there were not the first and signal *fact* of gnostic minds. It is not the "main currents" that evoke them and bring them together; it is they that decree the existence of a particular current and bring about their own meeting.

Probably, then, the word "fact," as just used, does not signify quite what our current speech commonly means by the word; rather, it signifies what current speech makes its opposite, when it distinguishes between persons and facts, men and events. For us, the first and last *fact,* the initial and final event, are precisely these persons, without whom there could never be anything that we call "event." Hence we must reverse the perspectives of the usual optics, substitute the hermeneutics of the human individual for the pseudodialectic of facts, which today is accepted, everywhere and by everyone, as objective evidence. For it was only by submitting to the "necessity of the facts" that it became possible to imagine in them an autonomous causality that "explains" them. Now, to explain does not yet necessarily mean to "understand." To understand is, rather, to "imply." There is no explaining the initial fact of which we are speaking, for it is individual and singular, and the individual can be neither deduced nor explained; *individuum est ineffabile.*

On the contrary, it is the individual who explains very many things to us, namely all the things that he *implies* and that would not have existed without him, if he had not begun to be. For him to explain them to us, we must understand him, and to understand is to perceive the *meaning* of the thing itself, that is, the manner in which its presence determines a certain constellation of things, which hence would have been entirely different if there had not first been this presence. This is a very different matter from deducing the thing from assumed causal relations, that is, from taking it back to something other than itself. And it is doubtless here that the reader will most readily mark the contrast with our current modes of thought, those represented by all the attempts toward philosophies of history or toward the socialization of consciousnesses: anonymity, depersonalization, the abdication of the human will before the dialectic net that it began to weave itself, only to fall into its own snare.

What concretely exists is wills and relations between wills: failing will, imperious or imperialistic will, blind will, will serene and conscious of itself. But these wills are not abstract energies. Or rather, they are and designate nothing but the willing subjects themselves, the subjects whose real existence postulates that we recognize the individual, and the individual as the first and only concrete reality. I should gladly admit that I am here in affinity with an aspect of Stoic thought,* for is not one of the characteristic symptoms in the history of philosophy in the West precisely the overshadowing of the Stoic premises by the dialectic that derived from Peripateticism? Stoic thought is hermeneutic; it would have resisted all the dialectical constructions that burden our most current representations: in history, in philosophy, in politics. It would not have surrendered to the fiction of "main currents," the "meaning of history," "collective wills," of which, moreover, no one can say exactly what their mode of being may be.

For the fact is that, outside of the first and final reality, the individual,

* See Victor Goldschmidt's excellent book *Le Système stoïcien et l'idée du temps* (Paris, 1953).

there are only ways of being, in relation to the individual himself or in relation to what surrounds him; and this means *attributes* that have no substantial reality in themselves if they are detached from the individual or individuals who are their agents. What we call "events" are likewise the attributes of acting subjects; they are not beings but ways of being. As actions of a subject, they are expressed in a verb; now, a verb acquires meaning and reality only from the acting subject who conjugates it. Events, psychic or physical, do not assume existence, do not "take shape," except through the reality that realizes them and from which they derive; and this reality is the acting individual subjects, who conjugate them "in their tense," "in their time," give them their own tense and time, which is always essentially the present tense and time.

Hence, detached from the real subject who realizes them, facts, events, are merely something *unreal.* This is the order which had to be inverted to alienate the real subject: to give, instead, all reality to facts, to speak of the laws, the lesson, the materiality of facts, in short, to let ourselves be trapped in the system of unrealities that we have ourselves constructed and whose weight falls on us in turn in the form of history, as the only scientific "objectivity" that we can conceive, as the source of a causal determinism the idea of which would never have occurred to a humanity that had preserved the sense of the real subject. Detached from the real subject, facts "pass away." There is past, and there is past that has been "passed beyond," "transcended." Hence the resentment against the yoke of the past, the illusions of progressivism, and, conversely, the complexes of reaction.

Yet *past* and *future* are themselves attributes expressed by verbs; they presuppose the subject who conjugates those verbs, a subject for whom and by whom the only existing tense and time is the *present,* and on each occasion the present. Thus dimensions of the past and future are also, on each occasion, measured and conditioned by the capacity of the subject who perceives them, by his instant. They are dimensional to that person, for it depends upon him, on the scope of his intelligence and his largeness of heart, to embrace the whole of life, *totius vitae cursum,* to totalize, to imply in himself, all worlds, by falling back to the farthest limit of the dimension of his present. This is to *understand,* and it is a totally different matter from constructing a dialectic of things that have ceased to exist in the past. It is "interpreting" the *signs,* explaining not material facts but ways of being, that reveals beings. Hermeneutics as science of the individual stands in opposition to historical dialectics as alienation of the person.

Past and future thus become *signs,* because a sign is perceived precisely *in the present.* The past must be "put in the present" to be perceived as "showing a sign." (If the wound, for example, is a sign, it is so because it indicates not that such and such a one *has been* wounded, in an abstract time, but that he *is* having been wounded.) The genuine transcending the past can only be "putting it in the present" as *sign.* And I believe it can be said that the entire work of Eranos is, in this sense, a *putting in the present.* Neither the contents of this book, nor that of all the other volumes previously published, offer the character of a simple historical dictionary. All the themes treated acquire the value of *signs* in them. And if it is true that, even at some future date, the act of Eranos, whose initiative has persisted for twenty-five years, could not be explained simply by deducing it from the circumstances that would justify the historian in saying that it was "very much of its time," this is because Eranos is itself a *sign.* It cannot now or in future be understood unless it is interpreted as a *sign,* that is, as a presence that ceaselessly and on each occasion puts "in the present." It *is* its time because it puts in the present, just as each acting subject *is* his time, that is, a presence that puts in the present whatever is related to it. An active presence does not fall "into its time," that is, it is not "of its time" in the sense of the oversimple theory that thinks it explains a being by situating it in an abstract time which is "everybody's" time and hence no one's.

In short, the whole contrast lies here. With *signs,* with hierophanies and theophanies, there is no making history. Or rather, the subject that is at once the organ and the *place* of history is the concrete psychological individuality. The only "historical causality" is the relations of will between acting subjects. "Facts" are on each occasion a *new creation;* there is discontinuity between them. Hence to perceive their connections is neither to formulate laws nor to deduce causes, but to understand a *meaning,* interpret *signs,* a composite structure. So it was fitting that C. G. Jung's study of synchronicity should be the center of the present book, since that study is itself the center of a new problematics of time. To perceive a causality in "facts" by detaching them from persons is doubtless to make a philosophy of history possible; it is to affirm dogmatically the rational meaning of history on which our contemporaries have built up a whole mythology.

But it is likewise to reduce real time to abstract physical time, to the essentially *quantitative* time which is that of the objectivity of mundane calendars from which the *signs* that gave a sacred qualification to every present have disappeared.

It remains for us to gain a better awareness of the abdication of the subject who thus alienates himself in objective history. The first step will necessarily have been ceasing to perceive events on the plane of *signs* and putting them on the plane of *data*. It is in this way that signs have been laicized. But our entire theology will, by an unconscious and fatal complicity, itself have had to prepare the laicization of which it is the victim. The meaning of history: no longer need a God be born in the flesh to reveal it. A textbook philosophy claims to be in possession of it and to impose it, because that philosophy is after all only a lay theology of the social incarnation.

The caricature of our own Image (Ivan Karamazov seeing himself in the looking glass) fills us with all the more terror because we have nothing to oppose to it except precisely our own features, which it mirrors to us in caricature. Now, it is impossible to compete with and against a scientific, materialistic, and atheistic socialization by a conformism of well-meaning people who can find no justification for their being except in their social activity nor any foundation for their knowledge except the "social sciences." The *no* that must be cried aloud proceeds from a different imperative. It draws its energy from the lightning flash whose vertical joins heaven with earth, not from some horizontal line of force that loses itself in a limitlessness from which no meaning arises. For what is called "evolution" would have *meaning* only on the cosmic scale; but our philosophers are too serious to make themselves responsible for the curiosity that is, at most, excusable in Gnostics and Orientals.

And yet, will the reader be so good as to consider for a moment the signature at the end of these few pages? Together with the name of a place, it comprises a double date incorporating three calendars: a date of the Christian era, an Iranian date in which the official name of the month corresponds to that of the ancient pre-Islamic Persian calendar, while the year is that of the solar Hegira (all the rest of Islam, outside of Persia, reckons in lunar years). This is a mere example. Is it to be supposed that putting these eras in correspondence, putting them together "in the present," conjugating them in the present, can result from a simple mathematical equation, with the aid of a table of correspondences? The answer will be *yes,* if one is naïve enough to suppose that all human beings everywhere are of the same age, have the same desires, the same aspirations, the same sense of responsibility, and that good-will and proper hygiene would suffice to bring them into accord in the frame of abstract objective time, the uniform mathematical time of universal history.

But the answer will certainly be *no,* if one has an acute awareness of differences, a concern for the rights of pluralism against all monism, whether a well-intentioned or a brutal and unavowed monism. What is in question is a relation between *qualitative times*. The Occidental may be much the elder, and he may often be younger than the Oriental, according to the realms in which they meet. But it is perhaps also true that only the Occidental is able to secrete the antidote, and to help the Oriental to surmount the spiritual crisis that the impact of the West has provoked in him, and which has already forever ruined several traditional civilizations.

This simple example suggests the true task of which we have perhaps not yet even begun to be aware. It is a matter of perceiving the same *signs* together; it is a matter of each one of us on each occasion interpreting them according to the meaning of his own being, but it is also a matter of constituting a harmonious hermeneutics of signs, as once the fourfold and sevenfold meanings of the Scriptures were in harmony. To accomplish this, there must be no more escaping into an abstract time, the time of anonymous collectivities; there must be a rediscovery of concrete time, the time of persons. And this, at bottom, is only opening the living spring of unconditioned *sympathy,* the sympathy that, existing before our deliberate and conscious purpose, causes the grouping of human beings and alone makes them "contemporaries."

What we should wish to call the *meaning* of Eranos, which is also the entire secret of Eranos, is this: it is our present being, the time that we act personally, our way of being. This is why we are perhaps not "of our time," but are something better and greater: we are our time. And this is why Eranos has not even an official denomination nor any collective name. It is neither an academy nor an institute, it is not even something that, in the fashion of the day, can be designated by initials. No, it is really not a phenomenon "of our time." And this is why it is likely to confound the future dialectical and deductive historian. It will not even interest the devotees of statistics, the probers into opinion.

If curves and graphs are demanded at any cost, I can suggest only one reference: the great planisphere that Dr. Daniel Brody, our courageous publisher, had the idea of displaying on the walls of the exhibition commemorating the twentieth anniversary of the *Eranos-Jahrbuch* in the offices of the Rhein-Verlag, at Zurich. It was a planisphere scored by lines in many colors, all meeting at the same center: an invisible point on the vast map, Ascona, on the shore of Lake Maggiore. The uninitiate would at once have supposed it something familiar—curves indicating airplane routes, the great lines of traffic. Nevertheless it expressed nothing of the kind, but simply the journey that each one of us had taken, from various points in the world, to the center that unites us. The lines had no statistical meaning: they were signs, the sign made *to* each of us, and *by* each of us.

The result of the response to that sign was the meeting of acting, autonomous individualities, each in complete freedom revealing and expressing his original and personal way of thinking and being, outside of all dogmatism and all academicism; a constellation of those wills, and a constellation of the worlds that they bring with them, that they have taken in charge by putting them into the present, the present of Eranos. A composite whole, a structure, not a result conditioned by the laws of the period or by fashionable crazes, but a whole made strong by its one inner and central norm: a woman's generous, energetic, tenacious will, that of Mme Olga Froebe-Kapteyn, every year propounding a new theme and thus inviting to a new creation.

And that is why even those who in the sense of current speech "are no more" nevertheless do not cease to be present in the present of Eranos. An immense work has been accomplished: essays, books, have seen the light of day, books that perhaps would not have come to birth if Eranos had not put them in the present. Its meaning, finally: that of a sym-phony whose performance would each time be repeated in fuller and deeper sonorities—that of a microcosm, which the world cannot be expected to resemble but whose example, one may hope, will spread throughout the world.

Teheran HENRY CORBIN
21 December 1956
30 Āzar 1335

MAN AND TIME

Erich Neumann

Art and Time

Art and time is a vast theme; I am sure you do not expect an exhaustive treatment of it in one lecture. Here we shall not concern ourselves with the phenomenon of time as it enters into man's experience or into his actual works of art; in other words, we shall not concern ourselves with the relation of the ego to the living stream of time, to eternity or the moment, to the swirling eddies of time, or to repose in time. Our discussion will deal principally with the relation of art to its epoch; the second part of our lecture will take up the specific relation of modern art to our own time.

However, I shall speak neither as an artist nor as an art critic; I shall not even speak of the artistic phenomena with which I come into contact as a psychologist, the more or less artistic productions which arise in the course of analytical therapy. Our present inquiry lies within the psychology of culture; it aims at an understanding of art as a psychological phenomenon of central importance to the collectivity as well as the individual.

We shall start from the creative function of the unconscious, which produces its forms spontaneously, in a manner analogous to nature, which—from atom and crystal through organic life to the world of the stars and planets—spontaneously creates forms susceptible of impressing man as beautiful. Because this substratum and background of the psychophysical world is forever bringing forth forms, we call it creative. And to the unknown in nature which engenders its forms of the external world there corresponds another unknown, the collective unconscious, which is the source of all psychic creation: religion and rite, social organization, consciousness, and finally art.

The archetypes of the collective unconscious are intrinsically formless psychic structures which become visible in art. The archetypes are varied by the media through which they pass—that is, their form changes according to the time, the place, and the psychological constellation of the individual in whom they are manifested. Thus, for example, the mother archetype, as a dynamic entity in the psychic substratum, always retains its identity, but it takes on different *styles*—different aspects or emotional color—depending on whether it is manifested in Egypt, Mexico, or Spain, or in ancient, medieval or modern times. The paradoxical multiplicity of its eternal presence, which makes possible an infinite variety of forms of expression, is crystallized in its realization by man in time; its archetypal eternity enters into a unique synthesis with a specific historical situation.

Today we shall neither inquire into the development of specific archetypes in *one* culture, nor follow the different forms of the same archetype in diverse cultures. Anyone wishing to convince himself of the reality of this overwhelming phenomenon need only consult the Eranos Archive, [1] a pioneer effort in this direction.

Nor shall we take up the aesthetic aspect, the history of styles, which inquires into the forms assumed by the archetypes in the various periods, although it would be exceedingly interesting to show, for example, how the archetypal world of Egypt was shaped by a static conception of eternity and time, while in Central America the same archetypal world is almost submerged in a jungle of ornament because here the all-devouring aspect of the Terrible Mother is dominant. Our effort will begin and end with the question of what art means for mankind and what position it occupies in human development.

At the beginning of the development of human consciousness the original psychic situation prevails: unconscious, collective, and transpersonal factors are more significant and evident than conscious and individual factors. Art is at this stage a collective phenomenon, which cannot be isolated from the context of collective existence but is integrated with the life of the group. Each individual is artist, dancer, singer, poet, painter, and sculptor; everything he does and his way of doing it, even where a recognized individual possession is involved, remains an expression of the group's collective situation.

Although from the very outset the collective receives its primary impulse from "Great Individuals," even they themselves, in accordance with the dialectic of their relation to the group, never give themselves as individuals

1 [Now in the Warburg Institute, London. A duplicate is at Bollingen Foundation, New York.—Ed.]

credit for what they have done but impute it to their inspiring predecessors, to the spirits of their ancestors, to the totem, or to whatever aspect of the collective spirit has inspired them individually.

Not only is the creative situation numinous, it is also experienced as such, for all existence was originally shaped by experience of the transpersonal. The festivals and rites are the nodal points of the numinosum, which shapes everything that comes into contact with its sacral sphere: cult implement and mask, figure and image, vessel and ornament, song and dance, myth and poetry. The original integration of all these into life and the numinous context as a whole is shown by the fact that a certain "style" is Oceanic or African, Indian or Nordic, and that it is manifested in the kinship between ornamented door post and ritual vessel, between tattoo motif and mask, fetish and spear shaft.

This unity is a symptom of the individual's immersion in a group context that transcends him; however, when we say that the group is unconsciously directed by the collective psyche, we do not mean that it is directed by urges or instincts. True, the individual's consciousness is almost blind to the underlying forces: his reaction to the creative impulse of the psyche is not to reflect, it is to obey and execute its commands. But the psychic undercurrents which determine man's feeling and image of the world are manifested through colors and forms, tones and words, which crystallize into symbolic spiritual figures expressing man's relation both to the archetypal world and to the world in which he lives.

Thus from the very outset man is a creator of symbols; he constructs his characteristic spiritual-psychic world from the symbols in which he speaks and thinks of the world around him, but also from the forms and images which his numinous experience arouses in him.

In the original situation man's emotion in the presence of the numinosum leads to expression, for the unconscious, as part of its creative function, carries with it its own expression. But the emotional drives which move the group and the individual within it must not be conceived as a dynamic without content. For every symbol, like every archetype, has a specific content, and when the whole of a man is seized by the collective unconscious, his consciousness is included. Consequently we find from the very start that the creative function of the psyche is accompanied by a reaction of consciousness, which seeks, at first in slight degree but then increasingly, to understand, to interpret, and to assimilate the thing by which it was at first overwhelmed. Thus at a very early stage there is a relative fixation of expression and style, and so definite traditions arise.

In our time, with its developed or overdeveloped consciousness, feeling and emotion seem to be bound up with an artistic nature; for an undeveloped consciousness this is by no means the case. For primitive and early cultures, the creative force of the numinosum supports or even engenders consciousness; it brings differentiation and order into an indeterminate world driven by chaotic powers and enables man to orient himself.

In the creative sphere of the psyche, which we call the unconscious, significant differentiations have been effected in the direction which will be characteristic of subsequent elaborations by the consciousness. The very appearance of a psychic image represents a synthetic interpretation of the world, and the same is true of artistic creation in the period of origination. Artistic creation has magic power, it is experience and perception, insight and differentiation in one.

Whether the image is naturalistic or not is immaterial; even the extremely naturalistic animal paintings of the Ice Age are, in our sense, symbols. For a primitive, magical conception of the world, each of these painted animals is a numinosum; it is the embodiment and essence of the animal species. The individual bison, for example, is a spiritual-psychic symbol; he is in a sense the "father of the bison," the idea of the bison, the "bison as such," and this is why he is an object of ritual. The subjugation and killing, the conciliation and fertilization of the animal, which are enacted in the psychic sphere between the human group and the image which symbolically represents the animal group, have a reality-transforming—that is, magical—significance, because this image-symbol encompasses the numinous heart and center of the animal living in the world, whose symbolic figuration constitutes an authentic manifestation of the numinous animal.

In the period of origination, the forms of expression and driving archetypal contents of a culture remain unconscious; but with the development and systematization of consciousness and the reinforcement of the individual ego there arises a collective consciousness, a cultural canon characteristic for each culture and cultural epoch. There arises, in other words, a configuration of definite archetypes, symbols, values, and attitudes, upon which the unconscious archetypal contents are projected and which, fixated as myth and cult, becomes the dogmatic heritage of the group. No longer do unconscious and unknown powers determine the life of the group; instead, transpersonal figures and contents, known to the group, direct the life of the community as well as the conscious behavior of the individual in festival and cult, religion and usage.

This does not mean that man suspects a connection between this transpersonal world and the depths of his own human psyche, although the transpersonal can express itself only through the medium of man and takes form in him through creative processes.

But even when the cultural canon develops, art in all its forms remains at first integrated with the whole of the group life, and when the cultural canon is observed in religious festival, all creative activity is articulated with this integral event. As expressions of archetypal reality, the art and music, dance and poetry of the cult are inner possessions of the collective.

Whether the epiphany of the numinosum occurs in a drawing scratched on bone, in a sculptured stone, in a medieval cathedral centuries in the building, or in a mask, fashioned for *one* festival and burned after it, in every case the epiphany of the numinosum, the rapture of those who give it form, and the rapture of the group celebrating the epiphany constitute an indivisible unit.

But the breakdown of this original situation in the course of history is revealed also by the phenomenon of the individual creator in art. With the growth of individuality and the relative independence of consciousness, the integral situation in which the creative element in art is one with the life of the group disintegrates. An extensive differentiation occurs; poets, painters, sculptors, musicians, dancers, actors, architects, etc. become professional groups, practicing particular functions of artistic expression. The majority of the group, it would appear, preserves only a receptive relation, if any, to the creative achievement of the artist.

But neither is the individual so isolated—nor are art and the artist so far separated—from the collective as first appears. We have learned to see the consciousness of the individual as the high voice in a polyphony whose lower voice, the collective unconscious, does not merely accompany but actually determines the theme. And this reorientation is not limited to the psychic structure of the individual: it also necessitates a new approach to the relations between men.

We see the group as an integral psychic field, in which the reality of the individual is embedded, so that he is organ and instrument of the collective.

But not only through his consciousness or his education by the collective is the individual embedded in this psychic field. The separate structures of the human organism regulate one another in a highly complex way, and in dreams those structures necessary for the whole of the individual personality are animated in such a way as to compensate for the onesidedness of conscious life; similarly, in the group there exists between its members a compensatory mechanism which—quite apart from the directives of the individual consciousness and of the cultural authorities—tends to round out the group life.

In the group as in the individual, two psychic systems are at work, which can function smoothly only when they are attuned to each other. The one is the collective consciousness, the cultural canon, the system of the culture's supreme values toward which its education is oriented and which set their decisive stamp on the development of the individual consciousness. But side by side with this is the living substratum, the collective unconscious, in which new developments, transformations, revolutions, and renewals are at all times foreshadowed and prepared, and whose perpetual eruptions prevent the stagnation and death of a culture. But even if we see the group as an integral psychic field, the men in whom reside the compensatory unconscious forces necessary to the cultural canon and the culture of the particular time are also essential elements of this constellation. However, only the historian—and he, too, is limited by his personal equation and his ties with his epoch—can evaluate the authentic historical significance of a group, a movement, or an individual. For there is no necessary relation between the true importance of a man and that imputed to him by his own time—that is, by the representatives of his own cultural canon. In the course of time, "leaders" and "geniuses" are exposed as frauds, while outsiders, outlaws, nobodies, are found to have been the true vehicles of reality.

Not the ego and consciousness but the collective unconscious and the self are the determining forces; the development of mankind and its consciousness is dependent on the spontaneity and inner order of the unconscious and remains so even after consciousness and unconscious have entered into a fruitful dialectical relation to each other.

There is a continuous interchange between the collective unconscious (which is alive in the unconscious of every individual in the group), the cultural canon (which represents the group's collective consciousness of those archetypal values which have become dogma), and the creative individuals of the group (in whom the new constellations of the collective unconscious achieve form and expression).[2]

Our attempt to distinguish different forms of relation between art and the artist and their epoch is based upon the unity of the group's psychic field, in which consciously or unconsciously, willingly or unwillingly, every single individual, and every sphere of culture as well, takes its place.[3] This unity—like that of the individual psyche—is composed of collective consciousness and collective unconscious.

The first stage in the relation of art to its epoch is, as we have suggested, the self-representation of the unconscious in the symbolic expression of the numinosum, characteristic of the situation of origination and of early cultures. The self-representation of the unconscious in art always presupposes a greater or lesser degree of unity, whether conscious or not, in the creative man's personality; and it presupposes that he must be embedded in his group. Moreover, the product of this phase is also characterized by unity; it is an art integrated with the group as a whole.

In the representation of the cultural canon, the second stage in the relation of art to its epoch, this is no longer the case. And here it is immaterial whether it is an ancestor, a god, or a Buddha who appears in the cultural canon, and whether it is the awakening of Osiris, a crucifixion, or the cutting out of the god's heart that figures as a part of the savior myth.

As you know, such canonical forms are also grounded in archetypes; that is, even in its representative form, art is a symbolic expression of the collective unconscious and, although it is essentially a representation of symbols close to consciousness, it has a decisive therapeutic function for the life of the group. For the fact that the symbol is consciously represented does not necessarily mean that it has been made fully conscious or that it has been dissolved through conscious assimilation.

True, the representation of the archetype in a cultural canon is closer to

2 We must leave out of account here the fact that the same constellations may appear in Great Individuals and in borderline cases of neurosis and insanity.

3 The psychological evaluation of the individual within the group as a whole presents an analogy to his sociological position. But the two evaluations, as we have stressed, can be utterly divergent. Since an insight into these compensatory relations is necessary to an estimate of the individual's importance to the community, we must, in judging the individual, use the notion of "social adaptation" much more cautiously than was previously the case when—quite understandably—adaptation to the values of the cultural canon was regarded as the sole criterion. The dilemma which this circumstance creates for depth psychology in its relation to the collective cannot be discussed here.

consciousness than the pure self-representation of the unconscious; the numinous power becomes less unknown. But since every symbol also expresses an essential unknown component of the psyche, its unconscious workings continue for a long time, even when it is interpreted and understood as part of the cultural canon.

Thus in all cultures the archetypes of the canon are the numinous points at which the collective unconscious extends into the living reality of the group.[4] Whether this be a temple or a statue of the godhead, a mask or a fetish, a ritual or sacral music—it remains the function of art to represent the archetypal and to manifest it symbolically as a high point of existence.

This artistic representation of the cultural canon resembles the digging and walling in of deep wells, around which the group gathers and from whose waters it lives. Every such well is adorned with traditional symbols in which lives the religious consciousness of the epoch.

But the cultural canon is not only a bond with the archetypal substratum of the unconscious. As "canon" it is also a means of limiting and fixating the intervention of the numinosum and excluding unpredictable creative forces. Thus the cultural canon is always a fortress of security; and since it is a systematic restriction to a dogmatic section of the numinosum, it carries with it the danger of onesidedness and congealment. For the archetypal world is a dynamic world of change, and even the numinosum and the divine are mortal in the contingent form which can be apprehended by man.

The archetypal as such is imageless and nameless, and the form which the formless assumes at any time is, as an image arising in the medium of man, transient. And just as the archetypal cultural canon must arise and take form, so likewise its representation is transient and must undergo change and transformations.

For the artist, whose vocation it is to represent the cultural canon, it is a question of growing into a tradition—that is, into the situation of his time and into the collective consciousness—rather than of receiving a direct mandate from the powers of the unconscious. Of course, an image of the canon can also be full of inner experience, but its archetypal reality may no longer encompass the whole of the artistic personality. An art which is oriented toward those sectors of the archetypal world that have already

4 Cf. my *The Origins and History of Consciousness* (New York and London, 1954), 371–75.

entered into consciousness through representation will never realize the supreme possibilities of art.

However, the creative process need not consist of an outward shattering of the cultural canon; it can operate underground, within the canon. Accordingly, the object depicted in a work of art cannot tell us whether we have to do with a representation of the cultural canon or with an evolution or revolution from it. If, within the Christian canon that has dominated the West for nearly two thousand years, we compare a Gothic, a Renaissance, and a modern Madonna, we see at once the revolutionary transformation of this archetypal figure. And a Byzantine Christ-Pantocrator and Grünewald's Christ on the Cross have their source in different worlds of God and man. One might almost say that they were no longer related.

The next stage in the relation of art to its epoch is the stage of compensation for the cultural canon, the significance of which has repeatedly been stressed by Professor Jung.[5] It is grounded in the vitality of the collective unconscious, which is opposed to the collective consciousness in the integral psychic field of the group. This stage presupposes the existence of an established opposition of consciousness to the unconscious, characteristic of the modern world. In it we go back to the immediate presence of the creative numinosum. Great art of this type almost necessarily implies tragedy. Compensation for the cultural canon means opposition to it—that is, opposition to the epoch's consciousness and sense of values. The creative artist, whose mission it is to compensate for consciousness and the cultural canon, is usually an isolated individual, a hero who must destroy the old in order to make possible the dawn of the new.

When unconscious forces break through in the artist, when the archetypes striving to be born into the light of the world take form in him, he is as far from the men around him as he is close to their destiny. For he expresses and gives form to the future of his epoch.

For example, the realism which emerged in Renaissance painting and which for centuries dominated our art has a significance far beyond such purely artistic considerations as mobility of the figure, perspective, plasticity, color, etc. Renaissance art did not, as it might appear, abandon medieval symbolism in order to reproduce the objective outside world; what

5 Cf. especially his articles on Picasso and the novel *Ulysses* (in *Wirklichkeit der Seele*, Zurich, 1934; tr. W. Stanley Dell in *Nimbus*, London, II, 1953, no. 2, 25–27, and no. 1, 7–20).

actually took place—and it is a phenomenon decisive for this epoch—was the reappearance of the earth archetype, in opposition to the heaven archetype that had dominated the Middle Ages. In other words, this naturalism is the symbolic expression of a revolution in the archetypal structure of the unconscious.

The beginning of natural science and sociology, the discovery of the individual and of classical antiquity, the schism in Christianity, the social revolution, etc., are all a part of the integral transformation of the psychic field, which seized upon the unconscious of all men—particularly of creative men. Thus a Dutch genre painting is not merely a representation of a fragment of external reality: it is a glorification of this world as opposed to the next, a discovery of the sanctity, the beauty, and the vitality of the material world, a praise of life in this world and of earthly man, in opposition to the praise of heaven, which had hitherto passed for the "real" world.

And whereas man's relation to this transcendent "real" world had led to a life burdened with original sin, with a sense of guilt and eternal inadequacy, man now came to feel that he was a son of the earth, at home on earth.

This intense conflict governed the work of Bosch, one of the most magnificent painters ever to have announced the coming of a new era.[6] He clung consciously to the old medieval canon, but beneath his hand the world transformed itself. It became demonic and gnostic; everything was temptation, and in the paranoiac despair of his ascetic, medieval consciousness he experienced the revival of the earth archetype around him, glittering demonically in every color. Paradoxically enough, although, and precisely because, for him Satan—in the form of an owl—had stood from the very first at the heart of creation, his earth transformed itself into an "earthly paradise." And all the colors and forms of this ostensibly accursed earthly paradise shine alluringly in a wealth of archetypal and classical ritual symbols, with such beauty that, although he himself did not know it, the curse, like Balaam's, has turned unexpectedly to blessing.

In his attempt to represent the demon-infested earth in the earthly colors of his unique palette, the earth magnificently triumphed over his medieval

6 See Wilhelm Fränger, *Hieronymus Bosch. Das tausendjährige Reich;* tr. Eithne Wilkins and Ernst Kaiser, *The Millennium of Hieronymus Bosch: Outlines of a New Interpretation* (London, 1952). I have intentionally avoided consideration of Fränger's interpretations, since it is impossible to judge at the present moment to what degree they are tenable.

conception. Consequently, for example, his *Christ Bearing the Cross*, and the Veronica in this same painting, disclose nothing medieval but on the contrary point to one of the most modern problems of future generations: the Great Individual with his soul, alone in the mass of men.

The workings of this ascendant earth archetype, which was to become a central component of the new cultural canon, extended down to the French Revolution, to philosophical materialism, and to the Madonna's rather belated dogmatic assumption into heaven. Only today has this process begun to be intelligible, but concurrently this archetype is beginning in turn to undergo a transformation: the projection is being dissolved and the content reintegrated into the psyche. As one of the greatest poets of our time has written:

> Earth, isn't this what you want: an invisible
> re-arising in us? Is it not your dream
> to be one day invisible? Earth! invisible!
> What is your urgent command, if not transformation?
> Earth, you darling, I will! [7]

The need of his times works inside the artist without his wanting it, seeing it, or understanding its true significance. In this sense he is close to the seer, the prophet, the mystic. And it is precisely when he does not represent the existing canon but transforms and overturns it that his function rises to the level of the sacral, for he then gives utterance to the authentic and direct revelation of the numinosum.

The advance of specialization and differentiation has destroyed the closeness of every individual to the psychic substratum, characteristic of the original situation. Since culture is in part a safeguard against the numinosum, the representatives of the cultural canon have lost contact with the primal fire of direct inner experience. Nor is this inner experience their function, for they represent the conscious and rational aspect of the archetypal world, the striving to safeguard and secure the artificial, cultural shell of life. Consequently, the creative struggle with the numinosum has fallen to the lot of the individual, and an essential arena of this struggle is art, in which the relation of the creative individual to the numinosum takes form.

In following the drive of the psychic substratum, the artist fulfills not only himself but his epoch. In the original situation the artist, or any

7 R. M. Rilke, *Duino Elegies*, IX; tr. J. B. Leishman and Stephen Spender (London and New York, 1939), pp. 86f.

individual proposing to shape a cult object, had to cleanse himself in order to achieve an exalted and detached transpersonal state, in which alone he could become the creative instrument of the powers. In the original situation this ritual preparation was undertaken in accord with the collective. To the modern artist it happens involuntarily; an outsider in society, he stands alone, delivered over to the creative impulse in himself.

We know that the creative power of the unconscious seizes upon the individual with the autonomous force of an instinctual drive and takes possession of him without the least consideration for the individual, his life, his happiness, or his health. The creative impulse springs from the collective; like every instinct it serves the will of the species and not of the individual. Thus the creative man is an instrument of the transpersonal, but as an individual he comes into conflict with the numinosum that takes hold of him.

Creative phenomena range from the lowest, unconscious stages of ecstatic frenzy and somnambulism to the highest level of conscious acceptance, in which the artist takes full responsibility and a formative, interpreting consciousness plays an essential part.

A similar conflict dominates the relation of the artist to his collective and his time. If he is driven to compensate for the cultural canon, there is an implication that he has been captured by it and has survived and transcended it in himself. Only by suffering, perhaps unconsciously, under the poverty of his culture and his time can he arrive at the freshly opening source which is destined to quench the thirst of his time. In other words, the creative man (though often this is not evident) is deeply bound up with his group and its culture, more deeply than the common man who lives in the security of the cultural shell, and even more deeply than the actual representatives of this culture.

And because of the predominance of the transpersonal in the psychic substratum of creative men, their psychic field is integral. For although creative men usually live unknown to one another, without influence on one another, a common force seems to drive all those men who ever compensate for a cultural canon at a given time or shape a new one. They are all moved in the same direction, though they follow an unknown impulse in themselves rather than any new road charted in advance. This phenomenon is called simply *Zeitgeist*, and no further attempt is made to account for it.

At a later day we can analyze and set up all sorts of chains of causality to explain the *Zeitgeist*, but these explanations after the fact are only in part convincing. Perhaps the least presumptuous of them states that the force which breaks through at one and the same time in philosophy and literature, painting and music, science and politics, and in innumerable creative individuals—the force that sets its imprint on the spirit of a time, of *any* time—is transpersonal and unconscious. Here again we do not wish to underestimate the role of the consciousness which responds to conscious problems, but we must attach great significance, crucial significance, to the directives of the collective unconscious.

In all these stages in the relation of art to its time—self-representation of the unconscious, representation of the cultural canon, and compensation for the cultural canon—the psychic field in which the individual is embedded remains the decisive factor. Despite all the changes brought about in the course of human development, the individual's relation to the collective remains his destiny.

But in the course of human history the artist becomes constantly more individualized and loses his original anonymity. As the ego and consciousness develop, the physiognomy of the individual artist is liberated from the anonymity of the current style. This individualization of creative man is the beginning of his individuation—that is, of the last form of relation between art and its epoch.

We shall designate this last phase as the transcendence of art. It rests, we believe, on an individual development of the artist, which makes him into the Great Individual who, precisely, transcends his bond with the collective both outwardly and inwardly. It is no longer his function to express the creative will of the unconscious or to depict a sector of the archetypal world, or to regenerate or compensate for the existing culture out of the depths of the collective unconscious.

What is fundamentally new and different in this stage is that the artist here attains to the level of timelessness. And reluctant as we are to use such terms, this stage of artistic creation cannot be characterized without such words as "eternity," "intuition of essence" [*Wesensschau*], and "metaphysical experience."

Although every creative representation of an archetype is a representation of something eternal, and although the archetypes are the real content of art, the eternal quality in a work of art can by no means be apprehended at first glance. Precisely because art is devoted to such a great extent to the representation of the cultural canon, its understanding requires historical knowledge, an orientation in the assumptions of the cultural canon to which the work belongs. Here perhaps you will disagree, but consider how we take the greatness of Asiatic or primitive art for granted today, and then recall Goethe's judgment on the horrid idols of India and the general opinion of primitives held up to a generation ago. Only in our own time has it become possible to experience and appreciate a "world art."

And consider that nearly all the great artists of our own culture, from Rembrandt to Bach, from the Gothic sculptors to El Greco, have had to be rediscovered. Here, too, we are the heirs of a tradition which taught us to see, hear, and experience anew. Where there is new knowledge of man, new art will be discovered, and the eternal in the art of the past will be discovered afresh.

In this sense, the timelessness of art can be experienced only by an enhanced consciousness, for what figure of Christ can be fully understood without knowledge of Christianity, what Buddha without Buddhism, what Shiva without the Hindu conception of cosmic cycles?

Is then the stage of transcendent art an illusion? Can we really know nothing more than the relation of the work of art to ourselves and to its own time? And is the most we can say of an artist that, if we disregard the eternity of the archetype he represented, he was a hair's breadth in advance of his own time?

Perhaps I can best explain what I mean by "transcendent" if I refer to the works of the great artists' old age.

We are accustomed—and this, too, is an acquisition of the last Western century, with its emphasis on the individual—to take an interest in the biographies of artists. We approach their lives like the mythological lives of prehistoric heroes, except that these Great Individuals are closer to us and we feel more related to their sufferings and victories, so that, far above us as they may be, they seem to offer a pledge of the dignity of our own individual existence.

It is no idle curiosity that makes us follow the course of their lives. They serve us as models in the sense that their work and lives form the unity which we call individuation and for which we must strive on the smaller scale allotted to us.

Each of these artists seems to pass through all the stages that we have attempted to characterize. He begins by responding to a creative impulse within him, which, as in the stage of the self-expression of the unconscious, strives to find form of whatever kind. Then, maturing, he grows into the contingency of his epoch; through study, he becomes the heir and son of his cultural tradition.

But whether the artist grows slowly away from the tradition of his time or passes over it at one bound and brings the new element the epoch lacked, ultimately, if he does not stop at the stage of representation of the cultural canon—and no truly great artist has ever done so—he finds himself alone. He is alone regardless of whether he is worshiped as an Olympian, whether he is an organist respected in a small circle, or whether he ends in deafness, poverty, or madness.

The struggle of these great men with the powers inside them and the times outside them seems to result in a statement which transcends the artistic and symbolic reality of their creative life. In music, painting, sculpture, and poetry they penetrate to the archetypal transcendence which is the inner life of the world. What speaks to us from a self-portrait of the aged Rembrandt, from the end of *Faust*, Part II, from Shakespeare's last plays or Titian's late paintings, from *The Art of Fugue* or a late Beethoven quartet, is a strange transfiguration, a breakthrough into the realm of essence. And this transfiguration is independent of content, form, matter, or style, although the transcendence of form would seem to be one of its elements.

In these works of man a numinous world is manifested in which the polarity of outward and inward—nature and art—seems to be resolved. Their secret alchemy achieves a synthesis of the numinosum at the heart of nature and psyche.

These aged masters seem to have attained the image and likeness of a primal creative force, prior to the world and outside the world, which, though split from the very beginning into the polarity of nature and psyche, is in essence one undivided whole.

In the creative solitude of the Great Old Men the limitations of the epoch are passed over; they have escaped the prison of time and the ego-bound consciousness. We begin to see that the supreme alchemical transformation of art merely reflects the alchemical transformation of the Great Individual's personality. At first, whether carried along by the powers or resisting them, he had remained distinct from them. But now, as his ego itself is integrated by the creative self, which from the very outset was the directing force of his existence, the center of gravity shifts. The original tension between his ego, the numinous substratum, and the outside world is annulled and, in the highest form of this transcending art, replaced by a creative act which is spirit-nature and transfigured nature.

For this reason it is not possible to characterize the style of these works of advanced age, for the creative integration of the personality transcends the contingency of any time-bound form.

This art no longer relates either consciously or unconsciously to any historical time; the solitary monologue of these "extreme" works is spoken, as it were, into the void. And one cannot quite tell whether it is a monologue or a dialogue between man and the ultimate. Hence the alienation of these great men from their contemporaries—they all, like the aged Laotse, have left the mountain pass of the world behind them.

If we call this transcendent art religious it is because the faith of Bach and the atheistic infinity of a Chinese landscape would seem to be two kindred forms of transcendence, and because we regard these ultimate works and many others of different kinds as the supreme religious act of which creative mankind is capable.

And here again we must declare that a feeling for this universal kinship has become possible only in our own ostensibly irreligious time, a time, as we often hear, that is fit only to be destroyed. Wherever traditional art apprehends the essence of the archetype, it does so by fitting the archetype into a fixed framework oriented toward the human world—even when this archetype consists of the death of the Saviour, the meditation of the Buddha, or the emanation of the divine. As object of worship, as example, and as representation of the transpersonal, it always signifies a descent of the eternal into the reality of a secure world of faith.

But in the rare instances when the phenomenon of transcendence occurs, the transpersonal seems, even though it has passed through the medium of the human, to have achieved its own objectivity—to speak, one might say, with itself. It is no longer oriented toward the world or man, the ego or the collective, security or insecurity; instead, the creative act which mysteriously creates form and life in nature as in the human psyche seems to have perceived itself and to shine forth with its own incandescence. The creative impulse seems to have liberated itself. United on the plane of artistic creation, the self which man experiences within him and the world-creative self which is manifested outwardly achieve the transparency of symbolic reality.

Of course, it is impossible to state objectively that everyone can find this transcendence in certain specific works of art. It suffices to note that the level exists and it is possible to experience it in some works of art. One of us will find it in a landscape by Leonardo or a poem by Goethe, another will find it elsewhere. But in any event we may say that this experience can be gained only through a few of the very greatest works and only by those who are open and prepared for it. For even when the highest form of artistic reality has achieved objective existence in a work, it must be reborn in subjective human experience.

And it seems to us that one of the principal functions of all art is precisely to set in motion the archetypal reality of the transpersonal within the individual and on the highest level of artistic experience to bring the individual himself to transcendence—that is, to raise him above time and epoch and also above the limited eternity realized in any limited archetypal form—to lead him to the timeless radiant dynamic that is at the heart of the world.

In this sense the greatest art is a learning to see in the way described by "Rabbi Nachman" of Bratislava: "Just as a hand held before the eyes conceals the greatest mountain, so does petty earthly life conceal from view the vast lights and mysteries of which the world is full, and he who can withdraw it from his eyes, as one withdraws a hand, will behold the great light of the innermost world." [8]

II

It is difficult if not impossible to analyze the art of our own time, because we ourselves still live entirely within the psychic field of which it is a part. You will therefore forgive me for returning briefly to matters we have already touched upon.

In Figure 1, you will find a diagram of a "balanced" culture, showing a collectivity and an epoch integrated with a cultural canon. The semicircle is the arch supporting the supreme values of the time, the symbols, images, ideals which constitute the transpersonal medium in which the psychic-spiritual existence of the collectivity is rooted. An archetype of the collective unconscious is associated with each of these supreme values. And we may say that the depth and force of an archetype, which is perceived through its projection into a supreme value of the cultural canon, are

8 Martin Buber, *Die Chassidischen Bücher* (Hellerau, 1928), p. 32.

Fig. 1
Culture in Balance

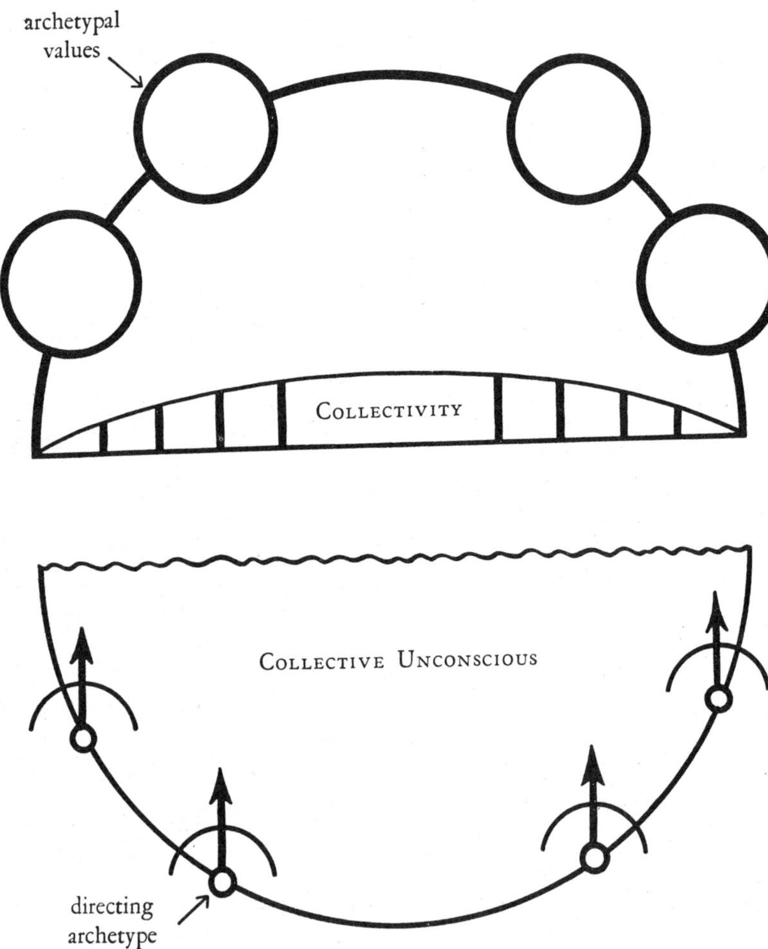

commensurate with the elevation of its position in the celestial arch.

For the collectivity the world of the cultural canon is as transpersonal as the world of the collective unconscious. The bond between the upper and lower semicircles, and between those two and the psyche of the group and of the individual, is unconscious.

The unity of life in this relatively self-contained sphere is secure and ordered as long as the higher corresponds to the lower. For in a balanced culture the collectivity and the individual integrated with the group are fed by the forces of the unconscious. In part, these forces flow into the personality through the consciousness, which stands in direct communication with the constellations of the cultural canon in religion, art, custom, science, and daily life; in part, the unconscious is set in motion by the archetypes embodied in the cultural canon.

The diagram in Figure 2 represents the disintegration of the canon, characteristic of our time and the century or two preceding it. The equilibrium in the tension of the psychic field has been lost. In my figure the archetypes forming the canon seem to be fading out. The symbols corresponding to them disintegrate and the arch collapses, because the underlying order has broken down. Just as a hive of termites or bees falls into chaos and panic as soon as the central power vested in the queen is destroyed, here too chaos and panic arise when the canonic order crumbles.

This chaos and the attendant atmosphere of doom are by no means diminished by the approach of other archetypes, which may actually have ushered in the collapse of the old cultural canon. Just as in antiquity and the Middle Ages, men today are afraid when stars fall, when comets move across the heavens, and when terrifying changes in the firmament and other signs announce the end of an epoch, which for the generation in question seems to be the end of the whole world.

For just as, archetypally, every New Year—or as in Aztec Mexico the beginning of every new end-of-year week [8a]—is a perilous time of judgment and doom, so is the beginning of every new cultural epoch bound up with all the phenomena that characterize the end of an era. Only at rare intervals, when the clouds part in the dark sky of the crumbling canon, do a few individuals discern a new constellation, which already belongs to the new canon of transpersonal values and foreshadows its configuration.

8a [Cf. Neumann, *The Great Mother* (New York and London, 1955), p. 185, and G. C. Vaillant, *The Aztecs of Mexico* (Penguin edn., 1950), pp. 195f.—Ed.]

Fig. 2

Disintegration of the Canon

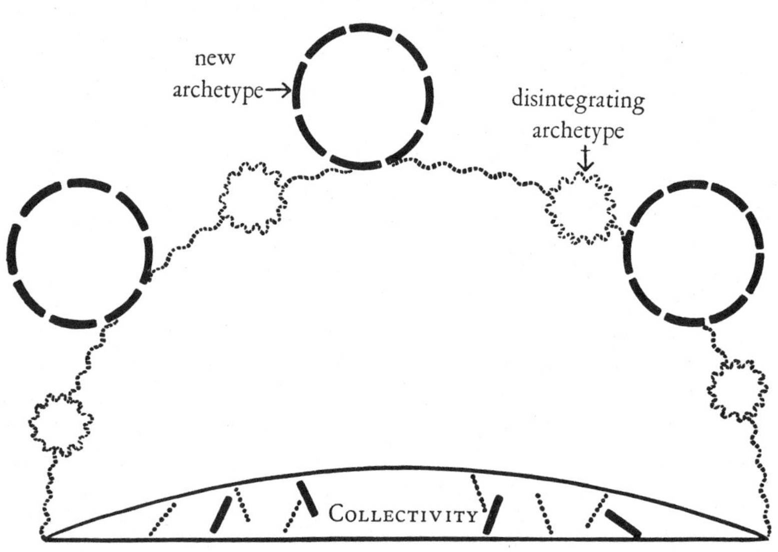

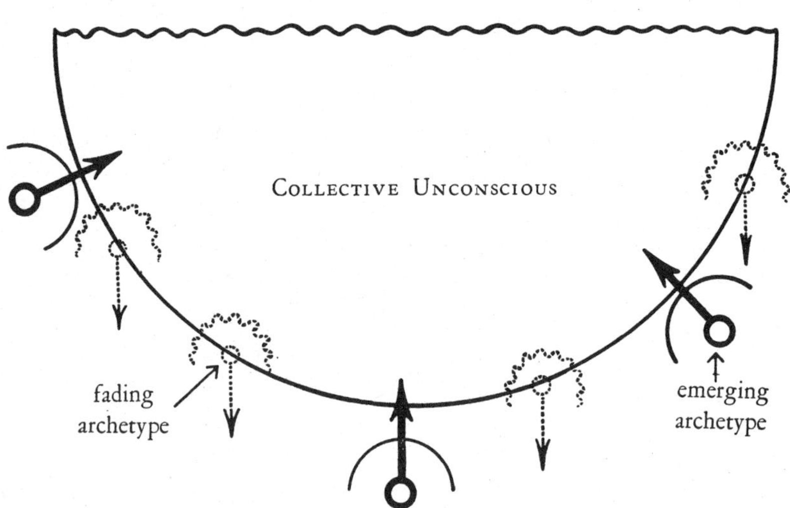

We need not dwell at length on the trend of Western culture in the most recent centuries and particularly the last. This work of cultural critique has been done by great thinkers, particularly by Marx, Kierkegaard, Nietzsche, and Freud. The self-assurance and smugness of this age; its hypocrisy; its certainty of possessing everything that was good, true, noble, and beautiful; its indifference to the misery next door; the missionary and imperialist arrogance of this age, which thought it represented the peak and summit of humanity; its Victorianism, against a background of prostitution and French cancan—all this was an expression of the inner hollowness of values which had once held meaning and which mankind had built up at the cost of endless effort.

Since then, all these stage properties have rotted away; today the disintegration of our cultural canon is evident, and it is the general symptoms of this disintegration which characterize our time and its expression in art. It seems to me that on the whole this disintegration is similar to that which occurs in an individual when for some reason his individual canon, his conscious world of values, collapses.

The disappearance of the certainty and security once conferred by the cultural canon shows itself primarily in a sense of isolation, of forlornness, of homelessness and alienation, which has vastly increased in the course of the last hundred years. Probably never before in the history of literature or painting have there been so many isolated individuals. The concepts of school, tradition, and unity of style seem to have vanished. At a distance, of course, we can discover certain kinships; yet each individual seems to have felt the necessity of starting from the very beginning.

Consider, to mention only a few of the painters of the last sixty years, such figures as Cézanne, Van Gogh, Gauguin, Rousseau, Munch, Klee, Matisse, Chagall, Picasso—there has never been anything similar in history. Each of them is a world in himself, endeavoring alone to ward off the chaos that menaces him or to give it form, each with his own characteristic desperation. It is no accident that we hear so much today of the forlornness of the individual and of the void. And the profound anxiety, the sense of insecurity, uprootedness, and world dissolution at work in these painters also moves modern composers and poets.

True, just as there is still a pre-analytical psychology, there still exists an art that belongs to the day before yesterday. But the false innocence of this pseudo art, which strives to illuminate life with the light of stars that set long ago, is no less disquieting than the modern art that belongs to our time. To this day-before-yesterday's beauty the words of the *I Ching* apply: "But [the superior man] dare not decide controversial issues in this way [that is, according to beauty of form]." [9] And indeed today we are confronted with great and controversial questions.

Thus in our age, as never before, truth implies the courage to face chaos. In his *Dr. Faustus*, in which he embodies the profoundest insight into the character of our time, Thomas Mann says of Leverkühn's *Apocalypse*, that expression of modern despair: "The whole work is dominated by the paradox (if it is a paradox) that in it dissonance stands for the expression of everything lofty, solemn, pious, everything of the spirit; while consonance and firm tonality are reserved for the world of hell, in this context a world of banality and commonplace." [10]

When the world of security crumbles, man is inevitably devoured by *nigredo*, the blackness and chaos of the *prima materia*, and the two great archetypal figures of the Devil and the Terrible Mother dominate the world. The Devil is shadow, evil, depression, darkening of the light, harsh dissonance. Elsewhere I have discussed at greater length this incursion of the dark aspect into the Western world and, to the displeasure of those who like to see the world through rose-colored glasses, attempted to draw its ethical consequences.[11]

Consider the great line which begins with Goethe's *Faust* and the Romantic Doppelgänger literature: Melville's *Moby Dick*, Poe, Baudelaire, Trakl, Heym, Kubin, Kafka, and their heirs in modern crime fiction and films. Consider how the dark prophecies of misery, sickness, crime, and madness have been realized, how the black hordes of darkest mankind have shaken the world. Hell, *nigredo*, has been let loose and, as in the paintings of Bosch, peoples our reality. Those whom this blackness has almost blinded do not believe that nature is good, man noble, progress natural, or the godhead a good God.

This darkening brings with it dissonance, the "beautiful" is abandoned in favor of the true, of so-called ugliness. And the dissonance characteristic of the modern world has not only carried its dark, negative *content* into our

9 *The I Ching, or Book of Changes*, tr. Cary F. Baynes from the German tr. of Richard Wilhelm (New York and London, 1950), Hexagram 22: *Pi* (Grace), p. 97. Also cf. Wilhelm, *Der Mensch und das Sein* (Jena, 1931), p. 211.

10 Tr. H. T. Lowe-Porter (New York, 1948), p. 375.

11 My *Tiefenpsychologie und neue Ethik* (Zurich, 1949).

consciousness but has concurrently brought about a general disintegration of form. Behind the archetype of Satan and the blackness surrounding him, at whose impact the crumbling world of the old cultural canon has collapsed, rises the devouring Terrible Great Mother, tearing and rending and bringing madness. And everywhere in modern art we see this dissolution in the breakdown and decay of form.

The libido would seem to have withdrawn from the once round and solidly modeled outside world and flowed inward. In painting, the world, formerly seen as real, has become one of appearance and illusion. This process began with the Impressionists, who abandoned the "illusory depth" of perspective, optical surface, objective color, and outward unity. Similarly in literature, the laws of composition have broken down. The line from Goethe to Dostoevski to Proust and Joyce is not a line of degeneration, but it does mark the increasingly conscious dissolution of style, human personality, and the unified work.

In Dostoevski's novels, for example, we have no longer a plastic individuality but a psychic movement which shatters all form, even that of the individual; what he essentially reveals is not any single man but the numinous powers of the inner world.

Even in such great portrayers of character as Balzac and Tolstoi we find an analogous dissolution of the plastic individual. A collective process, the group or the epoch replaces the individual as the actual "hero." This does not mean that the individual is no longer characterized as an individual or that there is no emphasis on literary form. But the central character is a collective entity, which is seen not only in sociological but in much more universal terms: war, money, marriage, etc. The novel has ceased to be purely personal and is peopled with transpersonal powers. And where the family novel does appear as such, its emphasis is on the passing generations, the changing times, and epochs and their decay.

Unity of time, place, and action; unity of character; plasticity of the individual; the *Bildungsroman*—how harmless and dated they all seem at a time when chaos threatens to engulf us and every serious work of art must directly or indirectly come to grips with this problem. For even where the problem is formulated differently, even where it assumes a philosophical or sociological, a theological or psychological, coloration—if we consider it as a whole, we perceive an immense anxiety and indeed a clear consciousness of great danger. And this was true long before our own epoch of world wars and atom bombs.[12] The chaos was first discernible within; this danger threatened from within; and perhaps more than any art before it, modern art is turned inward.

If we have abandoned outward unity, quasi-reality, it is in response to an overwhelming force from within us; the annihilation of everything that passed as good has brought with it the devastation of all that was held to be real. Outstandingly in Joyce this force from within is manifested as an erupting stream of language, as involuntary creation.

It is at this point that psychoanalysis and depth psychology, which are analogous phenomena from another part of our psychic field, invaded modern art as a whole—not merely literature—and have fructified its development in every sphere. The method of free association is an instrument for the discovery of unconscious contents and their movement, and it is also a destroyer of form and of conscious systematization, which now seems a fraud and façade, a figment of the "outside world," without inner truth.

In reality this incursion of the irrational into art was a legitimate expression of the time long before the Surrealists made a dogma of it. The surrender of conscious control is only a consequence of the disintegration of the cultural canon and of the values by which alone consciousness had oriented itself. And if the Surrealists made dreams, sickness, and madness the central content of art and tried to make their writing and painting flow directly from the unconscious, this was merely a late caricature of what was suffered by the great creative personalities, for they all stand under the sign of Orpheus, who was rent to pieces by the maenads. And in consequence the art which expresses our time seems to consist only of fragments, not of complete works. For the swarms of "little" artists the absence of canon imposed by the situation has itself become canon, and this is what gives rise to all our current "isms."

Here again the Great Men differ from the little. The great artists make conscious use of the situation, dissolving configured outward reality into a stream of feeling and action which, though coming from within, is neverthe-

12 It is highly questionable whether we can derive all these manifestations from the decay of our social structure. We can equally well demonstrate the contrary, that the disintegration of the cultural canon, originating in the unconscious, leads to the collapse of the social structure. More significant than any typologically determined overemphasis of inward or outward causality, in my opinion, is the realization that we have to do with an integral psychic field embracing two worlds in which changes occur simultaneously. Such prophecies regarding the future of our culture as those of Heine and Nietzsche show that the disease of the times can be diagnosed from within as well as from without.

less directed; this is equally true of Klee or Chagall, of Joyce or Thomas Mann. The lesser artists make a program of this principle; they amuse themselves and the world with the literary and artistic expression of their incontinence, with an exhibition of their private complexes. For example, Dali.

The modern painters of the last sixty years have been captured by a power which threatens to destroy them. These painters are not masters in the old sense, but victims, even when they dominate this situation. Because the form of the outside world has been shattered, an identifiable and learnable artistic technique has almost ceased to exist. All these artists suffer the demonic violence of the inward powers. Whether they are driven like Munch into solitude and sickness, like Van Gogh into the release of madness, like Gauguin to the distant isles of primitivism, or like Picasso into the amorphous world of inner transformation—their despair and the strain under which they work contrast sharply with the tranquillity of earlier artists, who felt that they were carrying on a tradition.

We find in Kubin and the early Klee the grotesque distortion, the anxiety and distress, that come of inundation by the unconscious; we find it in Odilon Redon and Ensor, in Lautrec and Munch. A sinister quality, a fear of world catastrophe, are apparent not only in the fractured lines of the paintings of Picasso and Braque but equally in much modern sculpture, with its disorganized fragments of shattered bodies.

The dream world of Chirico and the spirit world of Barlach are interrelated, just as they are related to Rimbaud and Rilke, to *The Magic Mountain* despite its totally different configuration, and to Hesse's *Steppenwolf*. Over them all stands anxiety, the incursion of *Die andere Seite* (The Other Side), which Kubin intuitively anticipated.

As our daytime world is devoured by the Terrible Mother, torn to pieces in the bloody rituals that are our wars, demonic, magical, and elemental irrationality invades us. The stream of the libido flows inward, from the crumbling canon into the unconscious, and activates its latent images of past and future.

This is why the art of primitive peoples, of children, and of the insane arouses so much interest today; everything is still in mixture and almost unarticulated. It is almost impossible to render this phase of the world faithfully, because we are still in a formless state of creative disintegration: protoplasm, mingling decay and new birth—amorphous, atonal, disharmonious, primeval.

Blackness, *nigredo*, means the breakdown of distinctions and forms, of all that is known and certain. When the psychic libido of the individual drains off into the darkness, he falls back into *prima materia*, into a chaos in which the psychic state of origination, of *participation mystique*, is reactivated. And in modern art we find the same phenomenon. The dissolution of the outside world, of form and the individual, leads to a dehumanization of art.

The vital energy leaves the human form which was hitherto its highest embodiment and awakens extrahuman and prehuman forms. The human figure that corresponds in a psychological sense to the personality centered in the ego and the system of consciousness is replaced by the anonymous vitality of the flowing unconscious, of the creative force in nature and the psyche.

This process is evident in the landscapes of the Impressionists. The transformation begins with the outside world, which becomes psychic and gradually loses its objective character. Instead of painting a segment of the outside world, the artist paints for painting's sake, concerning himself only with the inherent modality of the picture, with color and form; the psychic symbol has replaced the object. But through *participation mystique* this psychic symbol has a closer, more effective, and more inward contact with the segment of world to which it relates than a naturalistic, objective picture, dictated by consciousness and "made" with detachment.

We find in modern paintings a strange mixture, a unity of world and psyche, in which fragments of landscapes, cubes, circles, forms, colors, parts of human figures, organic and inorganic components, curves, tatters of dreams, memories, deconcretized objects and concretized symbols seem to float in a strange continuum. We are reminded of the myth that before the world was created with its familiar figures, fragments came into being, arms, heads, eyes, torsos, etc. without interconnection, which appeared only in a later birth.

Whether Picasso represents this world of the beginning or whether in his cubist efforts he opposes its chaos, whether in harmony with the life stream of color Chagall hovers lyrically over this world, or Klee, with the knowledge of an initiate, chisels out the secret counterpoint of its inner order, the driving force is in every case the *participation mystique*, the inner stream which follows its own laws, detached from the illusion of outward reality.

All this is deconcretized; and if corks and cookies, scraps of paper, or other articles are pasted on the picture, this quasi-concreteness only makes the spectral quality of the whole even more evident. Dynamics replaces composition, the energy of color and form replaces the illusion of outward reality, the amorphous replaces the conventional and matter-of-fact, and disintegration and the abyss banish comfort and "still life."

This deconcretization is also expressed in the two-dimensional trend of painting, which relinquishes the corporeality of world and body for a dynamic of form and color—a trend, by the way, which has its analogy in science, in both physics and psychology.

The human becomes demonic, things become human: a face dissolves into colors and forms, a blob of paint looks at us with a human eye. Everything shifts and leaps, now into empty banality, now into an abyss of cosmic suffering, now into a mystical transfiguration of color. Whip all this together and mix it with the unintelligible—isn't that just what life really looks like? But even if we recognize that this modern art is an authentic expression of our time, the question arises: Is it still art in the same sense as all previous art? And although those who first called it "degenerate art" were themselves degenerates, has our art not really gone astray?

But let us be careful! We are speaking of ourselves. If this art is degenerate, we too are degenerate, for innumerable individuals are suffering the same collapse of the cultural canon, the same alienation, the same loneliness—the rising blackness with its shadow and devouring dragon. The disintegration and dissonance of this art are our own; to understand them is to understand ourselves.

If the need for expression has its source in the intensity of the experience, how can modern man, whose world is menaced by chaos, do other than give creative form to this chaos? Only where chaos is overcome can what lies behind it emerge, and the seed of the fruit of chaos is perhaps more precious than the seed of any other fruit. Today there can be no hope for the future in any religion, art, or ethic that has not faced this threat of chaos.

That a new ethic is needed is neither a philosophical whim nor merely the product of an unfortunate disposition; it is a profound concern of our time.[13] Here the men of today and the men of yesterday must part company. Anyone whose ears do not burn, whose eyes do not cloud over at the thought of the concentration camps, the crematoriums, the atomic explosions which make up our reality—at the dissonances of our music, the broken, tattered forms of our painting, the lament of Dr. Faustus—is free to

13 Cf. my *Tiefenpsychologie und neue Ethik.*

crawl into the shelter of the safe old methods and rot. The rest of us must again taste the fruit of the tree of knowledge, which will redeem us from the paradise in which it is believed that man and the world are wholly good. It is true that we run the risk of choking on it. But there is no other way. We must acknowledge the evil, the blackness, the disintegration which cry to us so desperately from the art of our time, and whose presence it so desperately affirms.

Paradoxical as it may sound when formulated in theological terms, it seems today that we must redeem a bit of Satan. It is not without significance that I have never met any man for whom the idea of hell as eternal punishment, the idea of absolute damnation, was not absolutely inconceivable. Hell no longer seems an inhuman, alien conception, for all of us are too close to this hell within us and outside us; all of us are consciously or unconsciously dominated by the numinous law of transformation, which leads to hell, and also through it and beyond it.

Again I must quote from *Dr. Faustus*, this time Frau Schweigestill's words, with which the tragedy ends: "Often he talked of eternal grace, the poor man, and I don't know if it will be enough. But an understanding heart, believe me, is enough for everything."

Let us understand these words correctly. They are not proud or arrogant; on the contrary they are desperately modest. We really do not know any longer whether grace is enough, precisely because we are as we are and are beginning to see ourselves as we are. But at a time of overwhelming crisis, the questionable nature of grace, or rather our knowledge that we are unworthy of grace, compels us to understand and love mankind, the fallible mankind that we ourselves are. Behind this abysmal crisis, the archetype of the Eternal Feminine as earth and as Sophia would seem to be discernible; it is no accident that these words are spoken by Frau Schweigestill, the mother. That is to say, it is precisely in chaos, in hell, that the New makes its appearance. Did not Kwanyin descend into hell rather than spend her time with the serene music makers in heaven?

Modern art, then, is not concerned with beauty, much less with aesthetic pleasure. Modern paintings are no museum pieces. Since they are not primarily the product of a directing consciousness, they can only be effective and fruitful when the beholder himself is in an adequate psychic situation—that is, not centered in his ego-consciousness but turned toward his own unconscious, or at least open to it.

There is in modern art a psychic current which descends like a waterfall into the chasm of the unconscious, into a nonobjective, impersonal world. With their animism that brings to life the inner world and the realm of *participation mystique*, many of these works are charged with a demonic force that can suddenly leap out at the overwhelmed and terrified beholder at any time, in any place, and strike him like lightning, for modern art lives in a world between chaos and archetype; it is filled with plasmatic forces out of which such an archetype can suddenly be constellated.

Sometimes the powers themselves appear, as in the spectral, demonic world of Kubin, in Ensor's masks, and to a lesser degree in Dali. True, most modern artists deprecate realistic, objective representations of demonic forces, and indeed there are countless other ways of expressing the powers. They range from Barlach's picture of a world dominated by unseen forces to the plastic abstractions of Henry Moore and Picasso's abstract grotesque demonism.

Distortion, crookedness, and grotesque horror form an archetypal aspect of the demonic. If modern art is characterized by the disintegration of external reality and an activation of the transpersonal psychic world, it becomes understandable that the artist should feel a compulsion to depict the powers in their own realm—which is, of course, a psychic realm—and not as they appear, disguised, in nature. And in the art of primitives also, abstraction is often the form corresponding to the world of spirits and the dead.

As magnets order a field of iron filings, so do the archetypes order our psychic life; a similar process takes place in modern painting. Among primitive peoples the powers are projected into strange forms and symbols, and modern art has returned to this primordial phase of exorcism.

In Western culture the artist first set out to represent the world implied in the idea of the beautiful; he strove to concretize this transfigured vision, and later, with the emergence of the earth archetype, the idea of the beautiful seemed to have been imprinted on life itself. The modern development, however, has been to shatter all these static, ontological conceptions. The powers become visible as pure dynamic, no longer incarnated in man and object.

He who has perceived the numinosum which destroys every canon, dissolves every fixed system, and reduces every form to relativity tends to see the godhead as an irrupting power, a lord of destruction who dances like

Shiva himself over a collapsing world. And it is easy to misinterpret our world and its art in this sense—as annihilation. For all of us are still accustomed to believe in set images, in absolute ideas and values, to see the archetype only as eternal presence and not as formless dynamic, to forget the central commandment of the godhead, which is: "Thou shalt not make unto thyself any graven image."

But it is a total misunderstanding of our time and our art to regard their relation to chaos as purely negative. For all these artists have one thing in common: they have all experienced the creative truth that the spirit blows where it will, and even where they seem to be playing and leaving things to chance, it is not only because the perplexed ego has renounced all hope of knowledge but because they believe profoundly that in and behind chance a greater truth may be at work. Conscious renunciation of form is often falsely interpreted as inability to give form, as incompetence. Actually the breakdown of consciousness, carrying the artist backward to an all-embracing *participation* with the world, contains the constructive, creative elements of a new world vision.

The deflation of man makes for a sense of world and life far transcending the common bond which unites all men on earth. It is no accident that a human element appears so seldom at the center of the modern mandala, and so frequently a flower, a star, a spring, a light, an eye, or the void itself. The center of gravity has shifted from consciousness toward the creative matrix where something new is in preparation.

This shift is perhaps most evident in Chagall's paintings, which reflect most clearly the synthetic force of the soul's emotional reality. The luminous power of the inward colors, an inward movement guided by a stream of symbols, produces paintings which are an authentic metaphor for the inward life of the psyche. And beyond all chaos, yet profoundly bound up with it, there arises a new kind of psychic beauty, psychic movement, and irrational unity, whose flowerlike growth—otherwise found only in Klee, and here in a different form—is rooted in the profoundest and most secret depths of the soul.

Our art contains as many revelations of the archetype as of chaos. Only the simplest form of this reawakened archetypal world is reflected among the neoprimitives, whether like Gauguin they seek archaic form or like Rousseau represent the archetypes in naïve splendor: the desert, the forest primeval, the Great Mother as snake charmer, the battle in the jungle, or, contrasting with all this, the *petit bourgeois* world, the nosegay, etc.

An animistic, pantheistic sense of a world animated by the archetypes is revealed in the autonomous dynamic of natural form, as in Cézanne, the cubists, and modern plastic art. Not only in Van Gogh and Munch, but actually in all moderns, whether they paint portraits, landscapes, or abstractions, this autonomous dynamic creates psychic landscapes whose mood, emotion, color—the inner music of primal feeling, line and form, and the primal constellations of form and color—are the authentic expression of the powers. These powers everywhere, in wind and cube, in the ugly and absurd as well as in stone or stream—and ultimately in the human as well—are manifested as movement, never as given and fixed things.

For the art of our time inclines toward a radical spiritualism, a solemnization of the secret transpersonal and suprapersonal forces of life and death, which surge up from within to compensate for the materialism dominating the outward picture of our times, a materialism conditioned by the rise of the earth archetype during the Renaissance.

Thus it is a great misunderstanding to characterize this art as intellectual —for only its hangers-on are intellectual—and to underestimate its religious and, in the true sense of the word, metaphysical impetus. The anonymous creative drive itself is the essential reality of a human art independent of any external world. Our art, like our times, is characterized by the old Chinese saying quoted by Richard Wilhelm: "The heavens battle with the creatures in the sign of the Creative." [14]

In compensation for the decay of our cultural canon and our permanent values, both the individual and the group are experiencing an awakening of the collective unconscious. Its inward, psychic expression is modern art, but it is also outwardly discernible in the flood of religious, spiritual, and artistic forms that are erupting from the collective unconscious into Western consciousness.

The art of diverse epochs and religions, peoples and cultures, tends to merge in our modern experience. In the symbols of their worshipers' rapture the gods of all times confront us, and we stand overwhelmed by this inward pantheon of mankind. Its expression is the world's art, that prodigious net of numinous creation in which man is captured, although he himself has brought it forth.

14 Wilhelm, *Der Mensch und das Sein*, p. 234.

The dignity of man now appears to us in his creative power, whether in the modern or the Indian, in the medieval Christian or the Bushman. All together are the creators of a higher reality, of a transpersonal existence, whose emanation, transcending times and cultures, shows man in his creative reality and spurs him toward it.

The revelation of the numinosum speaks out of every creative man regardless of his cultural level, for there are different aspects of the transpersonal, which leads one individual to a religious calling, another to art, still another to a scientific or an ethical vocation. The fraternity of *all* those who have been seized by the numinosum is one of the great human phenomena we are beginning to perceive in this era which, more than any other before it, is gaining an awareness of the immensity of man's works.

The religions of the world, the saviors of the world, the revolutionaries, the prophets, and not least the artists of the world—all these great figures and what they have created form for us a single whole. We all—and not just individuals among us—are beginning not to free ourselves from our personal determinants, for that is impossible, but to see them in perspective. The African medicine man and the Siberian shaman assume for us the same human dignity as Moses and the Buddha; an Aztec fresco takes its place beside a Chinese landscape and an Egyptian sculpture, the Upanishads beside the Bible and the Book of Changes.

At the center of each culture and time stand different numinous—or as we say, archetypal—powers, but all are eternal, and all touch upon the eternal existence of man and the world. Whether it be Egypt's striving for permanence, Mexico's primitive terror, the human radiance and clarity of Greece; whether it be the faith of the Psalmist, the transfigured suffering of Jesus or the Buddha withdrawing into the infinite, the power of death in Shiva, Rembrandt's light, the emptiness of an Islamic mosque, the flowering earth of the Renaissance, the flaming earth of Van Gogh, or the dark earth of the African demons—all bear witness to the timelessness of man's seizure by the numinosum.

For the source of the creative drive is not nature, not the collective, not a definite cultural canon, but something which moves through generations and peoples, epochs and individuals, which calls the individual with the rigor of an absolute; and whoever he may be and wherever he may be, it compels him to travel the road of Abraham, to leave the land of his birth, his mother, and the house of his father, and seek out the land to which the godhead leads him.

In our time two forms of integration appear side by side, an outward and an inward, a collective and an individual. Much as they may seem to differ, they are essentially related. The one is the integration incumbent upon our culture, an integration with world culture and all its contents. Inundation by the world's collective contents leads first to chaos—in the individual as in the group as a whole. How can the individual, how can our culture, integrate Christianity and antiquity, China and India, the primitive and the modern, the prophet and the atomic physicist, into *one* humanity? Yet that is just what the individual and our culture must do. Though wars rage and peoples exterminate one another in our atavistic world, the reality living within us tends, whether we know it or not, whether we wish to admit it or not, toward a universal humanism. But there is an inward process of integration which compensates for the outward one; this is individuation. This inner integration does not consist merely in the integration of the individual's personal unconscious: when the collective unconscious emerges, the individual must inwardly come to grips with the very same powers whose integration and assimilation as world culture are his outward tasks.

Our conception of man is beginning to change. Up to now we saw him chiefly in a historical or horizontal perspective, embedded in his group, his time, and his cultural canon, and determined by his position in the world—that is, in his particular epoch. There is truth in this vision, no doubt, but today we are beginning to see man in a new perspective—vertically—in his relation to the absolute.

The roots of every man's personality extend beyond the historical area of his factual existence into the world of the numinosum. And if we follow the course of these roots, we pass through every stratum of history and prehistory. We encounter within ourselves the savage with his masks and rites; within ourselves we find the roots of our own culture, but we also find the meditation of Asia and the magical world of the Stone Age medicine man. The challenge of this transpersonal world of powers must be met by modern man, despite his characteristic sense of inadequacy.

We must face our own problems and our own imperfections; and at the same time we must integrate a superabundant outward and inward world that is shaped by no canon. This is the conflict which torments the modern era: modern man and his art.

This integration of chaos, however, is not possible in any single act or constellation; the individuation it requires is a process of growth, embracing the transformations of a whole lifetime; during such a process each individual's capacity for resolving conflict is repeatedly strained to the utmost. This perhaps is why the careers of the great artists of our time are all, in greater or lesser degree, Calvaries. The task of integration facing the great artist today can no longer be performed in a single work but more than ever before requires a unity of life and work. Van Gogh's pictures cease in this sense to be individual paintings; they are a storm of painting bound up with his life, and each picture is only a part of it. But often it has even ceased to be the painter's intention—if we can speak here of intention—to make a complete statement in any one picture; his orientation is toward the work as a whole, which is meant to express a reality that transcends painting.

All modern artists—in contrast to the fulfilled artists of normal times—have the sacred enthusiasm of which the *I Ching* says: "Thunder comes resounding out of the earth: the image of enthusiasm," and "Devotion to movement: this is enthusiasm." [15]

Whether we consider Picasso, with his single-minded devotion to a great creative impulse—whose work represents a significant reality only when taken as a whole, each part being problematic, questionable, and incomplete; or Rilke, whose development leads from delicate sound arrangements through the catastrophe of ten years' silence to the gigantic dome of the *Duino Elegies;* or the even-paced building of Thomas Mann's work, increasingly preoccupied with what is evil, diseased, and archaic in man, which he (who, more than any other artist of our time, has achieved the unity of life and work that is individuation) uniquely integrated; when we consider the tragic frenzy of Van Gogh or the mysterious transformation of Klee—all of them belong to us; they are we, or rather we are fragments of them all.

We know that the core of the neuroses of our time is the religious problem or, stated in more universal terms, the search for the self. In this sense neuroses, like the mass phenomena resulting from this situation, are a kind of sacred disease. Our whole epoch is full of it, but behind it stand the power of a numinous center, which seems to direct not only the normal development of the individual but his psychic crises and transformations as well—not only the disease but also its cure, both in the individual and in the collective.

This centroversion has great consequences in the great and small con-

15 Tr. Baynes, Vol. I, 71; Vol. II, 105.

sequences in the small. However, our whole art, which may be called neurotic in its rapture and "sacred" in its neurosis, is unconsciously or—in its highest summits—consciously directed by this central force. And so it is with each one of us.

Just as the psychic totality of the individual takes form around a mysterious center, the mandala of modern art, in all its vast diversity, unfolds around a mysterious center, which as chaos and blackness, as numinosum and as change, is pregnant with a new doom, but also with a new world. In the *Duino Elegies* Rilke wrote:

> For Beauty's nothing
> but beginning of Terror we're still just able to bear,
> and why we adore it so is because it serenely
> disdains to destroy us.[16]

More than to any other beauty in art, these words apply to the terrible beauty of modern art, which itself denies that it is beauty. Never before was the beautiful so close to the terrible. The masters of Zen Buddhism often twisted their disciples' noses or struck them in the face in order to bring them illumination by thrusting them back on themselves. Similarly our time and our destiny, and often our art as well, strike us in the face, perhaps also in order to fling us into the void of the center, which is the center of transformation and birth.

For despite all the despair and darkness which are still more evident in us and our art than the secret forces of the new birth and the new synthesis, we must not forget that no epoch, amid the greatest danger to its existence, has shown so much readiness to burst the narrow limits of its horizon and open itself to the great power which is striving to rise out of the unknown, here and everywhere in the world. Menaced as we are by our own atom bombs, every act of destruction will be answered by a rebuilding, in which the unity of everything human will be affirmed more strongly than ever.

This is surely no prophecy, it is the reality of the road which we travel, or rather which we are compelled to travel. Upon this road the horizons are changing in a way we ourselves scarcely realize, and we along with them are moving toward the New, all of us, on this side and that side of the iron curtains that divide us today.

Let us not forget that, despite all the darkness and danger, the man of our time, like the art that belongs to him, is a great fulfillment and a still greater hope.

16 *Duino Elegies*, I, tr. Leishman and Spender, pp. 24f.

Henri-Charles Puech

Gnosis and Time

If I open this discussion with a few preliminary remarks which may seem long, it is because the problem involved in our title, "Gnosis and Time," is perhaps more difficult to formulate than to solve; or more accurately because it is only when we have defined our terms that we shall be able to deal with the problem and suggest a solution.

One of the principal obstacles in our path is this: except for a handful of texts that I shall mention shortly, we possess no document in which a Gnostic has explicitly set forth his conception of time. For the Gnostics, time was not a particular, specific, or relatively autonomous problem, needful or even susceptible of being examined and resolved independently. This does not mean that for them the question was not essential, that they were not deeply preoccupied with it. Quite the opposite. But the Gnostic's attitude toward time was a part of his general attitude toward the state of man here below and consequently toward the world as a whole, its history past and future, and the drama that is being enacted in it. Accordingly, we shall be able to discern and understand the Gnostic attitude toward time only as a function of the total Gnostic vision of the world, the Gnostic *Weltanschauung*. And since the parts of this world view are inseparable, our inquiry must ultimately be directed toward Gnosis as a whole, considered in its essence, its structure, and its mechanisms. This and this alone will enable us to observe that despite appearances, despite the almost total absence of explicit testimony, the problem of time lies at the very heart of Gnosis. Indeed, the word "heart" evokes the essence of the whole organism; and it is to the heart of the Gnostic sensibility and the Gnostic system that we must penetrate in our search for the facts bearing on our theme as well as their explanation.

A second difficulty lies in another aspect of our question: it seems at first sight to be stated only negatively, by contrast to, or at least in terms of, something else. The Gnostic vision of the universe can be situated and understood only in relation to other contemporary *Weltanschauungen*, from which it borrowed certain of its elements but against which it reacted, often violently. To anticipate briefly what we shall discuss in greater detail further on, the attitude of the Gnostics toward time, and more generally, toward the world, is characterized from the first by a movement of revolt against time and the world as conceived by Hellenism and Christianity—that is to say, by the divergent philosophies and religions of the circles in which Gnosticism spread and to which it adapted itself in the first centuries of our era. Here, as on many other points, the Gnostic attitude is chiefly one of negation. We can define it only in relation to what it negates, and consequently we must begin by determining the nature of these Greek and Christian conceptions which Gnosticism opposed. In so doing we shall apprehend its originality, its specificity, and thus, transcending the negative aspect, we shall arrive at its positive core and independent character.

A last difficulty has its source in the very term "Gnosis." There is a danger that this word will evoke only vague or confused ideas, for indeed it can be taken in several different senses. Here it will be necessary to define the sense in which we mean to employ it now; it will be necessary to circumscribe the field of historical realities which it covers and in which we shall gather the facts and proofs on which to support our hypotheses.

First, I shall undertake to sketch the view of time held by the Greeks and early Christians; then, in order to clarify and justify my use of the term Gnosticism, I shall explain what it has come to mean to modern historians and phenomenologists of religion. Slow as it may seem, such a course will lead us little by little to the heart of our subject. It will provide us with the best possible approach to a problem which proves baffling and elusive when we seek to confront it directly.

*

Our first point might be summed up as follows: [1] the Greek world conceived of time as above all cyclical or circular, returning perpetually upon itself,

1 The following pages on Hellenism and Christianity adhere to the text of a paper read on September 5, 1950, at the Seventh International Congress for the History of Religions and published in the *Proceedings of the 7th Congress for the History of Religions* (Amsterdam, 1951), pp. 33–52. Certain passages have been abridged, summarized, or deleted; the parts retained have been slightly revised and augmented here and there by small additions and brief notes.

self-enclosed, under the influence of astronomical movements which command and regulate its course with necessity. For Christianity, on the contrary, time is bound up with the Creation and continuous action of God; it unfolds unilaterally in one direction, beginning at a single source and aiming toward a single goal: it is oriented and represents a progression from the past toward the future; it is one, organic and progressive; consequently it has a full reality. Then comes Gnosticism. With its need for immediate salvation, it rejects the servitude and repetition of Greek cyclical time as well as the organic continuity of Christian unilinear time; it shatters them both into bits (the figure is no exaggeration). More succinctly, we might speak of a game among three opposing conceptions, the first representing time by a circle, the second by a straight line, the third by a broken line.

For the Greeks, indeed, the passage of time is cyclical and not rectilinear. Dominated by an ideal of intelligibility which finds authentic and full being only in that which is in itself and remains identical with itself, in the eternal and immutable, the Greeks regarded movement and change as inferior degrees of reality, in which, at best, identity can be apprehended in the form of permanence and perpetuity, hence of recurrence. The circular movement which assures the survival of the same things by repeating them, by bringing about their continuous return, is the perfect and most immediate expression (hence that which is closest to the divine) of the absolute immobility at the summit of the hierarchy.[2] According to the famous Platonic definition,[3] the time which is determined and measured by the revolution of the celestial spheres is the mobile image of immobile eternity which it imitates by moving in a circle. Consequently both the entire cosmic process and the time of our world of generation and decay develop in a circle or according to an indefinite succession of cycles, in the course of which the same reality is made, unmade, and remade, in conformity with an immutable law and determinate alternations. The same sum of being is preserved; nothing is created and nothing lost (*eadem sunt omnia semper nec magis id nunc est neque erit mox quam fuit*

2 On the primacy of *kuklophoria* and the inferiority of the movement of translation in a straight line, cf., for example, Aristotle, *Physics*, VIII, 9, 265a–266a or Olympiodorus, *Commentary on the Phaedo*, ed. William Norvin (Leipzig, 1913), pp. 192, 4–6; 195, 27–196, 9; 197, 4–5; 236, 9–11. Selected from among hundreds of such passages, these two are particularly instructive.

3 Plato, *Timaeus*, 37c–38a.

ante);[4] moreover, certain thinkers of dying antiquity—Pythagoreans, Stoics, Platonists—went so far as to maintain that within each of these cycles of time, of these *aiones*, these *aeva*, the same situations recur that have already occurred in the preceding cycles and will occur in subsequent cycles—and so *ad infinitum*. No event is unique, nothing is enacted but once (for example the condemnation of Socrates); every event has been enacted, is enacted, and will be enacted perpetually; the same individuals have appeared, appear, and will appear at every turn of the circle.[5] Cosmic time is repetition and *anakuklosis*, eternal return.

From this follow grave consequences. No point in a circle is beginning or middle or end in the absolute sense; or else all points are these indifferently. The starting point to which the "apocatastasis" or the completion of the "Great Year" restores the course of things in a movement which is regression as well as progression is never anything but relative. In other words there

4 Lucretius, *De rerum natura*, III, 945, and V, 1135. Cf. in the same sense, Manilius, *Astronomica*, I, 518–21 (tr. Thomas Creech, *The Five Books of M. Manilius*, London, 1700, p. 22):

> "Yet safe the world, and free from change doth last,
> No years decrease it, and no years can waste;
> Its course it urges on, and keeps its frame,
> And still will be, because 'twas still the same."

Or Censorinus, *De die natali*, ed. Friedrich Hultsch (Leipzig, 1867), IV, p. 7, li. 11–15. Censorinus, after declaring that all the Pythagoreans, a number of Platonists and members of the Old Academy, and many Peripatetics agree in affirming the eternity of the human race, writes: "Therefore also they say that of all those things which in that eternal world always have been and are to be, there was no beginning, but there is a kind of cycle of things being generated and born, in which is to be seen both the beginning and the end of each race [*variant and usual reading:* of everything that is born]." (Tr. A.S.B.G.) Similarly Marcus Aurelius, *Meditations*, VI, 37; VII, 1; VIII, 1; IX, 35 and 37; X, 27; XI, 1; XII, 26; for him the thesis is attached to the theory of the permanent circular movement of all things (e.g., II, 14; VII, 19; IX, 28).

5 Cf. for example Tatian, *Oratio ad Graecos* (Migne, *PG*, VI), 3; Origen, *Contra Celsum*, IV, 68, and V, 20–21. Also the references indicated by Paul Koetschau in his edn. of *Contra Celsum* (*GCS*, Vol. I, p. 338, li. 3, and Vol. II, p. 21, li. 23); Simplicius, *On Aristotle's Physics*, V, 4; ed. Hermann Diels, *Simplicii in Aristotelis Physicorum Libros . . . Commentaria* (Commentaria in Aristotelem Graeca, Vols. IX, X; Berlin, 1882–95), p. 886. Or the following reflections of Synesius ("An Egyptian Tale" or "On Providence," in Migne, *PG*, LXVI, 1277), who speculates on the analogy between the history of his time and the myth of Osiris and Typhon: "Why so troubling a likeness? It has no cause other than the unity of a wholly perfect world in which a close dependence necessarily unites the part which we inhabit and the heavenly bodies that surround us. When the heavenly bodies conclude their cycle and resume their course—we may place our trust in the doctrine common to the Egyptians and the Greeks—the return of their influence restores the conjunctures of former times on this earth."

can never, strictly speaking, be a beginning and end of the world; it has always moved in an infinite succession of circles and is eternal: any Creation or Consummation of the universe is inconceivable. Passage of time can never be represented by a straight line limited at its beginning and end by an initial and final event. And secondly, though by virtue of the successive cycles that compose it, time has a rhythm, it can never have an absolutely defined direction. As Aristotle remarks, we may say at our present point on the revolving circle that we are "after" the Trojan War; but the circle continues to rotate and "after" us it will once more bring the very same Trojan War, so that in this sense we may just as well say that we precede this event.[6] There is no absolute chronological "before" and "after." Finally, since all things are repeated and preserved identically, it is impossible that anything radically new should arise in the course of history.

Moreover, whatever may have been said to the contrary,[7] the Greeks never succeeded in developing a philosophy and still less a theology of history. Their farthest step in this direction—and even this occurred at a very late date, with Polybius and Diodorus—was to attribute a certain convergence in the facts of universal history (at last conceived as forming a

6 Aristotle, *Problemata*, XVII, 3; tr. W. S. Hett, *Problems* (LCL, 1936–37), Vol. I, p. 367: "How should one define the terms 'before' and 'after' [τὸ πρότερον καὶ τὸ ὕστερον]? Should it be in the sense that the people of Troy are before us, and those previous to them before them, and so on continuously? Or if it is true that everything has a beginning, a middle, and an end, and when a man grows old he reaches his limit and reverts again to the beginning, and those things which are nearer the beginning merit the term 'before,' what is there to prevent us from regarding ourselves as nearer the beginning [than the men of Troy]? If that is true, then we should be 'before.' As therefore in the movement of the heavens and of each star there is a circle, what is there to prevent birth and death of the mortal from being of this nature, so that mortals are born and destroyed again? So they say there is a cycle in human affairs [καθάπερ καὶ φασὶ κύκλον εἶναι τὰ ἀνθρώπινα]. The suggestion that those who are continually being born are numerically [τῷ ἀριθμῷ] identical is absurd, but we could accept that they are the same in 'form' [τῷ εἴδει]. [And actually Aristotle, for his part, admitted only the eternal recurrence of the species or type, and not of the individuals.] In that sense we should be 'before' [the men of Troy], and we should assume the arrangement of the series to be of the type [τὴν τοῦ εἱρμοῦ τάξιν] which returns [πάλιν ἐπανακάμπτειν] to the starting-point and produces continuity and is always acting in the same way [συνεχὲς ποιεῖν καὶ ἀεὶ κατὰ ταὐτὰ ἔχειν.] For Alcmaeon tells us that men die because they cannot connect the beginning with the end—a clever saying, if one supposes him to be speaking in a metaphor, and not to wish his words to be taken literally. If, then, there is a circle, and a circle has neither beginning nor end, men would not be 'before' because they are nearer the beginning, nor should we be 'before' them, nor they 'before' us."

7 Cf. in particular Wilhelm Nestle, "Griechische Geschichtsphilosophie," *Archiv für Geschichte der Philosophie* (Berlin), XLI (1932), 80–114.

single body) to the wholly natural "physical" action of *Tyche*, Fortune, or Chance or to look for a rhythm (still cyclical) in historical events or in the development of political regimes. Or else, with Plato for example, they speculated on the models or ideal schemata of states or social forms, from which they derived a necessary, a temporal succession applicable to any event whatever. The resultant laws were "laws of decadence rather than of development": [8] they represent change as a fall from an ideal primitive state conceived in terms of myth; political states do not improve, they become corrupted; and the history of governments is a history of decadence. Here we perceive the core of the Greek's feeling about time: it was experienced as a "degenerescence"—the notion of a continuous progress in time was unheard of. It could hardly have been otherwise in a conception for which perfection, the total and supreme expression of being, is given once and for all a world of essences or of intelligible models, transcending time.

In the light of what we have said, it is not difficult to account for the inability of the Greek mind to develop an authentic philosophy of history. The singular and contingent does not interest the Greek philosopher: it is not a subject for knowledge which retains only the general and reproducible aspects of sensuous reality. But above all, the Greek's view that events repeat themselves in the form of a circle every point in which is indifferently beginning, middle, and end—without any absolute relation of "before" and "after"—deprives him of a central reference point by which to define and orient a historical past and future. For him there is no unique event which has occurred once and for all, to provide this indispensable reference point and so enable him to give a single irreversible direction to the course of history.

Such, in its broad outlines, is the Greek conception of time and consequently of history. It is an essentially cosmological conception. Time is perceived and considered in the light of a hierarchized vision of the universe, in which the inferior realities are only degraded and necessary reflections of the superior realities which give them being and life and govern their movements. Time is part of a cosmic order; on its own level it is an effect and an expression of that order. If it moves in a circle, it is because, in its own way,

8 Emile Bréhier, "Quelques traits de la philosophie de l'histoire dans l'antiquité classique," *Revue d'Histoire et de Philosophie Religieuses* (Strasbourg), XIV (1934), 40; and, for the preceding, p. 38, n. 2. Cf. also Jean Guitton, *Le Temps et l'éternité chez Plotin et Saint Augustin* (Paris, 1933), p. 358, n. 1, and Nestle, "Griechische Geschichtsphilosophie," pp. 93–94.

it imitates the cyclical course of the stars on which it depends. Its endlessness, its repetition of conjunctures, are, in a mobile form, images of the unchanging, perfect order of an eternal universe, eternally regulated by fixed laws, an order of which the heavens, with the uniform revolution of their luminaries, offer still more sublime images.

The spectacle of a world so infallibly ordered from all eternity and the idea of a time recurring for ever and ever might inspire either of two sentiments in a Greek. One was admiration—an admiration that was rational, aesthetic, and religious, and might on occasion go so far as ecstasy. Everything in this grandiose universe has its place, where each event occurs at its appointed time, everything is just, beautiful, and good, or should be regarded as such, because it results from a necessary and intelligible order. What the individual might be tempted to consider evil or defective is mere "nonbeing" or a secondary accident, a note whose apparent discord blends and disappears in the organic movement of the symphony as a whole. Taken as a whole, the *kosmos*—and in Greek the word signifies "order" as well as "world," the two notions being inseparable—is divine, or the reflection of the divine; for some it is even the "son of God," a "second god" or a third.[9] And *a fortiori* the stars, whose exact regularity proves them to be animated and intelligent, moved by gods or gifted with an intelligence superior to ours, must be of divine nature if they are not actually gods.[10] This explains the form which Greek religion preserved from Plato's old age

9 Cf., among others, Harpocration and Numenius, references in my article, "Numenius d'Apamée et les théologies orientales au second siècle," *Annuaire de l'Institut de Philologie et d'Histoire Orientales* (Brussels), II (1934), 756; or Celsus in Origen, *Contra Celsum*, VI, 47, and the testimony of Origen himself, V, 7. The doctrine and formulas recur in certain treatises of the *Corpus hermeticum:* VIII, 1–2; X, 14; XII, 15; ed. and tr. Walter Scott, *Hermetica* (4 vols., Oxford, 1924–36), Vol. I, pp. 175, 197, 233, and in the *Asclepius*, 8, 10, and 39; ed. Scott, I, pp. 299–303, 305, 363. Note also in the same corpus (VI, 2; X, 10; ed. Scott, I, pp. 167, 195) other passages more in conformance with the general theory of Gnosis, declaring the world to be evil.

10 Cf. for example, Franz Cumont, "Le Mysticisme astral dans l'antiquité," *Bulletin de l'Académie Royale de Belgique, Classe des Lettres* (1909), pp. 256–86, or Hugo Gressmann, *Die hellenistische Gestirnreligion* (Leipzig, 1925). In the *Epinomis*, which now seems definitely attributable to Plato (cf. also *Laws*, X, 899b), the proof of the intelligence and divinity of the heavenly bodies is drawn from the regularity and invariable uniformity of their orbits (982a–e). Epicurus is the only philosopher of pagan antiquity who claimed that the stars moved in a straight line: Theon, *Commentary on the Almagest*, in A. Rome, ed., *Commentaires de Pappus et de Théon d'Alexandrie sur l'Almageste*, etc., Vol. II (Studi e testi, no. 72; Rome, 1931), p. 233; but this is precisely because he wished to destroy the belief in the divinity and will of the stars: A.-J. Festugière, *Epicurus and His Gods*, tr. C. W. Chilton (Oxford, 1956).

down to the end of paganism, the form of a cosmic religion that has been so well characterized in a recent work.[11]

The other attitude occurs only rarely and in a late period. Here, instead of —or rather on the fringe of—admiration we find a certain melancholy and weariness,[12] a more or less intense feeling of anguish and servitude. This inflexible order, this time which repeats itself periodically without beginning or end or goal, now appears monotonous or crushing. Things are forever the same; history revolves around itself; our life is not unique: we have already come to life many times and may return again, endlessly in the course of perpetual cycles of reincarnations, of *metensomatoses* or *metempsychoses*.[13] It is, above all, the stars, their positions and their movements, that govern and regulate the destiny of man. The astronomical order, its rigor enhanced by the *mathematici* or the astrologers, becomes strict determinism, predestination, fatality, *Heimarmene*, *Fatum*. At a late date, in the Greco-Roman era, we encounter a somewhat disillusioned or despairing fatalism. Many seek to escape this *douleia*, this slavery to the Destiny that is written in the stars, "sealed" in heaven, since the whole universe with all its events is of one piece.[14] But since the order and laws of the *kosmos* are immutable and eternal, the best part is to submit, to resign oneself; in awareness of the inevitable, one can build up frugal, self-sufficient wisdom with an aftertaste

11 Festugière, *La Révélation d'Hermès Trismégiste,* II: "Le Dieu Cosmique" (Paris, 1949).

12 The attitude of Marcus Aurelius is remarkable in this connection. As a convinced Stoic, the emperor believed in universal determinism and, as has already been indicated above, n. 4, in the circular recurrence of time; in him these beliefs are combined with a keen and often expressed sense of the transience and fragility of things and events, subjected by fatal vicissitudes to perpetual change (for example, *Confessions*, V, 13; VI, 15; VII, 25; IX, 19; X, 7), of the vanity and nullity of man's state on this "clod of earth" that is the world (V, 33; X, 17 and 34; XII, 7 and 32). Still he endeavors to "love" this poor and heavy *destiny* that is ours (VII, 67, and cf. X, 21).

13 The organic connection between the two Greek theses—infinity of the world and metempsychosis—is clearly noted by Origen, who shows that they are both incompatible with the Christian doctrine of the creation and end of the world: *Commentaria in Matthaeum*, XIII, 1; ed. Ernst Benz and Erich Klostermann, *Origenes Werke* (*GCS*, X, 1935), p. 176, li. 5–15; passage quoted by Pamphilus in his *Apology for Origen*, ch. 10, and tr. Rufinus, ed. Benz and Klostermann, XII (1941), p. 9, li. 43–50.

14 Cf. for example, Cumont, "Fatalisme astral et religions antiques," in *Revue d'histoire et de littérature religieuses*, new series, III (1912), 513–43, and *Les Religions orientales dans le paganisme romain* (4th edn., Paris, 1929), pp. 166–68, and the notes relative to these pages, pp. 289–90 (bibliography, p. 289, n. 58); or Festugière, *L'Idéal religieux des Grecs et l'Evangile* (Paris, 1932), pp. 101–15. On astrological fatalism and the sense of anguish it provokes even in some Christians, cf. Origen, *Commentaria in Genesim*, in Migne, *PG*, XII, 48–52. On Destiny, the "supreme concept of Western paganism," see Theodor Haecker, *Der Christ und die Geschichte* (Leipzig, 1935), p. 122.

of bitterness, an austere ethic based on lucid acceptance of all things and sustained by the obstinate tension of an energetic will, free from illusion. Rebellion against the course of the universe and against the universe itself, denial of the primacy and divinity of the visible firmament and the heavenly bodies—these are out of the question. Such attitudes are reserved for the Gnostics.

*

Christianity brings with it a wholly different conception of time.

Here time runs no longer in a circle but in a straight line, finite at its two extremities, having a beginning and an absolute end. Willed and governed by God, the total history of the human race considered as a single indistinct block is enacted between this beginning and this end. Here the direction of time is irreversible: it progresses toward an end, a goal, and it is the medium of a continuous progress. Now time has a full reality and a significance; in other words, it has not only a definite orientation but also an intrinsic meaning.

This Christian conception of time rests on a vision of the world very different from that of the Greeks. As opposed to the Greek view, the world of the Christians is created in time and must end in time. It begins with the first chapter of Genesis and ends in the eschatological perspectives of the Apocalypse. Moreover the Creation, the Last Judgment, and the intermediary period extending from one to the other are all unique. This created, unique world, which began, which endures, and which will end in time, is finite, limited at both extremities of its history. It is neither eternal nor infinite in its duration; it will never be repeated, nor will the events that occur in it. The world is wholly immersed in time.

This world and its destiny stand in a direct relation to the will of God. The perspectives which Hellenism interposed between God and his creature are swept away. Gone are the divinity of the firmament, astral fatality, the hierarchical superiority and circular domination of the heavenly bodies. The Greeks, as we have just seen, held the planets to be divine because they have a regular and rational course. The Christian Lactantius replies with this quaint but significant argument: "Precisely because the planets cannot depart from their prescribed orbits, it is evident that they are not gods; if they were gods, we should see them moving here and there like animate beings on the earth, who go where they wish because their wills are free."[15] On the contrary, man has been created free and stands directly in the presence of his creator. God is manifested in time. Each of his acts marks a *kairos*, a solemn and decisive moment of history. And this history is apprehended as universal, since in Christian eyes the mankind descended from Adam forms a unique whole, without distinction of race, language, or culture. The mighty hand of God—in the form of his Word or his Wisdom—never ceases to guide the world it has formed and the man it has kneaded of clay. As for the creature, he can know God only in these temporal manifestations: in history he discerns the accomplishment of the Creator's designs, the successive realization of a plan conceived by God for the benefit of mankind. The vertical interpretation of the world's changing appearances through the fixed and atemporal, archetypal realities of the upper, intelligible world, gives way—in ancient Christianity at least—to a horizontal interpretation of the segments of time through one another: the past announces and prepares the future, the future accomplishes and explains the past; or, to use the technical terminology of the Christian authors of the first centuries, the earlier events are the "types" or "prefigurations" of the subsequent events, and these in turn are the realization of the events which precede them and which are related to them as the "shadow" is related to full, authentic reality. Thus one might say that here the image anticipates

15 *Institutiones divinae*, II, 5, ed. Migne, *PL*, VI, 278–79; tr. E. Bréhier, *Histoire de la philosophie*, Vol. I (Paris, 1927), p. 511. Cf. Plato, *Epinomis*, 982c–e, tr. W. R. M. Lamb (LCL, 1927), p. 455: "And men ought to have found proof of the stars and the whole of that travelling system being possessed of mind in the fact that they always do the same things because they do what has been decided long ago for an incalculable time, not deciding differently this way and that, and doing sometimes one thing, sometimes another, in wanderings and changes of circuit. Most of us have thought just the opposite—that because they do the same things in the same way they have no soul; the multitude followed the lead of the unintelligent so far as to suppose that, whereas humanity was intelligent and living because it moved about, divinity was unintelligent because it abode in the same courses. But if man had sided with the fairer and better and friendly part, he might have concluded that he ought to regard as intelligent—and for this very reason—that which acts always in the same respects, in the same way, and for the same reasons; and that this is the nature of the stars, fairest to see, and passing along, dancing the fairest and most magnificent of all dances in the world, they make good the needs of all living creatures." For Methodius, bishop of Olympus or Philippi—*De autexusio*, ed. and tr. A. Vaillant in *Patrologia Orientalis* (Paris), XXII (1930), 795–97—man is, by virtue of his freedom, superior to the heavens, the sun, and the earth, which slavishly execute the will of God. On the "humiliation" of the heavenly bodies in ancient Christianity see the references drawn from Origen in H. de Lubac, *Surnaturel* (Paris, 1946), p. 192, n. 6.

the model, while in Greek thought the transcendent model is for all eternity prior to the image. Greek exemplarism is diametrically reversed.

Finally, with Christianity the human creature becomes the immediate, if not exclusive, object of divine Providence, a Providence conceived as in every instance "particular." History is definitely teleological and anthropocentric: an outrage and an absurdity for a mind as Greek as that of Celsus, the anti-Christian polemicist![16]

On the basis of this schematic representation of time there soon grew up a philosophy, or rather a theology, of history, the most perfect examples of which are provided by St. Irenaeus' *Adversus haereses*, published in the year 185, and St. Augustine's *City of God*, published from 413 to 426. Here we find one of the original contributions of Christianity and another of its differences from Hellenism. We have seen that the Greek mind was virtually unable to develop a philosophy of history, because it had no absolute center or fixed reference points by which to order and interpret historical events. Christianity possessed such a center in the coming of Jesus. This concrete, datable event binds and unbinds the entire perspective of human history. It divides this history into two periods which at the same time it joins together: a preliminary period, ushered in by the Creation and the Fall, converging toward the *Parousia*, which it prepares and prophesies; and a second period, of restoration and accomplishment, leading to the second coming of Christ in glory. With Jesus history has taken a decisive step, crossed an essential threshold: "the kingdom of God," awaited during the past centuries, "is at hand"; the *aiōn mellōn* has begun in the *aiōn houtos* or *enestōs*. Hence the web of history can be woven backward as well as forward from this basic point: from Jesus, the new Adam, to the creation of the world and the first man, a regressive continuity of the past, marked by the prophecies and "typical" events of the Old Testament: from Jesus to his second coming and to the end of the world a progressive continuity of the future.

16 Passage from the "True Discourse" cited by Origen, *Contra Celsum*, IV, 23. Some of the principal theses in regard to which Hellenism and Christianity proved irreconcilable are enumerated in Origen, *In Genesim homilia*, XIV, 3, p. 124, 6–10, ed. W. A. Baehrens (*Origenes Werke*, Vol. VI; Leipzig, 1920): "But (philosophy) differs from us, in saying that matter is coeternal with God. It differs by denying that God is concerned with mortal affairs, and saying that his providence is confined to the supralunar realms. They (the philosophers) differ from us, in making the lives of those who are born depend on the courses of the heavenly bodies. They differ by saying that this world is everlasting and will not be brought to a conclusion by any final event." (Tr. A.S.B.G.) Cf. *Commentarium in Epistolam ad Romanos*, III, 1, in Migne, *PG*, XIV, 926f.

A straight line marks the march of humanity from the initial Fall to the final Redemption. And the direction of this history is unique, because the Incarnation is a unique fact. Indeed, as Chapter 9 of the Epistle to the Hebrews and I Peter 3 : 18 insist, Christ died but once for our sins, once and for all (*hapax*, *ephapax*, *semel*); this is not an event that can be repeated, that can be reproduced several times (*pollakis*). Thus the development of history is governed and oriented by a unique and radically singular fact. And the destiny of all mankind, as well as the particular destiny of each one of us, is likewise enacted but once, once and for all, in a concrete, irreplaceable time, which is the time of history and of life.

This Christian conception of a rectilinear time in which nothing is seen twice, dominated by the Cross implanted in its center—the Cross on which, "under Pontius Pilate," a Passion was enacted which will never take place again and whose repercussions on the whole of history, past and future, are definitive—this conception is diametrically opposed to the Greek theory of circular time. True, an Origen in the third century and a Siger of Brabant in the thirteenth were not wholly free from the notion of a time moving in successive cycles.[17] But did Origen—as his accusers claimed—go so far as to

17 For Origen, see the texts collected by Paul Koetschau in his edition of the *De principiis* (*Origenes Werke*, Vol. V; Leipzig, 1913), p. 344, n. to li. 6ff.; in addition see Augustine, *De haeresibus*, XLIII (Migne, *PL*, XLII):

"But there are other teachings of this Origen which the Catholic Church altogether rejects, and as regards which it does not accuse him falsely and is not to be put off by those who defend him; in particular, his teachings regarding purging and deliverance, and the cyclical return of the rational creation after a long period of time to the same evils. For what Catholic Christian, learned or unlearned, is not utterly repelled by what he calls the purging of evils, namely, that even those who have ended this life in crime and wickedness and sacrilege and the greatest of impieties—yea, more, the very devil himself and his angels—shall, though after a very long time, be purged and set free and restored to the kingdom and the light of God; and again that after a very long time all those who have been set free shall once more fall and return to these evils; and that these alternate cycles of blessedness and misery for the rational creation always have been and always will be? Against the philosophers from whom Origen learnt this empty impiety I have argued strenuously in my book 'The City of God.'" (Tr. A.S.B.G.)

For a recent discussion of the problem, accompanied by numerous references to Origen's own works, see Martin Werner, *Die Entstehung des christlichen Dogmas* (Bern and Leipzig, 1941), p. 114 and n. 37. Werner also points out that Clement of Alexandria (*Eclogae prophetarum*, XXIII, 3) attributes to the Valentinians the idea of a new reproduction of the incarnation of the Savior and that, according to Hippolytus and Epiphanius (Cf. Werner, n. 36) the Elkesaites—inspired, according to the first of these heresiologists, by the Pythagorean doctrine of metempsychosis—professed the periodic return of Christ in the course of diverse reincarnations. For Siger of Brabant, cf.

maintain that the Passion is being repeated and will be repeated within each one of these circles? Here, in any case, we have an instructive counterproof: to believe in the repetition of the drama of Golgotha is regarded by the Church as the error par excellence, and if Origen succumbed to this heresy, it was precisely under the influence of Hellenism, whose influence Siger too felt, through Averroës and Aristotelianism. Be that as it may, anyone who wishes to apprehend the opposition between Christian rectilinear time and Greek circular time in all its living depth can do no better than consult Book 12, Chapters 10 to 14, of St. Augustine's *City of God.* Over against the secular periods of the philosophers, the *circuitus temporum in quibus eadem semper fuisse renovata atque repetita in rerum natura atque ita deinceps fore sine cessatione asseverarent* (*philosophi*), over against the *falsi circuli* or *falsus circulus*, Augustine sets forth the *rectum iter*, the *via recta*, which is the Christ. Over against Greek repetition he sets the Christian *novitas, nullo repetita, nullo repetenda circuitu.* Over against the despair of the pagans who walk in a circle—*in circuitu impii ambulant*, says Psalm 11 [AV 12] : 9—the beatitude of the Christians for whom, thanks to the Lord, "the circle is shattered"—*in adjutorio Domini Dei nostri hos volubiles circulos, quos opinio confingit, ratio manifeste confringit.* The whole culminates in the formulation of I Peter, which we have just mentioned: "*semel enim Christus mortuus est pro peccatis nostris*"—"for Christ hath *once* suffered for our sins."

This notion is fundamental in every respect. Yet other, more pragmatic factors also helped to imbue Christianity with the idea of an organic, oriented time and to guide it toward a theology of history. I shall not insist on this point, which I mean to develop elsewhere. But I must state the essentials, for certain of these factors bear directly on our subject.

First of all, Christianity, a new religion and in the eyes of the pagans a *superstitio nova*, had to provide itself with a past and furnish proofs of its authenticity. This it could do only by attaching itself to Judaism, by situating itself—as a true Israel— at the end of the long preceding development of Jewish history. By adopting this history it was able to claim a lineage going

Etienne Gilson, *History of Christian Philosophy in the Middle Ages* (London, 1955), p. 392. If Origen actually put forward the theory for which he was attacked, there would be every reason for repeating with Jean Gerson (who, it might be mentioned, borrowed the formula from St. Jerome, *Epistola 133, ad Ctesiphontem 3;* Migne, *PL*, XXII, 1152) that he "drank too deeply of the golden cup of Babylon."

back to the very origin of the world as recorded in Genesis.[18] The advantage was twofold: Christianity was thus enabled to represent itself as the oldest, most pristine of religions, having its sources and seeds in an age far predating the most ancient events narrated in the profane annals of the classical, Babylonian, or Egyptian civilizations. And indeed, taking as its basis the Bible and a comparative chronology, Christian historiography, born of apologetic requirements, was soon employed in demonstrating the legitimacy of such a pretension. Moreover, the sacred literature of Israel provided the Christian apologists with the testimony they required in order to prove that the coming of Jesus had been foreshadowed, foreseen, and prophesied in the past. Thus although the early Christians were sorely tempted for a time to break with Judaism and affirm the entire novelty, the absolute originality, of the Gospel, the Church finally annexed the Hebrew books to its corpus of canonical scriptures, set the New Testament after the Old, and established a line between its own history and that of ancient Israel which prepared the way for Christianity and prefigured it. In this way it succeeded in creating an organic, continuous bond between the present and the past. We shall see that in Gnosis, on the contrary, this bond is broken—and with it the organic continuity of time.

Still another factor led the Church to establish a close bond between the present and the future: this was eschatology, the eschatological feeling. Christianity was born of an apocalyptic ferment. It was dominated—exclusively at first, according to certain critics—by an expectation of the end of the world, an expectation which oriented the mind of the believer toward the future, toward a concrete event which would complete that other great event, the first coming. The present seemed to be of one piece with a future so imminent that it had perhaps already begun. There is no doubt that as time went on, the End seemed to recede more and more; the expectation, whether impatient or fearful, gradually dwindled. But even then—even with the postponement of the apocalyptic prospects—the Christians of the first centuries retained a kind of movement toward the future, a tension toward the end of a time which flows in a definite direction and whose instants are numbered. Whether near or far, the eschatological end orients

18 Cf. Tertullian, *De pallio*, 2 (Migne, *PL*, II, col. 1035: "From the Assyrians, it may be, the histories of 'recorded time' begin to open. We, however, who are habitual readers of *divine* histories, are masters of the subject from the nativity of the universe itself." (Tr. S. Thelwall, *The Writings of Tertullian*, Vol. III, ANCL, XVIII, 1870, p. 185.)

the past toward the future and binds the two together in such a way as to make the unilateral direction of time a certainty.

One last feature of this Christian picture of time remains to be noted. If time here has a direction, it also has a meaning for the salvation of all mankind and of each man in particular. History is *Heilsgeschichte*. Not only is it the progressive realization of universal redemption, not only is it the stage on which this drama is enacted, but beginning with St. Paul it appears also as a *paidagogia*, a pedagogical instrument employed by God to form and educate mankind, little by little, and lead it to a glorious maturity. Salvation, which is brought about by two concrete events, the Incarnation and Resurrection of the Saviour, also concerns the concrete totality that is man in time. For Christianity, what is saved, the object of Salvation, is not as in Hellenism and Gnosis only the *nous*, the atemporal "self," susceptible of taking on a multiplicity of temporal bodies in the course of many cycles of reincarnations; it is an individual unique in his flesh as well as his soul, the union of a body, a soul, and a spirit. Each individual enacts his destiny but once, once and for all, in the lifetime that is given him in the present and that will never be repeated. He is plunged into time, body and soul, and he will be resurrected, body and soul, at the end of time.

To sum up, the Christians of the first centuries conceived of time as rectilinear, continuous, irreversible, and progressive; they saw in it a true, direct, and meaningful manifestation of God's will. In this organic whole each event—past, present, future—has its place and its meaning; each event forms a unity with those that preceded and with those that will follow. In time and by time, to employ the language of the period, there is accomplished a divine "disposition" or "dispensation," an *oikonomia*—a word which designates both the providential development of history according to the plans of God and, in a more restricted sense, the Incarnation, the central point in this development, through which all things are ordered and explained.

It would be interesting to follow the fortunes of this specific conception of time throughout the development of Christian theology. We should have occasion to note that little by little the perspectives changed and that this view of time was thrust into the background, precisely under the influence of the Greek philosophy or mentality which increasingly contaminated Christian thought. We should also have occasion to analyze the body of converging phenomena which with the Church Fathers—particularly Origen and the Alexandrians—culminated in a more or less exclusive effort to understand Christianity, man, and the world, no longer according to strictly historical—and if the term is permissible, horizontal—views but atemporally, according to the hierarchical and vertical schema of Greek rationalism.[19] We should most particularly note the transformation of the primitive biblical typology into allegorism in the strict sense. We should see how an exegesis which remained faithful to the plan of history, which interpreted earlier events in the light of later ones—regarding the former as types or prefigurations of the latter—was more or less replaced (but not eliminated) by a method which in temporal events sought to discover the images or symbols of unchanging and atemporal, transcendent or interior, truths. However, this subject would take us too far.

*

We are now equipped to analyze and understand the third conception of time which appeared in the first centuries of our era, sometimes in combination with the Greek and Christian conceptions, and sometimes in opposition to them: the conception peculiar to Gnosis or Gnosticism. But first of all, what is Gnosis? What is it that we call "Gnosticism"?

Historically [20] the term was first used to designate a heretical movement—hence a movement posterior and interior to Christianity—particularly active in the second century. Its chief representatives at this time were Basilides, Valentinus, Marcion, perhaps also Bardesanes, who were regarded more or less as the successors of Simon Magus and Saturnilus of Antioch—a movement which survived at least until the seventh century among many

19 Useful data are furnished particularly by the works of Jean Daniélou, *Origène* (Paris, 1948), pp. 137–98; and *Sacramentum futuri: Etudes sur les origines de la typologie biblique* (Paris, 1950); and of H. de Lubac, *Histoire et Esprit: L'Intelligence de l'Ecriture d'après Origène* (Paris, 1950), especially pp. 267–94. The two authors differ, it must be said, on the essential point, the former maintaining that in places Origen shows the influence of an "anagogical" and "Gnostic" type of exegesis "along the lines of Platonic exemplarism," the second denying that any such interpretation could ever have so contaminated Origen's exegesis as to make it lose all eschatological character. In any case, certain passages in Origen remain alarming; among them, *In Johannem*, X, 18 (13) (Migne, *PG*, XIV), § 110: "One must not suppose historical realities to be figures for other historical realities and corporeal things for other corporeal realities; rather, corporeal things are figures for spiritual realities and historical realities for intelligible realities" (*οὐ γὰρ νομιστέον τὰ ἱστορικὰ ἱστορικῶν εἶναι τύπους καὶ τὰ σωματικὰ σωματικῶν, ἀλλὰ τὰ σωματικὰ πνευματικῶν καὶ τὰ ἱστορικὰ νοητῶν*).

20 Cf. my paper, "Ou en est le problème du Gnosticisme?" in *Revue de l'Université de Bruxelles*, XXXIX (1934–35), 137–58, 295–314.

diverse groups: Ophites or Naassenes, "Gnostics" in the strict sense, Sethians, Archontics, Audians—and it goes without saying, Basilidians, Valentinians, Marcionites, and Bardesanites. Invoking revelations or secret traditions allegedly coming from Christ and his Apostles, these heresiarchs and sectarians claimed to give a transcendent and exhaustive interpretation of Christianity and of the entire visible and invisible world—an interpretation accessible only to the initiate or to an élite, to a class of *gnostikoi*, "knowers," or of *pneumatikoi*, "spiritual men." These *gnostikoi* or *pneumatikoi* were held to be superior by nature to the two other classes of mankind, namely the "psychics" (the common Christians, the simple "believers," who have a soul but lack the Spirit) and still lower down, the "hylics," enslaved to the body and to matter. Of course such pretensions—which resulted in a veritable galaxy of systems, all apparently fantastic, mutually contradictory, and contrary to the Catholic faith—could appear to the Great Church only as monstrosities, born or nurtured in its bosom, which as its duty it must reject and condemn as heterodox.

But after long accepting the view of ecclesiastical writers that Gnosticism was a heresy of early Christianity, students of religion gradually began to find this conception too narrow. They discovered Gnostic systems other than those of the classical heresiologists and soon developed a broader view of Gnosis. It came to be understood as a determinate genus, widely distributed in both space and time, of which heretical Christian Gnosis represented only a particular species. It was quite evident, for example, that Manichaeism, born in the third century partly under the influence of the theories of Marcion and Bardesanes, is a species of Gnosticism, and that this Babylonian Gnosis with ecumenical perspectives, containing Iranian and perhaps Buddhist elements, far exceeded the dimensions of a Christian heresy, although the Western Church treated it as such. Much attention was now given to purely pagan Gnosticisms: Hermeticism, for example, or that theosophy of "Chaldaean oracles" which, beginning with Iamblichus, exerted so strong an influence on late Neoplatonism. Mandaeism was discovered: an ancient baptist religion still surviving in Iraq and Iran. As is shown by its literature and by one of the names for its adherents (Mandaean: *mandaya* is the Aramaic equivalent of the Greek *gnostikos*, and *manda* of *gnosis*), this sect provided a new example of Gnosticism, and better still of a non-Christian, perhaps pre-Christian, and in any case anti-Christian Gnosticism. Wishing to remain within our historical horizon, I shall not even speak of the Jewish Gnoses, of the Cabala, of the Moslem Gnoses, or of the systems of the alchemists, occultists, or "illuminati," which have abounded in the Western world from the end of antiquity down to modern times. Finally, the work of the comparative religionists and of the *Religionsgeschichtliche Schule* suggested two important conclusions: first, that certain Gnostic systems denounced by the heresiologists were actually Christianized only on the surface and in their most recent stratum, the original core being purely pagan; and second, that all the Gnoses of the period in question, Christian or not, employed an identical body of figures—images and mythical themes—whose origins go back far beyond the first century of our era and are to be sought in the ancient Orient, perhaps in Egypt, more likely in Babylonia, or Iran, or even, according to the boldest contention, in India.

Whatever the value of some of these assertions, we see how the use of the word "gnosticism" has been broadened; we see that the problem of Gnosticism now appears in a new light. Gnosticism has now become a general religious phenomenon whose historical scope infinitely surpasses the limits of ancient Christianity and whose origins are exterior if not anterior to Christianity. If there have been Christian Gnosticisms, these were not properly speaking heresies immanent in Christianity but the results of an encounter and a fusion between the new religion and a Gnosticism which had existed before it, which was originally alien to it and in essence remained so. Here Gnosticism has assumed Christian forms, or forms which in the course of time became more and more profoundly Christianized, just as elsewhere it took on pagan forms, adapting itself to oriental mythologies, to mystery cult, to Greek philosophy, or to the occult arts and sciences. Despite the diversity of its historical forms, Gnosticism must be regarded as a specific phenomenon, a distinct type or category of philosophico-religious thought: it is an attitude which presents a general picture and structure, which has laws of its own; an attitude which analysis and comparison enable us to find—substantially identical and with the same articulations—at the base of all the diverse systems which this common foundation or "style" justify us in subsuming under a common head and calling "Gnostic."

How shall we define this attitude? If it were possible to do so in a few words, we should say that Gnosis (from the Greek word *gnosis*, "knowledge") is an absolute knowledge which in itself saves, or that Gnosticism is the theory that salvation is obtained by knowledge. But this definition, true and central as it may be, remains inadequate. It demands to be explained and completed by an exhaustive description of the consciousness of the Gnostic and of his behavior toward God, the world, and the human lot. This I shall try to supply in part. I shall consider the Gnosticism of the first Christian centuries as a whole, referring explicitly or implicitly to the Christian as well as the pagan Gnoses, to Valentinianism or Marcionism as well as Hermeticism, Mandaeism or Manichaeism, in an effort to establish their common and constant traits. And first of all I shall attempt to describe the Gnostic's relation to time, his typical attitude or reactions in the presence of time. The other problems will arrange themselves around this perspective.

*

Our first problem is still of a general nature: what, in principle, is the position of Gnosticism toward the Greek and the Christian conceptions of time? It might be presumed, after what has been said, that Gnosticism sometimes adopted one and sometimes the other according as it adapted itself to paganism or to Christianity. Or better still, if we consider the views that have successively prevailed in modern science, we may be tempted by two solutions. In line with Harnack and even with more recent authors such as Burkitt, Schaeder, or Casey, we may consider Gnosis as the outcome of an extreme Hellenization of Christianity[21]—a thesis which, in one sense, is merely a return to the traditional opinion of the ancient heresiologists that the Gnostic systems resulted from the contamination of Christianity by this or that school of Greek philosophy, that even Manichaeism was only a Hellenized or "Hellenizing" Christianity.[22] In this latter case we should expect the Gnostic attitude toward time to resemble that of the Greeks, to consist of an attempt to transpose the essentially historical vision of early Christianity into an atemporal perspective.

If on the other hand we accept the theories of the comparative religionists, of Bousset, Reitzenstein, Steffes, or Lietzmann, for example, we shall regard Gnosticism as the consequence of a penetration, an invasion of Christianity, by oriental influences or—to cite Lietzmann—a "regression of Christianity

21 Adolf Harnack, *Lehrbuch der Dogmengeschichte*, Vol. I (Tübingen, 1886): 1st edn., p. 162; 5th edn. (1931), pp. 250; 253, n. 1; 266; 267; 269; F. C. Burkitt, *Church and Gnosis* (Cambridge, 1932); H. H. Schaeder, "Bardesanes von Edessa," *Zeitschrift für Kirchengeschichte*, LI (1932), 23. The conception of Gnosticism as "the acute secularization, or Hellenization, of Christianity" goes back, according to Harnack himself (Vol. I, p. 250, n. 1), to Franz Overbeck, *Studien zur Geschichte der alten Kirche* (Chemnitz, 1875), p. 184.

22 Socrates, *Historia ecclesiastica*, I, 22 (Migne, *PG*, LXVII): ἑλληνίζων Χριστιανισμός.

toward its oriental origins," an "extreme reorientalization of Christianity."[23] This, I might add, would lead us to consider the pagan Gnoses as purely Oriental or as the products of a Greco-Oriental syncretism. Then the Gnostic conception of time will seem to reduce itself to that of the Oriental religions and accordingly be neither rational nor historical, but mythical. I reserve judgment on the Oriental origin of Gnostic time, which in certain of its aspects strikes us, too, as mythical. However, without taking sides here between these different hypotheses, I can safely say—a priori, if you wish, but the proof will be provided in the following—that whatever spiritual environment it penetrated, Gnosticism never wholly adopted the Greek or the Christian view of time: it not only preserved a basically autonomous attitude toward them, but actually opposed them both.

One of the permanent and fundamental features of Gnostic thought is indeed an opposition between the world, or Creation, and God. The entire sensuous universe is experienced and judged as evil. God is not held responsible either for the evil that is in this world or for the world itself, which is evil. He absolutely transcends the world: he has no relation to it, for any relation would debase and enslave him; it would sully his inalterable purity and make him cease to be God in the supreme sense of the term. God did not produce the world and he does not rule over it. He is not known by the world, by the intermediary of the world or in the world, which is not his work and the work of his government. If he intervenes in the world, it is to save men from the world, to encompass an escape out of the world, not to accomplish anything whatever through the world. Thus this transcendent God—compared by Christian polemicists to the *Deus otiosus* of Epicurus[24]—

23 Hans Lietzmann, *The Beginnings of the Christian Church*, tr. B. Lee-Woolf (2nd edn., London, 1949), p. 295: "Gnosis has been described as the 'acute Hellenization of Christianity'; we must recognize in addition an equally acute 'reorientalization.'" Cf. R. Reitzenstein and H. H. Schaeder, *Studien zum antiken Synkretismus aus Iran und Griechenland* (Studien der Bibliothek Warburg, VII; Leipzig and Berlin, 1926), p. 141: "Gnosis offers not a Hellenization but a further orientalization of Christianity." Similar views have been put forward by W. Bousset, *Hauptprobleme der Gnosis* (Göttingen, 1907), and his articles "Gnosis," "Gnostiker" in Pauly-Wissowa, VII, 1503–33, 1534–47; and popularized by Johann Peter Steffes, *Das Wesen des Gnostizismus und sein Verhältnis zum katholischen Dogma* (Paderborn, 1922). Cf. also the suggestion recently put forward by Gilles Quispel, "La Conception de l'homme dans la gnose valentinienne," *EJ 1947*, p. 271: "Thus Valentinus Hellenized and Christianized the Gnostic anthropology. One wonders whether his doctrine, contrary to what Harnack believes, was not a Christianization and Hellenization of oriental Gnosis."

24 Cf. notably, Irenaeus, *Adversus haereses*, III, 24, 2, and Tertullian, *Adversus Marcionem*, I, 25. Tertullian drew his inspiration from Irenaeus; both passages have in mind

is alien to both the world and its history: he is—to use the vocabulary of the Gnostics themselves—the "alien God" (*xenos*, *allotrios*, *extraneus*; *nukrāyā*, in Syriac and Mandaean); the "Other," He who is radically "other" (*allos*, *heteros*, *alius*); the Unknown, Ineffable, Hidden God (*agnostos*, *ignotus*, *akatonomastos*, *apokekrummenos*), naturally unknown (*naturaliter ignotus*), that is to say, knowable not by nature but, beyond nature, by revelation; a God incommensurate with the daily course of things and the ordinary knowledge of men; hence a "strange" God and, when he manifests himself, totally "new" (*kainos*, *novus*).[25] Below him or opposed to him, depending on whether the dualism is mitigated or absolute—distinct from him, in any

---

Epicurus, I, 21 (*Epicurea*, ed. H. Usener, Leipzig, 1887), as has been shown by Gilles Quispel, *De Bronnen van Tertullianus' Adversus Marcionem* (Leiden, 1943), pp. 26–28. See also Tertullian, II, 16; ed. Emil Kroymann, in *CSEL*, XLVII (1906), p. 356, li. 14–18; IV, 15 (p. 463, li. 27–28); V, 19 (p. 645, li. 10–15); and less precisely II, 27 (p. 374, li. 1–3): "Whatever attributes therefore you require as worthy of God must be found in the Father, who is invisible and unapproachable, and placid, and (so to speak), the God of the philosophers." (Tr. Peter Holmes, *The Five Books . . . against Marcion*, ANCL, VII, 1868, p. 113.) In V, 4, Marcion's good God is expressly called *deus otiosus*. Cf. the *πρῶτος θεὸς ἀργὸς* of Numenius of Apamea, in Eusebius, *Praeparatio Evangelica*, XI, 18, 8 (Migne, *PG*, XXI) and my remarks in *Annuaire de l'Institut de Philologie et d'Histoire orientales* (Brussels), II (1934), 757, 761–67, 773–76.

25 Bibliographical indications in my book, *Le Manichéisme: son fondateur, sa doctrine* (Paris, 1949), p. 152, n. 273. I shall cite here a few texts particularly relevant to our discussion:

Irenaeus, *Adv. haer.*, III, 24, 2 (Migne, *PG*, VII, 967): "For they blaspheme the Creator, Him who is truly God, who also furnishes power to find [the truth]; imagining that they have discovered another God beyond God, or another Pleroma, or another dispensation. . . . but they dream of a non-existent being above Him, that they may be regarded as having found out the great God, whom nobody [they hold,] can recognize as holding communication with the human race, or as directing mundane matters." (Tr. A. Roberts and W. H. Rambaut, *The Writings of Irenaeus*, ANCL, V, 1868, p. 370.)

Most particularly Tertullian, *Adv. Marcion.*, I, 8 (ed. Kroymann, p. 300)—regarding the "New God" of the Marcionite: "Now when I hear of a new god, who was unknown and unheard of in the old world and in ancient times and under the old god—and whom, [accounted as] no one through so many centuries back, and ancient in men's very ignorance of him, one Jesus Christ (himself a novel being, [although decked] with ancient names) revealed, and none else before him."

I, 19 (p. 314): "Well, but our God, say the Marcionites, although he did not manifest himself from the beginning and by means of the creation, has yet revealed himself in Christ Jesus."

V, 16 (p. 630): "Now, to inflict punishment on the heathen, who very likely have never heard of the Gospel, is not the function of that God who is naturally unknown, and is revealed nowhere else than in the Gospel, and therefore cannot be known by all men. The Creator, however, ought to be known even by [the light of] nature, for He may be understood from His works, and may thereby become the object of a more widely spread knowledge."

(Tr. Holmes, pp. 13f., 33, 453.)

case—there is another God, inferior or essentially Evil, who created and dominates the world. This is a Demiurge, feeble, narrow-minded if not ignorant; or it may be the Devil himself, unengendered Principle or Prince of Darkness and incarnation of Evil as such, guilty of having produced the material universe and carnal man, and therefore, for certain sects, accursed.[26] The imperfection and wickedness of this God are known—only too well!—by such products and by the tyrannical laws he imposes upon the course of events and upon his wretched creatures. Two gods, then, whose activities are antagonistic: on the one hand a God of Salvation and Grace, on the other a God of Creation and of nature or matter; the one bringing deliverance from existence in time, the other inflicting temporal existence and dominating it. The universe is split into two heterogeneous and hostile domains: the one invisible or spiritual, the other visible or material.

What were the consequences of an encounter between this theme and the *Weltanschauungen* peculiar to Hellenism and Christianity?

Gnosticism, to be sure, adopts the notion (common to the entire Hellenistic and Roman era in the Near East as well as the West) of a hierarchical universe, descending by degrees from the celestial beings down to earthly

26 Cf. the "accursed god" (θεὸς κατηραμένος), chief of the Archons, mentioned by Celsus in connection with certain Gnostics (Ophites?): Origen, *Contra Celsum*, VI, 27 (ed. Koetschau, Vol. II, p. 97, li. 11); opposed to the "great God," VI, 51 (Koetschau, p. 122, li. 28–30), he is the god of the Jews, creator of this world, god of Moses and of Genesis ("who maintain that the God of the Jews is accursed, being the God who sends rain and thunder, and who is the Creator of this world and the God of Moses, described in his account of the creation of the world" [tr. H. Chadwick, Cambridge, 1953, p. 343]); see also VI, 27 (p. 97, li. 14–17), and cf. VI, 27 (p. 97, li. 20–21), VI, 28 (p. 98, li. 5–13), and VI, 29 (p. 99, li. 4–6)—god of the Mosaic Law. The Demiurge or Cosmocrator, the god of this world or this aeon, is knowable and known (γνωστός, *notus*) by his creation and his government, by a natural and historical means: cf., for example, Adamantius, *Dialogus de recta fide*, I, 13 (ed. W. H. van der Sande Bakhuyzen; *GCS*, 1901), or Tertullian, *Adv. Marcion.*, IV, 25 (ed. Kroymann, p. 506): "Other heretics . . . alleging in opposition to it that the Creator was known to all, both to Israel by familiar intercourse, and to the Gentiles by nature." (Tr. Holmes, p. 285.) It is precisely thereby, and also because his creation proves to be imperfect, that he renders himself despicable: Irenaeus, *Adv. haer.*, III, 24, 2 (Migne, *PG*, VII, 967): "They have dishonored and despised God, holding Him of small account, because, through His love and infinite benignity, He has come within reach of human knowledge." (Tr. Roberts and Rambaut, p. 370.) We are reminded almost in spite of ourselves, of Paul Valéry's words in *La Soirée avec Monsieur Teste:* "What they [most men] call a superior man is one who has made the wrong choice. If we are to marvel at him, we have to see him—and if he is to be seen, he has to show himself. . . . So every great man is tainted with an error. Every mind that people consider great took his start from the mistake of making himself known." (Tr. Jackson Mathews, unpublished.)

realities, a universe in which the superior rotation of the heavenly bodies regulates the inferior course of things and events. But though the frame is the same, it is distorted, and the picture it encloses is vastly changed. Greek thought, as we have seen, is essentially cosmological: for the Greek, the idea of a *kosmos*, a "world," is inseparable from that of "order," and this order is the work and expression of the divine. The godhead manifests its action and unchanging presence by the intermediary of the regular movement which never ceases to animate the astronomical world and which is transmitted in a graduated but continuous and evenly regulated manner to the rhythms of earthly time. The stars, by virtue of the regularity of their circular course, are divine; the world, in its harmonious totality, is divine; divine Providence is confounded with the eternal laws of the *kosmos*. But where the Greek exalts, accepts, agrees, the Gnostic condemns, rejects, rebels. The regularity strikes him as a monotonous and crushing repetition, order and law (the physical and moral *nomos*) as an insufferable yoke; the effect of the positions and orbits of the planets on earthly destinies impresses him as an unjust and tyrannical servitude. The firmament, the heavenly bodies, most particularly the planets which preside over Destiny, fatality, are evil beings or the seats of inferior entities such as the Demiurge and the creating angels, or of demoniacal rulers with bestial forms: the "Archons." In a word, the visible universe ceases to be divine and becomes diabolical.[27] Man stifles in it as in a prison, and far from being the manifestation of the true God, it bears the mark of his congenital infirmity or imperfection: it betrays the hand of a fallen, perverse being. The Greek says: "God *and* the world," linking the two terms indissolubly; the Gnostic says: "God *or* the world," dissociating the two terms, which for him represent two heterogeneous, independent, irreconcilable realities. The providential action of God no longer consists of preserving and executing the cosmic laws; on the contrary, it will intervene in order to contradict and break those laws. Certain Christian Gnostics maintained, for example, that Jesus—by his birth or by himself—broke the *Heimarmene* or utterly revolutionized its order by impressing on the planetary spheres a direction diametrically opposed to that which they had previously followed.[28] In short, Gnosis accepts the Greek view

27 Cf. Hans Jonas, *Gnosis und spätantiker Geist*, I: *Die mythologische Gnosis* (Göttingen 1934), pp. 146–99, 223–33, 251–55.

28 Thus in Christian Gnosticism Jesus is conceived as radically changing the order of *Heimarmene:* he revolutionizes it, impressing a wholly different direction on its usual fatal course. According to the Valentinian Theodotus (*Excerpta ex Theodoto*, 72–75),

of the universe only in order to despise, negate, and transcend it in the most typical cases; the Gnostic revolt against the world is indeed a revolt against the world of Greek science.[29] Or in a more profound aspect, the Gnostic attitude, as opposed to that of the Greeks, is—if I may be pardoned the use of such terms—anticosmic or acosmic.

From this we easily conclude that the Gnostic conceived the relations between the atemporal and the temporal quite differently from the Greek. The atemporal far transcends the temporal, but between them there is no common measure or passage by continuous and necessary degrees. Above all, cosmic time, included in the condemnation of the material world, is not the image of eternity—feeble and distant but faithful and, in its own degraded way, perfect. As we shall see, time, the work of the Creator God, is at best a caricature of eternity, a defective imitation far removed from its model; it is the consequence of a fall and, in the last analysis, a lie. Thus, even in close contact with Hellenism, Gnosticism preserves its irreducible and specific character; its conception of time remains basically distinct from the Greek conception, which it does not assimilate but tends to disorganize if not to demolish.

If we now confront Gnosticism with the Christian conception of time, we inevitably come to a similar conclusion. First let us consider the notion of the two Gods. What consequences will it have when transplanted into Christian ground? It goes without saying—and this operation finds its complete expression in Marcionism—that the Creator God will be identified with the God of the Old Testament, with the God of Genesis and the Torah, the organizer and legislator of a world which, as is shown by the Hebrew Bible itself, he subjects to his overbearing, jealous, angry, cruel domination that is harsh and inflexible even in its justice. The transcendent God, on the contrary, the unknown God of peace and goodness, is identified with the Father

---

the coming of the Savior shatters fatality; it is marked (§ 74, 2) by the appearance of a *ξένος αστὴρ καὶ καινός, καταλύων τὴν παλαιὰν ἀστροθεσίαν, καινῷ φωτί, οὐ κοσμικῷ λαμπόμενος*, transferring from fatality (*Εἱμαρμένη*) to Providence (*Πρόνοια*). Still more realistically, the *Pistis Sophia* (chs. 14, 15; cf. chs. 18, 23; and Hans Leisegang, *La Gnose*, French tr., Paris, 1951, pp. 253–54) declares that as a result of Jesus' intervention the course of the stars has been "deflected for the salvation of souls"; *Heimarmene* and its sphere have been compelled to exert their influence toward the right for six months, whereas their regular movement was from right to left, from East to West, and consequently their dominating influence was always exerted in a leftward direction.

29 Jonas, pp. 146–56.

of Jesus Christ, the new God who reveals the unprecedented message of the Gospel: this is a God who forgives and saves, incomparably superior to Yahweh, who judges and condemns. The consequences of this duality have a direct bearing on our theme. Christianity is detached from Judaism and hence from all historical perspective. It is novelty pure and simple, unrelated to the past, in which it was neither prepared nor announced.[30] Moreover, its revelation of a hitherto unknown God of love runs counter to everything that man could imagine concerning God before the coming of Jesus, whether by a natural knowledge drawn from the fact and spectacle of the creation or by the acts and declarations of the inferior or evil God, as recorded in the books of the Jews. The coming of Christ itself has nothing in common with the prophecies inspired by the Demiurge. The prophets, moreover, like all or almost all of the characters in the ancient history of Israel, were the servants of the Archons or of the false God of justice,[31] and certain sects even went so far as to exalt at their expense all the accursed creatures or persons of the Old Testament, all those who rebelled against the Creator and his Law: the Serpent, Cain, Korah, Dathan, Abiram, Esau, the Sodomites.[32] In other words, the past is condemned and rejected; the present is absolutely dissociated from it, as is the New Testament from the Old, which it contradicts and demolishes. All this is admirably summed up by St. Irenaeus when he writes that the Gnostic attitude culminates in a *contrarietas et dissolutio praeteritorum:* [33] far from being, as in the Christian theory championed

30 Cf., for example, the testimony in regard to Marcion collected by Adolf Harnack, *Marcion* (2nd edn., Leipzig, 1924), pp. 284*–85*, and Irenaeus, *Adv. haer.*, II, 9, 2 ("*Deus . . . sine teste*") and II, 10, 1 ("*Deus . . . qui a nemine unquam annuntiatus est*").

31 Cf., among other works, Irenaeus, *Adv. haer.*, I, 7, 3–4 (Valentinians), I, 23, 3 (Simonians), I, 24, 2 (Saturnilus), I, 24, 5 (Basilidians), I, 30, 10–11 (Ophites?), and more generally II, 35, 2–3. For the Marcionites, see Harnack, *Marcion*, 2nd edn., pp. 113–17, 284*–86*. For the Manichaeans, Paulicians, Bogomils, and medieval Catharists, see references in H.-C. Puech and A. Vaillant, trs., *Le Traité contre les Bogomiles de Cosmas le Prêtre* (Paris, 1945), pp. 168–72, 201–5.

32 Celsus in Origen, *Contra Celsum*, VI, 53; Irenaeus, *Adv. haer.*, I, 27, 3; Epiphanius, *Panarium*, XLII, 4, 3–4; Theodoret, *Haereticarum fabularum compendium* (Migne, *PG*, LXXXIII), I, 24 (Marcion); Irenaeus, *Adv. haer.*, I, 31, 1; Epiphanius, *Panarium*, XXXVII, 2, 4–5; Augustine, *De haeresibus*, XVIII; Theodoret, *Haereticarum fabularum compendium*, I, 15 (Cainites).

33 *Adv. haer.*, IV, 13, 1: "For all these do not contain or imply an opposition to an overturning of the [precepts] of the past, as Marcion's followers do strenuously maintain, but [they exhibit] a fulfilling and an extension of them." Cf. IV, 16, 4 (in connection with the "*decalogi verba*"): "And therefore, in like manner, do they remain permanently with us, receiving, by means of His advent in the flesh, extension and increase, but not abrogation." (Tr. Roberts and Rambaut, pp. 413, 424f.)

by the Bishop of Lyons, a continuity, unique, organic, and progressive, in which the present is *plenitudo et extensio*—expansion and accomplishment of the past—time here is broken into two parts which contradict each other, the second discrediting and annulling the first. To speak in more general terms, history is useless; it is, like the whole common economy of the world, the work of the lower God, and if the transcendent God suddenly intervenes at a certain moment, this event, which nothing attaches to any antecedent, shatters history into bits and reveals it to be an imposture.

The application of the theory of the two Gods to Christianity involves other consequences which we must investigate. But even now we see the incompatibility of such a position with the authentic Christian conception of time. For a time that is organic, willed, and continuously guided by God, from beginning to end, in which the perpetually present and direct action of God or of his word announces and prepares for the future by way of the past—for this effective providential bond—it substitutes an incoherent time, interrupted by the sudden intervention of a God alien to history and creation—a time from which the true God is absent, a time without value or efficacy, whose effect is error, ignorance, servitude. We have just pointed out that Gnostic thinking is essentially distinguished from Greek thinking by its anticosmic character, its acosmic indifference or hostility to the world. Now we may say that what sets it off against the original Christian *Weltanschauung*, which was grounded above all in history, is its antihistorical or ahistorical character, its indifference or hostility to history. In this respect a difference of attitude was necessary and fundamental; and indeed when Gnosticism and Christianity met, the adaptation of Gnosis to Christian forms brought about a revolution that was soon judged unacceptable by the Church.

*

What then—considered in itself—is this specific Gnostic conception of time?

Let us first analyze the Gnostic's feeling about time. Gnosticism is typically a religion of Salvation. But before being formulated and resolved in the fields of speculation and ritual, the problem of Salvation grows out of an emotional situation: it corresponds to a concrete and profound need, to a lived experience; it grows out of man's reaction to his given lot. Whence does the Gnostic derive this need? The answer is given by the heresiologists. The Gnostic is haunted by an obsessive sense of evil; he never stops asking himself: "Whence comes evil? Why evil?"[34] It is indeed more than likely that the enigma of the scandalous presence of evil in the world, the intolerable feeling of the precariousness, evil, or ignominy of the human lot, the difficulty of imputing a meaning to this existence of evil, of attributing it to God and of justifying God at the same time—that these are the source of the religious experience which gave rise to the Gnostic conception of Salvation. The Gnostic in this earthly life feels crushed by the weight of Destiny, subjected to the limitations and the servitude of time, of the body, of matter, exposed to their temptations and their degradation. For the Gnostic this feeling of servitude and inferiority could only be explained by a fall: the mere fact that he has or is capable of having such a feeling signifies that man must intrinsically be—or must originally have been—something other than what he is in this degraded world which he experiences as a prison and an exile and to which—like the transcendent God upon whom he projects his nostalgia for transcendence—he is and calls himself a "stranger" (*allogenes*, *nukrāyā*).[35] This gives rise first of all to a movement of revolt and rejection: the Gnostic refuses to accept the world or to accept himself in his present state. More particularly it inevitably gives rise to a sense of revulsion against time, in extreme cases to a passionate striving to negate time.

Time is perceived and conceived as strangeness, servitude, and evil. In itself, or through the situation in which it places the individual, it is misery, care, strife, a sense of being torn, an obstacle, an abasement. It is the abode of servitude, of exile, of oblivion, ignorance, and sleep;[36] and all these are states contrasting with that which we enjoyed—beyond the world or before there was a world—in our former existence, which along with Salvation will

34 Tertullian, *De praescriptione haereticorum*, VII, 5; Eusebius of Caesarea, *Historia ecclesiastica*, V, 27 (heretics in general); Tertullian, *Adv. Marcion.*, I, 2 (Marcion); Epiphanius, *Panarium*, XXIV, 6, 1 (Basilides); *Dialogue of John the Orthodox with a Manichaean*, Migne, *PG*, XCVI, 1325 (Manichaeans). See also what a Valentinian (?) relates or is supposed to have related regarding his encounters with evil and the reflections they inspired in him, in Methodius of Olympus (or of Philippi), *De autexusio*, III; Adamantius takes up the same ideas in *Dialogus de recta fide*, IV, 2.

35 Cf. my book, *Le Manichéisme* (Paris, 1949), p. 152, n. 273, and my paper, "Les Nouveaux Écrits gnostiques découverts en Haute-Égypte (premier inventaire et essai d'identification)," in *Coptic Studies in Honor of W. E. Crum* (Boston, 1950), pp. 126f.

36 The references on this point would be innumerable. For the sake of simplicity I refer the reader to Jonas, *Gnosis und spätantiker Geist*, I, pp. 105–20. Also C. R. C. Allberry, ed., *A Manichaean Psalm-book* (Stuttgart, 1938), part II, pp. 57, li. 19–25; 146, li. 14–26; 152, li. 12 (the desert of the world); 152, li. 14; 197, li. 16–25; 218, li. 18–219, li. 23; and the remarks of Festugière in connection with the *Excerpta ex Theodoto*, II, 2, in *Vigiliae Christianae*, Vol. III (Amsterdam, 1949), pp. 194–95.

be restored through rejection of our union with the body and through our mere consciousness of the abnormal nature of this union. And then we shall have freedom, total possession of our authentic being, full knowledge, sober lucidity, an awakening of ourselves to ourselves. Time is also a taint: we are plunged into it and participate in it through our body, which, like all material things, is the abject work of the lower Demiurge or of the principle of evil; in time and by time our true "self," spiritual or luminous in essence, is enchained to a stranger substance, to the flesh and its passions, or to the darkness of matter. Consequently our temporal state is a monstrous amalgam of spirit and matter, of light and darkness, of the divine and the diabolical, a mixture which threatens our soul with infection and assails it with suffering and sin.[37] Our birth introduces us into this degrading captivity to the body and to time, and our earthly existence perpetuates it. But this is not the end of our suffering. Aroused by the Creator or by matter, the instinct of generation impels carnal mankind to increase and multiply; having been cast into the trammels of this world, we in turn engender new captives, who will engender still others, and so on indefinitely. Thus according to the Manichaean doctrine, the captivity of the parcels of the divine substance hurled into the infernal abyss, into the night of the flesh, is prolonged from body to body, from generation to generation, in accordance with the designs of the Principle of Evil.[38] More generally, the Gnostics agree in professing that we are condemned to be reborn, to pass from prison to prison in the course of the long cycle of reincarnations (*metensōmatōseis*) or of transfusions (*metangismoi*), which in certain Manichaean texts is likened to the Buddhist *samsāra*.[39] A desperate prospect, which makes existence seem more than ever like a "growth of death." [40]

Present life with its infinite sufferings is not true Life. Still more, time, whose instants engender and destroy one another, in which each moment

37 Cf. Jonas, *Gnosis*, p. 104 (Mandaean texts) and pp. 299–301 (Manichaean texts). On the "mixture" or "amalgam" in the Manichaean doctrine I have given several references in *EJ 1936*, p. 202, n. 1, and in *Le Manichéisme*, p. 167, n. 308.

38 Cf. *EJ* 1936, pp. 229–30, 256.

39 References in my *Le Manichéisme*, p. 179, n. 360. On metempsychosis among the Gnostics, see Irenaeus, *Adv. haer.*, I, 23, 2–3 (Simonians); Origen, *Commentaria in epistolam ad Romanos*, V, 1, and VI, 8; Migne, *PG*, XIV, 1015, 1083 (Basilidians); Irenaeus, *Adv. haer.*, I, 25, 3–4, and Hippolytus, *Elenchos*, VII, 32 (Carpocratians), VIII, 10, 1–2 (Docetes).

40 The expression is frequent in the Manichaean Turfan fragments (for example, M38 v. in *Abhandlungen der preussischen Akademie der Wissenschaften*, Berlin, 1904, Appendix, p. 77).

arises only to be engulfed in the next moment, in which all things appear, disappear, and reappear in a twinkling, without order, without aim or cessation or end—time contains within it a rhythm of death beneath an appearance of life. As I have elsewhere attempted to show,[41] the Manichaeans, notably, conceived the life of hell—of the Kingdom of Darkness and of Evil—in the image of man plunged into pure time, into absolute change. The demoniacal beings who people the five superimposed regions of the Empire of the Prince of Darkness perceive only the immediate; their capacity for seeing and hearing is "narrow," limited to what is purely actual and close at hand. They react only to the instantaneous, without plan or repose. They appear, devour one another, and engender one another only to devour and destroy one another anew—perpetually, mechanically one might say—throughout a process of change without aim or term, which is disorder, confusion, folly or absurdity, abomination: a series of desperate skirmishes in the night, without reason, aroused by an insatiable, insensate, bestial hunger for annihilation, the *enthumēsis*, the "desire," for death.

Not only is this time which is hell and gehenna experienced as a fallen state; it is also regarded as the consequence of a fall. Like all creation, it results from an original disaster: according to Valentinian Gnosis, this was the fall of an Entity—Sophia—from the divine world of plenitude, out of the *pleroma;* according to Manichaean Gnosis it was the defeat of the primordial man who was driven from the Kingdom of Light and engulfed by Darkness. In a more or less remote era time was born from the *hysterema*, a *defectus* or *defectio*, a *labes*—a deficiency, error, or fault—from the collapse and dispersion in the void, in the *kenōma*, of a reality which had previously existed one and integral, within the pleroma. Bound to the world of "deficiency" and absence, the temporal process depends on the mediocre or evil "Workman" of this world. Sometimes even—for example, in that Gnosis, Bogomilism [42]—the Father, the Good God, abandons the present cycle of seven thousand years to the power of Satan.

It goes without saying that time is apprehended and suffered as a fatality,

41 "Le Prince des Ténèbres en son royaume," in *Etudes Carmélitaines* (Paris, 1948) (volume on Satan), pp. 136–74; tr. *Satan* (London and New York, 1951), pp. 127–57. The Mandaeans have a similar conception of Hell and the Demons, likewise studied in this article.

42 Cf. Euthymius Zigabenus, *Panoplia dogmatica*, tit. XXVII, in Migne, *PG*, CXXX, 1309; and "Interrogatio Iohannis," in Richard Reitzenstein, *Die Vorgeschichte der christlichen Taufe* (Leipzig and Berlin, 1929), pp. 300, 303.

a *Heimarmene*, and for the man who lives in it, as a *douleia*, a servitude ordained by a natural predestination.[43] Birth and becoming, *gennēsis* and genesis, are subjected to the crushing weight of Necessity, to the blind and inexorable domination of the Demiurge, the Cosmocrator, to the blows and counterblows of a Destiny governed by the translation, the "aspects," the "conjunctures"—the antagonisms or combined influences of the signs of the zodiac, the stars, the planets. The starry firmament is peopled with oppressors and despots (*arkhontes, kosmokratores, tyrannoi*); the planetary spheres are customs stations or jails—*maṭṭarātā*, say the Mandaeans—where demoniacal guards do their utmost to hold back the souls which strive to escape from the perpetually re-forming chains of becoming. In the eyes of the Gnostic the firmament which for the Greek evoked order and beauty and inspired sentiments of admiration and religious veneration has become the scene of a tragedy of a drama full of horror.[44]

And time is anguish. Horror takes possession of the man who feels engulfed and crushed in it, century after century, throughout the interminable expanse of his successive rebirths, rebirths which have been and are still to be. Hans Jonas goes so far as to say that the thought of time fills the Gnostic with a kind of "panic terror," [45] and in support of this statement he cites two texts, one Mandaean, the other Manichaean, both expressing the plaint of a soul exiled for centuries from its luminous home and forsaken here below in an alien universe: "In this world [of Darkness] I lived for a thousand myriad years and no one knew that I was there. . . . The years followed the years, the generations followed the generations: here I was and they did not know that I was living here, in their world" [46] and "Now, O gracious Father, innumerable myriads of years have passed since we were separated from Thee!" [47]

Abandoned in the midst of a hostile world that man cannot recognize as

43 Jonas, *Gnosis*, pp. 223–27. On predestination in Gnosis see Simone Pétrement, *Essai sur le dualisme chez Platon, les gnostiques et les manichéens* (Paris, 1947), pp. 244–59.

44 "Withdrawing from the tragic spectacle, as they see it, of the Cosmic spheres."—Plotinus, *Enneads*, II, 9, 13 (tr. S. MacKenna, London and New York, 1957, p. 145): this passage, like the entire treatise, is directed against the Gnostics.

45 Cf. p. 100: "*Das Panische des Zeit-Erlebnisses.*"

46 *Ginza*, V, 1, 137–38, German tr. Mark Lidzbarski (Göttingen and Leipzig, 1925), pp. 153, 154.

47 Turfan Fragment T II D173a, r., in A. von Le Coq, "Türkische Manichaica aus Chotscho, I," *Abhandlungen der preussischen Akademie der Wissenschaften*, Phil.-hist. Kl., 1911, Appendix VI, p. 10.

his own; fallen into an abominable misery; torn by grief and pain—such is the Gnostic's temporal state.

Disgust or hatred, terror, anguish and despair, and piercing nostalgia are the sentiments he experiences in his servitude to time. Marcion, for example, denounces in the most brutal terms the ignominy of the existence led by man, engendered in obscenity, born amid the unclean, excruciating, and grotesque convulsions of labor, into a body that is a "sack of excrement," until death turns him into carrion, a nameless corpse.[48] The Valentinians, on the other hand, project the image of their own torments upon the figure of fallen Sophia: sadness (*lupe*, *tristitia*), disgust (*taedium*), terror and anguish (*phobos*, *timor*, *ekplexis*, *stupor*, *pavor*, *expavescentia*), consternation and anguish (*aporia*, *consternatio*, *amekhania*), "all in ignorance (*agnoia*, *ignorantia*)," the pangs of an "agony," like that of Jesus.[49] Such quotations can be multiplied at will. The following passages from Manichaean hymns strike us as particularly significant. First these lines from a "Psalm of Jesus," in which the "living self," son of the Primordial Man, evokes all that he has endured—and that every man endures—in the infernal abyss that is this world:

Since I went forth into the Darkness,
I was given a water to drink
which [was bitter] to me.
I bear up beneath a burden which is not mine.

I am in the midst of my enemies,
the beast surrounding me;
the burden which I bear
is of the powers and principalities.

They burned(?) in their wrath,
they rose up against me,
they run to [seize] me,
like sheep that have no shepherd.

Matter and her sons
divided me up amongst them,

48 Cf. Tertullian, *Adv. Marcion.*, I, 29 (ed. Kroymann, p. 331, li. 2–4, and 332, li. 1–2); III, 10 (p. 392, li. 13–14); III, 11 (p. 394, li. 12–17); IV, 21 (p. 490, li. 19–22); and *De resurrectione*, 4 (pp. 30–31). This last passage is directed against heretics in general.

49 Cf. Irenaeus, *Adv. haer.*, I, 4, 1–3; 5, 4; and 8, 2; Hippolytus, *Elenchos*, VI, 32, 2–7. More generally, see Jonas, *Gnosis*, pp. 109–13 (*Angst, Irren, Heimweh*) and 119–20 (*Der Lärm der Welt*): Jonas particularly stresses Mandaean texts.

they burnt(?) me in their fire,
they gave me a bitter likeness.

The strangers with whom I mixed,
me they know not;
they tasted my sweetness,
they desired to keep me with them.

I was life to them,
but they were death to me. . . .[50]

Or the great lamentation of these lines:

Deliver me from this profound nothingness,
From the dark abyss which is a wasting away,
Which is all torment, wounds until death,
And in which there is neither helper nor friend!

Never, never is salvation found here;
All is full of darkness . . .
All is full of prisons; there is no issue,
And those who arrive here are struck with blows.

Parched with drought, burned by torrid wind,
And no green . . . is ever found here.
Who will deliver me hence, and from all that wounds,
And who will save me from infernal anguish?

And I weep for myself: "Let me be delivered hence,
And from the creatures who devour one another!
And the bodies of humans, the birds of space,
And the fishes of the seas, the beasts, the demons,
Who will remove me from them and free me
From the destroying hells, without detour(?) or issue?" [51]

50 Ps. 246, in *A Manichaean Psalm-book*, Part II, p. 54, li. 11–23. Tr. in Torgny Säve-Söderbergh, *Studies in the Coptic Manichaean Psalm-book* (Uppsala, 1949), pp. 71–72, and in Gilles Quispel, *Gnosis als Weltreligion* (Zurich, 1951), p. 67. The third verse of the first strophe is translated differently by these two authors: "which [was bitter] to me" (Säve-Söderbergh); "which [made me] forget" (Quispel).

51 Turfan Fragment T II D178, in *Abhandlungen der preussischen Akademie der Wissenschaften*, 1926, IV, 112–13. [Puech's version, here translated, is in the French of E. Benveniste, *Yggdrasill* (Paris), August 25, 1937, p. 9.—ED.]

Or this last poem, unfortunately incomplete:

Child of the Light and of the gods,
Behold, I am in exile, separated from them.

My enemies fell upon me,
And carried me off among the dead.
Blessed be he and find deliverance,
Who will deliver my soul from anguish!

I am a god and born of the gods,
Glittering, resplendent, luminous,
Radiant, perfumed and beautiful,
But now reduced to suffering.

Hideous devils without number
Seized me and deprived me of strength.
My soul lost consciousness.
They bit me, dismembered me, devoured me.

Demons, *yakshas* and *peris*,
Somber inexorable(?) dragons,
Repulsive, stinking and evil,
They made me see pain and death.

Roaring they rush upon me,
Pursue me and assail me . . .[52]

If such is the temporal existence of man, it goes without saying that time must inspire loathing and revolt. The constraint in which it holds our true "self," and which is seen as the form par excellence of Evil, engenders a need of Salvation or—what amounts to the same thing—of liberation, arouses a demand for total liberty, a nostalgia for a lost freedom. In the name of this freedom the Gnostic rebels against time, or more generally against the order of the *kosmos* and against every law and rule (physical, moral, or social), at the risk of falling into nihilism, anarchism, amoralism, or even licentious immoralism. In his struggle for deliverance, the "spiritual" or "perfect" man, assured of his transcendent origin, of his native superiority, seeks to shatter time, to destroy the world. The Marcionite violently

52 Turfan Fragment M7, in *Sitzungsberichte der preussischen Akademie der Wissenschaften* 1934, pp. 874–75. [From the French tr. of Benveniste, p. 8.—Ed.]

opposes the Demiurge, the "god of genesis"; he declares a *theomakhia*, a blasphemous battle against the Creator; all his acts tend to "afflict" or "destroy" the Creator, by destroying his works, by despising and hating them.[53] "You have been immortal from the beginning," says Valentinus to his initiates, "you are the sons of Eternal Life, and you have wished to share death in order to expend it and exhaust it, in order that death may die in you and through you. For you dissolve the world without being dissolved yourselves; you are the masters of creation and of all corruption." [54] And the blasphemies against the visible universe uttered by some of his Gnostic listeners horrified Plotinus as much as the sarcasms hurled by other sectarians against Yahweh's creation did the Church.

But was this emotional conception of time translated into a speculative theory of the origin and essence of time? On this aspect of the question, it must be admitted, we have little documentation. In a passage which occurs in both the extant versions of the *Apokryphon* or *Secret Book of John*,[55] Ialdabaoth, the "Protarchon," first and leader of the Archons, is "borne in ignorance" by Sophia, who casts him out; he desired to "possess the designs" of "the Mother," of a reality which surpasses him, that is, in all probability, to imitate them. "Being ignorant, he did not know that she was wiser than he: he took counsel with his Powers; they engendered Destiny (*Heimarmene*) and bound the gods of the heavens, the angels, the demons, and men in measure, duration, and time (or: in measures and times [*chronos*] and moments [*kairos*]), in order to subject them all to (the chain of Destiny), which governs all—an evil, tortuous thought." Time, the instrument of the servitude, thus becomes a product of ignorance, resulting from a wicked

53 Cf. Clement of Alexandria, *Stromateis*, III, 3, 12; 4, 25; Tertullian, *Adv. Marcion.*, I, 13, 29; Hippolytus, *Elenchos*, X, 19, 4; St. Jerome, *Adversus Jovinianum*, II, 16. The intervention of the Good God or of Christ also has as its aim the destruction of the Creator's work or of the created past; see, for example, Irenaeus, *Adv. haer.*, I, 27, 2; IV, 13, 1; Celsus in Origen, *Contra Celsum*, VI, 53; Tertullian, *Adv. Marcion.*, III, 4; IV, 25; Hippolytus, *Elenchos*, VII, 30, 3.

54 Fragment of homily quoted by Clement of Alexandria, *Stromateis*, IV, 13, 89, 1–3, ed. Otto Stählin, *GCS*, Vol. II (1906), p. 287, li. 10–15.

55 Berlin Papyrus 8502, fol. 71, 14–72, 12; Nag-Hammadi Papyrus (acquired in 1946 by the Coptic Museum in Cairo), fol. 37, 1–13. For a formulation of the passage cf. the *Gospel of Mary* (another Gnostic apocryphon contained in the Papyrus Berolinensis), fol. 17, 5–6: "*zur Zeit* (χρόνος) *des Zeitpunktes* (καιρός) *des Aeonen* (αἰών)"; Walter Till in *La Parola del passato* (Naples, 1946), fasc. II, p. 265 = Pap. Ryl. 463, fol. 21, 1–2 (τὸ λοιπὸν δρόμου καιροῦ χρόνου αἰῶνος); C. H. Roberts, *Catalogue of the Greek and Latin Papyri in the John Rylands Library*, Vol. III (Manchester, 1938), p. 21.

imitation (evil in its intention and execution) of a sort of prototype that is infinitely superior, of something wholly other. The same idea occurs, this time explicitly, in a text of St. Irenaeus, summing up the doctrine of the Marcosians, disciples of Valentinus.[56] The passage which I shall briefly analyze and comment upon is of great interest. As we know, Plato in his *Timaeus* represents the Demiurge modeling the universe, with his eyes fixed on the transcendent world of Ideas, seeking to give the most perfect possible imitation of it. Similarly, the Marcosian author gives his Demiurge the intention of imitating the pleroma and of reproducing the infinite, atemporal life after his fashion. In both cases the operation gives birth to cosmic time. But there is a radical difference: whereas in Plato the Demiurge knows the intelligible, eternal model exactly and directly, for the Gnostic theologian the Demiurge has only an enfeebled, distant knowledge of it, only a vague notion suggested by his mother, the fallen Sophia. Since he is himself "the fruit of a fall," of "error" or of "absence," he is separated from the pleroma by a gap, a profound caesura. Hence truth escapes him, and in the replica which he presumed to create, the eternity, stability, and infinity of the superior Ogdoad take the degraded form of a moving multiplicity, consisting of the successive moments, years, centuries which compose and divide time. In other words, there is no longer a continuity between the atemporal and the temporal as in Plato, but a chasm, and the time which results from the work of the Demiurge is no longer the most perfect image; it is no longer—according to its own rank—the most faithful imitation of eternity, but a *pseudos*, a "lie"—an imposture and a caricature verging on illusion. Time is a lie: even in the field of speculation this conception, traces of which may be discerned in Hermeticism or in Mazdaism,[57] reflects the loathing which time inspires in the Gnostic.

56 *Adv. haer.*, I, 17, 2 (Greek text in Hippolytus, *Elenchos*, VI, 54, 1–2):

"In addition to these things, they declare that the Demiurge, desiring to imitate the infinitude, and eternity, and immensity, and freedom from all measurement by time of the Ogdoad above, but, as he was the fruit of defect, being unable to express its permanence and eternity, had recourse to the expedient of spreading out its eternity into times, and seasons, and vast numbers of years, imagining, that by the multitude of such times he might imitate its immensity. They declare further, that the truth having escaped him, he followed that which was false, and that, for this reason, when the times are fulfilled, his work shall perish." (Tr. Roberts and Rambaut, p. 74.)

The passage should be compared on the one hand with Plato, *Timaeus*, 37c–38c, and on the other hand with the passage from the *Apokryphon of John* mentioned in n. 55, above.

57 Cf. *Asclepius*, 37: "For where things are discerned at intervals of time, there are falsehoods; and where things have an origin in time, there errors arise." (Tr. W. Scott,

Consequently we need not be surprised that Salvation, whose object it is to deliver man from the servitude, the suffering, the lie of time is here accomplished through an essentially atemporal mechanism.

As we have said, the Gnostic's need for Salvation grew from a sense of the strangeness of his present situation in the world. The mere existence of such a feeling proves that man must intrinsically be, and must originally have been, something other than what he is now. Accordingly, his refusal to accept the condition allotted him in time brings with it a nostalgia for a realm beyond or rather before the world, for an earlier existence in which his substance was pure of all mixture or adulteration, in which his power was infinitely free: a homesickness for a lost paradise which *gnosis* will enable him to regain. Thus in one and the same act of thought the Gnostic looks upon his present degradation as only accidental and provisional, and gains awareness of his innate superiority, which neither this body, this matter, or this time, to which he is fettered here on earth, has been able to destroy. Consequently the temporal situation that is unacceptable to his feeling becomes paradoxical for his intelligence. His emotional need for Salvation is transposed and formulated in terms of an intellectual requirement and an intellectual problem; it will find satisfaction in an act of consciousness and knowledge. This act is *gnosis*, "knowledge," which is also *epignosis*, "recognition." Knowledge or recognition of what? Ordinarily the term is used in an absolute sense. When it is accompanied by a genitive complement, it designates knowledge of oneself, of man, of God, or—what amounts more or less to the same thing—of the Way, of Joy, of Life.[58] In other words, the experience of evil is expressed, and requires explanation and solution, on the plane of consciousness. Side by side with the horror of evil there is, in the consciousness of the Gnostic, a desire—transformed into an overweening certainty, a certainty that is more than hope and faith—of possessing an absolute Truth, a total Knowledge, in which all the riddles raised by the existence of evil are solved.

How does it come about? According to the sectarians themselves, Gnosis provides an answer to the triple question "Who am I and where am I?

Hermetica, Vol. I, Oxford, 1924, p. 357.) For Mandaeanism see Ernst Percy, *Untersuchungen über den Ursprung der Johanneischen Theologie* (Lund, 1939), pp. 96–105: "Lüge in den mandäischen Schriften."

58 On all these points numerous texts with commentary will be found in E. Norden, *Agnostos Theos* (Leipzig, 1913), pp. 87–115, and in Richard Reitzenstein, *Die hellenistischen Mysterienreligionen* (3rd edn., Leipzig, 1927), pp. 66–67, 284–308.

Whence have I come and why have I come hither? Whither am I going?" [59] Thus it is an explanation of my present situation, but an explanation which will also be its dénouement. The explanation will consist in restoring me to a vast totality of which my present situation is the center, and it will take two directions determined by my two questions "What was I before this situation? What shall I be after it?" This explanation will have a bearing both on my origins and on my destiny. On the one hand, it will flower into a cosmological myth, whose successive episodes will culminate in the history of man and in my present history. This myth will have the function of explaining that God did not will evil, but that evil is either increate and pre-existent in its opposition to Good (this is the dualist solution), or born of a series of degradations of the divine essence or of the fall of a transcendent Being, an "aeon," which broke the peace and the perfection of the pleroma and, more or less directly, produced an incomplete world outside of the Light, the prison of mankind subjected to fatality and sin (this is the emanatist solution). And on the other hand, the Gnostic explanation will find

59 The classical formula is provided by the Valentinian Theodotus (*Excerpta ex Theodoto*, 78, 2): "The knowledge of who we were, what we have become; whither we are hastening, whence we were redeemed; what is birth, what is re-birth." (Tr. from Hastings, *ERE*, VI, p. 231.) In the *Acts of Thomas*, XV (ed. Max Bonnet, Leipzig and Paris, 1883, p. 121, li. 12–13) on the other hand, the hero says to Jesus: "Who . . . hast shown me how to seek myself and know who I was, and who and in what manner I now am, that I may again become that which I was." (Tr. James, *ANT*, pp. 370f.) The first part of this definition of Gnosis is contained implicitly in a Gnostic liturgical text cited by Irenaeus (*Adv. haer.*, I, 21, 5), in which the soul of the Perfect Man, having been delivered and restored to its heavenly home, declares: "I know myself and am whence I came" (tr. Roberts and Rambaut, p. 84). The second part may be read in the *Corpus hermeticum* (IV, 4); here the soul that has received baptism in the vessel of the *Nous* and which thereby partakes of *gnosis*, is informed that "[you] recognize for what purpose you have been made"; the other beings, on the contrary, "know not for what purpose they have been made, nor by whom" (tr. Scott, pp. 151, 153). This formula is studied by E. Norden in *Agnostos Theos*, pp. 102ff. Similar definitions in the religious literature of Iran (*Škand-Gumāṇīk Vicār*, X, 2–11; ed. P. J. de Menasce (Fribourg, 1945), p. 114; and above all in *Pand-Namak i Zartušt*, cited by de Menasce, p. 120. Also, in the philosophical literature of the Roman epoch. Arthur D. Nock, review of Jonas, *Gnosis und spätantiker Geist*, in *Gnomon*, XII (1936), 609, and his "Sarcophagi and Symbolism," *American Journal of Archaeology*, L (1946), 156, notes two examples in Porphyry (*De abstinentia*, I, 27) and in Aristides Quintilianus (III, 7). In a sense we may add Macrobius, *Commentarium in Somnium Scipionis*, I, 9, 1; ed. Franz Eyssenhardt (Leipzig, 1893), p. 509, li. 24–28: "Philosophers whose views are correct do not hesitate to agree that souls originate in the sky; moreover, this is the perfect wisdom of the soul, while it occupies a body, that it recognizes from what source it came." And I, 9, 3 (p. 510, li. 6–8): "A man has but one way of knowing himself, as we have just remarked; if he will look back to his first beginning and origin." (Tr. W. H. Stahl, *Commentary on the Dream of Scipio*, New York, 1952, p. 124.)

its expression in a soteriological myth, counterpart of the cosmological myth but intimately bound up with it. The principal function of such a myth will be to assure us (1) that though we are now degraded, we nevertheless derive our origin and true being from the transcendent world; (2) that by our essence we remain allied and "consubstantial" with this transcendent world or with the fallen entity which will finally be saved and whose destiny is therefore ours and vice versa;[60] and (3) that thereby our own divine substance has remained intact in the accidental episodic mixture that is our existence here on earth. Thus our main task will be to regain awareness of ourselves, to reawaken in ourselves the divine "parcel" or "spark" that is present in us or configured by the "spirit" (the *pneuma* or the *nous*), to reintegrate ourselves with the entity or the superior world that is consubstantial with us. In short, we shall separate from the material *kosmos*, we shall find ourselves once again in our full pristine truth, or rather in our eternal, permanent truth, which for the present has simply been forgotten or clouded over.

As a knowledge or recognition of oneself, as revelation of oneself to oneself, *gnosis* is a knowledge of the whole universe, visible and invisible, of the structure and development of the divine as well as the physical world. Some of the Gnostics actually call it a total "science"—in the positive sense of the word—or even, in Manichaeism, an exhaustive and purely rational explanation of all things.[61] Yet everywhere and always this "science" is resolved in myths of soteriological purport, myths intended not only to explain man's situation *hic et nunc* but also to reveal to him his origin and authentic reality and to bring him the certainty of salvation as a gift eternally given and requiring only to be found again. Knowledge of oneself implies redemption from oneself, just as knowledge of the universe implies the means of freeing oneself from the world and of dominating it.

60 This is the case among the Valentinians, for whom, according to Irenaeus (*Adv. haer.*, I, 5, 6), the "pneumatic generation" (τὸ κύημα πνευματικόν) is and remains consubstantial with the "Mother," the feminine entity who is an Aeon of the pleroma (ὁμοούσιον ὑπάρχον τῇ μητρί). And above all among the Manichaeans, where the individual souls which have fallen into the darkness of matter, or of the bodies, are "parts," "portions," "parcels" of the luminous God, consubstantial with the soul of the "Primordial Man," himself an incarnation of the soul of the "Father of Greatness" (numerous references in *Le Manichéisme*, p. 154, n. 275). More generally on the consubstantiality of God and man in Gnosticism, see Clement of Alexandria, *Stromateis*, II, 16, 74, 1, ed. Stählin, Vol. II, p. 152, 6–10.

61 Cf. for example the *Wisdom of Solomon*, 7 : 17–22, and *Pistis Sophia*, ch. 92–93. See also my *Le Manichéisme*, p. 72, and p. 157, nn. 280–82.

Once we are familiar with this conception we shall easily understand the atemporal character of Gnostic Salvation.

To be sure, Salvation takes place in time, but the act on which it is founded is intrinsically atemporal. It is an interior and individual illumination, a revelation of oneself to oneself, a sudden, gratuitous act which is accomplished by a predestined individual and which presupposes no previous condition or preparation in time. This gratuitousness actually amounts to an absolute right that is in no way contingent on the acts and events preceding the abrupt revelation. The knowledge of self brought by *gnosis* is reminiscence of self, return to a primitive, permanent state, recovery of a being that has been elected for all time, that is saved by virtue of its origin, for all eternity. The "spiritual," the "perfect" man merely recovers an indestructible acquisition, an ontological state given once and for all, his true being which time has not affected, which existence in time has veiled but has not impaired or dissipated. In a fragment already quoted, Valentinus declares to the "pneumatic" men: "You are immortal and the children of eternal life." [62]

Moreover, Salvation here concerns only the atemporal, eternal part of ourselves. Neither flesh nor blood, which are material things and hence evil, can inherit the kingdom of God. There is no resurrection of the body or with the body; on the contrary, the spirit is absolutely detached from the body through its awakening to itself, or through the union, the "spiritual marriage," of the reflection that is our soul in this world, with our real self, our "angel," who is our transcendent personality. Only our *nous* or our *pneuma*, immanent in the atemporal substance of God or of a divine entity, is saved.[63]

In separating our spirit, our self, from the body, this Salvation places us

62 Clement of Alexandria, *Stromateis*, IV, 13, 89, 2, ed. Stählin, Vol. II, p. 287, 11–12. Cf. the anonymous treatise called the Codex Brucianus, LIX, tr. Charlotte A. Baynes, *A Coptic Gnostic Treatise Contained in the Codex Brucianus* (Cambridge, 1933), p. 177: "And I shall give you an authority proper to you, and none shall hinder you in that which you desire. And you shall possess aeons and worlds and heavens, so that the intelligible spirits come and they dwell in them. And you shall be deified, and you shall know that you came forth from God, and you shall see him that he is God within you: and he shall dwell in your aeon."

63 Concerning this denial of the resurrection of the flesh the texts are extremely abundant. I content myself with referring the reader to the very general testimony of Tertullian, *De praescriptione haereticorum*, XXIII, and with reproducing two formulas from ch. 6 of the *Adversus omnes haereses* of Pseudo-Tertullian, which, in speaking of Cerdo and of Apelles, sum up the entire theory in a few words: "A resurrection of the soul merely does he approve, denying that of the body" (ed. Kroymann, p. 222, li. 25f.); "This man denies the resurrection of the flesh, . . . he teaches the salvation of souls alone" (p. 224, li. 1–2) (tr. Thelwall, pp. 269, 271).

outside of time; it introduces us into a situation that transcends the limited, and therefore captive—the phenomenal, and therefore illusory—existence that has hitherto been ours. It consists not in fulfilling oneself in time but in finding oneself fulfilled beyond time and before time. It releases us from time in order to carry us back to our original, atemporal condition.[64]

Thus Salvation places us beyond all power of time, since the state that it restores to us is definitive. Salvation is regeneration in the sense that it is a gathering together (*syllexis*) of our luminous, divine substance,[65] a recuperation of our authentic self, a return to our own primitive being and place, to our *idia*.[66] And it is liberation in the strongest sense. The *eleutheria*, the freedom, that it assures us is not only negative,[67] a detachment or liberation

64 In this connection we find in the *Acts of Thomas* (XLIII, p. 161, 9–10) a highly remarkable formula which has been well commented on by G. Bornkamm in his work *Mythos und Legende in den apokryphen Thomas-Akten* (Göttingen, 1933), pp. 121–22: "that I also may be set free and be gathered unto the nature that is mine from the beginning" (tr. James, p. 386). Here the self effects a return—through a gathering together and concentration—to its original, primordial nature. Along the same lines, cf. several significant expressions noted by E. Peterson, "La Libération d'Adam de l' Ἀνάγκη," *Revue biblique*, LV (1948), 203, in a magic papyrus, the pseudo "Liturgy of Mithra." Cf. Quispel, *Gnosis als Weltreligion*, p. 19: "The Valentinians declare programmatically: 'Once the spirit (that is, the spiritual man) comes to itself, it has returned to its origin.'" (Clement, *Paedagogus*, 32, 1).

65 Cf. in particular the passage in the "Gospel of Eve" reproduced by Epiphanius, *Panarium*, XXVI, 3, 1; ed. Karl Holl, *Epiphanius, Ancoratus und Panarium* (*GCS*, 1915–33), Vol. I, p. 278, li. 11f.: "I am thou and thou art I, and wherever thou art, there am I, and I am scattered through all things. And whencesoever thou wilt thou gatherest me together, and gathering me together thou gatherest together thyself." (Tr. A.S.B.G.) And the quotation from the "Gospel of Philip" in the same heresiologist (*Panarium*, XXVI, 13, 2 (Vol. I, p. 292, li. 16–20): "I have taken knowledge (it [the soul] saith) of myself, and have gathered myself together out of every quarter and have not begotten (sown) children unto the Ruler, but have rooted out his roots and gathered together the members that were scattered abroad. And I know thee who thou art." (Tr. James, p. 12.) Cf. also in this connection Leonhard Fendt, *Gnostische Mysterien* (Munich, 1922), pp. 4–12, 76–77; as well as Jonas, *Gnosis*, Vol. I, pp. 139–40.

66 Cf. the liturgical fragment cited by Irenaeus (*Adv. haer.*, I, 21, 5), in which the liberated soul declares on its return to its supracelestial home: "I derive being from Him who is pre-existent, and I come again to my own place whence I went forth." (Tr. Roberts and Rambaut, p. 84.) Numerous Manichaean passages along the same lines are indicated in my *Le Manichéisme*, p. 156, n. 278.

67 Consult on this point Jacques Dupont, *Gnosis: La Connaissance religieuse dans les Epîtres de Saint Paul* (Louvain and Paris, 1949), pp. 282–327, which gives a bibliography and sums up the interpretations of the modern critics. On the two directions (strict asceticism or extreme libertinism) that the application of Gnostic *eleutheria* or *exousia* can take, cf. my remarks in H.-C. Puech and A. Vaillant, eds., *Le Traité contre les Bogomiles de Cosmas le Prêtre* (Paris, 1945), pp. 333–35, and H. J. Schoeps' study, "Gnostischer Nihilismus," in *Aus frühchristlicher Zeit: Religionsgeschichtliche Untersuchungen* (Tübingen, 1950), pp. 255–70.

from the tyranny of Destiny and the slavery of the body and of matter (*apolutrōsis*); it is also a positive freedom, *exousia*, an absolute power or licence to do whatever we please (whence the Gnostic amoralism that is sometimes translated into deeds), an independence by right of birth (the Gnostic proclaims himself a "king's son"),[68] from the laws and the masters of this world, and later, on departure from the body, from the planetary Archons and from the Creator and Judge of the universe, the Cosmocrator. At the beginning of this life, *gnosis* clothes the spiritual man in *adiaphoria*, "indifference," and *apatheia*, "impeccability," and this state is inalienable, regardless of what he may subsequently do. The Gnostic is free in all things and judges all things. He is a *bythos exousias*, an "abyss of liberty." [69] The image has been revived by Nietzsche: [70] like the sea which without harm swallows up all the filth cast into it by a thousand watercourses, he can receive and absorb all things without ever being sullied, he can engage in all sorts of action, and still no sin may ever be imputed to him. He is saved by nature and not by works, and none of the acts that he may perform indifferently in an alien world can alter or destroy his status as a chosen and saved being; [71] though plunged in the mire, a block of gold remains eternally gold.[72] Here again time has no effect on the transcendent, definitive state

68 Cf. for classical Gnosticism, Clement of Alexandria, *Stromateis*, III, 3, 30, 1; for Mandaeism, *From the John-Book of the Mandaeans*, tr. from the German of Mark Lidzbarski (London, 1924). For Manichaeism see Turfan Fragment M liturg., *Abhandlungen der preussischen Akademie der Wissenschaften*, 1904, Appendix, p. 29, and one of the *Psalms of Thomas* of the Fayoum Psalter, in *A Manichaean Psalm-book*, part II, p. 216, li. 2–3. Nor should we forget the "Kings' Sons" who are the heroes of the famous "Song of the Pearl" in the *Acts of Thomas*, 108–13.

69 According to a passage from Porphyry's *De abstinentia* (I, 42), which in my opinion is not directed against the Cynics, as J. Dupont maintains (op. cit., pp. 295–98), but against the Gnostics, as is shown by the close resemblance between its language and that of the Gnostics as disclosed in various passages of the *Stromateis* of Clement of Alexandria.

70 *Thus Spake Zarathustra*, tr. Thomas Common, rev. by O. Levy and J. L. Beevers (London, 1932), p. 68: "Verily, a polluted stream is man. One must be a sea, to receive a polluted stream without becoming impure."

71 As Irenaeus reports (*Adv. haer.*, I, 6, 2) concerning the Valentinians, the πνευματικοὶ who have the τελεία γνῶσις are absolutely saved "by nature," and not by their works ("but as to themselves, they hold that they shall be entirely and undoubtedly saved, not by means of conduct, but because they are spiritual by nature"). Hence the Gnostic can suffer no harm or taint of corruption, regardless of what acts he performs ("it is impossible that spiritual substance, by which they mean themselves, should ever come under the power of corruption, whatever the sort of actions in which they indulged"). (Tr. Roberts and Rambaut, p. 26.)

72 Irenaeus, *Adv. haer.*, I, 6, 2: "For even as gold, when submersed in filth, loses not on that account its beauty, but retains its own native qualities, the filth having no

achieved through *gnosis*. On the contrary, the Gnostic may either ignore time or dominate it and bend it to his whim. And he stands in a similar relation to the body and to matter: he may either detach himself from them, guard against their taints, remain aloof from them through the strictest asceticism, or else demonstrate his contempt for them, his revolt or superiority, by indulging in unrestrained debauch, by exhausting the flesh and his carnal desires. Only the "psychic" men—the intermediary category who are neither saved by nature like the "pneumatics" nor fatally damned like the "hylics"—require an education to achieve Salvation, require a succession of efforts and good works, hence a progress in time or through a series of reincarnations.[73]

*

It would be inaccurate to say that Gnostic Salvation, though intrinsically atemporal both in its object and in its effects, is wholly exempt from temporal conditions. But where time does enter in, its role is reduced to a minimum and the tendency is to annul it.

Actually the saving revelation that gives Gnosis its content is sometimes represented—in Valentinus or Basilides, for example [74]—as a *paradosis*, a tradition transmitted in time or—as in Manichaeism [75]—is based on the authority of a long line of precursors, or successive "prophets of humanity," who have appeared since Adam at certain moments of history: Shem, Seth, and Enoch among others, or Zoroaster, Buddha, and Jesus. But in the first case this tradition is secret, usually without outward guaranty, and paralleled by individual revelations. The very idea of tradition is threatened if not replaced by that of a discontinuous, independent, anarchic revelation.

---

power to injure the gold, so they affirm that they cannot in any measure suffer hurt, and lose their spiritual substance, whatever the material actions in which they may be involved." (Tr. ibid.)

73 So it was among the Valentinians (Irenaeus, *Adv. haer.*, I, 6, 1–2, and 7, 5, or *Excerpta ex Theodoto*, 54–57. And the same is true of the Manichaean "Catechumen" or "Hearer," who corresponds more or less to the "Psychic" of classical Gnosticism (cf. my *Le Manichéisme*, pp. 88–91, and 186–95, nn. 374–92).

74 Cf. Clement of Alexandria, *Stromateis*, VII, 17, 106, and *Letter from Ptolemy to Flora* in Epiphanius, *Panarion*, XXXIII, 7, 9 (Valentinians); Clement of Alexandria, *Stromateis*, VII, 17, 106, and Hippolytus, *Elenchos*, VII, 20, 1 (Basilidians); Hippolytus, *Elenchos*, V, 7, 1 (Naassenes). More generally, Irenaeus, *Adv. haer.*, I, 25, 5 (= Theodoret, *Haereticarum fabularum compendium*, I, 5).

75 Cf. my *Le Manichéisme*, pp. 61–63 and p. 144, n. 241 (in which the references are given). On the Manichaean theory of the successive eclipses of the Revelation, see ibid., pp. 66, 149, nn. 259, 260.

In the second case, the revelation provided in diverse epochs by various envoys is itself discontinuous; each of the successive messages proclaimed before the appearance of Mani was engulfed in a diabolical catastrophe and eclipsed along with the truth (a partial truth to be sure) that it contained. Precursors there are, but no continuous or progressive tradition. From time to time the revelations interrupt the course of history, but they do not extend continuously from its beginning to the coming of the Paraclete.

Yet in so far as the inner revelation has to be awakened or reawakened by a Revealer, Salvation depends on a Savior who intervenes in time. But the Gnostic attaches no importance to the historical aspect of this intervention. First of all, the Savior—and this is stated very clearly in Mandaeism and Manichaeism—is conceived above all as the personification of the transcendent *Nous*, a sort of projection or configuration of the individual *nous*, which also plays the role of "Saved Savior," a savior who saves himself within each man. The mythical aspect of the Savior overshadows his historical aspect where he is not, like the Mandaean Manda d'Hayye—"Gnosis of Life"—a purely mythical being. Moreover, the Savior is conceived exclusively as a Revealer, an "awakener." He is a master or illuminator (*phōstēr*), an example; he is the instructor who brings *gnosis*, the prototype who shows how one can release the *nous* from matter through Gnosis. It is not his acts that save, but the symbols that materialize his acts, or the teaching he dispenses. No value of sacrifice, of expiation for the sins and the flesh, no significance of redemption is attached to the sufferings or Passion of the Savior, whether he be Jesus or Mani. The essential is not the concrete, realistic, historical character of the drama that is the Savior's earthly life but the intellectual, exemplary, atemporal character of the revelation divulged by the Savior. This is particularly evident in the Christian Gnoses, which could not help taking the historical figure of Jesus into account. The Christian Gnostics—and the Manichaeans—establish a duality, a *hiatus* between the metaphysical Christ and the Jesus who appeared in Judaea. They attach the appearance of the latter to no historical event: for Marcion, Jesus appeared suddenly (*subito*) in the form of a man of thirty; [76] more generally, his coming is a *coup de théâtre* which breaks history into two pieces and which nothing in the past has foreshadowed or prepared the way for; it has nothing to do with the prophecies of the Old Testament. Above all, Christ

76 Tertullian, *Adv. Marcion.*, III, 2 (ed. Kroymann, p. 378, li. 16–17): "*Subito filius et subito missus et subito Christus*"; and III, 3 (p. 378, li. 28): "*statim.*"

was not really incarnated: his substance was purely spiritual, "pneumatic." Jesus was not, in any true and profound sense, placed in a concrete segment of time. There was only a phantom Savior (*putativus*, says St. Irenaeus) who appeared at a certain moment but did not enter into any real flesh or integral historical man. His body and consequently his sufferings and his Passion were only apparent—except where, as in Basilides, another man is substituted for him on the Cross. Thus the miracles, the Crucifixion, the Resurrection have neither full reality nor concrete efficacy: at most they are symbols or examples. Either a fantastic drama was enacted behind the historical reality or else the historical setting was illusory, so that the reality expressed through it remains atemporal. Fundamentally, this Gnostic conception, designated as "docetism," negates the historical, temporal character of the life and work of Jesus.

There is a last point in which Gnostic soteriology might imply a temporal perspective, and that is eschatology. As a matter of fact, Christian and—at least in Manichaeism—Iranian influence did result in Gnostic theories and visions bearing on ultimate ends, on the End of the Epochs and the disappearance of the present world. Yet what could these views of the future mean to spirits so impatient of all concrete time? The Gnostic expected no particular or general resurrection: as we have seen, he held that the flesh could not be resurrected; moreover, since he identified resurrection with the awakening of the spirit to truth and with inner regeneration through knowledge, he held the spiritual man, once illuminated, to be already resurrected and forever. To cite the second Epistle of Timothy (2 : 18), which sums up the theory in order to condemn it, "the resurrection is *already* come." [77] On

77 On this instantaneous resurrection, conceived as a definitive state which immediately locates the saved being beyond death, we can do no better than consider the testimony regarding those heretics who were looked upon—rightly or wrongly—as the ancestors of Gnosticism: Nicholas and Menander. Regarding the first, Hippolytus, in fr. I of *De resurrectione*, preserved in Syriac (ed. Hans Achelis, *Hippolytus Werke*, Vol. I, part II, p. 251, li. 10–17), writes, precisely after quoting from II Tim. 2 : 18: "This Nicholas . . . impelled by an alien (diabolical) spirit, was the first to affirm that the resurrection has already come, meaning by 'resurrection' the fact that we believe in Christ and receive baptism, but he denied the resurrection of the flesh. And at his instigation several men founded sects. These included above all the so-called Gnostics, to whom belonged Hymenaeus and Philetus (combated by the Apostle)." On Menander, see Tertullian, *De anima*, 50, 2 (ed. August Reifferscheid and Georg Wissowa, in *CSEL*, XX, 1890): "But the insane opinion of the Samaritan heretic Menander is also rejected, who will have it that death has not only nothing to do with his disciples, but in fact never reaches them. He pretends to have received such a commission from the secret power of One above, that all who partake of his baptism become immortal,

the other hand, the Gnostic seeks to anticipate the final Consummation to come by accomplishing it in himself and for himself; he participates in it *hic et nunc*, enacting the event through the medium of the rite. The Manichaean *Bēma* is an anticipated rehearsal of the Last Judgment; the Valentinian or Marcosian *apolutrōsis*, the *consolamentum* of the medieval Catharists, and without doubt the "spiritual baptism" of the Bogomils on which it was probably modeled are prefigurations of the souls' return to their transcendent home and of their heavenly marriage with their angel or true "self," their eternal prototype. And the eschatological events are turned inward: the *teleiōsis*, the *syntēleia*, the *apokatastasis*, the *consummatio* are already present and accomplished in the person of the Gnostic; the "perfect" man, the *teleios*, is already "consummated." He has in himself attained the state which, temporally speaking, must, in the future, follow the end of the ages.

Thus the Gnostic spirit tends, in all its manifestations, to negate time or at least to dispense with it and surpass it. Confronted with historical elements, it spontaneously reduces them to atemporal, or more accurately to mythical, terms. In connection with the figure of the Christian Jesus the operation is unequivocal. But the remark may be generalized. Gnostic thinking is fundamentally mythical. It is dominated by the nostalgia for an initial situation which commands all actuality, by a myth of the *Urzeit* and *Ursprung*.[78] It is incapable of considering the particular persons and events of history rationally in concepts or concretely by apprehension. For Gnostic thinking, concepts become ill-defined schemas, entities half abstract, half concrete, half personal, half impersonal; "aeons," *aiōn*, *'ōlām* (Mand. *almā*) —fragments of time or spatialized and hypostatized periods of time—the elements or characters in a mythological drama; and for their part, historical individuals and facts are sublimated into something half way between the real and the symbolic. Even the course of time is moved into a mythical perspective: according to the Manichaean theory, for example, it corresponds to the second stage of a mythical process that unfolds in three "moments": an anterior moment, in which Light and Darkness lived separately; a median

---

incorruptible, and instantaneously invested with resurrection-life." (Tr. Holmes, p. 521.) And see the texts of Justin Martyr, *Apologia*, I, 26, 4, and Irenaeus, *Adv. haer.*, I, 23, 5: "His disciples obtain the *resurrection* by being baptized into him, and can die no more, but remain in the possession of immortal youth" (tr. Roberts and Rambaut, p. 89)—indicated by J. H. Waszink in his edition with commentary of Tertullian's *De anima* (Amsterdam, 1947), p. 519.

78 I shall not develop this point, which has already been treated by K. Kerényi in his two papers on mythology and gnosis, *EJ 1940–41*, pp. 157–229.

moment, in which Light is attacked and conquered by Darkness and the two unengendered and atemporal substances are mixed; and a posterior moment, in which their original disjunction will be re-established. On the margin of historical time and parallel to it there is enacted a mythical drama whose actors are the "Aeons" or transcendent Entities. In Valentinian Gnosis we have strife in the pleroma, Passion, the fall and mishaps of Sophia, and her salvation and return to the pleroma; in Manichaeism or in the vision of the alchemist Zosimos we have the fall of the Primordial Man and his captivity in the Darkness, and the entire historical process consists in the recovery and reshaping of his luminous substance that has been dispersed among all living creatures. It is the diverse phases of this mythical drama that give to history whatever meaning it can have, or rather that interrupt the course of concrete time, chopping it into an incoherent succession of dramatic episodes: sudden interventions of the transcendent in human affairs, sudden acts of God, which nothing justifies and nothing prepares the way for, arbitrary irruptions which put the finishing touches to the inorganic picture of Gnostic time. "*Subito Christus, subito Iohannes: sic sunt omnia apud Marcionem,*" writes Tertullian.[79] And, we might add, so is everything connected with Gnostic time.

*

What shall we conclude from all this? The picture resulting from our investigation of time as conceived by Gnosticism may appear confused, unbalanced, even contradictory, and so indeed it is. Time exists, but on the one hand it is a captive, heavy with the chains of evil Destiny, while on the other it is inorganic, broken by the interventions of Revelation and by the Gnostic's will to break it in order to break with it. This dramatic time has a certain affinity with the Christian conception of concrete, historical time: it has a beginning and an end, and in it a kind of special Providence is effected in favor of mankind (with, to be sure, the difference that Gnostic time has no full reality and that Providence or what might here be called by that name operates only for the benefit of an élite). But Gnostic time is only the consequence and the reflection of the adventures or conflict of transcendent realities, an episodic copy of an atemporal tragedy, and the Gnostic's effort is to transcend time in order to establish himself, as absolutely as

79 *Adv. Marcion.*, IV, 11 (ed. Kroymann, p. 449, li. 22–24). ("Christ suddenly, and just as suddenly, John! After this fashion occur all things in Marcion's system."—Tr. Holmes, p. 211.)

possible, in the world of atemporal realities, in a universe that is intelligible and given eternally. In this sense the Gnostic attitude seems to approach that of Hellenism, except that where the Greek sees the necessary and true image of eternity, the Gnostic sees a caricature and a lie. The Gnostic conceives neither pure temporality like the Christian nor pure atemporality like the Hellene. For him history is paralleled and finally in large part absorbed by myth; and the atemporal is also treated mythically. Or we might say that the atemporal and intelligible world, the pleroma, loses some of its immobility to become the theater of the successive and changing adventures of the Aeons, while the concrete events of historical time are transformed into properties, echoes, or symbols of the episodes in this atemporal drama that is prolonged in them. Thus the temporal (as mobility or succession) seems to penetrate the atemporal, while conversely the atemporal (in the form of transcendence) tends to absorb the temporal. For in both realms we actually find an atemporality and a temporality conceived by a fundamentally mythical thinking. It is myth which gives the visions, both of the transcendent world and of historical time, their structure—myth which is intrinsically neither eternity and intelligibility after the Greek fashion, nor history and time of the Christian type. Myth is articulated atemporality. It narrates events and adventures, but they are undatable and occur outside of any concrete time, although they seem to partake of time by their successive character. Hence, applied to the intelligible world and to Creation, mythical thinking can only contaminate and transform them both in equal measure. Compared with the Greek and Christian conceptions, this mythical time of Gnosticism might consequently appear to be a bastard conception, sharing in them both, straddling them and clumsily uniting them. In reality, it is neither Greek nor Christian but corresponds to an autonomous attitude which, in attempting to adapt itself to Greek opinions and beliefs, disfigured them both. Consider how absurd the adventures of an Aeon, of immutable Eternity, must have been for a Greek mind; and how scandalously impious a Christ detached from history, a phantom Savior in revolt against the Creator, must have seemed to an adherent of the Great Church.

Gilles Quispel

Time and History in Patristic Christianity

We write: "Anno Domini 1951." This means that we measure time from a center. This center determines the time that follows it, and the time which preceded it strove toward this center. Our historical numbering of the years tacitly presupposes a caesura between the era before the birth of Christ and the era which came after it. Our history is oriented toward a center.

It is true that for some years certain circles (Jan Romein and his adherents) have been trying to repress this fact. They speak with a special pathos of the year so-and-so "before our time reckoning." This term is hard to understand and suggests certain innocent Socratic questions. Is there, for example, any such thing as "after our time reckoning"? What will happen "after our time reckoning"? Or will nothing at all happen in the vacuum "after our time reckoning," a vacuum that will drop out of time so entirely as to lose all connection with tradition? Do these circles perhaps altogether deny the Western tradition that is so utterly saturated with history? And yet it must be admitted that their reluctance to speak of a center of history is understandable, for obviously such a term also implies the central fact of the Christian religion; it implies that past, present, and future are to be understood in terms of this center, that the world as history converges toward this point in a mysterious systole and diverges from it in an equally mysterious diastole. How has this come about? How was it possible that the belief in a universal history, a belief which, as we read in the Book of Daniel, was the dream of a Nebuchadnezzar in the year 168 "before our time reckoning," should have become the basic presupposition of European man?

The New Testament conception of time is wholly naïve: as in Judaism and to some extent in Parsiism, a distinction is made between the present aeon, which extends up to the second *Parousia*, and the coming, future aeon.

Thus the history of Salvation becomes a movement from the beginning in paradise to the end in the New Jerusalem.

In this historical unfolding the religious vision discovers the workings of an *oikonomia,* a divine plan of Salvation. (It is characteristic that in the later Christian idiom *oikonomia* signifies "Incarnation" as well as "plan of Salvation," and finally comes to designate the inner unfolding of God into the Trinity, because historically neither the inner life of the Godhead nor the *oikonomia* can be understood except from the perspective of the Incarnation.) And when man is placed in this *oikonomia,* he experiences his *kairos*—that is to say, a tension and a meaning enter into his inherently profane and aimless life "time," because it becomes related to the plan of Salvation and is thus in direct relation to God.

> Nowhere is what the New Testament means by *kairos* better expressed than in the passage from the Gospel of St. John (7 : 3ff.) (in this respect a truly classic passage) in which Jesus says to his unbelieving brethren: "My *kairos* [to go up to Jerusalem] is not yet come, but your *kairos* is alway ready" (verse 6). This means: For you there is no *kairos* in the historical, New Testament sense; there are no times appointed and specially singled out by God in his omnipotence with a view to his plan of salvation. For the others there exists only the profane usage of the word *kairos:* everything depends merely on the human decision as to whether a *kairos* is favorable or not. They can go up to Jerusalem at any time. But not so Christ, for he stands in the very midst of the divine plan of salvation, whose *kairoi* are exactly determined by God.[1]

To a certain degree this sense of time was determined by eschatology. The great discovery of Weiss and Albert Schweitzer was the significance of the expectation of the end for the teachings of Jesus, for beyond any doubt the first Christians expected and hoped that the kingdom of God would *soon* be manifested on earth. In the New Testament man stands in a process which draws its meaning and virtue from an invisible end; mankind, and the cosmos as well, has an *eschaton,* a *telos,* an end which draws events toward it like a magnet. How new this was is shown by a comparison with the Greeks. In his book *In the Grip of the Past,*[2] Bernhard A. van Groningen describes how the Greeks lived in the past and were fascinated by the

1 Oscar Cullmann, *Christus und die Zeit* (Zurich, 1946), p. 35. Cf. Théo Preiss, "The Vision of History in the New Testament," *Papers of the Ecumenical Institute* (Geneva), V (1950), 48.

2 In the series Philosophia antiqua, Vol. VI (Leiden, 1953).

repetition of the past; so much so that for them the future had no dimension of its own.

And yet we should misunderstand the special character of the early Christian sense of time if we attempted to see it wholly in terms of the *telos*. The decisive factor was, rather, the center, the life and death of Jesus. This is the unique, unrepeatable, essential fact, which gives rise to history and to the new sense of time. From it the course of time takes its direction; from it time strives toward an end. There is a divine *ephapax*, a "once and for all": "For in that [Christ] died, he died unto sin once" (Rom. 6 : 10). And wherever Christians forgather down to the present day, the significance of this act and this sacrifice for salvation is called to mind: "This do in remembrance of me" (Luke 22 : 19). Moreover, the kingdom of God is mysteriously and invisibly present with the first appearance of Jesus: "The time is fulfilled, and the kingdom of God is at hand" (Mark 1 : 15). Or, as in an interpolation to the Gospel of St. Mark, "The limit of the years of the power of Satan is fulfilled" (Mark 16 : 14, Western text). For there is no doubt that for Jesus the kingdom of God was already present in his person: "The blind receive their sight, and the lame walk, the lepers are cleansed, and the deaf hear, the dead are raised up, and the poor have the gospel preached to them" (Matthew 11 : 5). These are the signs of eschatological time. And it is particularly through and after the Passover that this knowledge that the end of time is at hand is fully formed in the disciples: "And it shall come to pass in the last days, saith God, I will pour out of my spirit upon all flesh" (Acts 2 : 17). The spirit had been poured forth and was the supreme reality in the life of the early Christians. It will come to pass at the end of days that the dead will rise again. Christ is risen. To be sure, the future aeon was not yet here in all its glory; but the Resurrection, the coming of the Holy Ghost, are anticipations of the end: "Beloved, now are we the sons of God, and it doth not yet appear what we shall be" (I John 3 : 2). Eschatological time breaks into present time. And just as the present has its own meaning and necessity in the announcement of the victory and in selfless charity, so the *pneuma* is already present as the ἀπαρχή of transfiguration. The early Christian sense of time was constituted by the *ephapax*—by proleptic eschatology and the meaning of the present for salvation—no less than by eschatology proper.

The thesis that this early Christian time feeling vanished completely in the patristic period is untenable. This notion is in keeping with Protestant or liberal dogma, but the facts speak a different language. Puech has shown that in the first centuries Christian thinkers developed the idea of rectilinear history and its unrepeatable uniqueness in even greater detail.[3] And indeed, the Church Fathers, in their polemics against heresy, expressed for the first time the idea that there exists a development in history, the idea that in the education of the human race certain forms were justified in their time, only to be rejected at a later epoch. Indeed, a study of the Church Fathers makes it clear that the pathos of progress is a secularization of early Christian conceptions. This historical vision of ancient Christianity grew out of the *ephapax*, the "once and for all."

Nor did the thread of proleptic eschatology ever break off. To be sure, patristic Christianity is not merely a continuation of early Christianity. The struggle against Gnosticism led to an overemphasis on free will, which gave patristic Christianity a different imprint from the early Christianity out of which it grew. However, it is a hasty simplification of a complex situation to say that vain waiting for the ardently hoped-for *Parousia* led to a total degeneration and secularization of Christianity—as though the dwindling of eschatological tension and the fading of the eschatological perspective were the causes of the so-called Hellenization of Christianity. In the first place, the texts give little evidence of any such weariness and disillusionment: nowhere is a breach in the tradition discernible. Moreover, such simple solutions for complex problems always tend to be false: it cannot be denied that the germs of the subsequent development were present in early Christianity.

In patristic Christianity we see the development of dogmatism, liturgy, asceticism, mysticism, and apologetics. Is this to be judged as a pseudomorphosis of the Gospel?

Concerning the origin of the trinitarian dogma, C. G. Jung writes:

> The sole reason for the dogma lies in the Christian "message," which caused a psychic revolution in Western man. On the evidence of the gospels, and of Paul's letters in particular, it announced the real and veracious appearance of the God-man in this humdrum human world, accompanied by all the marvellous portents worthy of the son of God. However obscure the historical core of this phenomenon may seem to us moderns, with our hankering for

3 Henri-Charles Puech, "Temps, histoire et mythe dans le christianisme des premiers siècles," *Proceedings of the 7th Congress for the History of Religions* (Amsterdam, 1951), pp. 33–52.

> factual accuracy, it is quite certain that those tremendous psychic effects, lasting for centuries, were not called forth causelessly, by just nothing at all.[4]

Thus Jung, too, believes that the dogmatic development is rooted in the *ephapax* and consequently has nothing to do with weariness and the disappearance of the eschatological perspective. As for the other phenomena, they can be shown to have developed at least in part from proleptic eschatology, so that, ironically enough, it would seem to have been through eschatology that elements having their origin in the mysteries, in philosophy, and in the Gnosis of antiquity became integrated with Christianity.

The early Christian Eucharist, a highly complex phenomenon, was not only an ethic of remembrance and the motif of sacrifice but also a Messianic banquet of rejoicing, an anticipation of the Lord's eschatological *beraka* with his disciples in the kingdom of God. Karl Barth writes: "It is the presence of Jesus in his congregation that is full of his future. For the congregation strives and yearns for his future, universal, and final revelation, which has occurred only in a particular and provisional sense in the Easter episode, so that even the full presence of Jesus in the spirit can only be a pledge and token of what the congregation, along with the whole cosmos, may and must still await: his return in glory." [5] Thus the divine service of the early Christians, like that of the Eastern Church to this day, is an anticipation of the end; it represents the kingdom of God here and now, living in concealment on earth. Cullmann also supports this view: "For the early Christians, the Eucharistic supper was an anticipation of the Messianic supper awaited by the Jews." [6] Barth calls the Last Supper "an anticipation of the universal, ultimate and definitive revelation, which had indeed begun with the resurrection of Jesus, but had only begun; the resurrection had been its ἀρραβών (pledge) and ἀπαρχή (beginning of sacrifice) but its wholeness was still absent, still to come, so that any celebration of the Last Supper can only look forward to it." [7] And concerning the author of the Apocalypse, Cullmann says: "Receiving his visions on the day of the Lord—that is, on the

4 "A Psychological Approach to the Dogma of the Trinity," in *Psychology and Religion: West and East*, tr. R. F. C. Hull (Collected Works, Vol. 11; New York and London, 1957), par. 222.
5 Karl Barth, *Die kirchliche Dogmatik*, Vol. III, part II (Zurich, 1948), p. 562.
6 Oscar Cullmann, *Les Sacrements dans l'évangile Johannique* (Paris, 1951), p. 40.
7 Barth, p. 604.

day in which the Christian congregation is united—the seer considers the Christian cult as a kind of anticipation of the events at the end of time, so that to describe the final drama, indescribable as it is in principle, he is justified in borrowing the terms and images of liturgical life." And concerning the intention of St. John the Evangelist, he writes: "Beginning with the events of the life of Jesus, he seeks to demonstrate the complete identity of the Lord present in the Christian congregation and of the historical Jesus." [8] Thus the *Kyrios* was present in the cult, *in praesentia reali,* but this was believed because the early Christians believed in the Easter episode, and he came as a prolepsis of the ultimate transfiguration.

Even if we reject the notion of influence, there is no doubt that this cult *eidos* discloses a certain parallelism with the Hellenistic mysteries. An account of the *inventio,* the great festival of the mysteries of Isis, that has come down to us tells how the *mater dolorosa* searched and how she found the dismembered Osiris.

> Isis grieves, laments, searches for her lost son with her dog's head [Anubis] and the shaven-headed priests; and the unhappy Isiaci beat their breasts and imitate the grief of the mournful mother; then, when the child is found, Isis is glad, the priests are beside themselves with joy, the dog's head who has found him is proud. And year after year they never cease to lose what they have found and to find what they have lost.[9]

Isis herself was present in the mystery: "It was she who was supposed to direct the rites." [10] And in this *praesentia realis* there lies a parallelism with the early Christian Eucharist. The Eucharist, too, knew sorrow when the Lord's death was announced. But it is also recorded that in the original Jerusalem congregation the festival was celebrated with rejoicing (ἐν ἀγαλλιάσει). This was joy at the presence of the *Kyrios.* The cry "*Maran atha*" implies, besides the prayer for the *Parousia* and the profession of the incarnation, the notion that the Lord is now present, in the divine service, and particularly in the rite of the Lord's supper.

The strange thing is, whereas the motif of remembrance was taken over from the Jewish feast of the Passover and the motif of sacrifice does not

8 Cullmann, p. 8.

9 Minucius Felix, *Octavius,* XXI (Migne, *PL,* III, col. 303).

10 Georges Lafaye, *Histoire du culte des divinités d'Alexandrie hors de l'Égypte* (Paris, 1884), p. 127.

appear to be paralleled at all in the mysteries,[11] this most central idea, most native of all, it would seem, to Christianity, this intuition of the Lord's presence in the cult has its correspondence in the Hellenistic mysteries.[12]

But how different is the time sense: the celebration of the Lord's presence is linked to historical events in the most recent past; it is an anticipation of the future—a point, so to speak, on a line between two points. And for this reason it is celebrated on a Sunday, which is the day of Resurrection but also anticipates the ultimate "day of the Lord," God's eschatological day of rest after the cosmic week. The celebrants of the mysteries of Isis, however, never cease, year after year, to lose what they have found, and to find what they have lost. This rite represents a timeless, primordial myth, an eternal repetition of the cycle of nature. The totality of the circle is the mystery of the ancient religions; proleptic eschatology, on the other hand, connotes an anticipation of the end. And the same relationship stands out in another detail. Isis collects the scattered members (*sparsa membra*) of Osiris, and in the Didache, the Christians prayed for the regathering of the dispersed members of the *corpus Christi:* "As this piece [of bread] was scattered over the hills and then was brought together and made one, so let your Church be brought together from the ends of the earth into your Kingdom." [13] And in the Gospel of St. John (11 : 51–52): ". . . that Jesus should die for that nation; and not for that nation only, but that also he should gather together in one the children of God that were scattered abroad." This symbolism attaches to the historical fact of the Diaspora and to the eschatological hope that at the coming of the kingdom of heaven the people of God will return to Jerusalem, the center of the earth, because Christ, too, was expected to return to Jerusalem at his second coming. The theme of the *dispersio* has been elevated from the realm of nature to that of history.

It would seem to be more difficult to understand apologetics from the standpoint of eschatology. For on the one hand Christian apologetics is a continuation of Jewish apologetics, while on the other hand it is so saturated with Greek popular philosophy that here at least one is justified in speaking

11 New discoveries show that the adepts of Mithras ate the sacrificed bull, but nothing indicates that Mithras was identical with the bull: M. J. Vermaseren, "De Mithrasmaaltyd," *Annalen van het Thymgenootschap*, XXXVIII (1950), part 1, pp. 26ff.

12 Arthur D. Nock, "Hellenistic Mysteries and Christian Sacraments," *Proceedings of the 7th Congress for the History of Religions*, pp. 53–66, shows without acrimony that Christian sacramentalism was not influenced by the mystery religions.

13 *Didache*, IX, 4; tr. Cyril C. Richardson, *Early Christian Fathers* (Library of Christian Classics, Vol. I; London, 1953), p. 175.

of a penetration of the Greek spirit. Certain hotheads have even gone so far as to speak of pre-existent Renans and Strausses. For some of the apologists do not so much as mention the name of Christ, but expatiate indefinitely on providence and free will, terms that do not even occur in the Bible. But here most particularly we must guard against optical illusion. For the apologists do not expound a philosophical doctrine but speak the language of the schools of rhetoric and of the anthologies: this gives us, who know the sources which were surely unknown to them, the impression that they mastered philosophy, just as an Italian can impress us tremendously with his knowledge because he has just finished reading that wonderful weekly, *l'Europeo.*

But why did the apologists speak in this way? For one thing, because otherwise they would not have been understood. With their exaggerated penchant for aesthetic effects the people of late antiquity could not tolerate clear, simple language: even St. Augustine complained that the Gospels were unbeautiful. And by way of entertaining their readers, the apologists proceed to discuss providence a little. Minucius Felix actually wrote that golden booklet, *Octavius*, containing arguments for and against the idea of providence. It should be borne in mind that this was a topic in a rhetorical thesis which every schoolboy had to compose, and Minucius merely repeated in an elegant style what everyone had long since known. And another apologist who took up a rhetorical thesis of this sort openly declared that he did so in order to show that in following this method one becomes entangled in antinomies; he annuls rhetoric in order to make room for faith.[14] For one of the purposes of apologetics was to convert the heathen. It was also a form of mission. And the literary genres invoked by the apologists had a long and venerable tradition; there were certain things you had to say—just as in fox hunting you have to say "Tallyho"—and certain things you were positively not supposed to say. That is why some of the apologists, for example, did not like to speak of a revolutionary's cross. Nevertheless, at the end of Minucius Felix's *Octavius* the pagan is converted to Christianity, while at the end of Cicero's dialogues the contestants go home just as they came. The purpose was after all the mission.[15] But in

14 Pseudo-Clement, *Recognitiones*, VIII, 5 (Migne, *PG*, III, cols. 1572–73), tr. Thomas Smith, "Recognitions of Clement," in *Tatian, Theophilus, and the Clementine Recognitions* (Edinburgh, 1867), p. 362.

15 My "Anima naturaliter christiana," in *Latomus* (Brussels), X (1951), 163.

early Christianity the mission had very little to do with importunateness and nothing at all to do with sentimental pietism. There was something very different behind it, namely eschatology. It was believed that the kingdom of God could not come before the joyous tidings were proclaimed to all the nations. Not that the early Christians wanted everyone to be a Christian; the Constantinian national church was foisted upon the Ecclesia and amounted to a monstrous falsification of its intentions. Originally, the early Christians regarded themselves as heralds, who proclaimed the coming of the king of the world and recruited for the army of Christ; and this eschatological perspective seems to account for St. Paul's missionary journeys, which followed from the prophecy of a famine, interpreted as a harbinger of the end. Thus eschatology created the mission and the mission produced its apologetics.

Here I shall not speak of the eschatological origins of asceticism and mysticism, because this has recently been done by Peterson[16] and von Unnik.[17] Instead, we shall turn to theology.

Can eschatology be said to have played a part in Christian theology and specifically in the Augustinian theology, which for obvious reasons is of particular interest to us here? There is no doubt that in theology we find ourselves on a very different plane from that of liturgy or mysticism, and that the wind that blows in St. Augustine is very different from that of early Christianity. If it is the task of the theologian to provide a scientific and systematic exposition of what he finds or thinks he finds in the documents of revelation, St. Augustine was assuredly a theologian. And perhaps for this very reason his thinking was so elastic and fruitful. Compared to a philosopher, he was seemingly at a disadvantage, for the philosopher has only his reason to reckon with and rejects what his reason does not recognize. Augustine, however, had to start from the Bible, which relates the most impossible things, which often seems to mock at reason, and which is in general exceedingly obscure. And he literally believed first, in order to understand afterward: *Credo ut intellegam.* But this method proved remarkably beneficial to Augustine's thinking. He himself says more than once that even with the greatest effort it is impossible to determine the author's intention; yet (he goes on to say) if one immerses oneself in the "profound obscurities" of Scripture, truths arise in one's spirit which are valid even if

16 Erik Peterson, *Euntes docete* (Rome), I (1948), 195.

17 W. C. von Unnik, "Gregorius van Nyssa," *Oratio Catechetica* (Amsterdam, 1949), pp. 22ff.

they do not reflect the author's meaning. I have never been able to find a single important doctrine in Augustine which is not based on an error in Bible translation. This is true of his theory of visions, which contains the profoundest psychological insights; it is true of his principle of *credo ut intellegam;* it even applies to his fundamental concept of *justitia* and to his theory of predestination. The same may be said of his ideas on time: we shall see that his analysis of time as *distentio* and *intentio* is based on a mistake in translation. Yet though Augustine teaches us how productive such misunderstandings can be, it remains a miracle how, precisely because he did not understand the Bible, he could discover so much by taking the Bible rather than reason as his starting point. But whatever we may think of Augustine's theological thinking, there is no doubt that it *is* theology, and for this reason we find ourselves with Augustine on a different plane from early Christianity or the liturgy.

For, among other things, theology is a demythologization. In our own day, Rudolf Bultmann has made the brand-new discovery that Christianity must be demythologized because the modern consciousness demands it. Why anything so questionable and ambiguous as the modern consciousness (whose consciousness? and why, precisely, consciousness?) should have been elected Pope is not easy to see: there are cleverer Popes and there always have been. If one wants to demythologize at any cost, one must be able to tell what is a myth and what is a fact established by scholarship. And, furthermore, one must bear in mind that history means history, that *theos* means *theos*, and that consequently *anthropos* also means *anthropos*. When I consider all this, it seems to me that the reduction of the Christian religion to Heideggerian existentialism, illuminating and suggestive as it may be, cannot be called demythologization, for one thing because this philosophy gives no answer to the question of what myth is.

Meanwhile, we can learn a good deal about demythologization from St. Augustine, who designates God as he who is *interior intimo meo et superior summo meo* ("more inward than my inwardness and higher than my height"). Where evil is no longer, as the Manichaeans supposed, situated in the cosmos—or in matter, as the Neoplatonists thought—but in the human will; where grace is infused and not forensically imputed; where the criterion for truth is found in an inward and yet not intrapsychic divine master; where Holy Scripture is inwardly inspired by the Holy Ghost; where history is interpreted as the conflict between the love of God and the love of self, and time as subjective; where visions are taken as products of the memory—a long step has been taken toward demythologization. And not so much because the contemporary consciousness dictated such thinking as because reflection on the content of religious beliefs was a feature immanent in theism. For St. Paul (I Cor. 15) *nous* and *pneuma* belong together, and Augustine remembered this passage when he turned his attention to the *visio mentis* and the *visio spiritus* in *De Genesi ad Litteram* (XII, 8). This method of demythologizing can be exemplified by Augustine's treatment of the problems of time and history: the contemporary consciousness caused the question to be raised and proposed the problem, and its influence was merely heuristic; moreover, Augustine exposed the hollowness and archaism of this consciousness. The point of departure was *faith:* faith in creation, in the *ephapax*, and in the experience of the end, jutting into time. He could justify this faith only by refuting the Hellenistic concept of time. This happens in successive stages. First, in the *Confessions*, time is taken into the soul; then, in the *City of God*, he refutes the cyclical conception of history, the belief in the eternal recurrence of all things and in reincarnation; finally, in *De Genesi ad Litteram*, he so extends the Greek concept of nature that side by side with the natural phenomena which are subservient to law he is able to recognize the rare and unique events, such as miracles, magic, and parapsychological phenomena, as well as, through his doctrine of *rationes seminales*,[18] something akin to a history of nature.

It has become customary to lift Augustine's reflections on time out of their context and compare them with the findings of modern scholars. When this is done, Augustine is often said to have anticipated Kant's discovery of the subjectivity of time. Emil Brunner goes so far as to compare him with Einstein and Planck. He writes glibly:

> It is certain that Augustine made a great discovery in venturing to state for the first time (in his *Confessions*) that the world is neither atemporal and eternal, nor created at a certain moment in the succession of time, but that world and time were created together, that world and time thus have their beginning in creation; so that it is meaningless to ask what God did before the Creation of the world. The entire schema of before and after—that is to say, the schema of time—is given only with creation, which is thus posited as a temporal creation. We cannot sufficiently admire the depth

18 Jacques de Blic, "Le Processus de la création d'après Saint Augustin," *Mélanges offerts au R. P. Ferdinand Cavallera* (Toulouse, 1948), pp. 179–89.

> and boldness of this thought: and if we consider the most recent findings of astrophysics, we can only be astounded at the brilliance of the thinker who through faith and without any scientific foundation intuitively arrived at an idea which, paradoxical as it may seem, imposes itself as the truth upon the scientific thinking of our day; since it follows both from Einstein's theory of relativity and from Planck's quantum physics.[19]

But experience teaches that such parallels with modern science are dangerous. Perhaps it will be worth while to place St. Augustine's ideas, especially his conception of time, strictly in their own setting, to ask whom he is attacking and with what intention he says what he says.

Augustine speaks of time because his adversaries asked him: What did God do before he created heaven and earth? This theatrical question had made itself at home in philosophy long before Christ and was an old stand-by of the rhetorical curriculum. The Epicureans and Manichaeans had taken it over, although in the mouths of the latter this argument could have no more than a rhetorical significance, because according to them the world had a beginning in time. No, the adversaries at whom Augustine aimed were others, profane philosophers who busied themselves with the *controversia de initio rerum temporalium* (controversy on the beginning of time). And as a comparison between the *City of God* (XI, 4, 5, and XII, 18) and *Confessions* (XI, 12) shows, these were the Neoplatonists of his day. Thus speculation on time became a motif in the great struggle between a cyclical and a historical view of the world, between archaism and Christianity, which was being enacted in those truly apocalyptic times. The battle was not about the academic problem of *tempus* but about *Christiana tempora.*

Augustine's Neoplatonic adversaries are to be sought in the city of Rome in the ranks of the national reaction once led by Symmachus, who wished to lay the blame for the sacking of Rome (A.D. 410) upon the Christians. It was they who by raising this question of responsibility led Augustine to write his *City of God.* Their shibboleth was criticism of the *Christiana tempora:* ah the golden days of the heroes Horace and Cicero! To the Christian view of history they opposed their own, a doctrine of the eternal recurrence of all things, a cyclical law of history which reminds us somewhat of Nietzsche and Spengler. In cosmic periods the same process is forever re-

19 Emil Brunner, "La Conception chrétienne du temps," *Dieu Vivant* (Paris), XIV (1949), p. 18. A Christological grounding of time is in Barth, *Kirchliche Dogmatik,* III, 11, pp. 524ff.

peated. As Plato once taught in Athens, so he will teach once again; indeed he will teach innumerable times, in the same city and in the same school.

Similarly all human life is repeated over and over again in endless metempsychoses, from heavenly bliss to earthly misery, from earthly misery to heavenly bliss. The logical ground for this theory is that only knowledge of the finite is possible: thus God, too, has only a finite number of causes for the finite number of things that he creates. Hence there is no beginning and no *telos*, no *novum*, no unique fact, no irreversible time, no evolution; and man, so to speak, is a squirrel in a cage—eternity is immanent. In their refutation of Christianity the Neoplatonists opposed the cycle to the straight line, the *circuitus* to the *via recta:* "these arguments, with which the impious seek to turn our simple faith away from the straight way, in order that we may walk in a circle with them." [20] Thus an entire philosophy of history is concealed in their question about the beginning of time.

This question preoccupied Augustine because the theme of time and eternity evoked by his vision in Ostia, where he experienced eternity, runs through his whole opus.[21] In *De Genesi ad Litteram* he elaborates the relationship of time and eternity in the creation of the cosmos; in the *City of God* he attacks the cyclical view of history in order to free eternity from the embrace of time; and in the *Confessions* he shows that the question was false, because time is within the soul and presupposes the movement of the cosmos, so that before the creation there was no time.

In the *City of God* (XII) he attempts, not unsuccessfully, to undermine the cyclical sense of the cosmos by showing that even a Platonist must admit that in the continuous repetition of the reincarnated soul there must be some *novum;* for either we assume that this circuit has an end, or we must, in order to avoid being caught in an endless chain, assume that the soul once upon a time fell from the spiritual world. In both cases a *novum* appears. But if there is a *novum* in human life, a *novum* enters automatically into history as well.[22] But then the eternal recurrence of all things proves false and our eyes open to the *ephapax* and the *eschaton*. And Augustine cries out: "Where are our revolutions, that admit nothing new, but keep all in one course?" (XII, 20). The spell of determinism is broken, the circle is shat-

20 *City of God*, XII, 10-20.

21 To have demonstrated this is Guitton's great achievement: Jean Guitton, *Le Temps et l'éternité chez Plotin et Augustin* (Paris, 1933).

22 John F. Callahan, *Four Views of Time in Ancient Philosophy* (Cambridge, Mass., 1948), deals with Plato, Aristotle, Plotinus, and Augustine.

tered. And whereas Herodotus, the first important historian among the Greeks, spoke of the cycle of human events, the last great historian of ancient times leads his readers from the *falsus circuitus* to the *trames recti itineris*, the straight line of history.

After thus demolishing the cyclic view of history, Augustine could proceed to develop his own vision of the two kingdoms, of God and of the Devil, which have existed side by side from the very beginning and will exist down to the last judgment; and the mixture of the two constitutes the history which, guided by an admirable providence, makes the universe into a picture containing darkness as a necessary component, so that the passage of the centuries becomes a wonderful song of antitheses: "So making the world's course, like a fair poem, more gracious by antithetic figures."[23] In developing this universal vision, he revived old Judeo-Christian eschatological conceptions, particularly that of the heavenly Jerusalem which would come at the end of time. It should also be borne in mind that in his anti-Manichaean works he had become versed in the historical themes of the heresy fighters and in this respect shows himself very much dependent on the tradition. However, he abandoned the chiliasm—still very much alive in Western tradition—which gave a very vivid picture of the future paradise on earth, in other words, confused time and eternity. The City of God remains an *eschaton*, a goal of the cosmic, historical, and individual process, but it is still *eternal* life. Yet Augustine would not have been what he was if he had not derived the two kingdoms from their psychological roots, *amor Dei* and *amor sui*, love of God and love of self, and sought the source of the second kingdom in *superbia*, pride and lust for power, which for him was the beginning of all sin: *initium omnis peccati superbia est.* Here he speaks from personal experience. And this is how Augustine demythologized history. In general we may characterize his theology as demythologized eschatology.

It is against this background that we must view his remarks on time in the eleventh book of the *Confessions*.[24] Here again he comes to grips with the Neoplatonists and turns time inward in order to make room for eschatology. In this connection it should be remembered that the Neoplatonism he was fighting was a mixture of Platonic, Aristotelian, and Stoic elements, so that

23 *City of God*, XI, 18; tr. John Healey, ed. R. V. G. Tasker (2 vols., London and New York, 1945).

24 Peter Brunner, "Zur Auseinandersetzung zwischen antikem und christlichem Zeit- und Geschichtsverständnis bei Augustin," *Zeitschrift für Theologie und Kirche* (Tübingen), new series, XIV (1933), 1–25.

he was actually attacking the whole ancient concept of time. Augustine's arguments are best understood in the perspective of the Aristotelian concept of time, to which he also refers in his text. According to Aristotle, time is the number of motion; time and motion exist in an indissoluble togetherness (ἅμα): "Time is, if not motion (κίνησις), at least something in it; it is the number of motion, hence an event (πάθος) and a state (ἕξις) of motion. 'Αριθμός—it is explicitly stated—does not, in this definition of time, signify that with which we count, but that which is itself counted."[25] In order to detach this most common and banal phenomenon from its exteriority, Augustine must make it into a riddle. "What then is time? If no one asks me, I know; if I want to explain it to a questioner, I do not know."[26] We speak of past, present, and future; the past is no longer, the future is not yet; if the present endured, it would not be time but eternity: in order to be time, it must become the past; it owes its being to nonbeing; it is time only if it tends toward nonbeing. "An *X* hurtles from a nothingness to a nothingness through a nothingness."

If there is any such thing as past and future, they must be presence, present in the soul. And indeed, the past is present in the memory as an image. Is this also true of the future? Here Augustine begins to hesitate with that magnificent, inspired hesitation which so often veils his profoundest intimations. Yes, it must be so, the future exists for me only as presence in my soul. But how can this be? Are existent images, images that are already present in the memory, anticipated? Is there a kind of *arcana praesensio futurorum* (mysterious prescience of things future) which would explain biblical prophecy as well as pagan divination? This he does not know at this point. But he does know that the future as expectation arises through rational induction from the present.

Thus past, present, and future are in the soul as *memoria, contuitus* (sight), and *exspectatio*. We measure times. But how can we measure what does not exist? The past is no longer, the future is not yet. And what of the present? The present has no duration. *Praesens nullum habet spatium.* It has vanished before one can apply the measure. *Implicatissimum aenigma!* A very intricate riddle!

After thus leading his belated Horaces, "cyclists," and guilt specialists around by the nose for a time, Augustine gives the solution of the riddle.

25 Ibid., p. 8.
26 *Confessions*, XI, 14; tr. F. J. Sheed (London and New York, 1951).

How shall I measure time? In order that we may compare a short and a long syllable, both must have died away. Thus I do not measure the syllables themselves, but the images of the two tones in my *memory*. "In thee, my soul, I measure my times." Thus when I measure time, I measure impressions, modifications of consciousness.

When I deliver a lecture, my expectation is directed toward what I wish to say, my attention toward what I am saying, and my memory toward what I have said. Time consists precisely in the present regard of a comparing consciousness. My attention is broadened, becomes extensive, a *distentio*. Time is a *distentio animi*. And this extensivity of the soul signifies at the same time its dismemberment, for it is hurled back and forth between memory, expectation, and attention until nothing more is to be expected, because death has come. My whole life is *distentio!* The time of all men in the world draws to an end. I have succumbed to time: "I am divided up in time, whose order I do not know, and my thoughts are torn with every kind of tumult." [27]

And now at last Augustine is where he wants to be. For he has transposed time into the soul, in order to recover the soul from its externalization and dispersion in the world. With an allusion to one of the profoundest eschatological passages in St. Paul he says:

> But Thy mercy is better than lives, and behold my life is but a scattering. Thy right hand has held me up in my Lord, the Son of Man who is the Mediator in many things and in divers manners—that I may apprehend by Him in whom I am apprehended and may be set free from what I once was, following your Oneness: forgetting the things that are behind and not poured out upon things to come and things transient, but stretching forth to those that are before (not by dispersal but by concentration of energy) I press towards the prize of the supernal vocation, where I may hear the voice of Thy praise and contemplate Thy delight which neither comes nor passes away.[28]

And Peter Brunner remarks:

> I myself am *distentus*, I am in the dispersion of my temporality. Is there still a salvation, a healing? Can the self, shattered in its temporality, still find its wholeness and unity? Yes, but never within its own temporality, but only if the self looks out from its own

27 Ibid., XI, 29; tr. Sheed.
28 Ibid.

> temporal fragmentation toward the eschatological, eternal *ante* of all time which is manifested in the Mediator; only by reaching and striving out of time toward *ea quae ante sunt*, beyond our temporality. Only when I look toward this eternal *ante* am I no longer *distentus*, but *extentus*, reaching out of this temporality and toward the *superna vocatio*.[29]

Beside *distentio* into past, present, and future, we have *intentio* toward eternity. And there can be no doubt that Augustine regards outward time without relation to God as "lost time." For from the very outset it has been his purpose, in fact the aim of all his reflections on time, to free the inner eye for this dimension, to show that his adversaries' cyclical conception of time comprehends no true eternity but only a circular, static finiteness, and that eternity, or rather the all-embracing Eternal One, constitutes time and encompasses it in his incomparable otherness, and that man, if he withdraws from the outside world, can in some way, through his *intentio*, come into contact with this eternity, this original, genuine, creative time of God. It has not been sufficiently taken into account that Augustine himself sounds this programmatic theme at the beginning of his philosophy of time:

> Those who speak thus do not yet understand You, O Wisdom of God, light of minds: they do not yet understand how the things are made that are made by You and in You. They strive for the savor of eternity, but their mind is still tossing about in the past and future movements of things, and is still vain. Who shall lay hold upon their mind and hold it still, that it may stand a little while, and a little while glimpse the splendor of eternity which stands for ever: and compare it with time whose moments never stand, and see that it is not comparable.[30]

This *intentio*, this inner relation to eternity, is the heart of the matter. And this precisely is an idea that could not have been held by Kant, whose precursor Augustine is said to be.

A comparison between modern thinkers and Augustine would seem to pass by what is most essential. And this also seems to apply to the distinction between "lived time" and "thought time," which Emil Brunner misses in Augustine. "No sooner has something passed from the future into the

29 P. Brunner, p. 15. In *Kirchliche Dogmatik*, Vol. I, part II, p. 51, Barth gives us the following misjudgment: "A problematization of the time arising in the act of the human spirit through the consideration that the time which we think we 'have' might be lost time, does not seem to come within his scope."

30 *Confessions*, XI, 11; tr. Sheed.

present," Brunner writes, "than it has become the past. On this, too, Augustine made definitive statements. But if I am not mistaken, he failed to take one of the most important facts into account, namely that lived time is something other than thought time. Lived time, to use Bergson's term, is real time (*durée réelle*)." [31] And Brunner goes on to explain how this deficiency in St. Augustine is to be understood.

Here again time as *intentio* is not taken into account. And it seems to me that it would be more fruitful for an understanding of Augustine to compare him with himself than to indulge in such excursions into vitalism. Here our ways part from those of Karl Barth and Emil Brunner, who lift Augustine's philosophy of time from its phenomenological context, as though the old theology of loci, based on quoting disconnected passages, had not long been superseded. For on all sides we are admonished to consider the whole, the fundamental structure. In this sense and only in this sense can it be illuminating to compare Augustine with Bergson. If I understand Bergson correctly and if it is permissible to demythologize this thinker too, he believed that when I close my eyes I "intuit" that I endure; he believed that duration is the experience of the "time that passes," whereas for the intelligence this experience congeals into a "past time." [32] Now this can in some degree be compared with the first phase of *intentio*, the imaged vision of the *visio spiritus*. The *intentio* turns away, detaches itself from the sense organs, and enters into ecstasy, so that even where the senses are unobstructed, no things are seen, no words are heard, and the soul is entirely with the images (*De Genesi ad Litteram*, XII, 12). But Augustine has a still profounder vision, *visio mentis*, the imageless contemplation of God, the experience of eternity, the highest intensity and inwardness of the soul, illumination. Here the intention is directed toward eternity, and God speaks ineffably, more withdrawn and yet more intensely present than in the image, and directly (*De Genesi ad Litteram*, XII, 27: "in that manifestation, in which God is, He speaks ineffably, being unspeakably far more hidden and yet more present"). In this sense, to be sure, Augustine does know two modes of time, *distentio* and *intentio*, distraction and intensity of the soul, but it is eternity, the eternal, which is experienced in a realm beyond images. "Why," writes Guitton, "might there not for some men be moments in

31 E. Brunner, p. 28.

32 Cf. C. H. de Goeje, *What Is Time?* (Leiden, 1949), though de Goeje's remarks are also in need of demythologizing.

which they would, through grace, be sufficiently present to themselves, not of course to coincide with God's eternity, but at least to savor their eternity in God in hope and anticipation?"[33]

In his account of his conversation on eternal life with his mother, shortly before her death, Augustine makes it clear to us why he was so concerned with the relationship between time and eternity, and why he later spoke in so sublime a tone of the vision of God:

> When the day was approaching on which she was to depart this life—a day that You knew though we did not—it came about, as I believe by Your secret arrangement, that she and I stood alone leaning in a window, which looked inwards to the garden within the house where we were staying, at Ostia on the Tiber; for there we were away from everybody, resting for the sea-voyage from the weariness of our long journey by land. There we talked together, she and I alone, in deep joy; and forgetting the things that were behind and looking forward to those that were before, we were discussing in the presence of Truth, which You are, what the eternal life of the saints could be like, which eye has not seen nor ear heard, nor has it entered into the heart of man. But with the mouth of our heart we panted for the high waters of Your fountain, the fountain of the life which is with You; that being sprinkled from that fountain according to our capacity, we might in some sense meditate upon so great a matter.
>
> And our conversation had brought us to this point that any pleasure whatsoever of the bodily senses, in any brightness whatsoever of corporeal light, seemed to us not worthy of comparison with the pleasure of that eternal Light, not worthy even of mention. Rising as our love flamed upwards towards that Selfsame, we passed in review the various levels of bodily things, up to the heavens themselves, whence sun and moon and stars shine upon this earth. And higher still we soared, thinking in our minds and speaking and marvelling at Your works; and so we came to our own souls, and went beyond them to come at last to that region of richness unending, where You feed Israel forever with the food of truth: and there life is that Wisdom by which all things are made, both the things that have been and the things that are yet to be. But this Wisdom itself is not made: it is as it has ever been, and so it shall be forever: indeed "has ever been" and "shall be forever" have no place in it, for it simply is, for it is eternal: whereas "to have been" and "to be going to be" are not eternal. And while we

33 *Le Temps et l'éternité*, p. 198.

> were thus talking of His Wisdom and panting for it, with all the effort of our heart we did for one instant attain to touch it; then sighing, and leaving the first fruits of our spirit bound to it, we returned to the sound of our own tongue, in which a word has both beginning and ending. For what is like to your Word, Our Lord, who abides in Himself forever, yet grows not old and makes all things new!
>
> So we said: If to any man the tumult of the flesh grew silent, silent the images of earth and sea and air; and if the heavens grew silent, and the very soul grew silent to herself and by not thinking of self mounted beyond self; if all dreams and imagined visions grew silent, and every tongue and every sign and whatsoever is transient—for indeed if any man could hear them, he should hear them saying with one voice: We did not make ourselves, but He made us who abides forever: but if, having uttered this and so set us listening to Him who made them, they all grew silent, and in their silence He alone spoke to us, not by them but by Himself: so that we should hear His word, not by any tongue of flesh nor the voice of an angel nor the sound of thunder nor in the darkness of a parable, but that we should hear Himself whom in all these things we love, should hear Himself and not them; just as we two had but now reached forth and in a flash of the mind attained to touch the eternal Wisdom which abides over all: and if this could continue, and all other visions so different be quite taken away, and this one should so ravish and absorb and wrap the beholder in inward joys that his life should eternally be such as that one moment of understanding for which we had been sighing—would not this be: *Enter thou into the joy of thy Lord?* [34]

So much has been written about this vision that one scarcely dares say any more. If I nevertheless do so, it is certainly not in order to refute earlier scholars. There are good reasons for the attempt to view this passage in the light of mysticism, and it is established fact that Augustine made use of Neoplatonic models in describing his experience. But it is a mistake to seek here only a mystical experience or only a philosophical intuition as though the two were mutually exclusive and as though St. Augustine's illumination (for that is the core of the matter) could be defined so clearly. For in the ancient Christian consciousness the elements that we differentiate and delimit, and even set off against one another, were indissolubly connected—as the whole of the patristic literature, and particularly Augustine's theory

34 *Confessions*, IX, 10; tr. Sheed.

of illumination, shows. Even so, we shall attempt to take a third path and ask what Augustine himself thought of his vision. This can be done, because in the twelfth book of *De Genesi ad Litteram* he delivered a very detailed judgment on visions in reference to his experience at Ostia.

Here we find that formally Augustine would have designated this event, with a term going back to the Neoplatonist Porphyry, as a *visio mentis*, a rational vision. But from the standpoint of content he takes a deeper view, for according to Augustine it is precisely in this moment that man becomes aware of his createdness, his limitation, and absolute dependence: "however little the mind, which is not what God is . . . can comprehend Him" (XII, 26). And moreover, it was very well known to Augustine that man walks by faith on this earth, even though he live justly.[35] But man cannot achieve such a vision through intellectual exertion; it is a revelation, a charisma of God: *secundum assumentis Dei gratiam* (XII, 26).

And precisely for this reason, because from the very beginning the living God sent man on this road, guided him in this direction, man can be held worthy to drink beatitude at the source in this life and to preserve the memory of it: "Then the one and only virtue is to love what you see, and the highest happiness is to have what you love, for then the blessed life is drunk in its source, whence some part of this human life is watered" (XII,

35 *De Genesi ad Litteram*, XII, 26 (Migne, *PL*, XXXIV, col. 478): *secundum assumentis Dei gratiam*. Ibid., 28: *Unde dictum est: Beati mundo corde quia ipsi Deum videbunt, non per aliquam corporaliter vel spiritualiter figuratam significationem tamquam per speculum in aenigmate, sed facie ad faciem, quod de Moyse dictum est, est "os ad os," per speciem scilicet, qua Deus est quidquid est, quantulumcumque eum mens, quae non est quod ipse, etiam ab omni terrena labe mundata, et ab omni corpore et similitudine corporis alienata et abrepta capere potest: a quo peregrinamur mortali et corruptibili onere gravati, quamdiu per fidem ambulamus, non per speciem, et cum hic iuste vivimus. Cur autem non credamus, quod tanto apostolo gentium doctori, rapto usque ad istam excellentissimam visionem, voluerit Deus demonstrare vitam, in qua post hanc vitam vivendum est in aeternum?* ("according to the grace of God who takes him up." / "Wherefore it is said: Blessed are the pure of heart, for they shall see God, not in any figurative appearance whether bodily or spiritual, as though in a glass darkly, but face to face, or, as is said of Moses, 'mouth to mouth'; namely, in that manifestation in which God is whatsoever He is, however little the mind, which is not what He is, even though it be cleansed of all earthly dross, and cut off and set free from all body and all that is bodily, be able to comprehend Him; for we are on pilgrimage away from Him, weighed down with a mortal and corruptible burden, so long as we walk by faith, not by sight, and live righteously here. For why should we not find it credible that to so great an apostle, the Doctor of the Gentiles, rapt in that most excelling vision of his, God willed to show that life in which after this life we are to live for ever?"—Tr. A.S.B.G.)

Barth's remarks in *Kirchliche Dogmatik*, Vol. II, pt. 1, p. 9, are in need of revision to conform with this passage.

26). When Augustine speaks of the *visio mentis*, he is thinking of the Apostle Paul, who in a vision heard "unspeakable words which it is not lawful for a man to utter" (II Cor. 12 : 4). He aspires not to the idea of the Good, which is an "object of understanding," but to the living God who is the subject of the encounter. Where grace and revelation are concerned, he went beyond Plotinus, spiritual empiricism seeing more deeply than rational metaphysics into the heart of religion.[36]

And if it is true that the art of writing consists of keeping something silent, we may go farther in our judgment of the vision in Ostia. And then, "with all the effort of our heart we did for one instant attain to touch it; then sighing, and leaving the first fruits of our spirit bound to it, we returned. . . ." [37] "It" means the heavenly Jerusalem, which he remembers on his pilgrimage through life, which is his home and is his mother, the place of God's presence, "so that I shall not turn away but shall come to the peace of that Jerusalem, my dear mother, where are the first fruits of my spirit, . . . and there Thou shalt collect from my present scatteredness and deformity all that I am." [38] Then suddenly we see what lies behind the *distentio* and *intentio:* here we find a recurrence of those original themes of the Judeo-Christian eschatology—diaspora and return to Jerusalem—but in a new, more inward sense: only through the restoration of his relation with God, only by being overpowered by God, can man achieve his wholeness. The theme of the *dispersio* is transferred into the soul.

And more: when Augustine, both in his reflections on time and in his account of his vision at Ostia, repeatedly echoes one of the finest eschatological passages in St. Paul: "forgetting those things which are behind, and reaching forth unto those things which are before, I press toward the mark (*secundum intentionem*) for the prize of the high calling," we should not forget what immediately precedes these words in the epistle: "I count not myself to have apprehended" (Phil. 3 : 13).

And this is crucial, for St. Augustine as well. Jean Guitton, the eminent student of St. Augustine, has compared Augustine's experience of time and eternity with the conception of Plotinus and Spinoza, and sums up what is characteristic for Augustine in the following words: "But in it he sees not

36 On Neoplatonism, Gnosis, and Christianity cf. my *Die Gnosis als Weltreligion* (Zurich, 1951), p. 16.

37 *Confessions*, IX, 10; tr. Sheed.

38 Ibid.

salvation, but only a foretaste of it."[39] As in early Christianity, as in St. Paul, so also in St. Augustine, the *οὔπω λογίζομαι κατειληφέναι* (I count not myself to have apprehended) stands beside the *οἶδα ἄνθρωπον ἐν Χριστῷ* (I know a man in Christ). And one wonders: is this utter detachment of soul, which experiences God's eternity with absolute evidence and yet hovers between "already fulfilled" and "not yet fulfilled"—is this not an anticipation of the end, is it not proleptic eschatology?

39 *Le Temps et l'éternité*, p. 199.

Louis Massignon

Time in Islamic Thought

Since Kant, mathematics has accustomed us to consider time as an *a priori* form of our intuition; joined to three-dimensional space, time constitutes the fourth dimension of an expanding universe. Nevertheless, we feel a kind of contraction in our thinking when it aspires to apprehend time; we feel that the possible exceeds the existential,[1] that the data of the problem go beyond the solutions, that the quest surpasses the findings. Minkowski's "time as a fourth dimension" remains open to discussion.

A religious thought wholly oriented toward a transcendent monotheism, such as Islam, has an entirely different vision of time. There is no question here of inventing time; it is time that reveals to us the order (*amr*) of God, the fiat (*kun, kūnī*), which releases the acts we perform as responsible beings. Thus for the Musulman theologian time is not a continuous "duration," but a constellation, a "galaxy" of instants (and similarly there is no space, but only points). The heresiographers condemn as materialists the "Dahriyūn," the philosophers who divinize Duration (*dahr*).

For Islam, which is occasionalist, and apprehends the divine causality only in its actual "efficacy," there exists only the instant, *hīn* (Koran 21 : 111; 26 : 218; 37 : 174, 178), *ān* (K. 16 : 22), the "twinkling of an eye" (K. 16 : 79: *lamh al-basar*), the laconic announcement of a judicial decision of God, conferring on our nascent act His decree (*hukm*), which will be proclaimed on the day when the cry of Justice (K. 50 : 41) is heard.

This discontinuous perception of time in "instants" is not pure religious subjectivity. The instant appears to the entire Musulman community as an authoritative reminder of the Law, as inevitable as it is unexpected. The fundamental instant in the life of Islam appears at nightfall with the

1 Leibniz' dictum, borrowed from Ghazālī: "there is nothing more in the possibles [*imkān*] than what exists."

new moon, *ghurrat al-hilāl*, which declares "open" a period of variable duration for the liturgical accomplishment of various legal observances (pilgrimage, period of widowhood, etc.).[2] It is not permissible to foresee the new moon by means of theoretical tables; it must be watched for and established by two "witnesses of the instant." This method is still observed by all Islam (except for the Ismailians). It is the *iltimās al-hilāl.* In this Islam accords with the most primitive peoples of mankind, who, in the very irregularity of the phases of the moon, revere the manifestation of a mysterious Will independent of the solar seasons.[3] The most that Islam tolerates is a very primitive calendar, consisting in the twenty-eight lunar mansions (364 days), furnishing empirically the name of the star (*Najm*), or rather of the zodiacal constellation, in which the rising of the new moon must be watched for at the end of each lunar month. This instant, at nightfall, marks the beginning of a day, *yawm*, which establishes an indiction or *epoche*, the beginning of an era: such as July 16, A.D. 622, the first day of the Musulman hegira to Medina; or such as, in earlier times, the "*ayyām al-'Arab*," the tribal battles that constituted the only real calendar of the Arabs before Islam. These are "stopping places" for the minds of men, implying "introversion" into the memory.

But the only perfect, self-sufficient instant is the Hour (*Sâ'a*), the hour of the Last Judgment, the final summation of the decrees of all responsibilities incurred; this Hour must be awaited with a sacred awe (K. 42 : 17), for the "witness of this instant" is the divine Judge (according to the Shi'ites and the Sūfīs, all instants from those of the Five Prayers to the Stations of the Pilgrimage can be personified in their Witnesses). This Ultimate Day (*yawm akhīr*) is preceded by other premonitory "catastrophic days" (*yawm 'asīb, wāqi' a*, etc.), whose aspects are described in the Apocalyptic collections (King Abdullah of Jordan, recently assassinated, read me one of them one evening two years ago at Amman [4]); the Ultimate Day is their culmination and conclusion.

All the other "days" are imperfect, insufficient to themselves; for the decree they proclaim is fulfilled only after a delay (*imhāl*), at the end of a

2 That is why the liturgical 24-hour day is a nychthemeron.

3 Cf. the rejoicing at the full moon of the Passover in Israel (= the coming of the Messiah).

4 This was a Shiite Apocalypse in which Ja'far Sādiq advised Nafs Zakiya against rising up on behalf of justice, before the Hour. [King Abdullah was assassinated July 20, 1951.—ED.]

certain period (*labath:* K. 18 : 24;[5] 20 : 42). It is actually through this idea of a "period" that the notion of "duration" was introduced obliquely into Islamic thought; here "duration" is the silent interval between two divine instants, the announcement and the sanction; it is this variable period that the responsible man must utilize for expiation in order to conjure the sanction (which remains inevitable); it is the "sounding board" between the two sonorous "instants."

In the Koran the second "instant," that of the sanction, is called the term (*ajal*), or more precisely the marked term (*ajal musammā*). This was one of the first theological notions to be studied in Islam, in connection with the "decree" concerning a murdered man. Did he die at the "term marked" by God? Should God not bring him back to life *before* the Universal Judgment in order to "pay" him publicly the "price of his blood" at the expense of his murderer? This is what the Koran teaches through the Return of Jesus and the Awakening of the Seven Sleepers of Ephesus; the *Raj'a*, as the Shi'ites call it, the Return for the Vengeance of Justice, which is not yet the Resurrection but its prodrome: the rising of eschatological time which "accelerates" (*tajaddud*) the process of decomposition of a world of corruption.

*

Thus the first Musulman thought knows nothing of continuous duration, and considers only atoms of time, "instants," *ānāt* (pl. of *ān*), *awqāt* (pl. of *waqt:* cf. K. 15 : 38). They are not "states." Arabic grammar does not conceive of "verbal times" [tenses] as states; in principle it knows only "verbal aspects," the finished [perfect] (*māḍī*) and the unfinished [imperfect] (*muḍāri'*) which mark, outside of our time, the degree in which the (divine) action has been made real. But little by little, particularly in the spoken language, Arabic grammar has come to consider verbal time in relation to the responsible agent, that is, present, past, and future. It applies the term "*ḥāl*" (modality) to the subjective consciousness that we form of the instant surrounded by the "halo" of beauty (cf. Jullabi, 369) that it evokes for us.[6] This *ḥāl* is not strictly speaking a state. The primitive mystics (among

5 The 309 years of "sanctifying" slumber of the Seven Sleepers. The twelve lunar months (*ahilla*, pl. of *hilāl*; K. 2 : 185; 9 : 38), composing the Hegirian year (*sana*) on the *ajal;* cf. the Shiite Mufīd; and the word *ḥusbān* (K. 18 : 37).

6 The "*ḥāl*" taken as a proper name: "Yahya" (= he lives = John), "Yamūt" (he dies), "Yazūl" (he passes).

them Junayd), as we shall see, regard it as an instant without duration, colored by a fugitive virtue.—Let us consider, rather, the grammatical analyses of the instant (*waqt*): according to Qushayrī (*risāla* 37) the phrase "I come at dawn" marks an instant, because it announces an imagined event (*hādith mawhūm*) by means of a verifiable event (*hādith mutahaqqiq*). In the analyses of a later theologian, Fakhr Rāzī, who with Aristotle regards time (*zomān*) as an instant that elapses (*ān sayyāl*), (*mabahith mashr.*, I, 647), the same phrase announces a well-known recurrence (*mutajaddid ma'lūm:* at dawn) in order to date another, imagined recurrence (*mutajaddid mawhūm:* "I come" = simple possibility). Jurjani was to revive this second definition (*sh. mawāq.*, 219, *istil.* 119).

First of all we observe that although Qushayrī and Fakhr Rāzī are both predestinarians, Qushayrī places the accent on the realization of the believer's hope through mysterious divine omnipotence;[7] whereas the very Hellenized Fakhr Rāzī has recourse to a knowledge of the laws (recurrence) of nature, contingent or otherwise. Possibly Qushayrī still believed, like his predecessor Ibn al-Qāss (d. 945) that the sun's movement is discontinuous, that it has each night a resting place (*mustaqarr:* K. 36 : 38; 18 : 84), which it leaves only at divine order.

Secondly, the word *mutajaddid* in Fakhr Rāzī is highly interesting; it is an attenuating Hellenization of the word *tajaddudāt* (innovations) conceived by his adversaries, the Karrāmiya, and by Abū'l-barakāt, in order to stress (in opposition to the Greeks) the idea that God is interested in particulars, and that He excites our free acts by His grace; and in order to inject into the divine Essence (as Will to create our acts) an infinity of modalizations of His "fiat," corresponding to each of the instants in which He makes us responsible for new acts (*ihdāth fi'l Dhāt*).[8] Abū'l-barakāt even believed that these modalizations or innovations in the divine Essence constitute the only real proofs of God's existence. For him then there was an *ordinal* plurality of events in God; and for this reason he wrote that "time is the dimension of Existence" (*al-zamān miqdār al-Wujūd;* cf. K. 32 : 4 for "*miqdār*"). Whereas like a good scholastic Fakhr Rāzī admitted only a *cardinal* plurality in God, relating to the ideas of His Knowledge "which creates things."

7 The recurrence that is an appointment, *mī'ād* (K. 28 : 85; 34 : 29).—The incidence (*hulūl*) of the accident of inflection, the infusion of grace.

8 Cf. Ibn abī'lhadīd, *sharh Nahj al-balāgha;* Ibn Taymiya, *minhāj*, *al-sunna*, whence the problem: Is what is not foreseen by the Law *licit a priori* (*bara'a asliya, ibāha*).—On the *hikāya*, cf. *letta'līq;* and the *af'āl qalbiya*.

And this leads him, according to Ghazālī (*mi'yār*, 172, *maqāsid*), to the Aristotelian definition of time as "the number of movement according to the before and after" (*Physics*, IV, 11, 219b, 1–2).

Tempted by Neoplatonism, the later mystics of "existential monism" (as opposed to the "testimonial monism" of the primitives) returned to the Platonic notion of a divine Duration: Jurjani said: "*al-dahr imtidād al-Hadrat al-ilāhiya*"—"Duration is the expansion of the Divine Presence" (*ist.* 111). Plato (followed by Crescas in the fourteenth century) saw "Chronos" as a cyclical movement of the Uppermost Heaven, a living and numbered reflection of intelligible Eternity.

The later mystics adapted three very ancient Arabic technical terms to this notion of divine duration: *sarmad*, the absolutely fixed (opp. *dahr*, the fixed in relation to change); *azal*, the pre-eternal; *abad*, post-eternity. Hallāj, however, said that *azal* and *abad* are mere embryos from the standpoint of the *yaqīn* (the instant of divine certainty perceived in the heart).

*

In seeking to determine the essential Musulman idea of time, it seems most profitable to turn away from the theorists' oscillations between Platonic "duration" and Aristotelian "number of movement," and to consult the experimental testimony of the "practitioners": grammarians and fundamentalists (in canon law), physicians, psychologists of ecstasy, and musicians.

The grammarians, we recall, use the term *hāl* for the time that is "subjective" relative to the agent, to the "now" to which it testifies immediately; this instant is without duration; for when retrospective allusion is made to it by means of the historical present (*'alā'lhikāya:* according to the narrative mode), the allusion is powerless to revive this "now."

Beginning with Shāfi'ī, the fundamentalists, who use the methods of the syntaxists (*sarfiyūn*) but do not yet resort to Stoic (or Aristotelian) logic, apply to the *hāl* the principle of the *ta'mīm al-hukm*, the generalization of a decree (in the domain of its legitimacy); this is the *istishāb al-hāl* (extremely limited among the Hanbalites), a kind of tacit renewal of the status quo, i.e., to perpetuate (*ibqā*) the momentary description (*wasf:* a Khariyite word, hence having a Qadarite flavor) of a juridical case observed, so that it could legitimately apply to other analogous cases the canonical decree (*hukm*) that has been attributed to it. — This is an implicit recourse to a kind of conceptualism, substituting for the "description" (*wasf*) a "quality" (*sifa*), an "idea" susceptible of logical universality (*kulliya*) to the extent compatible with the data revealed (cf. the very strange arithmetic of the division of inheritances according to the Koran).— Nevertheless, this is a kind of virtual, immaterial duration, which leads Islam to admit that everlasting spiritual substances can exist "outside" of God (angels, souls).

Rāzī, the great physician, who was a *Dahrī*, a partisan of the eternal Duration of the universe, denied any duration to psychic phenomena such as pleasure (*ladhdha*); in a special work he affirmed clinically that pleasure is a state *without* duration; for it is simply the threshold of convalescence, the passage between sickness and health. Thus the religions are wrong in speaking of "eternal bliss."

The first psychologists of ecstasy, *wajd*, gave it this name to signify a sudden shock of grace, perceived as an instant of anguish (*wajada* = to find; *wajida* = to suffer), without duration but endowed with a variety of mental colors (joy, sorrow; gratitude, patience; dilation, constriction; etc.).[9] The first mystics denied these states (*ahwāl*, pl. of *hāl*) any real duration; then Muhāsibī, taking a step very like that of the fundamentalist Shāfi'ī, gave the *hāl* a virtual, ideal "duration"; and Ibn 'Atā maintained that after interruption, a "resumption" of the *hāl* was possible (*'awd:* contra Junayd);[10] that it remained the same. Thus the disappearance of the instant of anguish could leave the heart with a kind of "rhythmic impulse" and an enduring promise of plenitude, the beginning of a Wisdom situated outside of time. "What is the instant?" Hallāj was asked.—"It is a breeze of joy (*farja*) blown by pain—and Wisdom is waves which submerge, rise, and fall, so that the *instant* of the Sage is black and obscured" (Kalābādhī, No. 52). He also said: "The instant is a pearl-bearing shell, sealed at the bottom of the ocean of a human heart; tomorrow, at the rising tide of Judgment, all the shells will be cast on the beach; and we shall see if any pearl emerges from them" ('Attār, *Tadhkirat al-Awliyā'*).

Thus the instant of anguish can in some sense survive, but like a germ of hidden immortality, buried at the bottom the heart (*tadmīn*), not like those virtues worshiped by certain fanatical ascetics, who, through wishing to keep them as emblems, forsake for them the God who made them desire them. We can form an idea of this "hidden" persistence if we recall that the

9 Shāfi'ī was first to posit the permanence of the *wujūd*, of a status quo, an intelligible qualification.
10 On this *'awd*, cf. *ta'arruf*, 96.

duality of the *annunciatory instant* is not symmetrical, but oriented toward the future, toward the marked term (*ajal musammā*) that has been "announced" to us, and that the "empty" dimensions of the period of this expectation engender a kind of spiritual rhythm destined to impress on each creature its personal melodic mark in the symphony of the Beyond.

Starting with the (wooden) percussion instruments, the Musulman musicians, the "practitioners," produce the rhythm (*īqā'*) by differentiating the *dīh* (dull blow on the *edge* of the darabukka) from the *tā'* (sonorous stroke on the *center*); the irregularity in the alternation of these two strokes (*naqra*) creates a rhythmical movement, a dance (left foot, right foot). The systems of silences (*sukūn*), broken by such alternating strokes to form distinct rhythmic patterns (*mas, mūdī, murabba'*, etc.), elevate us beyond the phonetics of noises toward a phonology of sounds, toward a consideration of the structure of immaterial harmonies.

Similarly, the ambivalence of the instant of anguish, understood as an otherness oriented toward its "marked term," makes us transcend it; leading us to that finality (*nihāya*), that "piercing through," which is more than our original "rising up" (*bidāya*); for as Hallāj remarked, it is the "Realization" (*tahqīq*). The instant of anguish (*yawm al-hasra*, K. 19 : 40) is essentially prophetic—it does not scan the passage of time in linear fashion as the Aristotelian water clock does, nor does it periodically invert the many-phased cycles of astral time, caused by the "fall of Psyche," as the hemispherical gnomon of the Chaldeans does; rather, it announces the final stopping of the pendulum of our vital pulse on the tonic of its scale, on the "place of its salvation" (St. Augustine). It is not a fragment of duration, it is beyond doubt a divine "touch" of theologal hope, which transfigures our memory forever.

Henry Corbin

Cyclical Time in Mazdaism and Ismailism

1. Cyclical Time in Mazdaism

THE AGES OF THE WORLD IN ZOROASTRIAN MAZDAISM

A little manual of Mazdean doctrine, written in Pahlavi and dating from the fourth century of our era, contains a number of questions the answers to which everyone over the age of fifteen is supposed to know. The first questions are: "Who am I and to whom do I belong? Whence have I come and whither am I returning? What is my lineage and what is my race? What is my proper calling in earthly existence? . . . Did I come from the celestial world, or is it in the earthly world that I began to be? Do I belong to Ōhrmazd or to Ahriman? To the angels or the demons?" [1]

And here are the answers:

> I came from the celestial world (*mēnōk*), it is not in the terrestrial world (*gētīk*) that I began to be. I was originally manifested in the spiritual state, my original state is not the terrestrial state.[2]

1 *Pand Nāmak i Zartusht* (The Book of Counsels of Zartusht). The short treatise is also entitled *Čitak Handarz i Pōryōtkeshān* (Selected Instructions of the First Doctors of the Faith). Its authorship remains doubtful. One tradition attributes it to the Grand Mōbaδ Āturpat i Mahraspandān, a high dignitary of the Mazdean clergy whom the Sassanid King Shapur II (A.D. 309–79) had empowered to establish the definitive canonical text of the Avesta, divided into twenty-one books or *nask*. A little "book of counsels" by this author has come down to us. It is dedicated to his son Zartusht (so named to assure him of the holy prophet Zarathustra's spiritual sponsorship). But a "book of counsels" is also attributed to his son, who in his turn was Grand Mōbaδ under Ardashir II (A.D. 379–83). A critical edition of our *Pand Nāmak* has been published by H. S. Nyberg in *Hilfsbuch des Pehlevi*, Vol. I (Uppsala, 1928), pp. 17–30, 68–69. Cf. also J. C. Tarapore, *Pahlavi Andarz-Nāmak* (Bombay, 1933). The questions quoted here occur in Strophe 1.

2 On the contrast between the meanings of the verbs *āfrītan* and *būtan*, cf. Nyberg, *Hilfsbuch des Pehlevi*, Vol. II (Uppsala and Leipzig, 1931), Glossary, *s.v.;* and Heinrich Junker, "Über iranische Quellen der hellenistischen Aion-Vorstellung," *Vorträge der Bibliothek Warburg* (Leipzig), I (1923), 133–34.

> I belong to Ōhrmazd (Ahura Mazda, the Lord Wisdom), not to Ahriman (the Spirit of Evil and of Darkness); I belong to the angels, not to the demons. . . . I am the creature of Ōhrmazd, not the creature of Ahriman. I hold my lineage and my race from Gayōmart (primordial Man, Anthropos). My mother is Spandarmat (Angel of the Earth), my father is Ōhrmazd. . . . The accomplishment of my vocation consists in this: to think of Ōhrmazd as present Existence (*hastīh*), which has always existed (*hamē-būtīh*), and will always exist (*hamē-bāvetīh*). To think of him as immortal sovereignty, as Unlimitation and Purity. To think of Ahriman as pure negativity (*nestīh*), exhausting himself in nothingness (*avīn-būtīh*), as the Evil Spirit who formerly did not exist in this Creation, and who one day will cease to exist in Ōhrmazd's Creation and who will collapse at the final time.[3] To consider my true self as belonging to Ōhrmazd and the Archangels (*Amahraspandān*).

These few simple but decisive formulas project the responses simultaneously on a horizon both of pre-existence and of superexistence. They imply that the moment of birth and the moment of death, recorded so carefully in our vital statistics, are neither our absolute beginning nor our absolute end. They imply that time, as we commonly conceive of it, as a line of indeterminate length, losing itself in the mists of the past and the future, has literally no sense, but is simply the absurd. If a modern mathematical philosophy has taught us to conceive of time as a fourth dimension added to the three dimensions of space, we may say that the myth of Mazdean cosmogony reveals to us something in the nature of still another dimension (a fifth dimension?), the one which situates a being's "elevation" of light or depth of darkness.

The terms "elevation," or "height," and "depth" suggest the dimensions of visual space,[4] and the exigencies of language compel the myth to place the power of light and the opposing power of darkness in this sort of spatial relation to one another. Yet any geometrical representation is doomed to failure, since we must conceive of a space both infinite and limited. For in point of fact, the primordial Light and Darkness do not occupy a space

3 Strophes 2, 3. Cf. the somewhat different translation in Junker, p. 133 (*avīn būtīh,* to have become invisible).

4 Or better still, since this light has been announced to us as vibrating eternally with the voice of Ōhrmazd (cf. below), we might evoke the idea of a sonorous space: a being in whom the archetypal dimension that shines through resembles a musical motif which, in marking its own outline, also utters the promise of its metamorphoses. In it the limited and the unlimited coincide.

that is situated and defined in advance; they establish a space that is absolutely peculiar to themselves, that can only be measured in terms of light and darkness. The height or depth of light may be designated as eternal Time, and the space of light, in which awaken the creatures of light, who fulfill the thoughts of this light, is eternally born from this eternal Time.

It is then in this depth of light that originates the personal existence of the being who recognizes himself on earth "as belonging to Ōhrmazd and the Archangels." But the time in which are inscribed the moment of his coming into the earthly form of existence and the moment of his final departure from it is not the eternal Time of this depth of light. It is a time which originated in it, which is in its image, but which is necessitated and limited by the acts of a cosmic drama of which it marks the prelude and whose conclusion will also be its own. Deriving from this eternal Time it returns to its origin,[5] taking with it the beings who intervene as the cast of characters in its cycle, because in this drama each one of them "personifies" a permanent role which was assigned them by another Time. Essentially a "time of return," it has the form of a cycle. The Mazdean cosmogony tells us that time has two essential aspects: the Time without shore, without origin (*Zervān-i akanārak*), eternal Time; and limited time or "the time of long domination" (*Zervān-i deranγ xvatāi*), the Αἰών in the strict sense, although eternal Time also tends to assume this name. Eternal Time is the paradigm, the model of limited time that was made in its image. And that is why our time itself, as a dimension of earthly existence, gives an intimation of a dimension other than its own chronological dimension—a dimension of light which determines its form and meaning. Inversely, the absence or annihilation of this dimension measures the depth of darkness of one who is in this time. Since it discloses this relation with the origin, the dimension of light may be called the archetypal dimension; as such, it characterizes and situates a being of Light, a being of Ohrmazdean essence. Forming a bond between this being and an eternal Time to which the limited time of his actual form of existence carries him back, this archetypal di-

5 Cf. H. S. Nyberg, "Questions de cosmogonie et de cosmologie mazdéennes," *Journal asiatique* (Paris), CCXIV : 2 (Apr.–June, 1929) ["Questions," I], p. 214, li. 9. Note the use of the verb *gumečit* for the return of limited time into unlimited Time; this is the same word which serves to designate the "mixture" (*gumečishn*) of Darkness with Light. Cf. also R. C. Zaehner, "Zurvanica," III, *Bulletin of the School of Oriental Studies* (London), IX (1937–39), *Dēnkart* text 228 on p. 880, and the long extract from *Dēnkart* 282 on pp. 883–84.

mension commands a very specific experience of eternity, or rather the anticipation which makes possible—or which translates—the conception of a cyclical time that is not the Time of an eternal return, but the time of a return to an eternal origin.

The concept of this dimension of light, an archetypal dimension because it grounds every being in another self which keeps eternally ahead of him, can provide us with the key to a celestial world inhabited by figures who are constituted and governed in their being by a law of their own, a law with its very own logic. The responses we have just read refer to the twofold plane or twofold state of being which characterizes Mazdean ontology, and which is designated by the two terms *mēnōk* and *gētīk*. We must take care not to reduce the contrast they express to a Platonic schema pure and simple. We are not dealing precisely with an opposition between idea and matter, or between the universal and the perceptible. *Mēnōk* should, rather, be translated by a celestial, invisible, spiritual, but perfectly concrete state. *Gētīk*[6] designates an earthly visible, material state, but of a matter which is in itself wholly luminous, a matter immaterial in relation to the matter that we actually know.[7] For, and this is the peculiarly Mazdean conception, a transition to the state of *gētīk* means in itself not a fall but rather fulfillment and plenitude. The state of infirmity, of lesser being and darkness represented by the present condition of the material world, results not from its material condition as such but from the fact that it is the zone invaded by the demonic Contrary Powers, the arena of struggle and also the prize. Here the stranger to this creation is not the God of Light but the Principle of Darkness. Redemption will bring the flowering of the *tan i pasen*, the "body to come," the *corpus resurrectionis;* it does not tend to destroy the *gētīk* world, but to restore it to its luminous state, its archetypal dimension.

This dimension of light constitutes every being, every physical or moral entity of the earthly world, as the counterpart of a celestial (or *mēnōk*) reality with which it forms a pair; this *mēnōk* is its spiritual entity, its archetype, its "angel." It is by establishing this dimension that the Mazdean metaphysical imagination attests its characteristic aptitude for configuring hypostases, for making the features of a celestial Person shine through all reality. This representative norm is so fundamental that Time itself, in

6 On these two concepts cf. Nyberg, *Journal asiatique*, CCXIX: 1 (Jul.–Sept., 1931) ["Questions," II], pp. 31–36.

7 Cf. also *Shkand-Gumāṇīk Vicār* . . . , ed. Jean de Menasce (Fribourg, Switzerland, 1945), Vol. IV, pp. 16–20, and the remarks on "Questions," II, 12–18, on p. 36.

either of its aspects, will be apprehended as a person with definite traits. It is precisely in this personal guise that we mean to consider it, and let us now, for a few moments, reflect on this point.

Logic, if it is not to be discomfited, must conform to the requirements of this norm, for the characteristic of such hypostases is to exist both in themselves and in what they accomplish. What results is not a confusion of the planes of being, but a communicability of names, that sometimes creates difficulties for our thinking—and the worst solution to these difficulties would be to degrade these figures into simple allegories. All our efforts must be directed toward safeguarding and justifying the play of "transparitions" which are made possible in this new dimension of depth in light precisely here and not otherwise or elsewhere. It will become clear to us that if time can be apprehended as a person, it is because, far from being our familiar, abstract notion, it is an archetypal Person—that is to say, this time configures and prefigures the form that a luminous being must take or regain—and because, as time of trial and of combat, it is the mediator of this metamorphosis. Thus is established a homology between the time of action of each personal being and the Time of the total cycle; between fulfilled personal being and the "Person" of eternal Time.

Once these premises have been established, it would seem that by giving our attention to this "person of time" and the variations of its features as manifested to mental vision, we may also distinguish, beneath the variants of the cosmogonic schema, the anthropological differentials characterizing pure Mazdaism on the one hand and the dramaturgy that has been designated as Zervanism on the other, because of the central role played by Zervān in it (and because its schema in turn discloses important variants).

Let us roughly outline the ideal schematization of the possible conceptions. For the pure dualist vision, that of Zoroastrian Mazdaism, the precosmic drama in which the cycle of our "aeon" originated is provoked by the attack and invasion of a Contrary Power, exterior and alien to Ōhrmazd, God of Light. Ahriman, Spirit of Evil, of negation and darkness, rises up from a bottomless abyss of undisclosed origin, existing prior to all cause. For the Zervanist vision, the drama takes place within the very person of Zervān, eternal Time or absolute Time, as the supreme godhead which by itself gives rise both to the principle of light and to the antagonist. Here, it seems to me, we have a much more serious differential than that between two different theological interpretations of an identical situation.[8] Nevertheless, from the standpoint of pure Mazdaism, an attempt at reduction was conceivable; such an attempt results in a schema that might be designated as Mazdeanized Zervanism or as Zervanized Mazdaism.

The schema of integral Zervanism undergoes in turn certain dramaturgical changes: the idea of a mediation appears in the person of the Angel Mithras, who, according to the Zoroastrian theology of our times, shows certain points of resemblance to the Archangel Michael.[9] Finally, the unity that gives rise to the two Contraries is situated no longer at the level of the supreme godhead but at the level of an emanated angelic hypostasis: this hypostasis will assume the role of a Saved Savior, a kind of Archangel Michael who has had to gain his own victory over himself, and the periods of cyclical time must mark this victory in the person of all his followers. This is the form that the drama and the role of the angel of humanity will assume in Ishmaelite Gnosis.

In the mythohistory of pure Mazdaism, cyclical time is punctuated by three great acts which extend over twelve millennia and constitute the ages of the world. The first of these acts is the primordial Creation (*Bundahishn*), encompassing the prelude of the first three millennia, during which the Creation is established in its *mēnōk*, subtle and celestial, state. In the ensuing period from the fourth to the sixth millennium, the Creation is transferred to the *gētīk*, or earthly, state. Then comes the second act: the catastrophe. The Negator, whose menace had risen up from the abyss at the very outset of the spiritual Creation, succeeds in entering and ravaging material creation. This second act constitutes the period of the "mixture" (*gume-*

8 A. Christensen tends toward a reduction of this sort in *L'Iran sous les Sassanides* (2nd edn., Copenhagen, 1944), p. 154, n. 4; p. 437. Cf. Nyberg, "Questions," II, pp. 81, 82; and *Die Religionen des alten Irans*, German tr. by H. H. Schaeder (Leipzig, 1938), pp. 388ff. (Zervanism as the cosmogonic doctrine of the Median magi before they became Zoroastrians). J. Bidez and F. Cumont, *Les Mages hellênisés* (Paris, 1938), Vol. I, pp. 63ff. E. Benveniste, *The Persian Religion according to the Chief Greek Texts* (Paris, 1929), ch. 4 (Zervanism as the doctrine of the Magi recorded by Plutarch); Cumont's arguments to the contrary—*Les Mages hellênisés*, Vol. I, pp. 65–66, and Vol. II, p. 72, n. 1—are not conclusive. See also Benveniste, pp. 77, 97: Zervān in Soghdian Buddhism and in Manichaeism; here, we may note, the question of the historical existence of a "Zervanite church" does not arise, for we have set out to consider only the pure philosophical schematization of certain concepts and their phenomenological connection with the mode of existence that they indicate.

9 J. J. Modi, "St. Michael of the Christians and Mithra of the Zoroastrians," in *Anthropological Papers*, Part 1 (Bombay, 1911), pp. 173–90; cf. below, nn. 51 and 55, and Part 2, p. 155, n. 47.

čishn), which we are still experiencing.[10] It will end with the act of final "separation" (*vičarishn*), ushered in by the *Saoshyant* or Saviors born from the race of Zarathustra in the course of the three last millennia, and by the "transfiguration" of the world (*frashokart*).[11]

In the Mazdean book of Genesis, the Bundahishn, we read as follows:

> It hath been revealed that during the unlimited Time, Ōhrmazd was in the heights, adorned with omniscience and goodness and surrounded by light. This light is the place and abode of Ōhrmazd. Some call it the infinite Light (*asar roshnīh*). This omniscience and this goodness are the garment of Ōhrmazd. Some call it the Religion (*Dēn*). . . . The Time of the garment is infinite, for the goodness and religion of Ōhrmazd have existed as long as Ōhrmazd himself; they still exist and they will always exist." [12]

Here the unlimited Time is neither a principle superior to Ōhrmazd nor is it his creation; it is an aspect of his illimitableness; it expresses his very being, which is also expressed by his omniscience and by the infinite light in which he resides. However, a play of transparitions, which, as we have said, are possible only in this dimension of thought, ultimately put us in the presence of time as a plastically defined figure. From eternal Time and in the image of eternal Time, Ōhrmazd created the limited Time he required to frustrate the challenge of Ahriman; he was said to have created it "in the form of a youth of fifteen, luminous, clear-eyed, of tall stature, full of a vigor resulting from a perfect endowment and not from a brutal and violent nature." [13] If in this vision of a youth we seem to discern a Mazdean form of the *puer aeternus* motif, we need only recall that the age of fifteen connotes the aspect which our texts give to the "resuscitated ones," [14] in order to realize that the "Person of Time" merely exemplifies the ideal dimension of a being of Light.

But more than this: if we give heed to the equivalences that are sub-

10 On the six millennia as the duration of the actual world, cf. "Apocalypse d'Hystaspe," in Bidez and Cumont, *Les Mages hellénisés*, Vol. II, p. 364.

11 Cf. Nyberg, "Questions," I, pp. 210-11; G. Messina, *Libro apocalittico persiano Āyātkār i Žāmāspīk* (Rome, 1939), pp. 118–20.

12 "Questions," I, pp. 206–7; for a somewhat different translation see Messina, *Žāmāspīk*, p. 85, n. 3; cf. the text of the Zātsparam, ch. 1, in Zaehner, "Zurvanica," II, pp. 576–77; A. V. W. Jackson, *Zoroastrian Studies* (New York, 1928), pp. 114–15; and Junker "Iranische Quellen," pp. 127–28.

13 Cf. Nyberg, "Questions," I, p. 231.

14 *Āyātkār i Žāmāspīk*, ch. 17, verse 16.

stituted for the denomination of Zervān, we shall perceive the intrinsic form of personal experience, the expectation projected in a vision whose "figures" present transparitions of one another. The text cited above has taught us that Religion (*Dēn*), as omniscience and goodness in infinite Time, is the garment of Ōhrmazd, which surrounds and configures his being. Other texts teach us that "what has always been is the voice of Ōhrmazd in the Light," and that from this eternal vibration of the Light, the religion of Ōhrmazd [15] vibrates eternally. This eternal Voice which is the Creative Logos of Ōhrmazd is also designated as the celestial (*mēnōk*) archetype of the Zoroastrian prayer formula par excellence, the formula known from its first words (*yaθa ahu vairyo*) as the *Ahuvar*.[16] But this celestial archetype is also said to be *Dēn*, the eternal Religion. A late Persian translation expressly gives to Ahuvar the name of Zervān.[17] Thus there is an equivalence, a reciprocal transparition, between eternal Time, the celestial archetype of creative prayer, and the eternal Religion.

The substitution of *Dēn* for the celestial archetype of Ahuvar suggests that *Dēn* is precisely the uttering of the eternal Utterance, in which are grounded the melodic themes which state the modality of each being. But the representation of eternal Religion, which is also Omniscience and Goodness as typified in a hypostasis, suffices to orient us toward a whole body of speculations concerning Wisdom, or the divine Sophia. Actually *Dēn* (Religion) does not designate a simple institutional abstraction. The figure of Daēnā (Avestan form of the Pahlavi word *dēn*) is the principle of a whole strictly Mazdean sophiology.[18] Its extreme complexity makes a complete

15 Ibid., ch. 2, verse 2.

16 Cf. the whole of Chapter XIX of the Yasna. Each of the words composing this prayer designates symbolically one of the *nasks* of the Avesta. Held to have existed before the Creation, this prayer is conceived as a hypostasis, a veritable Logos-Sophia (just as Zarathustra's *Gathas* or psalms (cf. Yasna LIV) appear as angelic hypostases; it may be said that to recite them is literally to "recite an angel"). Cf. I. J. S. Taraporevala, *The Holy Word of the Religion of Zarathustra and the Holy Immortals* (Bombay, 1947); J. J. Modi, *The Religious Ceremonies and Customs of the Parsees* (2nd edn., Bombay, 1937), pp. 200–1; Nyberg, *Die Religionen*, pp. 268–69; J. Hertel, *Die Awestischen Herrschafts- und Siegesfeuer* (Leipzig, 1931), p. 58. Unfortunately no two authorities agree about the translation.

17 Cf. in E. B. N. Dhabhar, *The Persian Rivayats of Hormozyar Framarz* (Bombay, 1932), p. 438, the little Persian text in which Zarathustra asks Ōhrmazd: "What was it that already existed when the world became existent?" Answer: "I and Ahunvar (Ahuvar), we both existed." A gloss adds: "Zervān is called 'Ahunvar.'"

18 Cf. W. Bousset, *Die Religion des Judentums im späthellenistischen Zeitalter* (3rd edn., Tübingen, 1926), pp. 37, 344ff., and 520, n. 3 (I expect to come back to this question elsewhere). Cf. also a Mazdean figure of Wisdom in *Mēnōkē Xrat* (the Book of Celestial

exposition difficult; like all the configurations of the Mazdean "imagination," it designates both an angelic hypostasis with personal traits, and its operating counterpart in the earthly being: here it is the visionary soul, the organ of the religious vision of wisdom,[19] in short that attribute of the earthly (*gētīk*) human being which enables him to be coupled with his celestial (*mēnōk*) reality. Let us simply compare two visions: Daēnā-Sophia is the garment and eternal Time of Ōhrmazd. But she is also the feminine Angel who appears after death to the Mazdean soul that has battled faithfully, presenting herself to it as the celestial Self, the light-Self of that soul. Thus the soul incarnated on earth recognizes its celestial partner, or *paredros*, as a figure through which eternal Time is discernible. This comparison grants us a brief glimpse of the dimension of being presupposed by the representation of time in its Sophianic aspect.

Concentrating on the origin, which is also the direction of return, the imagination can face the combat.

"Ahriman rose from his depths," says the Bundahishn,[20] "and arrived at the frontier where the star of Lights (*star-i rōshnān*) is situated." His envious and hateful nature and his bloodthirstiness leap forward, but perceiving "a splendor and an ascendancy superior to his own," he falls back into his darkness to produce his Counter-Creation, the multitude of his demons dedicated to the work of destruction. Ōhrmazd, in his gentleness characteristic of a being of Light (omniscient but not all-powerful), proposes peace to the Antagonist. But is it in his power to convert him into a being of Light? Ahriman replies with a bitter challenge: "I will rise up, I will urge thy creation to fall off from thee and become enamored of me." Ōhrmazd knows that it is not in Ahriman's power to beguile all his creatures. But he also knows that to reduce the Contrary Power of Ahriman to impotence, he will need time, the limited time which he creates in the image of eternal Time; and for the struggle he suggests a period of nine millennia. His Adversary accepts, for his knowledge is of the kind that can only "retard," and he is thus unable to foresee the issue of the cosmic drama whose three great acts we have just mentioned.

Wisdom), Nyberg, "Questions," I, ch. 8, pp. 198–99. For the equivalence of *Dēn* and Sophia in Manichaeism, cf. "Questions," II, pp. 48ff. Cf. also Junker, "Iranische Quellen," p. 164, the end of his n. 50; R. Reitzenstein, *Das Iranische Erlösungsmysterium* (Bonn, 1921), pp. 102ff., 241–42.

19 Cf. Nyberg, *Die Religionen*, pp. 114–20.

20 Cf. Bundahishn, I, in Nyberg, "Questions," I, pp. 208–9.

And in still another grandiose episode the myth suggests that the "cycle of time," the "aeon," is for Ōhrmazd the instrument of his victory over the Antagonist. Taking up Ahriman's challenge, Ōhrmazd inflicts upon him a vision of the future, which Ahriman rejects but which nevertheless overwhelms him: in this vision he beholds the destruction of his demons, the coming of the Resurrection and of the "Future Body" (*tan i pasen*). Then Ōhrmazd sings the *Ahuvar* stanza,[21] the resounding incantation shatters the space intervening between them, and Ahriman falls prostrate to the bottom of Darkness, where he remains for three millennia (the fourth, fifth, and sixth, during which Ōhrmazd aided by the Archangels transfers his Creation from the *mēnōk* to the *gētīk* state). But we have seen that the celestial archetype of the sacred *Ahuvar* stanza is a personification of Ōhrmazd's Time and eternal Wisdom. Thus time is the mediator of Ahriman's defeat.

This episode reveals the hieratic nature of time; and this hieratic nature will give it a privileged position for the unveiling of the world of the archetypes. There is only one sure weapon, the hieratic weapon, the vibration of glorious Light in which Daēnā-Sophia, the wisdom of Ōhrmazd, is eternally embodied. The fact that the sacred stanza of an eternal liturgy within the being of Ōhrmazd is the "person" of time, instrument of the ruin of the demons, also defines the essentially liturgical character of this time. From end to end, the work of Creation and the work of Redemption constitute a cosmic liturgy. It is in celebrating the celestial liturgy (*mēnōk yazishn*) that Ōhrmazd and his Archangels establish all creation, and notably awaken the Fravartis (at once the celestial prototypes and the tutelary angels of men [22]) to the individuality and differentiated consciousness of their enduring Self. And it is by the ultimate celebration of the five liturgies of the *nychthemeron* that the last Saoshyant will accomplish the Resurrection.[23] The total time of the cycle which by the cooperation of all the luminous beings, of all the Fravartis coming to the aid of Ōhrmazd, must ensure the defeat of Ahriman and the subjugation of his demons — this time is a liturgical time.

Of course the fractions of this time (years, months, days, hours) are in turn liturgical moments, homologous to the cycle of the aeon, because they themselves were first created in the celestial (*mēnōk*) state. We have the

21 Ibid., p. 210, li. 18ff.

22 Ibid., p. 236, li. 15ff. (at the hour of the eternal celestial noon); 216, li. 20ff. (from the *Ahuvar* was created the celestial year). See also Junker, pp. 135–36, on time and creation as an epiphany of Ōhrmazd.

23 *Žāmāspīk*, ch. 17, verses 14, 15.

celestial Year, the five celestial sections of the Day, etc. That is why the duration of the millennia cannot be evaluated in the uniform time of our calendars; it is a liturgical time, that is to say, a continuity of liturgical moments.[24] And it is because this is a liturgical time, and because such a time is in essence cyclical, that the time of our cycle is actually conceived in the image of eternal Time. It is the epiphany of eternal Time: the created order as a temporal succession epiphanizes the eternal order which hierarchizes all celestial beings. Carried back to its transcendent origin, the temporal relation exemplifies the multiple organic relations between celestial archetypes; Creation in itself, as an epiphany of the *mēnōk* in the *gētīk*, places the order of succession in limited time.[25] That is why the order of festivals, the entire cycle of the liturgic ceremonial, will be an image, a repetition of the cosmogony: six great solemn festivals (*Gāhambar*) correspond to the six great periods or creations distributed among the six supreme archangels (Ōhrmazd is added to them as a seventh, just as the year encloses the totality of these festivals and with them forms a heptad).[26]

And henceforth, since each of the fractions of time has its celestial archetype and since the liturgical succession of these moments merely exemplifies the relations between these celestial hypostases, their very nomenclature will reveal a communicability of names in conformity with the norm of Mazdean ontology. Each of the twelve months of the year is named after a supreme Archangel (*Amahraspand*, the "Immortal Saints") or after one of the angels (*Yazata*, "venerable"); and so likewise each of the thirty days of the month. Finally, each of the canonical hours is also entrusted to the celestial being or angel who is its archetype, and takes his name;[27] and in its celestial

24 On this concept of hierophanic time cf. Mircea Eliade, *Traité d'histoire des religions* (Paris, 1949), pp. 334–35 (the only possible horizon for an understanding, for example, of the tradition dating the appearance of Zoroaster at 6,000 years before Plato).

25 Cf. Junker, "Iranische Quellen," p. 135, text of the *Dēnkart* in n. 31; on the relation between time and eternity, see Zaehner, "Zurvanica," I, p. 319 (for the quotation from Nāṣir-e Khosraw, cf. H. Corbin and M. Moïn, eds., *Jāmi' al-Ḥikmatain* (Bibliothèque Iranienne, A, 3; Teheran and Paris, 1953), p. 118, li. 8; "Zurvanica," III, p. 885; and de Menasce, *Shkand-Gumāṇīk Vicār*, pp. 250–51. Limited cosmogonic time is the condition and foundation of Creation; it will be reabsorbed into infinite Time. Not that the world will disappear: "on the contrary, it remains, but transfigured and exempt from the taint of growing old, restored to the transcendent state which was its first state" (p. 251).

26 Cf. Nyberg, "Questions," I, pp. 227–35; Modi, *The Religious Ceremonies*, pp. 419–28.

27 "Questions," I, p. 229 (Bundahishn, end of ch. I and ch. III); on the number of "thirty" *Amahraspands* (or "Archangels") cf. Dhalla (n. 44 below), pp. 357ff. On the canonical hours, see "Questions," I, p. 237 (celestial dawn, celestial noon, celestial sunset, etc.);

(*mēnōk*) entity each of these fractions of time is apprehended as a Person. It is this Person who gives the moments of earthly time their dimension as liturgical moments: one may say that the event of this day *is* this Person, the essence of this day is to be the day of this or that angel after whom it is named (e.g., the day of Ōhrmazd of the month of Farvardīn). This relation to the angel is the archetypal dimension which gives to each fraction of limited time its dimension of height or depth in Light, its dimension of eternal Time. Finally, it is by this same token that the celestial partner of a human being of Light who has completed his cycle of earthly time may be manifested to him as an angelic Form, beneath whose name (Daēnā, Dēn) we have discerned eternal Time. When the angel says to the soul: "I am thy Daēnā," it is tantamount to saying: "I am thine Eternity, thine eternal Time."

To be sure, these notions present difficulties, for here thought operates not with concepts or abstract signs, but with concrete personal figures; their imperative presence fills the individual who, to contemplate them, must reflect them in himself. Then, without confusion of their persons, their reciprocal presence must compose a single whole. Time is not the abstract measure of the succession of days, but a celestial figure in which a creature projects his own totality, anticipates his own eternity, experiences himself in his own archetypal dimension. For although Time reveals itself in two aspects, one of which is an image of the other, it also reveals the disparity, the gap between the celestial Person and the earthly person which strives, or rather fails, to be its image. In view of all this, it is essential to consider how the variable relations between pure Mazdaism and Zervanism and the possible variations within Zervanism itself in regard to the relative degradation or preponderance of the person of time, enable the being who projects his own person into the person of time to anticipate his own eternity.

THE ABSOLUTE TIME OF ZERVANISM

We have characterized these variants as Zervanized Mazdaism and Mazdeanized Zervanism. Both schemas present a kind of attempt at a reduction of integral Zervanism, which affirms the absolute preponderance of Zervān, unlimited Time, over the two principles which, as a superior entity, pregnant

---

Jackson, *Zoroastrian Studies*, p. 129; Modi, *The Religious Ceremonies*, p. 219; F. von Spiegel, *Erânische Alterthumskunde* (3 vols., Leipzig, 1871–78), Vol. II, p. 12.

with both of them, it generates. But Zoroastrian Mazdaism could not compromise in regard to the preponderance of Ōhrmazd over Ahriman and their absolute heterogeneity. In the pure Mazdean vision Zervān, the Unlimited, expresses the very norm of Ōhrmazd's being, which is also expressed by his Wisdom-Daēnā, his omniscience and his infinite Light. But if the figure of Zervān is removed from Ōhrmazd's being and given precedence over it, a first consequence will be that the peculiar dimension which we noted in the beings created by his Light will become accentuated in Ōhrmazd himself. And the second consequence will be that the two antagonistic principles will be reduced to the same inferior level with regard to Zervān. While this second consequence can only meet with absolute rejection on the part of pure Mazdaism, the first did not make a reduction of one schema to the other inconceivable, and perhaps even favored such a reduction.

What we may call Zervanized Mazdaism is attested principally by a Zervanite interpolation in the first chapter of the Bundahishn.[28] Here the subordination of Ōhrmazd is attenuated; that is, it is marked above all by the notion that Ōhrmazd became sovereign only through the Creation, conceived as an act of his thought.[29] This act of his thought first produces Creation in the celestial state and then exerts a kind of dialectic constraint over the ideal world of the Negating Spirit, by compelling it to manifest itself.[30] From the very outset Ōhrmazd embodies movement, restlessness, and struggle, and the Mazdean theosophy endows him with a vision which would be incompatible with a rationalist theology of the pure act.

As for Mazdeanized Zervanism, it clings without hesitation to the preponderance of Zervān but like pure Mazdaism relegates the power of Ahriman to an outer abyss. It accentuates the above-mentioned traits in the person of Ōhrmazd. This schema is attested principally by two texts. In

28 Cf. the penetrating analysis by which Nyberg discovered the exposé of Zervanite cosmology interpolated into ch. I of the Bundahishn, in "Questions," II, pp. 36ff. (text in "Questions," I, p. 212, li. 3ff.). Philosophical schematization here imposes a distinction between Zervanite Mazdaism (integrating the name and concept of Zervān, who is subordinated to Ōhrmazd, his maker) and Mazdeanized Zervanism (which subordinates Ōhrmazd to Zervān but, unlike integral Zervanism, maintains the exteriority of the Antagonist). The premises and consequences of these variations have the broadest implications. On the word *zurvān* or *zervān* cf. "Questions," II, p. 52; Nyberg, *Die Religionen*, pp. 380–88; L. H. Gray, *The Foundations of the Iranian Religions* (Bombay, 1925), pp. 124–29.

29 "Questions," I, p. 212, li. 1–4, 13–17 (creation of unlimited Time and of the Time of Long Domination as an instrument).

30 Ibid., li. 12–24; II, p. 40.

the Book of Celestial Wisdom,[31] Zervān appears as a sovereign of inalienable sovereignty: unaffected by Ahriman's Counter-Creation, he is exempt from old age, pain, and death, and it is with his approval that Ōhrmazd forms his own Light, this Creation, the Archangels, and the celestial Wisdom. And in this book the figure of Destiny—Fatum (*bakhsh*)—shines through the figure of Zervān.[32]

A short Mazdean treatise in Persian, a polemic against the doctors of Islam (whence its title: *'Olamā-ye Islām*[33]), is still more precise, for the author himself seems to profess the Zervanite doctrine. "In the religion of Zarathustra," he writes, "it is revealed that with the exception of Time all the rest is creature, while Time itself is the Creator."[34] It first produced Fire and Water; when they were joined, Ōhrmazd became existent. It is noteworthy that the eternal birth of the personal being of Ōhrmazd results here from the conjunction of those two elements which in Hermeticism are the symbol par excellence of the alchemical operation taken as the generation of divine mankind.[35] Ōhrmazd, wholly luminous, pure and fragrant, perceives his redoutable Adversary in the depths of the abyss. He is filled with surprise and alarm. He ponders how to set in motion forces which may defeat him, and he creates the "time of long duration,"[36] amounting to

31 On this book cf. W. Geiger and E. Kuhn, *Grundriss der Iranischen Philologie* (Strassburg, 1895–1904), Vol. II, pp. 107–8; on the form of the words of the title see Nyberg, "Questions," I, pp. 242–46; cf. principally the text, p. 198. Plastically speaking, Zervān, exempt from old age, imaged in created Time as a youth, resembles the "Ancient of Days" only very remotely.

32 Nyberg, "Questions," II, p. 54.

33 There are two different Persian recensions: cf. Dhabhar, *Rivayats*, pp. 437–57, and Junker, "Iranische Quellen," pp. 143ff.

34 In agreement with Junker, "Iranische Quellen," p. 143, li. 33–34, we must correct the following text (corresponding to *Rivayats*, p. 450, and to the edition, p. 81, li. 8): "There is no one we may call its Creator since it was not made by him who is himself Creation" (and not "because it had not yet made the Creation").

35 The alchemic doctrines of those who have been called the "Hellenized Magi" (Ostanes etc.) are already partially known. But little consideration seems to have been given to the alchemic doctrine implied in Zoroastrian orthodoxy. It is held, for example, that if the Ahrimanian smoke mingled with the Fire, it did not combine with its luminosity, whose antagonist it was (so that pure and purifying Fire could not be the substance of Hell). "Ōhrmazd's creatures (Water and Fire for example) cannot destroy one another." Cf. de Menasce, *Shkand-Gumāṇīk Vicār*, p. 36. Beings of the same essence form pairs and are complementary, but not so Light and Darkness, which are contradictory. And this is capital. Cf. also Hertel, *Die Awestischen Herrschafts- und Siegesfeuer*, index, *s.v. Gewässer*.

36 As we must read with Dhabhar, *Rivayats*, p. 451. Junker, "Iranische Quellen," pp. 143–44, has unfortunately read the exact opposite, and the schema becomes unintelligible.

twelve millennia, which is manifested in the celestial Sphere, constellated by the twelve signs of the zodiac.[37]

So far the drama has resulted from the clash between the Power of Light (aided by Zervān or subordinated to him) and a Contrary Power which is wholly external, as in pure Mazdaism. But now this clash is conceived as a drama within the supreme deity himself, because in the *person* of Zervān this supreme godhead contains both the elevation of Light and the depth of Darkness. This then is the vision of integral Zervanism. Its schema has been transmitted to us by Christian sources, notably by the Armenian writer Eznik. It need not surprise us that polemical considerations have dispelled every trace of great mythical inspiration and introduced a certain element of the ridiculous.[38]

Before anything existed, the heavens or the earth or any creation—the Magi are made to say in these texts—Zervān existed. And from the outset the name of Zervān holds a twofold meaning: that of Destiny (*bakhsh*) with which we are already familiar, and that other meaning, no less fraught with consequences, of celestial Glory or Light (*xvarr*), the keystone of Mazdean theosophy. It is further related that for one millennium Zervān performed sacrifices in order that a son might be born to him, a son who

37 Dhabhar, *Rivayats*, p. 451. Cf. *Mēnōkē Xrat* in "Questions," I, p. 198 (two last paragraphs); p. 214 (last four lines). I disregard the question as to which of the two figures, nine or twelve millennia, is of Zervanite rather than Mazdean origin. Concerning the difficulty created by the recognized Ahrimanian nature (in *Mēnōkē Xrat*) of the "seven" planets (thus including the sun and the moon, though they belong to Ōhrmazd's initial Creation), cf. Nyberg, "Questions," II, pp. 62–65, and the sketch on Iranian astrology given by de Menasce, *Shkand-Gumāṇīk Vicār*, pp. 45–49. The usual type of explanation with which too many students content themselves (degradation of gods as a result of the political circumstances attendant on an encounter between two religions) really misses the essential point, as Hans Jonas remarked in *Gnosis und spätantiker Geist* (Göttingen, 1934), Vol. I, pp. 29–31. As for the twelve signs of the zodiac considered as twelve generals (Pahlavi *spāhbat*) on the side of Ōhrmazd (and the seven planets as seven generals on the side of Ahriman), it should be noted that in the Ismailian Nāṣir-e Khosraw the seven Enunciatory Prophets, respectively inaugurating each of the seven periods of a cycle, are also "generals" commissioned by the prime Intelligence (*Jāmi' al-Ḥikmatain*, p. 121).

38 Cf. the texts in Nyberg, "Questions," II, pp. 71ff.; Bidez and Cumont, *Les Mages hellénisés*, Vol. II, pp. 88ff.; the text of the Nestorian monk Iohannan bar Penkayē, ed. de Menasce, "Autour d'un texte syriaque inédit de la religion des Mages," *Bulletin of The School of Oriental Studies*, IX (1937–39), 537–61. Cf. also Junker, pp. 142–43. This myth has been called puerile mythology, a gross and primitive myth. Whatever may be the responsibility of Eznik and the other Christian writers, one thing is certain: it is impossible to see why "spiritualization" must necessarily set in at the end of a long "evolution," and why an "evolution" might not equally well bring about the degradation of a so-called "primitive" spirituality.

would be called Ōhrmazd and who would be the Creator of the Heavens and the earth. But then a doubt arose in Zervān's mind: is this solitary liturgy not in vain? Is it effective? Would Ōhrmazd, the child of his thought and his desire, really be born? And then, from this thought *and* this doubt. two beings were conceived: one was Ōhrmazd, child of his liturgical act, the other Ahriman, the child of the Shadow, of the Darkness of his doubt. But at first Zervān knew only that they were two and vowed that he would bestow the sacerdotal kingdom upon the first one to appear.

This vow was known to Ōhrmazd; with the loyalty and simplicity of a being of Light, he informed Ahriman, who by himself, with his "retarded knowledge," would have known nothing. No sooner did he learn this than he found a way of being born prematurely, as it were, and appeared before his father (who was also his mother).[39] Zervān asked him: "Who art thou?" "I am thy son." And the enraged Zervān replied: "My son is fragrant and luminous, thou art dark and foul-smelling." And now Ōhrmazd, born in due time, presented himself luminous and fragrant to Zervān, who realized at once that this was his son, for whom he had performed long liturgical rites. He wished to invest him with the royal priesthood and gave him his blessing. But Ahriman intervened and reminded Zervān of his vow. In order not to break the vow, Zervān resolved on a compromise: "O false, maleficent one, to thee will be given a reign of 9,000 years, and Ōhrmazd will be sovereign over thee.[40] After 9,000 years, Ōhrmazd will reign, and all that he desires to do, that he will do."

Thus the dominant theme of Zervanism imposes a thesis which would be intolerable to pure Zoroastrian Mazdaism: the primogeniture of Ahriman. Still more serious, Ahriman is the prince of this world and his reign is legitimate, since Zervān, to avoid breaking his vow, was himself compelled to confer the kingship upon him. Ōhrmazd is sovereign, to be sure, but he does not reign; he will reign only at the end of this aeon, at the end of the 9,000 years. The cycle of the millennia is not even imposed by Ōhrmazd himself as in the Mazdean dramaturgy. It is decided upon by Zervān as a

39 The Bundahishn also declares that Ōhrmazd "acquired the position of father and mother of Creation" ("Questions," I, p. 221). Another opinion, however, attributes to Ōhrmazd and Ahriman a celestial mother named Xvashīzag (an affectionate diminutive, signifying roughly "she who is wholly beautiful"), a kind of Iranian Venus Urania, as Nyberg says: "Questions," II, p. 83.

40 Concerning this translation, cf. the important note in Nyberg, "Questions," II, p. 73, n. 1.

compromise, because, to eliminate the Shadow, the Darkness engendered by his doubt, he must agree to limit himself: limited time, our aeon, the time of our world, is the repentance of Zervān the Eternal.

The dialectic of Yes and No thus introduced into the godhead brings forth a cosmogony comparable to that which Schelling set out to develop speculatively in his sketch on the Ages of the World.[41] Here likewise the contradiction of Yes and No, introduced into eternity itself, shatters eternity and sets a series of eternities or aeons in place of a single one. Eternity resolves into time.[42] It is in this contradiction that the succession of the "Ages of the world" originates. The cycle of Ahriman will be followed by a new aeon, that of Ōhrmazd. Similarly in the Ismailian theosophy it is the two phases, the Light and Darkness of the Angel who is the demiurge of our cosmos, which will motivate the alternation of cycles of epiphany and occultation.[43] The eschatological resolution of the present aeon, it is true, is similar in Zervanism and in pure Mazdaism; it is the elimination of the Power of Darkness. But infinite Time, detached from Ōhrmazd and rising above him on the horizon of all the creatures of Light, is also a whole new archetypal zone, which now, together with this Infinite, stretches out immeasurably.

We have already mentioned the Mazdean concept of the Fravartis (*fravashi*, *farvahar*, *ferouër*), celestial archetypes of the creatures of Light,[44] acting as the tutelary angels of earthly creatures. Ōhrmazd revealed to his prophet that without their aid and support he would be unable to defend his Creation against Ahriman's assault.[45] Now the episode of a pre-existential choice is at the root of the whole Mazdean anthropology and assuredly provides the clearest motive for the naming of these feminine archetypal

41 Schelling, *The Ages of the World*, tr. F. de W. Bolman, jr. (New York, 1942). In this work the religion of the Magi is referred to (pp. 102, 159, 173).

42 Ibid., p. 137. It must be noted that Mazdaism aspires not to a new beginning but to a restoration of all things, a return to the original state, an ἀποκατάστασις. But we also find (cf. below in the myth developed by Dion), tied up with the religion of the Magi, explicit mention of the idea of an indefinite succession of cycles (cf. below in Ismailism the succession of the cycles tending toward the final restoration, the Grand Resurrection).

43 With this difference, that the first cycle is a cycle of Light, not a cycle of Ahrimanian domination. Even though Darkness here has its origin in a being of Light, this being is no longer the supreme godhead. Cf. below, pp. 134ff., and Part 2.

44 Cf. a summary account in M. N. Dhalla, *History of Zoroastrianism* (New York, 1938), pp. 232–43, 375–78.

45 Ibid., p. 238, and Yasht, XIII, 12, 13, 28, 76, etc. H. W. Bailey, *Zoroastrian Problems in the Ninth-Century Books* (Oxford, 1943), p. 143.

entities as "those who have chosen."[46] In the prologue of the millennia belonging to the period of Mixture, Ōhrmazd confronted the Fravartis of human beings with a free choice, which is at the origin of their *destiny*, that is to say, their Time, their Aeon: either they might dwell in heaven, safe from the ravages of Ahriman, or they might descend and be incarnated in material bodies in order to combat Ahriman in the earthly world.[47] The Fravartis elect to join battle on earth. And now a kind of duplication occurs. In the end the incarnated Fravarti is identified with the soul; but this soul does not cease to possess an archetypal dimension, since its celestial condition was to *be* an archetype. It is in point of fact only the "person" and earthly part of a Whole, of a syzygy, completed by a celestial Person, another "self" which is its Destiny, the Angel-Soul, the celestial Self, which comes to meet it after death on the road to the Činvat Bridge, which is accordingly referred to in the texts as "the Soul on the road,"[48] and which calls itself Daēnā.

A whole chivalric ethic hangs from this conception.[49] To lose this archetypal dimension is literally to cease to have an angel, it is to die as a soul can die: to cease to answer for one's celestial partner, which can then no longer answer for its earthly soul. Ōhrmazd is not an all-powerful god imposing a Law, imposing trials and sufferings to which one submits without understanding. He is one whose companions share his combat, whose suffering they assume, and whom they do not betray. In the Zervanite ethics the Fravartis are no longer merely the knights of Ōhrmazd but are his suffering members, those in whom "he endures affliction,"[50] because here Ōhrmazd assumes the features of the active and suffering God, foreshadowing the primordial Man of Manichaeism.

But beyond this there is a surprising feature—to which philosophical reflection, which ought to draw its consequences, seems to have devoted little attention. The Mazdean ontology of the celestial archetypes accords

46 Cf. other etymologies, in Bailey, pp. 107ff.

47 Text of the Bundahishn, Bailey, p. 108; and "Questions," I, pp. 236–37.

48 Cf. Dhabhar, *Rivayats*, p. 511 (*Saddar Bundehesh*, ch. X, verse 9; *ravān-e rāh*). Cf. Bailey, p. 115 (*dēn = ruvān ī rās*). I shall have more to say of this central question later.

49 As Eugenio d'Ors says in commenting on the Avestan idea of the angel, "the Zoroastrian religion is translated into a sort of order of chivalry." *Introducción a la vida angélica* (Buenos Aires, 1941), p. 111.

50 "*anākīh . . . dīt.*" Cf. the just remarks of Nyberg, "Questions," II, pp. 80, 81. Ōhrmazd's creatures (and the same is true of Ahriman and his counter-creatures) are his "members"; they stand in a kind of *unio mystica* with him who has formed them, but the essence of Ōhrmazd as such is inaccessible to evil.

to each of them a Fravarti: the Archangels (Amerta Spanta), the Angels (Yazata, Izad) have each their Fravarti. More important still, Ōhrmazd himself has his Fravarti.[51] But this "Angel of Ōhrmazd" cannot then be like the Angel of Yahweh who stands before His Face and manifests Him to His creatures. Rather, it is the Angel who goes ahead of him because he reveals him to himself and manifests to him the horizon, the eternal advent of unlimited Zervān. Thus the archetypes have in turn their Angels, and Ōhrmazd himself, who conceived them as conscious and active Powers, also has his own archetypal Archangel—but this extraordinary intuition projecting the archetypes into a new archetypal dimension is intelligible only if this dimension opens up a *distance* and a distention within eternity itself. Then Ōhrmazd's being must not be an immutable and immobile existence, the pure act of the rational theodicies, but must be projected into the dimension of an eternal future. His Angel stands in the same relation to Ōhrmazd as Daēnā (the aeon) to the human being (the incarnate Fravarti), who—eschatologically speaking—attains to his angel only to be drawn with him into a new height, as though a new archetypal Archangel forever preceded their syzygy. Ōhrmazd and all the beings of the celestial universe are drawn into the ascending movement of limitless eternities toward horizons and toward creative acts of thought belonging to universes still informulable. Here then we may speak of a "Gothic style" of cosmology. In this sense the Zervanite horizon, that of absolute Time without shore, without origin, and without end, would truly be in keeping with the Mazdean universe of those archetypal Archangels who, far from being "fixed," multiply beyond themselves, always sending out another Angel ahead of themselves.

Still there remains something in the schema of integral Zervanism that cannot be reduced to the needs of uncompromising Mazdaism. In the Zer-

51 On the Fravartis of the Archangels cf. Yasht, XIII, 82–84; in Vendidād, XIX, 46–48, Zarathustra is enjoined to invoke the Fravarti of Ahura Mazda (cf. Yasht, XIII, 80). Unfortunately Dhalla's article "Ahura Mazda's Fravashi" (Fravarti) in *Indo-Iranian Studies in Honour of Darab Sanjana* (London, 1925), pp. 115–16, does not go to the bottom of the question. Here we are approaching an archetypal structure. The Parsee theologian J. J. Modi, referring to a vision of Catherine Emmerich, makes an allusion to what he calls Christ's "Fravarti"—cf. his *Dante Papers* (Bombay, 1914), 7: "Angelology," pp. 157–58. On the other hand we know the close relations in the ancient Church between Angelos Christos and the Archangel Michael. Cf. Hans Söderberg, *La Religion des Cathares* (Uppsala, 1949), pp. 77ff. (cf. also n. 9, above; and below, n. 55, and Part 2, p. 155, n. 47).

vanite dramaturgy there remains an ambiguity capable of compromising that prodigious infinite *élan*, an ambiguity capable of beguiling the incarnated Fravartis into a betrayal that will deprive them of their dimension of Light. For Ahriman is the legitimate prince of this world; moreover, although he is a Power of Darkness, this Darkness is an aspect of the supreme godhead itself. To affirm this world is assuredly to serve the Power of Darkness, but is it not also to serve the godhead which itself gave birth to this Darkness and made of this time the time of its wrath, of its renunciation of being itself? And such indeed seems to be the secret of the nocturnal cult which, according to Plutarch, certain Magi devoted to Ahriman. Thus the effort to surmount radical dualism ends by establishing the Darkness as the norm of the Day; what was the "Day of the Angel" is inverted into the "Day of Ahriman." In order that the dawn of Resurrection may shine upon the night of this false day, in order that the day which will be the negation of this negation may grow, the Zervanite schema must undergo certain dramaturgical alterations. Unlike Zervanized Mazdaism or Mazdeanized Zervanism, integral Zervanism may be preserved in an aspect of its essential idea, the idea of a unity mediating between the duality of Light and Darkness; but on condition that this unity shall cease to be at the level of the supreme godhead and regress to an ontologically subsequent rank.

DRAMATURGICAL ALTERATIONS

Here unfortunately we can speak of these dramaturgical changes only briefly, to the degree in which they prepare us for the periods and cycles of the Ismaili mythohistory.

The alterations of the Zervanite dramaturgy are attested by Greek and Islamic sources. In his thirty-sixth oration, Dion of Prusa has transmitted the famous myth of the chariot of the Magi, which seems to have come from a psalter belonging to Magi celebrating the mysteries of Mithras, and which might be compared to the famous vision of Ezekiel. The chariot is harnessed to four chargers typifying the elements, consecrated to the four gods which they respectively represent. One of them is endowed with wings and is of a beauty and splendor surpassing the apparent animal nature of its myth; it is the soul of the invisible guide, and it is forever in movement through all the periods that follow one upon another unceasingly throughout the eternities. In it we may recognize Ōhrmazd as the soul of Zervān (as he will be in Manichaeism), and here again Zervān is expressly identified with eternal Wisdom.[52]

In mentioning the astonishing Magian rite to which we shall refer below, Plutarch introduces a new figure among the *dramatis personae:* Mithras the mediator. Here a new Zervanite tetrad is presupposed: Zervān, Ōhrmazd, Ahriman, Mithras.[53]

It is precisely this idea of a mediator that is emphasized in the account of Zervanism given us by Shahrastānī (12th century), the estimable Persian historian of religions. It is this idea which radically alters the schema of integral Zervanism and puts an end to all ambiguity in its anthropology and ethics. Darkness and Light do not confront each other from the very origin in an irreducible dualism, but are born from the same being, who makes Time "temporalize" itself—an eminently Zervanite idea. Yet this being, the superior and mediating unity in which the contraries originate, is no longer the absolute original godhead. Zervān is one of the beings of Light, the greatest among the angels; thus there is a shift, a regression of the level at which duality—and with it cyclic time—bursts forth. The object of Zervān's doubt is expressed in more metaphysical terms than in Eznik's myth: "Perhaps this universe is nothing," or than in the words of those whom Shahrastānī calls the Gayōmartians (from Gayōmart, the primordial Anthropos): "If I had an adversary, what would he be like?" [54] Here we

52 Cf. Nyberg, "Questions," II, pp. 91–99 (recalling *Phaedrus* 246D–249D, the winged chariots of Zeus and the gods, the race of the souls); Bidez and Cumont, *Les Mages hellénisés*, Vol. I, pp. 91ff., and Vol. II, pp. 142ff.; F. Cumont, *Textes et monuments figurés relatifs aux mystères de Mithra* (Brussels, 1899), Vol. II, pp. 60–64 (cf. another exemplification of the myth of the chariot applied to the Angel Sraosha, in Yasna, LVI, 27–29). The chariot of the Magi has inspired comparisons with the celebrated vision of Ezekiel, which is the origin of the Jewish mysticism of the Merkabah; cf. Bousset, *Die Religion des Judentums*, pp. 355–57; Reitzenstein, *Das Iranische Erlösungsmysterium*, pp. 246ff.

53 *De Iside et Osiride*, 46–47. Cf. Benveniste, *The Persian Religion*, ch. 4 (above, n. 8), especially pp. 89ff.; Nyberg, *Die Religionen*, pp. 392ff. On the Zervanite tetrads see "Questions," II, pp. 108ff.

54 Shahrastānī, *Kitāb al-milal* (lithographed, Teheran, 1288 A.H.), pp. 113–14. I do not believe that we should go too far in denying the historical reality of this sect (R. Reitzenstein and H. Schaeder, *Studien zum antiken Synkretismus aus Iran und Griechentland* (Leipzig, 1926), pp. 236–39). True, the sect of the Gayōmartians is attested only by Shahrastānī, but nothing proves to us that he did not possess data which are no longer at our disposal. Though his effort at systematization is indeed discernible, his exegesis is itself a historical fact. Among the Gayōmartians the Angel Zervān al-kabīr (Zervān the Great) of Shahrastānī's Zervanites does not appear. It is Ōhrmazd himself (Yazdān) who by his doubt engenders his Antagonist. The mediating role of the angels is similar among the Zervanites and the Gayōmartians (note

have the fascination of the void, and the thought of the Other, a thought which as such engenders that Other, so unleashing a combat in heaven which will endure for three millennia. It is, then, the angels as a whole who here fulfill the function of Mithras or of the Archangel Michael, and their mediating role permits us to recognize also their features in those of the Angel Metatron, who dominates so great a part of the mystical literature of the Jews.[55] In the account of Shahrastānī, the angels decree for Ahriman a time of seven millennia, during which the world will be given over to him, but at the end of which he will be compelled to return it to the Light.[56]

We shall see that in the Ismaili schema of mythohistory the angel corresponding to the Angel Zervān not only is the mediator who gives rise to Light and Darkness as well as their respective cycles, but also is the mediator of the victory over Darkness, the mediator of his own victory over himself. To this victory all his companions, made in his image, must contribute, his companions whose archetype he is; this they must do by undertaking in turns a combat punctuated by heptads of millennia. In concluding his account of the angelic mediation, Shahrastānī recalls the fundamental episode of the Fravartis' choice and of their descent to earth. Here the combat of the Archangel Michael has its parallel not in the idea of a "fall of the angels" (never, in Mazdean terms, can an angel, *Izad, fereshta*, be "evil"), but in a voluntary descent, a voluntary renunciation of the Abode of Light, in favor of the perilous combat on earth. And a similar angelological structure will be formulated in the Ismaili anthropology.

TIME AS A PERSONAL ARCHETYPE

The episode of the descent of man's Fravartis to earth is thus both the consequence and the signal of the *shift* of eternal Time into limited time. Very opportunely Shahrastānī mentions this at the end of his account of modified Zervanism. And I believe that it is by concentrating our attention

---

that among the latter the motif of the descent of the Fravartis appears explicitly).

55 Cf. H. Odeberg, *3 Enoch or the Hebrew Book of Enoch* (Cambridge, 1928), pp. 131–33 (cf. above, n. 9, n. 51). It is not so much the historical derivations that are to be sought here; there will never be a decisive solution. To explore the meaning of an archetype's recurrence is in itself a sufficient and satisfying task.

56 I do not believe that the figure of seven millennia (instead of nine or twelve) is due to a copyist's error. It is no accident that this figure accords precisely with the Ismaili schema and the astrological correspondences of the Great Cycle.

upon this motif that we in turn shall best be able to gain an intimation of how eternal Time can be apprehended as a celestial Person, and what experience of time in its twofold aspect is expressed in this personalization. Let us briefly recall certain of our initial findings: every creature is composed of his earthly part and of his celestial counterpart, his archetype or angel. Hence through every reality it is possible to discern a person—that is, to grasp this reality *as* or *in* its celestial person. The fractions of time (months, days, hours) may themselves be visualized as persons (angels and archangels whose names they bear and who are their *event*). This relation to their angel constitutes precisely their archetypal dimension; it is this relation that makes it possible to apprehend them as a complete Whole and thereby to apprehend them as Persons. This norm applies *a fortiori* to the Fravarti incarnated as an earthly human soul whose celestial counterpart is the Soul of Light or Angel which it encounters "on the way" to the Činvat Bridge, which separates the two universes. Thus the visualization not only of all reality as a person but also of that person as transcendent and celestial depends essentially on the archetypal dimension constituted by the relation with the angel, a new "dimension of Light" which determines the entire structure of the Mazdean ontology.

Let us keep in mind this fundamental norm in seeking to follow the chain of relations that confronts us here. Not only do the fractions of time appear as celestial Persons—that is to say, as eternal individuations—but absolute Time itself, eternal Time, appears in multiple personal Figures: Zervān, eternal Time, is a sovereign; he is Wisdom-Daēnā; Zervān is Destiny; Zervān is Light and Glory, as we learn in the myth recorded by Eznik. Moreover, the Greek equivalents of these Iranian notions tend to fix the play of transparitions upon the vision of a determinate figure, namely that of the *Agathos Daimōn*—that is to say, upon a figure which in every case becomes the tutelary angel or celestial *paredros*. The transparition corresponds to that which in Zervān gives us an intimation of Daēnā, and in Daēnā of the celestial Self. And it is precisely this insistent and precise transparition which should enable us to ask with some hope of an answer: what mode of existence and experience is presupposed by the apparition (the phenomenon) of eternal Time as a personal figure, tending to become fixated in the form of the angel which is the celestial *paredros* and as such the archetype, the guide, and the destiny of life? This form of angel-*paredros* also signifies a totality that is consummated only by the conjunction of the earthly person and of the celestial Self which is its superior existence. Until the incarnated Fravarti is joined, upon her return, with the Angel who comes to meet her "on the road" to Činvat Bridge—up to this moment the earthly soul is lacking, it lags behind itself—that is, behind the totality of its being. In short, we are led to this conclusion: the visualization of eternal Time as of a person identifying himself with the archetypal Person of every earthly individual signifies literally that in compensation limited earthly time, the time Ōhrmazd needs in order to expel Ahriman from his Creation, in short the time that we ourselves are in (for us earthly creatures "time" pure and simple)—this time is *retarded eternity*.[57] That is why in the Angel's annunciation after death—"I am thy Daēnā"—we were able to perceive the equivalent of "I am thine Eternity."

At this point let us consolidate our general statements and illustrate them by examples. There are numerous texts that might enlighten us. But I shall be brief, condensing the themes as much as possible.

1. A first series of examples tends to show the epiphany of eternal Time as essentially multiform—that is to say, it shows the Αἰών as *παντόμορφος θεός*.[58] Not only does this modality provide a foundation for its numerous epiphanies; it also makes possible the exegetic transition leading the being from the hypostasis as such to the being in its function. It is thanks to this multiformity that eternal Time can in each instance manifest itself as an archetypal Figure, for this precisely is what assures its presence in that "instance." The idea of a unity which is the unity of each member of a Whole and also that of their totality may also be verified in connection with the archangelical heptad in Mazdaism, and in the earliest Christianity as well.[59] This idea makes possible a simultaneity of divine unity and divine plurality which avoids the simplest dilemma between monotheism and poly-

57 The term is that of Nédoncelle.

58 Cf. Reitzenstein, *Das Iranische Erlösungsmysterium*, pp. 172ff.

59 On the origins of this Iranian method of enumeration (which always considers the totality as a new unity added to the number of members composing it) cf. Reitzenstein, *Das Iranische Erlösungsmysterium*, pp. 154ff., and Nyberg, "Questions," II, pp. 54ff. This is by no means a naïve logic; cf. the remarks of Junker, "Iranische Quellen," pp. 160–61. Cf. also the Christian inscription at Miletus, where each of the seven archangel aeons is *also* the Whole (Deissmann in Reitzenstein, p. 175, n. 2; ibid., Christ as *auriga cherubim;* and cf. above, n. 52, the myth of the chariot). Also see Reitzenstein, "Eine frühchristliche Schrift von den dreierlei Früchten des christlichen Lebens," in *Zeitschrift für die neutestamentliche Wissenschaft* (Giessen), XV (1914), in which Christ is at the same time the sum of the seven Angels and one of them (pp. 67–68, 82).

theism. This might be an occasion to redefine the old term of "kathenotheism" as the hierophantic category of "every instance."[60] This means that given the figure in which the transparitions of the aeon tend to become fixated, the mode of existence of the soul for which eternal Time is epiphanized as a figure that is its archetypal dimension culminates neither in the void of its own isolation nor in a uniformly nameable divine presence, but in a rigorous and irreplaceable individuation (καθ' ἕνα, *singulatim*) of that divine presence.

The epiphanies of the aeon assume this aspect of an eternal individuation which is always a totality. We might conceive a predetermined number of such epiphanies, but each is multiplied in turn. There are, for example, the celestial archetypes or personal figures of the divisions of the Mazdean year, typifying personal creative powers. We find examples of a similar mental iconography in the Gnostic, Nosayrī, and Ismaili calendars;[61] in Manichaeism; and finally, we have the twelve maidens, Virtues, or "Majesties" —the "twelve glorious maidens of Zervān"—a mystery which in the twelve hours of Light leads the soul from earth to perfect Light. But in addition Time itself as an eternal totality is epiphanized in individuated figures, whose play of reciprocal transparitions are fixated in a figure which may enable us to define the mode of existence for which eternal Time announces itself in this manner.[62]

Zervān is eternal Wisdom: Zervān is Destiny (*bakhsh*) as an elected and imparted finality, leading back to itself (personal destiny or finality which is something other than what is popularly called fatalism). In his capacity of Destiny and personal Destiny, Zervān also appears as *xvarr* (Avestan *xvarenah*)—that is to say, as the celestial Light of Glory, the "fire of vic-

60 Cf. Betty Heimann, *Indian and Western Philosophy, a Study in Contrasts* (London, 1937), pp. 37ff. And this is not a problem peculiar to India.

61 Cf. R. Reitzenstein, *Poimandres* (Leipzig, 1904), p. 270, and our study, "Rituel sabéen et exégèse smaélienne," *EJ 1950*, pp. 235ff.

62 Cf. E. Waldschmidt and W. Lentz, *Die Stellung Jesu im Manichäismus* (Berlin, 1926), p. 127; Reitzenstein, *Das Iranische Erlösungsmysterium*, pp. 154–59; de Menasce, p. 255. On the three greatest periods of cosmic Time represented in three figures forming a unity we may compare (for the archetype) Gayōmart, Zarathustra, Saoshyant (Reitzenstein, pp. 99, 242); Nuriel, Enoch, Metatron (Odeberg, *3 Enoch*, p. 124); primordial Man, Archangel Michael, and Christ (Söderberg, *La Religion des Cathares*, p. 78). In the Ismaili theosophy the seven Imāms of the seven periods of a cycle epiphanize the essence of a unique and eternal Imām (cf., in Manichaeism, Adam, Seth, Enoch, Buddha, Zoroaster, Jesus, and Mani).

tory" which is primarily the property of the celestial Yazatas.[63] This Glory was visibly manifested as a nimbus and flame forming haloes round the heads of the princes of dynasties consecrated prior to our chronologies; it still retains this visibility in the stylized nimbus which accompanies it from the figure of the Mazdean Saoshyant to the Western representations of Christ, to the Eastern figures of Buddhas and Bodhisattvas. But it is not only the royal and sacerdotal charisma; it is the power which constitutes and knits together the existence of a being of Light. In this sense, this "Glory" signifies the soul itself insofar as it exists before the body.[64] Henceforth, if this Light of Glory, figure of eternal Time, is imparted to every being of Light as its very soul, we shall be justified in calling it the Destiny and Eternity of that being.

It should be mentioned that these alternating denominations in which we glimpse the Figure of Zervān in the myth recorded by Eznik were given precise Greek equivalents: Δόξα and Τύχη.[65] And the fact that this Light of Glory, which is also Destiny, was represented by the term Τύχη is of the greatest importance. For in the same context the figure Τύχη (fate, destiny) was identified with the figure which dominates the Hermetic horizon, *Agathos Daimōn*, who appears simultaneously as a Hermetic divinity and as the personal "good daemon," the *δαίμων πάρεδρος*, the celestial *paredros* or partner—that is to say, the helping, tutelary angel—a gratuitous gift obtained by prayer.[66]

In whatever sense we consider it, we perceive a figure with increasingly precise traits. On the one hand, Daēnā is Zervān and she is also the Angel-Self, the celestial archetype coming to meet the soul. In the *Corpus hermeticum* Sophia is the aeon; she is the mother of Anthropos—that is to say,

63 Cf. Gray, *Foundations*, pp. 120–23; Spiegel, *Erânische Alterthumskunde*, Vol. II, pp. 42–44; Hertel, *Die Awestischen Herrschafts- und Siegesfeuer*, pp. VIII, XIff., 12, 76.

64 Cf. Reitzenstein and Schaeder, *Studien*, p. 230, n. 2; pp. 17, 321; p. 320 (Iranian *xvarenah* and Hebrew *shekhina*).

65 Cumont, *Textes et monuments*, Vol. I, pp. 284–85; Bidez and Cumont, *Les Mages hellénisés*, Vol. I, pp. 68ff.; Vol. II, pp. 52, n. 5; 87; 89; 92, n. 2; Nyberg, "Questions," II, p. 71, and ch. 5, pp. 66–67. In the Pahlavi script, *xvarr* (glory) is represented by the Aramaic ideogram *gaddeh* (fortune, luck); Gray, *Foundations*, pp. 121, 128; it reappears in Ismailism under the Arabic form of *jadd* (= Persian *bakht* in Abū Ya'kūb Sejestānī (*Mawāzīn*, XII, and below, Part 2, p. 150, n. 27) characterizing the angel identified with Gabriel, who would correspond topologically to Zervān.

66 Cf. Reitzenstein, *Das Iranische Erlösungsmysterium*, pp. 192–93 (also p. 191, n. 1; and *Poimandres*, p. 18, n. 8; Agathoel, angel of victory and of rejoicing); *Corpus hermeticum*, text established by A. D. Nock and tr. A.-J. Festugière (Paris, 1945–54; 4 vols.), Vol. I, Treatise X, 22–23, and n. 78.

of the regenerated *mystes*, for she has given birth to his immortal body, *ἀθάνατον σῶμα*.[67] But in addition, the assurance of immortality is bound up with the attainment of the *daimōn paredros*, the celestial angel or partner. At the same time, Zervān is Τύχη, Personal Destiny; Τύχη is *Agathos Daimōn*, who is a divine figure as such and also a *daimōn paredros*, the personal angel of each soul.[68]

2. Now it is by this figure of the *daimōn paredros* that we may finally understand the characteristic mode of being of a soul for which time is epiphanized as a person. If all the transparitions or hierophanies of eternal Time tend to be fixated in this person, it is because the soul for which it is thus modalized has taken cognizance of its archetypal dimension and knows that the totality of its being can be fulfilled only in conjunction with its celestial *paredros*. But at the same time we perceive the "transitive" way in which a godhead, without ceasing to be in itself a hypostasis, can exist totally in each of its individuations; this is the case with the figures of the Mazdean angelology, such as the *agathos daimōn*, which is also a *daimōn paredros*, etc.

To this structure corresponds exactly that of the soul which exemplifies it, the being whose archetype this godhead is. So it is that the same name will designate the angelic hypostasis in itself and its presence in its earthly counterpart considered as a part or potency of it and revealing precisely its dual structure, its reference to the angel or celestial archetype. In Mazdaism, for example, *fravarti* (*farvahar*) and *daēnā* (*dēn*) are celestial entities and human potencies or faculties as well; more precisely they are that part of human beings which enables them to be coupled with these celestial entities. Similarly in Hermeticism the *Nous* is at once a god, the faculty of intuitive knowledge in man, and his tutelary angel (as *Agathos Daimōn*).[69] Here we do not have two inconsistent theories, but the dimension of an anthropology which is already an angelology: "the man without *Nous*" means the man deprived of that faculty of knowledge and precisely the "man without an angel," in short something which is no longer a human being.[70] But, on the other hand, to attain to the *angelos paredros* is to gain immortality,[71] to become aeon; and similarly the meeting with Daēnā "on

67 Ibid., XI, 3; Vol. II, XIII, 2. Cf. n. 2 of Vol. II, p. 268. Reitzenstein, *Poimandres*, p. 44; *Das Iranische Erlösungsmysterium*, p. 44. Junker, "Iranische Quellen," p. 164.
68 Reitzenstein, *Poimandres*, pp. 153; 156, n. 2; 365.
69 *Corpus hermeticum*, Vol. I, p. 134, n. 73, and p. 139.
70 Ibid., X, 24, and p. 139 (bottom).
71 Cf. above, n. 68.

the road" to the Činvat Bridge signifies the shift of limited time to eternal Time; the attainment of Destiny itself and the plenitude of the Light of Glory or *xvarenah.*

Thus it is only by anticipation that the soul can now be granted a vision of its eternal Time in the form of its Angel-Archetype; and this prevision, by showing the soul what it is *not yet* but has still to be, reveals to it its own being as "retarded eternity." In consequence, anticipation is the vital law of an existence which, by thus understanding itself, must tend toward its superexistence on pain of being *eternally retarded* over against itself. This anticipation is manifested in rites and injunctions, in the enchantments of a mental iconography or of ecstatic visions.

The symbolism of the *kosti* has rightly been interpreted in this sense.[72] The *kosti* is the sacred cord, woven of lamb's wool, which the Zoroastrians wear as a girdle and which is venerated as their distinctive religious sign. The cord is passed three times around the waist and knotted four times, twice in front and twice behind. The symbolic significance traditionally attached to these four knots makes it possible to identify them as a Zervanite tetrad to which, as in the myth of the "chariot of the Magi," is added a fifth member which fastens together and totalizes the tetrad; but here precisely Zervān or Wisdom, the invisible *auriga* of the chariot, is represented by the very person of the Mazdean believer. In this sense the symbolism of the *kosti* approaches the symbolism of the robe in which the *mystes* was clad: the *stola olympiaca* of which Apuleius speaks,[73] or the heavenly robe constellated with the signs of the zodiac, mentioned in the mysteries of Mithras, which was such that when the *mystes* donned it he in person became the god passing through the constellations.[74]

It is likewise as an injunction to abolish the delay, to convert retarded eternity into anticipated eternity that we may understand the solemn announcement of the *Nous* to Hermes: "If you do not make yourself like

72 Cf. Junker, "Iranische Quellen," pp. 136, and 160, n. 36; Modi, *Religious Ceremonies*, pp. 178–79. It should also be noted that the third knot itself refers to the sacrosanct Zoroastrian trilogy: "Good thought, good word, good action," projected spatially as forming the three levels of paradise: *Humat, Hūxt, Huvarsht* (*Mēnōkē Xrat*, II, 145; LVII, 13).

73 Reitzenstein, *Das Iranische Erlösungsmysterium*, p. 167.

74 Ibid., pp. 168, 239. Cf. also the motif of the heavenly girdle brocaded on the robe donned by the *mystes*, in Junker, "Iranische Quellen," p. 162: the *kosti* makes the Zoroastrian believer a symbol or exemplification of the aeon, an Anthropos, one reborn, a son of God like the "All in All, composed of all the powers" (*Corpus hermeticum*, Vol. II, XIII, 2).

unto God, you can not understand God, for the like is intelligible only to the like. Make yourself grow until you correspond to greatness without measure, by a leap that will free you from all body; raise yourself above all time, become aeon (become eternity); then will you understand God." [75]

There is, finally, a mental iconography that anticipates the supreme hierophany. Here the perpetual recurrence of one and the same figure, whose soul takes delight in foreseeing the encounter, might well form the basis of a comparative study. It is eminently in Mazdaism that we encounter the apparition of Daēnā at the entrance to Činvat Bridge, under the aspect of a heavenly Maiden whose beauty surpasses all imagination.[76] But the same vision occurs in Manichaeism [77] and in Sufism as well.[78] We find its equivalent in the Buddhism of the Pure Land.[79] And the Liturgy of Mithras contains an ecstatic anticipation of this eschatological vision when the *mystes*, having become aeon, sees the gates open before him, and the world of the gods and the angels becomes visible to him; when his soul, beside itself with joy, comes face to face with "the god of glittering presence, the god of the golden ringlets, in the flower of his youth, clad in a robe of splendor, crowned with a golden diadem." [80]

Ismaili gnosis will characterize this attainment of transcendence as a passage from the "angel *in potentia*" to the "angel *in actu*." Here we shall find the significance of angelology not only for a certain form of mystical experience but also for an entire anthropology, for a philosophy of the person and the personality. But precisely this philosophy is bound up with a cosmology in which cyclic time has its origin in a *retard*, a *passing beyond*, a relegation to the past. This origin is the drama that befell one of the angels of the pleroma, who will here play the role of the Angel Zervān in the schema of Shahrastānī; and the entire anthropocosmic dramaturgy

75 *Corpus hermeticum*, XI, 20.
76 *Hādoxt Nask*, II, 1–15 (= Yasht, XXII, 1–15); Vendidād, XIX, 98–104; *Mēnōkē Xrat*, II, 123–39 (cf. below, Part 2, p. 171, n. 102).
77 Cf. our "Récit d'initiation," *EJ 1949*, pp. 183–84.
78 'Abdolkarīm Gīlānī, in R. A. Nicholson, *Studies in Islamic Mysticism* (Cambridge, 1921), p. 117; and cf. Suhrawardī's hymn to Perfect Nature in our "Récit d'initiation," p. 160.
79 For the motif of the descent of Amida (Amitābha), cf. H. Minamoto, "L'Iconographie de la 'descente d'Amida,'" in *Etudes d'orientalisme* published by the Musée Guimet in memory of Raymonde Linossier (Paris, 1932), Vol. I, pp. 99–129.
80 Junker, "Iranische Quellen," p. 152; Reitzenstein, *Das Iranische Erlösungsmysterium*, pp. 238–40; G. R. S. Mead, *A Mithraic Ritual* (London and Benares, 1907), pp. 32, 61, 63.

will be carried toward its final act by the torment of a "retarded eternity." This will be the theme of our next discussion.

2. *Cyclical Time in Ismailism*

ABSOLUTE TIME AND LIMITED TIME IN THE ISMAILI COSMOLOGY

It was in the course of the tenth and eleventh centuries of our era (fourth and fifth centuries after the Hegira) that the Ismaili theosophy took form in great systematic works, chiefly under the influence of several great Iranian thinkers.[1] One of these thinkers, Abū Ḥātim Rāzī, whose work, like so many others, still exists only in manuscript, was a Fatimid dignitary (dāʿī) in the Dailam (region to the southwest of the Caspian Sea). He was a contemporary of the celebrated Moḥammad ibn Zakarīyā Rāzī (the Rhazes of the Latin writers of the Middle Ages, d. *ca.* 923–32), a physician and alchemist suspected of crypto-Manichaeism, whose philosophical work has today been in large part lost.[2] As their name indicates, both men have a bond with Rhages (the city mentioned in the book of Tobit, the Ragha of the Avesta, today Rayy, several kilometers south of Teheran). It is fortunate for philosophy that these two eminent contemporaries should have met and known each other and that, moreover, since Zakarīyā Rāzī was (even posthumously) the object of Ismaili attacks,[3] these two fine minds should have clashed in controversies which were no less intense for all their courtesy.

In one of his books Abū Ḥātim Rāzī left us a record of one of these discussions.[4] His adversary set his name to a cosmology in which he restored—or perhaps actually founded—an ideal Sabaean philosophy. This cosmology asserted the existence of five eternal principles: Demiurge, Soul, Matter, Space, and Time.[5] Here we shall be concerned solely with the passage regarding the eternity of Time.[6]

1 Abū Yaʿkūb Sejestānī, Mo'ayyad Shīrāzī, Ḥamīdaddīn Kermanī, Nāṣir-e Khosraw, etc.
2 On Abū Ḥātim Rāzī, cf. W. Ivanow, *A Guide to Ismaili Literature* (London, 1933), p. 32, VIII; *Studies in Early Persian Ismailism* (Leiden, 1948), p. 37 and passim; S. Pines, *Beitrage zur islamischen Atomenlehre* (Berlin, 1936), pp. 35ff. On Mohammad ibn Zakarīyā Rāzī cf. Pines, pp. 35, 69, and passim. The remains of his philosophical work have been collected by Paul Kraus, *Razis Opera philosophica fragmentaque quae supersunt*, Vol. I (Cairo, 1939).
3 Notably on the part of Nāṣir-e Khosraw.
4 In the *Kitāb Aʿlām al-Nobowwat* (Ivanow, *Guide*, n. 19).
5 Cf. our "Rituel sabéen."
6 Cf. Kraus, *Razis Opera*, p. 304; Pines, *Beiträge*, p. 53.

The bout opens with a loyal challenge:

> You have said then that the five principles are eternal (*qadīm*) and alone eternal? Well then, time is constituted by the motion of the spheres, the passage of days and nights, the number of years and months; are all these co-eternal with time, or are they produced in time?—The defender seeks to draw the assailant into a terrain where his weapons will be ineffectual. True, measured by the movement of the Heavens, all the things he has just named are produced in time. But in so arguing he is merely upholding the thesis of Aristotle. Who will venture to say that it has never been disproved? Moḥammad ben Zakarīyā Rāzī—but at this point let us give him back his old name of Rhazes to simplify matters and distinguish him from his homonym—Rhazes, then, who will end by invoking Plato, begins by stating his own thesis in simple terms: "For my part, I profess this: Time implies an absolute Time (*Zamān muṭlaq*) and a limited time (*Zamān maḥṣūr*). Absolute Time is eternal Duration (*mudda, dahr*); this is the time that is eternally in movement and never halts. Limited time is that which exists through the movements of the celestial spheres, the course of the sun and the heavenly bodies.

But Abū Ḥātim asks skeptically what substantial reality (*ḥaqīqa*) one can represent under the concept of this absolute Time. It is not so simple; his adversary asks him to compare the time of this world which is moving toward exhaustion and completion, with the absolute Time that can neither be completed nor destroyed.

What interests us here is neither the details nor the development of the discussion but essentially the statement of Rhazes' thesis. Here we have no wish to debate the question of a historical filiation running from the philosophemes of Mazdaism to those of Ismailism, nor to determine the "influences." [7] But we may say this much: in its terminology, Rhazes' distinction between an absolute Time and a limited time presents a direct and lateral correspondence with the two fundamental aspects of time in the Mazdean cosmogony.[8] The relation seems to have been suggested as early as the

7 This is a problem which in any case cannot be elucidated by the current methods of purely static and analytical exegesis, by a historicism limited to an essentially causal type of explanation which reads causality into things. With regard to the extreme complexity of the data and the seriousness of the irreparable gaps in our sources, cf. e.g. G. H. Sadighi, *Les Mouvements religieux iraniens au IIème et au IIIème siècle de l'Hégire* (Paris, 1938).

8 *Zamān* (= *Zervān*) *i akanārak* and *Zamān i kanārakomand* or *Zamān i derangxvatāi* have been studied in our first lecture.

eleventh century by Ibn Ḥazm, the celebrated Andalusian Arabic writer, in his critical history of religions.[9] On the other hand, as the historian Bīrūnī remarked, the doctrine of Rhazes borrowed from Neoplatonism [10] in so far as it distinguished between (1) the Time (*Zamān*, χρόνος) with which number is concerned and which corresponds to the definition of Aristotle; (2) Duration (*Mudda*), analogous to διάστασις τῆς ζωῆς, the distance that dis-tends the life of the soul (for the soul which is not attached as such to the movement and number of the Heavens is that which numbers this number); [11] and finally (3), the aeon (*dahr*), the time of the eternal intelligible world. Actually, the last two aspects tend to fuse into one, and in this respect the entire distinction of Rhazes' doctrine might be attributed to his master Irānshahrī, an Iranian philosopher who lived in the ninth century and who seems to have been a highly original thinker, but whose work is known to us only from a few quotations. Irānshahrī regarded the terms "time," "duration," and "eternity" as one and the same thing considered under two aspects: unmeasured Time (independent of the movements of the Heavens and even of the soul, since it refers to a plane of the intelligible universe that is superior to the soul) and Time measured by the movement of the heavens. Thus, since eternal Duration and Time are only two aspects of the same essence, the distinction made by Rhazes between absolute Time and limited time would correspond to that between separated time and unseparated Time: χώριστος χρόνος and ἀχώριστος χρόνος in the terminology of Proclus.[12]

Now the Ismaili theosophy of mythohistory presupposes precisely the representation of an eternal Time—whose eternity, however, erupts in cycles of successive times whose rotation carries them back to their origin. What, then, we cannot help wondering at this point, was the reason for the per-

9 *Kitāb al Fiṣal* (Cairo, 1348), Vol. I, p. 35.

10 Cf. Bīrūnī's text in Pines, pp. 49–52.

11 Ibid., p. 50, n. 2: the interpretations of Simplicius and Alexander of Aphrodisias. Cf. Nāṣir-e Khosraw, *Jāmi' al-Ḥikmatain*, ed. Corbin and Moïn, ch. 9, pp. 117–20, §§ 114–15; and ch. 17 (cf. below).

12 Cf. Pines, pp. 51–52; 41, n. 2; and 85, n. 4. The problem also attracted the attention of the philosophers of the Safawid period, Mīr Dāmād and Ṣadrā Shīrāzī. Cf. also Proclus, *The Elements of Theology*, ed. E. R. Dodds (Oxford, 1933), p. 228 (Αἰών-Zervān as hypostasis); and E. Zeller, *Die Philosophie der Griechen* (3rd edn., Leipzig, 1903–22), Vol. III, Part 2, p. 707 (Iamblichus). The powerful personality of Irānshahrī is indicated by the tradition according to which he rejected all religions and created one of his own. Do the words of sympathy and praise with which Nāṣir-e Khosraw refers to him suggest that this personal position was not without its affinity to Ismailism?

sistent attacks on Rhazes? Essentially he was attacked as the "Sabaean philosopher," the negator of Prophecy; not that Ismailism upheld the prophetology of official and orthodox Islam, but its entire technique of interior or spiritual exegesis (*ta'wīl*) presupposes the text transmitted by the Prophets (*Nāṭiq*). Similarly, the correspondence between celestial hierarchy and earthly hierarchy presupposes that the "mediators" of salvation are not merely the spiritual angels of ideal Sabaeanism.[13] Even when Rhazes sets out to describe absolute Time, the Ismaili thinker, under the stress of polemical considerations, seems to suppose that he is still speaking of the time of sensuous things, of the time that "is nothing other than the changing states of that which is body."[14] And there will be all the more indignation when Rhazes, positing Time as one of the five eternal principles, seems to make a thing, a substance, of it.[15] But once polemical ardors have abated, the motif of the twofold aspect of Time as a *single* essence will reappear with an imperious necessity.[16] This will be the case with the great Iranian Ismaili philosopher, Nāṣir-e Khosraw (eleventh century).

In a closely reasoned chapter of a work which is a synthesis of Greek and Ismaili philosophy,[17] Nāṣir compares the notions of eternity (*dahr*) and of time (*zamān*),[18] and sets forth this proposition: "Time is eternity measured by the movements of the heavens, whose name is day, night, month, year. Eternity is Time not measured, having neither beginning nor end." "It is the Time of Duration without end, absolute Duration."[19] The cause of this eternal Duration is the first divine Emanation, the first primordial Intelligence or Archangel: eternity is in the horizon (or in the sphere) of this Intelligence. The cause of time is the Soul of the World; but the Soul is itself in the horizon of the Archangel; it is not in time, for time is in the horizon of the Soul as its instrument, as the duration of the living mortal who is "the shadow of the Soul," while eternity is the duration of the living immortal—that is to say, of the Intelligence and of the Soul.[20]

13 Cf. our "Rituel sabéen," pp. 195ff.

14 Nāṣir-e Khosraw does this in *Kitāb Zād al-Mosāfirīn*, ed. Kaviānī (Berlin, n.d.), p. 111.

15 Ibid., pp. 112–13.

16 Ibid., p. 110. On the importance of Nāṣir-e Khosraw (d. *ca.* 481 A.H./A.D. 1088), who organized the Ismaili community of Badakhshan, the Oxus region at the eastern end of the Iranian world, cf. W. Ivanow's recent study, *Nāṣir-e Khosraw and Ismailism* (The Ismaili Society, series B, V, Leiden and Bombay, 1948).

17 This is the work cited above, n. 11, which is a synthesis of Greek and Ismaili philosophy.

18 Ibid., p. 118, li. 6, 7. Cf. § 109 and *Zād*, pp. 117–18, 364–65.

19 Ibid., p. 118, li. 8.

20 Ibid., p. 113, § 109; p. 117, § 114; cf. p. 188, § 192.

In declaring, "The Intelligence is one with eternal Time," Nāṣir-e Khosraw is also stating the secret of the speculative Ismaili cosmology: the eternal birth of the pleroma from the *Ibdāʿ* (eternal Existentiation), formed of archangelical hypostases originating in the first among them. This world is not of an immutability and immobility presenting a simple contrast to the perishability of sensuous things; there are Events in Heaven, archetypal Events preceding the Creation of things, and these Events are the very genesis of being. This ontological mystery is circumscribed by Nāṣir in three words (*azal, azalīyat, azalī*) the nuances of which we should have some difficulty in translating if the author, even though writing in Persian, did not relate them to Arabic paradigms. Thus we have an eternally-being (*azal*) as *nomen agentis* (present participle *fāʿil*); an eternal actuation of being (*azalīyat*) as *nomen verbi* (noun of action, *fiʿl*); an eternally being made-to-be (*azalī*) as *nomen patientis* (past participle, *mafʿūl*).[21] The text is marvelously abstruse, but it discloses the following: by being eternally, the eternally-being (*azal*) actuates precisely its own being-that-has-become, its being which has eternally been—that is to say, which is eternally made-to-be by its own act of being. We must bear in mind that in terms of Ismaili philosophy the eternally-being constitutes the supreme godhead, absolutely unknowable and unpredicable.[22] But what this godhead is eternally in actuating its being, in revealing it, is the first archangelical hypostasis (*al-mobdaʿ al-awwal*),[23] its eternal Personification, its very Ipseity, the Only One forever being revealed. This Archangel is the *Deus determinatus* (*al-Lāh*) to such a point that all the predicates which the exoteric religions would focus on the supreme godhead should actually be applied to this divine Epiphany within the first Intelligence (*ʿAql awwal*).

Here Nāṣir explicitly calls our attention to an ontological aspect with which the "speculative grammar" of our Middle Ages was very much concerned and which was designated as the *significatio passiva*. Here it is the aspect which action assumes in its end, in that wherein it is accomplished (*nomen patientis*), at the very point where action in being fulfilled is no longer distinguished from *passio*, since *passio* is its outcome (as, for example, writing and the thing written, *scriptio* and *scriptum*). As Nāṣir said: "The *significatio passiva* of the *nomen patientis* (*mafʿūlī-e mafʿūl*) consists in the

21 Ibid., ch. 17, pp. 187–89, §§ 191–93, much more precise than *Zād*, p. 195.

22 "He who cannot be attained by the boldness of thought." Cf. R. Strothmann, *Gnosis-Texte der Ismailiten* (Göttingen, 1943), p. 55.

23 Cf. *Jamiʿ al-Ḥikmatain*, p. 188, li. 9.

very action of the agent, which is accomplished in him." In this sense the Archangel of the primordial theophany considered as the end in which is accomplished the ontomorphosis of the eternal Being appears as eternal Action or divine Energy and as eternal, divine Passion (or divine "pathetism"). As eternally made-to-be, the Archangel is the eternal, divine Past. Since by this very token he is in his person Action-made-to-be, this active aspect of his eternal being summons to being, actuates the procession of archangelical entities that follow him; and the same duality of *actio* and *passio* is repeated at every degree, producing the eternal birth of a new Archangel.

In their very nature these premises are difficult to understand. But without them it is impossible to grasp the principle of the Ismaili cosmic dramaturgy, to understand why the consequence of the error of the angel which will take the role of the Angel Zervān (in the schema of Shahrastānī) will be described as a "retard"—the regression of a rank (that of the Angel) which lets itself be surpassed, put behind (*ta'akhkhor*, *takhallof*). Actually if this is true, the eternal Existentiation (*Ibdā'*) of the primordial Archangel, which is at the origin of the pleroma, is not only eternal actuation of being but also eternally to come, eternal advent. The eternal Past *is* eternally actuated; it does not *become* a past, it is not *thrust into* the past, it does not sink into a past that is more and more past, as we say that the past sinks into time. But then the intoxication that will seize the Angel in the illusion that he himself is the actuation of his being—precisely this intoxication will remove him from eternal actuation, from the eternal advent of being. His doubt stops him to himself, thrusts him into the past, and by this fall into the past his own rank is *surpassed* (here again space is born from time).[24] At this moment "temporal (or limited) Time" is born, a time in which there is a remoteness, a past that is no longer eternal, a past that is no longer.

Nevertheless, the Ismaili vision contains a repentance, a *conversion* already accomplished by the Angel; and through this conversion the temporal time originating in his fault has also *shifted back*. That is why this Time has the form of a cycle; it is not a rectilinear time indefinitely accumulating a past and leading nowhere, but a time leading back to the origin. There is redemption from the past: the angelic rank is surpassed, it falls into the

24 Or again visual space is only one aspect of space, perhaps a symbol of true space, just as the time of our chronologies is only an aspect or a symbol of Time; there is no opposition between Time and Eternity, there are only two aspects of Time as such, Αἰών and Αἰῶνες.

past, and then again becomes future. To lead back to the origin: this is the exact meaning of the word which designates esoteric spiritual exegesis (*ta'wīl*), the central operation of Ismaili thought, of which the alchemical operation is only a special case.[25] Thus cyclical Time leading back to the origin becomes itself an exegesis, the total exegesis of mankind, the archetype of all exegesis.

This generation of Time and this redemption by Time may be viewed differently according to the diversity of our sources: Iranian sources of the Fatimid period, Iranian sources of Persian Neo-Ismailism of the Alamūt tradition, Arabian Fatimid sources, or Yemenite sources in the Fatimid tradition.[26] In any event these schemata put forward a representation of Time as an instrument, making it possible to overcome a retard, a being-passed-by. But according to the greater or lesser amplitude seen in the archangelical pleroma, the generation of Time occurs peacefully, as it were, under the pressure of a sense of ontological imperfection—or else it occurs through a catastrophe ushering in a dramaturgy analogous to that of the Mazdean cosmology.

The first schema is drawn from Iranian sources, particularly Nāṣir-e Khosraw. He describes the procession of the five primordial archangelical hypostases, the first two of which are the Intelligence (*'Aql*) and the Soul (*Nafs*).[27] This eternal motion which moves the being of the first Intelligence or Archangel is an eternal movement of adoration of the Principle, which eternally actuates it toward being. From this eternal movement of adoration, from this cosmic liturgy, the Soul of the World eternally takes its birth.[28] This Soul is a second Archangel which is like the first in that it is

25 Cf. our study "Le Livre du Glorieux de Jābir ibn Ḥayyān," *EJ 1950*.

26 It is not possible to discuss the periods of Ismailism here in detail. For an orientation cf. L. Massignon's article "Karmates" in the *Encyclopédie de l'Islam;* W. Ivanow, "Ismā'īlīya" (ibid., *Supplément*), and the introduction to his *Guide;* Strothmann, *Texte*, pp. 1–8. The sources to which I have been constrained to limit myself here are essentially: for Fatimid Ismailism, Nāṣir-e Khosraw (Persian)—cf. above, n. 16; for the post-Fatimid Yemenite (Arabic) tradition, Sayyid-nā Idrīs 'Imādaddīn, 19th Yemenite dā'ī (d. 872/1462, cf. the *Guide*, LV, p. 62); for the Persian tradition of Alamūt, the *Rawdatu't-Taslīm* (Persian) attributed to Naṣīraddīn Ṭūsī (d. 672/1274).

27 The three others being *Jadd* (= Persian *bakht*—cf. above, Part 1, p. 140, n. 65), *Fatḥ*, and *Khayāl*, identified with the Archangels Gabriel, Michael, and Seraphiel, according to Abū Ya'kūb Sejestānī, *Kitāb al-Mawāzīn* (The Book of Balances, unpublished MS), ch. 12.

28 Cf. Nāṣir-e Khosraw, *Six Chapters or Shish Fasl, also called Rawshanā' ī-Nāma*, Persian text ed. and tr. into English by W. Ivanow (The Ismaili Society, series B, VI, Leiden, 1949), p. 42 (pp. 13, 14 in the pagination of the Persian text).

perfect (*in potentia*) but unlike it in that it is imperfect (*in actu*), since its being proceeds from the principle only through the intermediary of the first Archangel. Just as this Soul *is* the adoration of the primordial Archangel, so the Cosmos *is* in turn the adoration of the Soul—with this difference, that the Soul cannot complete its work, cannot make good the margin of imperfection and incompleteness that comes to it solely from Time.[29] That is why it starts the movement of the Cosmos; it tends toward its perfection through the great souls which appear from epoch to epoch in this world, not only the Prophets but in general all the members of the esoteric Church, up to the coming of the *Qā'im*, the Resurrector.[30] Here then the cycle of Time is measured by the Soul's effort to make good its own ontological imperfection.

Another schema develops the procession of ten archangelical hypostases.[31] With one of them, the third, a crisis occurs which shakes the celestial pleroma. This is the drama in Heaven, which is the origin of the drama on Earth; the earthly persons exemplify the eternal *dramatis personae* through the periods of an indefinite succession of cycles. This is the dramaturgy that we shall consider here.

THE PERIODS AND CYCLES OF MYTHOHISTORY

1. *The drama in heaven.* We have already stressed the idea that in eternal Time the eternal divine Past *is* eternally actuated and does not fall into the past as a time which "is no longer." Thus the procession of archangelical hypostases, which are the events of this past eternally in the present, is manifested to us as the harmony of a perfect hierarchy; there is no retard, no surpassing of one by the other.[32] If such a surpassing does occur, it will bring about a rupture of this eternal Presence in the present; there will be a sort of fraction of pure ether that has become impermeable to the Light. And it is always through the idea of surpassing and obfuscation, of

29 Ibid., pp. 50, 51, 66 of the translation. Cf. the fine ch. 54 of the *Khwān al-Ikhwān* (Table of the Brothers) of Nāṣir-e Khosraw, ed. Y. al-Khachab (Khashshāb) (Cairo, 1940), pp. 137–39, on the cosmic liturgy of the universal Intelligence or primordial Archangel.

30 Ibid., p. 49.

31 Described, notably, in a voluminous work by Ḥamīd Kermānī (*Rāḥat al-'Aql*) consecrated to the correspondences between the hierarchies of the celestial and earthly universes. Cf. below, n. 96.

32 Idrīs 'Imādaddīn (cf. above, n. 26), *Zahr al-Ma'ānī* (unpublished MS), ch. 4.

regression and opacity that our Ismaili theosophists describe the catastrophe that befell one of the Angels of the pleroma of the *Ibdāʿ*.

Thus the temporal dimension expressed as retard (we have just spoken of "retarded eternity") introduces into the pure Light an alien dimension which is translated as opacity and so alters a relation that could be measured and spatialized only in the dimension of pure Light. For a being of Light this temporal dimension is a falling off from himself, and that is why it is defined as the radical Evil.[33] Here lies the source of the entire Ismaili ethic, which enjoins upon man an unremitting effort to tear himself away from this heaviness, which in every surpassed excellence (*mafḍūl*) finds a reason for striving toward a higher excellence (*afḍal*), and which thus from step to step accomplishes in the mythical hierarchy a repetition of resurrections (*qiyāmāt*) whereby the mystic rises unremittingly above himself.

But how did the rupture take place? In contemplating itself, the prime Intelligence recognizes the mystery of its being; the act of eternally-being which actuates it constitutes it eternally in being; this is the act of which it is the *significatio passiva*, the *mafʿūl*, and which in itself, as something eternally made-to-be, it is not.[34] This recognition is its eternal adoration (its *tawḥīd*), which actuates the Angel who issues from it and who is the Soul of the World; it is the cosmic liturgy which is eternally celebrated by the Archangel[35] and in which beings of every form have their source. The mystery of its being, according to the Yemenite theologian Idrīs ʿImādaddīn (fifteenth century), is like the light (here *perfectio prima*) which, in penetrating the absolutely limpid ether, makes it Light (*significatio passiva*) and thus constitutes it in its own perfection of Light (*perfectio secunda*). And that is why the prime Intelligence is at the same time the veil (*ḥijāb*) and the supreme Name (*Ism aʿẓam*) of the eternally-Being.[36]

At once act and passion, at once the Veil that conceals and the Name that names and reveals, at once adoring (in respect to the Principle that actuates it) and adored (by those to whom it reveals the Principle), the

33 Ibid.

34 Here one must bear in mind the dialectic of the *mafʿūl* mentioned above (nn. 21, 23). The prime Intelligence is the *Mobdaʿ* of the *Ibdāʿ* of the *Mobdiʿ*. Now the *Mobdaʿīya* (=*mafʿūlīya*) of the *Mobdaʿ* (= *mafʿūl*) is only the passive aspect, the *significatio passiva* of the active *Ibdāʿ* (eternal existentiation).

35 Cf. above, n. 29.

36 The prime *ʿAql* is the Angel brought closer (*malak moqarrab*), the sacrosanct (*moqaddas*) Angel, the Lotus of the Limit, etc. Cf. Idrīs, *Zahr*, chs. 6, 7; Strothmann, *Texte*, III, 4–6.

prime Intelligence is constituted in its being by a simultaneity which conditions both its transparency and the potency by virtue of which all the beings of Light, the archangelical hypostases, emanate from its being. The second of these hypostases (called Enclosure of the Sacrosanct, Paradise of the Refuge, Universal Soul [37]) stands in the same relation to the prime Intelligence as the prime Intelligence to the Principle; in it is repeated the same simultaneity of obedience and prerogative. It is the first to hear the appeal of the prime Intelligence [38] (the *da'wat*, and this is the very word which denotes the esoteric *mission* of the Ismaili Church on earth), an appeal summoning all the other Intelligences to celebrate the same liturgy as itself. This appeal has been heard by innumerable worlds (*'awālim*) of angels, forming ten great divisions, each of which is peopled with innumerable angels and has an angel-prince at its head.[39]

Yet this obedience implied an exception, a transgression against it, and this was the prologue of the cosmic dramaturgy. From the dyad of the first and second Archangel, Intelligence and Soul of the World, issues a third Archangel,[40] who is called *Adam Rūḥānī*, the spiritual Adam; this is the Angel of mankind, demiurge of our world. He appears as a hypostasis of Arabo-Persian Neoplatonism, but also shows certain traits of the Manichaean and Gnostic Anthropos. Still more precisely, his role corresponds to that of the Angel Zervān. Let us recall this Angel's doubt as set forth in Shahrastānī: "If the entire universe were nothing . . ." (Ibn Ḥazm speaks of an excess of melancholy, a prostration).[41] But what universe could have been nothing? Zervān was an Angel of the pleroma existing before the physical universe. And Ismaili Gnosis states exactly what it was that the Angel's error placed in doubt: the eternal ontological anteriority of the two Archangels who mediate between the Principle and the third Archangel.

37 *Zahr*, ch. 7. It is by his adoration mingled with an eternal rejoicing that the first Angel (*Sābiq*) gives existence to the following Angel (*Tālī*), who is then actually the first Emanation (*Inbi'āth*), since the first is not *monba'ith* but *mobda'*. The *tawḥīd* of the second Angel consists in recognizing his ontological rank in the *Ibda'*, his *maf'ūlī* (*significatio passiva*) with regard to the first Angel. Thus we have the original dyad or syzygy, the pair *Sābiq-Tālī*.

38 Ibid., ch. 8.

39 Here I cannot develop the interesting comparisons that might be drawn with the angelogical schemata of *3 Enoch*, ed. Odeberg. Cf. also G. Scholem, *Major Trends in Jewish Mysticism* (3rd edn., New York, 1954), pp. 68ff.

40 And second Emanation (*al-Inbi'āth al-thānī*). On this angel's relation to the Angel Gabriel in the philosophy of Suhrawardī, cf. our "Récit d'initiation," *EJ 1950.*

41 *Istawḥasha*. Not so much a sin of "pride" as an attack of melancholy in forsakenness and solitude.

Is he not their equal? Does he not even precede them? Is he not first and alone, originating in himself? Hence his refusal to recognize their precedence, to hear the appeal, to testify to the Oneness (*tawḥīd*).[42]

Thus the third Angel stops at himself: he remains motionless in a stupor which gives rise to a gap, a distance between himself and the world of eternal Existentiation from which he cuts himself off. There comes to be a "Time which passes" and creates a remoteness. The transgression becomes a regression: this is the rupture of the eternal Future (*abad*) which eternally actuates the eternal Past (*azal*) in the Present. When the Angel tears himself free from this stupor, he sees himself "retarded," surpassed (*ta'akhkhor, takhallof*), fallen behind himself. From third he has become tenth. To the Time of his stupor that he must redeem corresponds the emanation of the seven other Intelligences which are called the seven Cherubim or the seven Divine Words.[43] Similarly seven periods will punctuate each of the cycles of cosmic Time. Because this drama of the Angel forms the prologue in Heaven of the drama of mankind whose Angel he is, writers have been pleased to find in his deed the archetype of Adam's transgression (his paradise was the world of the *Ibdāʿ*; the tree which he was not to touch was the rank of the Archangel preceding him, who is the mediator of his being, etc.). Moreover, as we have said, the retard, as a temporal dimension, introduces an opacity in the dimension of pure Light. Here, as in the Angel Zervān, the Imagination of the Angel who goes astray manifests his Darkness, his Ahriman, his Iblis.[44]

But here precisely we perceive the difference of which we have spoken. If this Iblis-Satan is born within the angelic being as Ahriman taking birth in Zervān, a no less decisive change occurs in the Zervanite dramaturgy. Externalized as Ahriman outside of Zervān, Iblis is not invested with any legitimacy whatsoever. No ambiguity remains. He is expelled from the Angel and becomes as radically alien from him as Ahriman to Ōhrmazd. More precisely, the Angel, freeing himself from his stupor, tears Iblis out of himself, like an Archangel Michael achieving his own victory over himself.[45]

42 Cf. Idrīs, *Zahr*, ch. 9, and the text of Sayyid-nā Ḥosain ibn 'Alī, eighth Yemenite dāʿī (d. 667 A.H./A.D. 1268: Ivanow, *Guide*, XLIX, p. 60), ed. Bernard Lewis, "An Ismaili Interpretation of the Fall of Adam," *Bulletin of the School of Oriental Studies*, IX (1937–39), 702. It should also be recalled that this drama in heaven derives from our sources of Fatimid or Western Ismaili tradition (the old *daʿwat*).

43 Cf. Strothmann, *Texte*, XIII, 1.

44 Cf. Lewis, "Ismaili Interpretation"; Idrīs, *Zahr*, ch. 13.

45 Lewis, p. 703; and Idrīs, *Zahr*, ch. 9.

Iblis is hurled to earth and his form subsists as the purely Demonic. Thus the being of the third Angel is the mediator, the medium through which Darkness is born, but through which it is also vanquished.

At the same time he is the Angel-prince of an entire universe of Angels who are formed in his image (*ṣuwaruhum ʿan ṣūratihi*); they follow his destiny and he is responsible for them. He has thus immobilized them by his own stupor; it is their entire universe that is *surpassed,* that is retarded. Thus the Angel's movement of *conversion* is accompanied by the appeal (*daʿwat*) which he finally transmits to them from the prime Intelligence (appeal to the esoteric *tawḥīd*), and which is also a calling to accomplish in themselves, in their being which is in his image, this conversion and victory of their Angel. Some hear the appeal, others persist in negation and denial. The former, who show a striking resemblance to the Mazdean Fravartis, are the celestial archetypes of the earthly heralds and proclaimers of the mystical *daʿwat;* they are the posterity of the spiritual Adam. The others are the posterity of Iblis, the implacable adversaries, demons with human faces, who appear from cycle to cycle until the form of Iblis-Ahriman is extinguished.[46]

The profound metaphysical idea that this temporal distance or dimension engenders space is here applied to the generation of the Cosmos. As our Yemenite theologian points out, the retard brought upon the Angels themselves by the fault of their Archangel places them in a situation where a threefold mental movement lends their being a tridimensionality adapted to an existence in the dense and opaque world of material nature. Not only because he is compassionate and merciful,[47] but also because he himself suffers in these Angels who are his members, their Archangel (far from being the wicked Archon of certain Gnostic systems) creates for them a cosmos which is the instrument of their purification and the scene of the combat which is at once theirs and his.[48]

46 Lewis, p. 703; Idrīs, *Zahr*, chs. 9, 10; Strothmann, *Texte*, XII, 38.

47 Cf. the nature of the Archangel Michael in I Enoch 40:9, in *The Book of Enoch*, tr. R. H. Charles (Oxford, 1912), p. 73; and *3 Enoch*, ed. Odeberg, intro., p. 98, n. 1 (Metatron). Cf. above, Part 1, nn. 9, 51, 55.

48 Idrīs, *Zahr*, ch. 10. The idea that in and through their existence and his metamorphoses all his fellow Angels are the time and place of the Angel's battle—and that their existence is equally a battle *for* the Angel—belongs to a chapter of mystical experience to which we are planning to devote a comparative study. Cf. e.g. the case of Johann Georg Gichtel of the school of Jacob Boehme: ch. 5, "Vom Streit Michaels und des Drachens" in *Eine kurze Eröffnung und Anweisung der dreyen Principien*

Here we have a magnificent symbol. The repentance and nostalgia of the Angel are conceived as an energy penetrating the entire universe: the spheres, the elements, and the adepts—that is to say, the human beings of the posterity of the spiritual Adam. This energy is the leaven of the original Existentiation (*al-khamīrat al-ibdā 'īya*); it is the eternal Eve of the Angel of mankind. It is at the same time his nostalgia and his return to Paradise; it is this energy which from cycle to cycle engenders all his fellows in the angelical state, and finally engenders the *Imām* of Resurrection, the *Qā'im* or Resurrector.[49] This nostalgia then presupposes a past time, something which is relegated to the past in time. But it is also the expectation of something to come. And this something to come is precisely what the fault, the retard of the Angel, has put into the past: the paradisiacal state of pure Light. The nostalgia and expectation lead back to this past, they are a conversion *toward* it. Here, then, the phenomenon of cyclical Time is the reverse of our linear time which accumulates the past. In its passing, cyclical Time abolishes the past, changes it into the future that approaches increasingly. It does not remove us from the source, but leads us back to it; in the being whose form it is and who is *converted* back to his origin, cyclical Time presupposes that special dimension which we have called archetypal and which has its original form in the primitive universe of the Angel.

This form of cyclical Time is subject to developments. The simplest primitive schema would seem to have been a single cycle, punctuated by seven periods or millennia, each ushered in by an Enunciator prophet (*Naṭiq*) of a new Revelation, assisted by a spiritual legate (*Waṣī*) who is the foundation (*Asās*) of the Imamate and who throughout his period transmits the secret or esoteric meaning of the doctrine to the Seven Imāms who are descended from him.[50] Later, astronomical and astrological speculations made it possible to conceive of a Grand Cycle (*dawr a'ẓam*) composed of cycles each governed by a planet and divided into seven periods of seven

---

und Welten im Menschen . . . durch Johann Georg Grabern . . . Johann Georg Gichtel (new edn., Berlin and Leipzig, 1779), pp. 91–98.

49 Idrīs, *Zahr*, ch. 10; and cf. Naṣīraddīn Ṭūsī, *The "Rawdatu't Taslim," Commonly Called Taṣawwurāt*, Persian text ed. and tr. into English by W. Ivanow (The Ismaili Society Series, A, 4, Leiden and Bombay, 1950), p. 70 of the tr.

50 It has already been observed that the fundamental doctrines professed by various Islamic and Christian Gnostic sects have certain elements in common. In regard to this periodicity of Revelation cf. the Clementine Homilies quoted in W. Ivanow, *The Alleged Founder of Ismailism* (The Ismaili Society Series, A, 1, Bombay, 1946), p. 131, No. 2. Cf. also below, n. 74.

millennia, the whole to be concluded by the Grand Resurrection.[51] The resulting figures are truly "astronomical" [52] (a Grand Cycle of 360,000 years; some of the sayings of the Imāms reckon the time past at 400,000 Grand Cycles, each including 400,000 periods). Furthermore, the cycles of Time were held to reflect the drama that they exemplified: just as the aeon of Ahriman was expected to be followed by the aeon of Ōhrmazd, so cycles of Epiphany or Unveiling (*dawr al-kashf*) were conceived as alternating with cycles of Occultation (*dawr al-satr*).

But here we discern the consequences of the alteration of the Zervanite dramaturgy. Iblis-Ahriman is never invested with a legitimate sovereignty, he is the Adversary pure and simple. During the cycles of Epiphany, the form of Iblis (*al-ṣūrat al-iblīsīya*) is held prisoner in the "world of the mothers," that is to say, in the world of the simple elements.[53] And because the Angel had defeated his Iblis, the Grand Cycle began with a cycle of Epiphany and not with a cycle of Occultation and Darkness. It was ushered in by the appearance of the earthly Anthropos, the universal Adam (on the island of Ceylon) in the sixth millennium (governed by Mercury-Hermes) of the first period of the first cycle (both governed by Saturn).[54] On earth this universal Adam typifies the spiritual Adam and is the prototype of the Adam of the Bible and the Koran. The cycle of Unveiling which he inaugurates is a beatific cycle in which the true Gnosis is openly preached, in which men are exempt from bodily infirmity and ugliness of soul.[55] It endured until the approach of the first cycle of Occultation, when the form of Iblis reappeared and the drama on earth actually began.

2. *The drama on earth.* But how many cycles, each inaugurated by a "partial Adam" (*Adam jūz'ī*), alternated prior to the cycle of Occultation whose rigors we are now experiencing? The Ismaili mythohistory does not record

51 *Qiyāmat al-Qiyāmāt* (literally the Resurrection of Resurrections). On the connections with Babylonian astrology (Planets, Metals, and Ages of the World) cf. W. Bousset, "Die Himmelsreise der Seele," *Archiv für Religionswissenschaft*, III (1900), 243–44.

52 Idrīs, *Zahr*, ch. 11; *Texte*, I, 8 (p. 12 of the text); II, 1 (p. 19), IV, 20 (p. 53); Naṣīr Tūsī, *Taṣawwurāt* (above, n. 49), pp. LXXV–LXXVI, and pp. 67–68 of the translation; *Kalāmi Pīr*, ed. and tr. W. Ivanow (Bombay, 1935), p. XXXV, and p. 19 of the text.

53 Cf. Strothmann, *Texte*, I, 6; IV, 2.

54 The πανάνθρωπος as substitute for the tenth Angel (cf. *Texte*, p. 56): *Ādam al-awwal al-kollī*, cf. Idrīs, *Zahr*, ch. 12. This is the primordial Imām, repository and foundation of the Imamate, the institution which by preserving the esoteric meaning of all the Revelations gives mankind the possibility of mystical salvation.

55 Cf. Strothmann, *Texte*, I, 5.

the exact number, but only the vastness of the perspective.[56] It merely registers the veiled memory of nameless upheavals and crimes which preceded the history of present mankind. No archive records them, but their trace has been found in every epoch by the activity of the metaphysical Imagination—from the ecstatic books of Enoch down to Franz von Baader.

The postulates of the Ismaili theosophy might here be amplified in the light of a comparative research.[57] First of all they present a decisive contrast to the idea of "primitive man" accepted by our human sciences. Present mankind is regarded not as a summit of progress but as descended from a superior mankind through a catastrophe of whose mystery we can gain only a distant intimation. It does not issue from the gloom of savagery, from a void and an absence of humanity; the most ancient monuments bear witness not to a babbling, nor even to a dawn, but rather to a twilight.[58] When the speculative Imagination encounters the proposition of vulgar exoteric theology "that there was a time when the world did not exist," it is fitting, declares Naṣīraddīn Ṭūsī (Iranian theologian of the thirteenth century) to remind these theologians that they have remained on a plane of fictitious representation, that in the sense in which they take the words *time* and *world* "there never was a time when this world did not exist." [59] Or rather, this proposition is intelligible only if we have in mind the universe constituted by 18,000 worlds—that is to say, successive cycles each of which is actually one world.[60] These worlds result not from a historical causality but from a homology between cycles exemplifying the same archetypes. In short, there was a race of human beings superior to ours, who were the educators of our race; to this race belonged the Adam of the Bible and Koran. Far from having been the first man on earth, Adam was one of the last survivors of the cycle of Epiphany preceding our cycle of Occultation.[61]

The idea of this *exegesis* from one cycle to another inspires all Ismaili exegesis of the Koran. At the approach of the cycle of Occultation, the form

56 Cf. ibid., B, 1 (pp. 142–43 of the Arabic text).
57 Cf. above, n. 47.
58 Cf. Schelling, *Essais*, tr. into French by S. Jankélévitch (Paris, 1946), pp. 213–15.
59 *Taṣawwurāt*, p. 48 of the text and pp. 65 and 67 of the translation. It should be noted that we also find this figure of 18,000 worlds in *3 Enoch* 24 : 17. Cf. also Hans Bietenhard, *Die himmlische Welt im Urchristentum und Spätjudentum* (Tübingen, 1951), pp. 72–73.
60 Ibid., pp. 65, 66–67.
61 One might well amplify this cyclical conception of history in which the idea of an intercyclical homology contrasts sharply with an evolutionist conception of rectilinear "progress." One cannot help thinking of Spengler's ideas.

of Iblis is liberated and is manifested by grave symptoms which disturb the state of harmony and innocence characterizing the angelical mankind of the ending cycle.[62] These disturbances oblige the dignitaries to restore the discipline of the arcanum at the threshold of a world and a mankind which the direct vision of the celestial figures would only incite to destructive fury. But those who had been the "Angels" of the cycle of Unveiling—that is to say, those initiated into the Gnosis of Resurrection (*da'wat-e Qiyāmat*) —cannot bear the prospect of renouncing the state of freedom and innocence, of direct intuition of all truth; they cannot defer to the demands of the new esotericism. Their horror at the strictures of a religious Law gives way, however, in the course of a dialogue full of prescience and sadness. In the literal Koran text the dialogue takes place between God and his Angels; the Ismaili *ta'wīl* transposes it by one octave: here it is the last Imām of the cycle who gravely declares to his earthly angels: "I know what you do not know" (Koran 2 : 28). One of them, the young Adam, is invested as Proclaimer (*Nāṭiq*) of the new religious Law.[63] Now begins a drama which must be understood as an imitation and exemplification of the drama in Heaven. It consists of two episodes: the revolt of Iblis and the vengeance of Iblis, having as corollary what may be called "the error of the hierophant."

At the beginning of the new cycle the form of Iblis was incarnated in one of the dignitaries named Ḥārith ibn Murra, one of those whose office it had been to initiate the earthly angels of the cycle of Unveiling in the Gnosis of Resurrection. His refusal to recognize the new religious Law is implacable: is he to begin the arduous pilgrimage of the degrees of initiation all over again? Was he not created of fire, whereas the young Adam, restricted to the science of symbols, is made only of clay? Why then should he and the other earthly angels bow down before Adam? [64] When the Angel tears his Iblis from within him and hurls it to earth, all the ambiguity that is still possible in Zervanism has ceased: Ḥārith incarnates an Iblis-Ahriman in the pure state, the No without the Yes, the contrary power of the Adversary.[65]

The temptation to which Iblis incarnated as Ḥārith ibn Murra subjects

62 Cf. Idrīs, *Zahr*, ch. 12, and Nāṣir Ṭūsī, *Taṣawwurāt*, ch. 16, p. 49 of the text. Here the versions of the two great Ismaili traditions are in agreement.

63 Cf. Koran 2:35. On the father of Adam, on Ḥonaid, his Imām *mostawda'* and their Ismaili descendants, cf. Strothmann, *Texte*, X, 26.

64 "They all bowed down except for Iblis, who was one of the genii" (Koran 18 : 48). Cf. the order to worship Adam in "Vita Adae et Evae," quoted in Wilhelm Lueken, *Michael* (Göttingen, 1898), p. 29.

65 Cf. *Taṣawwurāt*, pp. 68–69.

Adam, and through which he takes his vengeance, consists in persuading Adam that since the perfect science of Resurrection was revealed by the last Imām (Qā'im) of the preceding cycle to which they both belonged, and since the blissful men of that cycle owed their state of innocence and freedom to this gnosis, the men of the new cycle should not be deprived of it.[66] In his inexperience, the young Adam lets himself be convinced and commits the supreme "error of the hierophant": he reveals the secret to men who are unfit to receive it, betrays the symbols to the unworthy. And now the drama which befell the Angel of Mankind in heaven finds its earthly exemplification,[67] and here it is shared by two persons. Now Iblis represents only the Angel's *past*, which the Angel by his victory has cut off from himself and which Time, from cycle to cycle, carries toward its annulment. And Adam, having approached the forbidden tree—that is to say, the Gnosis of Resurrection (the divulging of which was reserved for the last Imām)—"escaped through the wide-open door of Mercy." Like the Angel readmitted to the pleroma, Adam by his repentance returns with his posterity to the "paradise *in potentia*" [68]—that is, the *da'wat*, the esoteric Ismaili Church on earth. Its members are the "Angels *in potentia*," like the incarnated Fravartis of Mazdaism, carrying on the battle against the demons with human faces, who are the posterity of Iblis-Ahriman.

And just as the repentance of the Angel, the spiritual Adam, was the eternal Eve, his nostalgia and return to Paradise, so, Naṣīr Ṭūsī declares, Eve, wife of the earthly Adam, is the spiritual and secret meaning of the positive religion (its *bāṭin*), for she had knowledge of the esoteric laws and hidden meanings (the *ta'wīl*).[69] Thus it is through the mystery of Adam-Eve—two beings in one, the text of the religious law *and* the esoteric exegesis

66 Cf. our "Rituel sabéen," pp. 204ff.

67 Cf. Idrīs, *Zahr*, ch. 13; the article of Lewis in *Bulletin of the School of Oriental Studies* (n. 42 above), pp. 702–3; *Taṣawwurāt*, p. 70. The texts of the Yemenite tradition relate Adam's error and repentance to those of the Angel; the prohibitions enjoined upon Adam are compared to the situation of the third Angel; the tree he was not to approach was the ontological rank of the *Tālī*, the second Angel who *follows* the first but who stands in the relation of *Sābiq* (of him who *precedes*) to the third, etc.

68 And on these ideas of "paradise *in potentia*" and "Angels *in potentia*" rest the entire Ismaili anthropology and ethic (cf. *Zahr*, ch. 12; *Jāmi' al-Ḥikmatain*, ch. 13; *Taṣawwurāt*, pp. 59–60, 93–94). Cf. below and our "Rituel sabéen," pp. 199–200, 243–44.

69 *Taṣawwurāt*, p. 70. Cf. the *Jāmi' al-Ḥikmatain* of Nāṣir-e Khosraw (ch. 19, § 226, p. 209): the *waṣī*, the repository of the esoteric sense of the symbols, is regarded as the spiritual mother of the adept, while the Prophet, proclaimer of the letter, is his father.

that transcends it, the Prophet *and* the Imām, the Proclaimer (*Nāṭiq*) *and* the Silent One (*Ṣāmit*)—that the fruit of the positive religion, and the final Resurrection (*qiyāmat*), can spring forth. It is worth noting that Ismaili esotericism here configures its supreme symbol as the conjunction of the masculine and the feminine, which was also the great symbol of Hermeticism. The consummation of this mystery will mark the completion of the Grand Cycle, when the last Imām will proclaim and accomplish the Grand Resurrection. All the adepts, distributed through all the ranks of the esoteric hierarchy, compose the mystical Body, the Temple of Light of this Imām-Resurrector.[70] It is the horizon of Resurrection which for each adept gives its meaning to the Time of combat; here too "the history of the universe is that of the kingdom of the Spirits." [71]

RESURRECTION AS THE HORIZON OF THE TIME OF "COMBAT FOR THE ANGEL"

It is evident that this conception of the Imām as lord of Resurrection, summit of the eternal Imāmate in which culminates the Ismaili vision of the aeon, is far above the political ideology of a final successor who will be a legitimate descendant of the Alids.[72] This political ideology was effaced by the Gnostic idea of the Imām as Anthropos or as the Perfect Child (*al-walad al-tāmm*) who engenders himself in the secret of the cycles of the aeon, and who, in his eschatological Epiphany, is expected to be the ultimate "exegete" of mankind, a member of the true posterity of Adam,[73]

70 Cf. Strothmann, *Texte,* I, 1; VI, 3; XIII, 2; *Taṣawwurāt,* pp. 149–54; *Jāmi' al-Ḥikmatain,* ch. 9, § 117, p. 121.

71 Schelling, *Essais,* p. 215.

72 With the transformation of the concept of the Imām, Persian Ismailism becomes eminently a religion of personal salvation, taken as a religion of Resurrection. Cf. the interesting remarks of W. Ivanow on the aspect of docetic Christology assumed by the doctrine of the Imām as divine epiphany, *Taṣawwurāt,* p. LXXVIII (cf. also below, n. 100). Here a vast field of inquiry opens. Unfortunately what one might call the "secret of Alamūt" still eludes us—that is to say, we do not know the reasons why August 8, 1164, was chosen as the date for the Grand Resurrection, for the advent of the Religion of Absolute Truth; cf. ibid., pp. LXXVI and LXXX, LXXVII, and LXXIX, and *Kalāmi Pīr,* p. XXXV. And perhaps there is a hopeless paradox, if not a *desperatio fiducialis,* in proclaiming the divulging of the esoteric meaning: in so becoming exoteric, will it not in turn necessitate a new *ta'wīl?* The danger of this *regressio ad infinitum* seems to have been discerned by the commentator on Avicenna's mystical tale entitled "Ḥayy ibn Yaqẓān" (cf. the translation following our study, *Avicenne et le Récit visionnaire* (Teheran and Paris, 1954).

73 This posterity, it should be recalled, does not include *all* human beings (for mankind also embraces the posterity of Iblis), but only those "whose Angel" by associating him-

which he will lead back (*ta'wīl*) to the celestial archetype in which it originated. Just as the universal primordial Adam is the first earthly manifestation of the spiritual Adam or Angel of mankind, exemplified in the partial Adam of each cycle, so the Imām Resurrector, blossom of the eternal Imāmate, will be its final *parousia*, as the ultimate primordial, earthly substitute for the Angel to whom he leads back. Among the spiritual Adam, the primordial earthly Adam, and the Resurrector (*Qā'im*), there is the same relation as among Gayōmart, Zarathustra, and the Saoshyant to come, who will be *Zarathustra redivivus.* Similarly each of the Imām's manifestations, the Imām of each period, is only the manifestation of a unique and eternal[74] Imām who, in the person of the last among them, will consummate the totality of the Aeon or Grand Cycle.

By projecting itself on the horizon of the Imām Resurrector, the expectation now commands a process of resurrection which shakes the entire esoteric sodality by a movement that is communicated from degree to degree: each adept must "resuscitate" (or "suscitate") an adept like himself—that is, by rising from degree to degree cause another at every step to rise to his own former rank.[75] The mystical Body, the Temple of Light (*Haykal al-nūr*) of the Imāmate is thus constituted by the totality of adepts; *each one* reflects it in himself, just as the pupil of the eye can contain the highest mountain.[76] And precisely this comparison gives us an idea of the experience of eternity that is offered the adept: to reflect the whole of the Temple of the Imāmate is to become in his own person an exemplification of the aeon; it is for each adept to attain to his own eternal person—that is to say, to angelicity *in actu;* it is, by a series of resurrections (*qiyāmāt*), to induce in himself the flowering of the Grand Resurrection (corresponding to the final Transfiguration, which in Mazdean Pehlevi is called *Frashokart*, *Restakhīz*).

This ethic of resurrection, to which we have already referred (as an ethic of struggle against a retard, against a being-surpassed), shows us each adept supporting the responsibility of the whole Temple of the Imāmate. By

---

self with the repentance of the third Angel at the time of the drama in Heaven, connects them archetypally with his battle against the posterity of Iblis.

74 *Taṣawwurāt*, p. LXXVI and p. 138; Strothmann, *Texte*, II, 5; cf. above, n. 50. Here one might compare the sequences: Gayōmart, Zarathustra, Saoshyant (= *Zarathustra redivivus*). Spiritual Adam (the third Angel), earthly Adam (universal and partial), the Imām *Qa'im* (the "Perfect Child," herald, or "Angel" of Resurrection). Nuriel, Enoch, Metatron. Cf. also below, n. 101 and above, Part 1, p. 140, n. 63.

75 Cf. Strothmann, *Texte*, I, 1; VIII, 3; XIII, 2.

76 Ibid., I, 1.

virtue of this responsibility the adept does not merely live *in* a fragment of measurable and measured Time. He is himself the total Time of his own measure, and that is why the entire combat constituting the essence of cyclical Time is carried on in the cycle of his own life. Since this Time is a retard, the gap between the fall and the reconquest of angelic rank is the Time of the combat for the Angel.[77] This expression (which results from our situation and reverses the famous image of the "combat *with* the Angel") is to be understood in a twofold sense. It is a combat *for* the person of the Angel of mankind (the third Angel who has become tenth), for the Angel does not carry on alone the combat which is to lead to the final reabsorption of Iblis-Ahriman, whose form reappears throughout the cycles of Occultation. But, since they have assumed his repentance and his nostalgia, his fellows, made in his image, become responsible in their own person for the combat that they wage *for him*. It is their own Iblis that they must hurl into the abyss, and in so doing they battle for the Angel who is in them *in potentia*. To reflect in oneself the Temple of the eternal Imāmate is to anticipate the consummation of the aeon; it is here "to become aeon," to produce in oneself the mutation of cyclical or measured Time, and for each adept this consists in assuming in his person an increasing exemplification of the Angel's being. This implies that what occurs in and by the person of each adept also affects the being of the Angel who is their archetype and who finds his exemplification in them.

Thus we are confronted with situations which reflect one another. The experience of Time lived as a totality here presents a character similar to that which we analyzed at the end of Part 1; here speculative foundation and spiritual experience meet. The Figures shine through one another and exemplify one another. The tenth Angel shines through the person of the

77 Unfortunately I cannot here discuss at any length the highly original aspect which the idea of this combat of and for the Angel assumes in the *Taṣawwurāt* (*jihād-e rūḥāni, ʿaqlāni, ḥaqīqī*), where it is related to the triple auto-intellection by which, according to the schema of Avicenna, each *ʿAql* or Angel, by understanding his own being, confers existence on three things: another Angel, a Heaven, and the Soul which is the mover of this Heaven. Ch. 14 (on good and evil) opens with a brief recollection of Zoroastrian dualism, which is rejected, it goes without saying, but reintroduced a few pages further on, where the primordial Inscience (*Jahl-e awwal*) is opposed to the primordial Intelligence (*ʿAql-e awwal*), and "a substance exhausting itself in nothingness" is opposed to a "true substance" these being the source respectively of evil and good creatures. The Ismaili *daʿwat* "separates" the antitheses (cf. the Mazdean *vičarishn*). It acts upon the primordial Intelligence and the true substance like the elixir of alchemy; upon their opposites it has no effect.

primordial Adam, through that of each partial Adam, and finally through the person of the Imām Resurrector; and similarly the Imām Resurrector is already manifested and announced in the person of every Imām of every period. One and the same archetypal Figure, the eternal Imām recurs in multiple exemplifications, just as all the adepts have their celestial archetype in the Angels who followed the tenth Angel in his repentance. This exemplification gives them their archetypal dimension and constitutes them as the cast of characters in a cyclical drama whose prologue was played in Heaven and whose antagonists meet again in every period, in every generation.[78]

The special and characteristic nature of the situation is shown in this process of *exemplification*, which constitutes the individual person and raises him to the dimension of an archetypal Person. Essentially, the perception of all reality becomes the perception, or visualization, of a concrete person. This situation creates the schema of a fundamental angelology, which is essentially the mode of self-understanding of an existence which undergoes what we may now call an *angelomorphosis*—that is to say, the passage from "angelicity *in potentia*" to "angelicity *in actu*," which is the positive culmination of the Ismaili anthropology.[79] On the other hand, this exemplification which personifies all reality in a concrete person presupposes both coincidence *and* distance, identity *and* difference, and for this reason the totality must also be present in the "every instance." This recurrence is the foundation of the *homology* between the total cycle of the aeon and the cycle of resurrections which in the life of the adept constitutes his ascension from one esoteric degree to another. In the Ismaili theosophy the idea of an exemplification of archetypal persons and the idea of a homology between the cycles define the religion of Resurrection (*da'wat-e qiyāmāt*) as an angelomorphosis.

1. *Archetypal Persons.* How is exemplification possible? It is to Naṣīraddīn Ṭūsī that we owe the elements of a brief and profound analysis. It seems to postulate that the aspect of action which we state in the infinitive, or the aspect of the event which we denote by an abstract noun, are by no means the true aspect of their reality, and that in the last analysis they refer back to the person of the *agent* who enacts the action or the event as the true reality of both. For all mental or ideal reality, every concept (*ma'nā*) in the

78 Cf. our study, "Le Livre du Glorieux," pp. 61–65.
79 Cf. "Rituel sabéen."

world of the universal has its counterpart in the world of the individual: a concrete person (*shakhṣ-e'aynī*) outside of which this ideal or mental reality remains virtuality and pure abstraction.[80] Everything takes place as though the question "Who is it?" were substituted for the question "What is it?"—as though to name the *person* were to define its *essence;* and it is to this person and not to the abstract, universal concept that the *ta'wīl* or internal exegesis leads back.[81] We gain this impression by juxtaposing propositions such as these: "Paradise is a *person* (or a human being)."[82] "Every thought, every word, every action *is* a person."[83] And finally: "Every true thought, every true word, every good action *has* an Angel."[84]

Around these propositions Naṣīr Ṭūsī develops an analysis which may well be called phenomenological. To be in Paradise, or to come into this world, designates above all different modes of being and understanding.[85] It means either to exist in true Reality (*ḥaqīqat*), or, on the contrary, to "come into this world"—that is to say, to pass into the plane of an existence which in relation to that other is merely a metaphoric existence (*majāz*). Measured time, too, is only a metaphor for absolute Time. Thus coming into this world has meaning only with a view to leading that which is metaphoric back to true being, and the external (exoteric, *ẓāhir*) back to the internal (esoteric, *bāṭin*), by means of an exegesis (*ta'wīl*) which is also an exodus from existence. Here, then, we have a mode of understanding (*modus intelligendi*) in which a mode of being (*modus essendi*) is expressed. Even while one is materially present in this world, there is a mode of being in Paradise;[86] but it goes without saying that this *mode of being*, Paradise, can be realized, can exist "in the true sense," only in a person who precisely

80 *Taṣawwurāt*, p. 62 (p. 46 of the Persian text). 81 Cf. "Rituel sabéen," p. 230.

82 *Taṣawwurāt*, pp. 39–60; and "Rituel sabéen," pp. 241–42.

83 *Taṣawwurāt*, p. 60. 84 Ibid.

85 Ibid., p. 91 (p. 63 of the text). This whole passage is of the greatest importance.

86 Such is the meaning of the "person of the (= that which is the) *sirāṭ mostaqīm*" (which corresponds eschatologically to the Činvat Bridge of Mazdaism); cf. *Taṣawwurāt*, pp. 62–63 (45–46 of the text). "The man whose head is raised toward the heavenly periphery (*moḥiṭ*), even while his feet are in the earthly center. Although in relation to the Angel he has not yet arrived at the World of absolute freedom, compared to the animal, he has already attained to it." The person who exemplifies this archetype of the "strait way" is the person who lives in the world beyond as though this beyond were already his present existence, and who carries all the aspects of this present existence back to something unique. This is the internal metamorphosis, the state of discerning lucidity accomplished by the secret of the *ta'wīl* (*bāṭin-e ta'wīl*), and such precisely is the Angel's (*fereshta*) mode of existence in contrast to that of the jinni (*perī*) or demon (*dīv*). Cf. ibid., pp. 64 (47 of the text), 81–82 (57–58 of the text).

is this Paradise—that is to say, who always personifies this mode of being. It is clear that because personification corresponds to an archetype, it is here the exact opposite of allegory.

Fundamentally we may say that since the reality of the act, of the event, is thus reduced to the person who enacts it and understood as that person's mode of existence, every *verb* is mentally conjugated in the middle voice (e.g., the ἀποφαινεῖσθαι of the phenomenology which shows *itself* the *phainomenon*). Or else we find a circuit of thought similar to that which in the Archangel's eternally actuated being (*azalī*) seizes upon the very act of eternally being (*azal*), which by eternally actuating his being (*azalīyat*) becomes personified in the Archangel.[87] Here action, thought, or word have their term in the agent: they are reflected and personified in him, by making him to be what they are. They are his modes of being; they are in "every instance" *this* person. In this light, the person in whom his own action is incarnated is the *significatio passiva* of his action—that is to say, he is what his action *makes him be*.

But that implies that this person is an *agent* only in a superficial and metaphoric sense. More active than the person himself is the thought that is thought through him, the word that is spoken by him (and personified in him). And this thought of his thought is precisely what Naṣīr Ṭūsī calls the Angel of this thought (or of this word or action).[88] This Angel endows the soul with the aptitude for thinking it and rising by it; he is the Archetype, the finality without which a cause would never be a cause. He is the "destiny" of that soul. The subjective case becomes an instrumental. The act of thinking is simultaneously a being-thought (*cogitor*) by the Angel,[89]

87 This is the "hermeneutic circuit" (cf. above, Part 2, sec. 1), the phenomenological rotation of which presents the action as a *fi'l* whose *maf'ūl* refers *to* the agent—that is to say, is done and concluded *in* and *for* the agent. The *intention* of the "middle voice" leads one to consider in the *maf'ūl* of every action the modification of the agent's mode of being, his event. It leads one to discover the transcendent subject, which is here the angel. The problem of the *intellectus agens* and the *intellectus patiens* in Arabo-Persian Neoplatonism might be considered in this connection. We shall return to it elsewhere.

88 *Taṣawwurāt*, p. 60 (p. 44 of the text, last par.): "Every true thought, every truthful word, every good action has a spiritual (*rūḥānīya*) entity—that is to say, the Angel (*fereshta*) who endows the soul, in its progressive rise, with the ability to pass easily through the successive degrees of perfection and return to its original source. Then this soul becomes a magnificent Angel (*fereshta-ye karīm*), and the Angels of its thought, speech, and action become integral parts of it, setting their imprint upon it."

89 In thinking this thought the person who thinks it is thought by the Angel, or on the contrary by a demon, for the alternative can only be the person "without an Angel." Cf. ibid.

causing the soul to be what he himself is. The ethic is posited not in terms of values but in terms of the Angel's modes of being. The propositions stated above (every thought *is* a person . . . every true thought *has* an Angel) describe a hermeneutic circle which fuses the schema of *angelology* with the process of *angelomorphosis*, and it is in this fusion that the possibility of exemplification resides.

The soul performs its action and understands it only beginning with the act which actuates the soul itself. It can become a magnificent Angel (*fereshta-ye karīm*) or an accursed demon,[90] deciding its eschatology through the very thing that it exemplifies. For its action is then its own form, which it sends out in advance of itself as its herald, and which is in the image of the Angel—or of the demon—who comes to meet it after death, announcing: "I am thyself." The burgeoning and growth in the soul of the angelical or demoniacal virtuality is the measure of its ascent (*mi'rāj*), or of its fall into the abyss. In the first case, as our author says: "Its thought becomes an Angel issuing from the original world; its word becomes a *spirit* issuing from that Angel; its action becomes a *body* issuing from this spirit." [91]

2. *The homology of the cycles of Resurrection* (*Qiyāmāt*). At the end of this ascension, the adept has completed the Time of his "combat for the Angel." The increasing exemplification of the angelical form which is potentially in the soul leads the soul back to its origin. It is the elimination of its own Iblis: as such, the individual existence of the adept forms a cycle homologous to the Grand Cycle by which the tenth Angel progressively annuls the form of Iblis which he tore out of himself at the time of the "drama in heaven." These are two aspects of one and the same combat, the combat which the heavenly Angel and the virtual or earthly Angels carry on together. Between the two there prevails the same homology as between all the degrees of being through which—by virtue of the Great Return, the *ta'wīl* that is the

90 To be made the "person of the Angel," or the "person of Salmān," to become the "Salmān of the microcosm," etc. Cf. our "Rituel sabéen," pp. 242ff., and "Le Livre du Glorieux," § 6.

91 *Taṣawwurāt*, p. 102 (70 of the text). Moreover, his "homogeneity with divine Reality implies that his *anima* (*nafs*) is conjoined with the light of the religion of the True Absolute (*da'wat-e ḥaqq*) and that through the energy of the Angel (*ruḥānīya*) of this religion, an Angel (*fereshta*) is appointed to guard over his thought, in which he preserves forever the ornament of the divine truth." Ibid. And man's angelomorphosis is correlative to an anthropomorphosis of the celestial universe, since the glorified human form is its form of light and that of all the other beings of Light. Cf. also Strothmann, *Texte*, I, 1; *Jāmi' al-Ḥikmatain*, last paragraph of ch. 11; Idrīs, *Zahr*, ch. 12 and above, n. 86.

cycle of combat for the Angel—the past is abolished and metamorphosed into the future of Resurrection (*Qiyāmāt*).

In a stirring vision Naṣīr Ṭūsī describes the contiguity of all the series of being, each communicating by its highest degree with the lowest degree of the series immediately above it. Thus the worlds of minerals, plants, and animals, the world of man, and the world of the Angel are graduated. And always the higher degree resembles Paradise for the degree below it. The same is true of the phases of a single being. The condition in which an infant cannot yet open his eyes in the sunlight is like his Hell in relation to the condition in which he can face the light, and the latter condition is then like his Paradise. But it is his Hell in relation to the condition in which he can walk and talk. Hell, again, is the condition in which the adult cannot yet attain to knowledge of the spiritual world through that of his own spirit and in which he is unable to experience the meaning of the adage: "He who knows himself (*nafsahu*, his *anima*), knows his Lord." When he attains to it, this state becomes his Paradise.[92] In this vision of an incessant rising from Hells, we see an *alchemy of Resurrection* operating from cycle to cycle. It offers a series of unfoldings, of divestments and revestments, to which one must consent on pain of falling backward, beneath oneself.

Here we may also speak of a "continual exaltation"[93] a cosmology "in Gothic style," or of a pursuit of "retarded eternity." Just as their Fravartis sustain the gods themselves (including Ōhrmazd and his Archangels) in this state of ascension, and just as the Fravartis incarnated on earth must there propagate this effort toward superexistence, so likewise, in the Ismaili schematization of the world,[94] the sum of the degrees of the esoteric hierarchy appears to the adept as a cycle of *resurrections*, each one of which must be transcended, as a succession of Paradises which must be surmounted on pain of falling back into a Hell. Each rank or spiritual degree is a resurrection (*qiyāmāt*) whereby the adept becomes conjoined with new immaterial forms which appear on his horizon.[95]

And just as each of the periods of our cycle is concluded by an Imām-

92 *Taṣawwurāt*, pp. 58–59 (43 of the text, bottom).

93 Cf. above, Part 1, end of sec. 2. Schelling, *The Ages of the World*, tr. Bolman, p. 149. Rudolf Otto, *Mysticism East and West*, tr. B. L. Bracey and R. C. Payne (New York, 1932), pp 184ff.

94 One should also remember the constantly affirmed homology among the mesocosmos (*'ālam-e Dīn*, the initiatic cosmos), the world of nature, and the celestial world.

95 Cf. Strothmann, *Texte*, IX, 5; Idāḥ 11 and Ism 2–3; Idrīs, *Zahr*, quoted in Ivanow, *The Rise of the Fatimids* (Bombay, 1942), p. 243 (54–55 of the Arabic text).

Qā'im, so likewise each of the adepts occupying an esoteric rank is a Qā'im, a Resurrector, in respect to the adept of the next lower rank: by a simultaneity of *action* and of *passion* he must "resuscitate" the following (*tālī*) adept to the rank which he himself had hitherto occupied, while he himself must "be resuscitated" to the next higher rank. The movement of perpetual elevation is propagated from the summit to the base of the mystical hierarchy. Finally, just as the seven periods of a cycle are closed by a Grand Resurrection (*Qiyāmat-e-Qiyāmāt*), instituted by the Qā'im par excellence, the "Perfect Child" who leads back (*ta'wīl*) to the Angel all those in the cycle who have belonged to his posterity—that is, who have borne his image and fought his battle—so, likewise, at the end of the cycle of his individual life, at the seventh degree of his ascension, the adept finds himself on the threshold of the perfect angelicity (*fereshtagī*) of the tenth Intelligence.[96] This is the dawn of his Grand Resurrection. Thus his own initiate's life reproduces the whole cycle or aeon whose totality the Imām Resurrector will complete in his person when limited time *reverts* to absolute Time. By this homology the adept also anticipates his eternity.

In the end the vision embraces all the universes and draws the physical universe of material bodies toward Resurrection.[97] When the highest degree of potency which consolidates the mineral universe is conjoined with the first degree of vegetal potency, the resurrection of mineral nature occurs. In a similar way, plants and animals are resurrected in the next higher order. And finally the angelical potency is the Resurrection of the human potency carried to its highest perfection. Just as the vital soul is like a *body* in relation to the imaginative soul; so the latter in turn is like a body in relation to the thinking human soul; and the latter, finally, is like a body in relation to the angel (the angelic Intelligence, *'aql*). When each of these souls is existentiated in the form immediately above it, this is the corporal resurrection (*ḥashr-e jasadānī*).[98]

96 The decade is completed by three superior esoteric ranks corresponding respectively to the third Angel, to the *Tālī*, and to the *Sābiq* (*Nafs* and *'Aql*, second and first Angels), the primordial pair from which issued the third Angel (become tenth after his error) and the Seven Cherubim Angels, or Words, of the pleroma of the *Ibdā'*. Cf. Ḥamīd Kermānī, above, n. 31.

97 Cf. *Taṣawwurāt*, pp. 93–94 (64–65 of the Persian text).

98 The text of the *Taṣawwurāt* recalls one of the doctrines which Shahrastānī attributes to Empedocles (*Kitāb al-milal*, lith., Teheran, 1288 A.H., p. 165, li. 11), though here *jasad*, body, is replaced by *qishr*, shell, rind, also garment. On this point P. Duhem pointed to the kinship in language and conception between this doctrine and that of the *Zohar;* cf. *Le Système du monde . . . de Platon à Copernic* (Paris, 1917), Vol. V, pp. 121–22.

At the end of our study we perceive a common typology in the horizons of Resurrection set forth in the Mazdean and Ismaili visions. In neither vision is Resurrection an event that simply occurs one fine day. In Ismailism it is accomplished in the person of all those who are "resuscitated" up to its triumphant unfolding in the person of the last Imām, the *parousia* of the tenth Angel. It is the work of each one of the adepts; its time is brought about by the involution of the time of each individual. Similarly in Mazdaism the Fravartis incarnated on earth to fight the combat of Ōhrmazd begin in their own person and action the event of the final Transfiguration. This is the sentiment expressed in the often repeated Zoroastrian prayer: "May we be those who bring about the Transfiguration of the world."[99]

In both doctrines we find a chivalrous ethic inspired by the feeling that evil and suffering are not inflicted by a divine being who consents to them while remaining aloof from them. This suffering is in the divine being himself since it is in his creatures; and by rejecting and combating it, all his followers make a rampart of their souls for him.[100] In both cases, the great moments of the cosmic drama are announced and "dated" in the homologous periods of the cycles by the apparition of figures which are conceived

---

Naṣīr Ṭūsī speaks of a kind of perpetual alchemy, a formation and unfolding of the spiritual Body. Here we can only mention in passing the fine texts in which Schelling speaks of the "general ability of matter to be raised again to spiritual properties" (*Ages of the World*, p. 173). "Thus man does not pass into the world of spirits with only his spirit in the restricted sense of the word, but also with that which in his body was himself, with what was spiritual in this body" (*Essais*, tr., pp. 357–58). *Reductio ad essentiam:* it is the task of soul to guide its corporeal senses to their perfection. Thus the soul resuscitates through the body, just as the body resuscitates through the soul. In the end, as Naṣīr Ṭūsī says, the spiritual and the corporeal will be one, and it is precisely because of this that "the Angel can become visible after death" (below, n. 102).

99 Yasna, XXX, 9.

100 The Persian word *Javānmard*, which recurs frequently in Shiite Sufism, is best translated by "spiritual knight." It corresponds to the piety and passionate devotion which the idea of the Imām, of the eternal Imām, inspires in the Friend of God exposed on earth to the implacable contradiction of men. Between the two branches of Ismailism, and even more so between them and Duodeciman Shiism, there are, to be sure, nuances and changes which profoundly modify the spiritual physiognomy. A proto-Ismailian treatise such as the *Omm al-Kitāb* (The Mother of the Book) abounds in precise Manichaean reminiscences and features borrowed from the apocryphal books of the Bible. On the other hand, as we have pointed out above (n. 72), the concept and the figure of the Imān led to a recurrence of the problems encountered in Christology. Indeed, all the positions from Arianism to the theology of St. Athanasius recur in speculative Imāmology. Cf. R. Strothmann, *Die Zwölfer-Schī'a* (Leipzig, 1926), pp. 79ff., 155ff.

as the recurrence of one and the same eternal Figure.[101] Finally, in both Mazdaism and Ismailism we have the same denouement of the individual eschatology: the face-to-face encounter between the human I and the celestial I, because the soul finally sees its "self." The episode of the feminine angel Daēnā in Mazdaism has its exact counterpart in Naṣīraddīn Ṭūsī's angel of the amiable and beautiful form, who becomes the companion of the soul for all the eternities.[102] It is the vision of the I knowing itself and finding itself in a transcendent I (a *paredros*), which is both the same and different, as in one same essence without confusion of persons, since a dialogue at once confirms the authenticity of the vision. But this celestial dimension of the Soul of the Perfect One is confirmed and visualized only after the cycle of his resurrections has been completed (after Time has ceased to "retard" over against Eternity); in both doctrines it completes the cycle of the Return, the combat "for the angel."

To the triple question of the little Mazdean catechism cited at the beginning of this study corresponds a situation which, as I have said, Naṣīr Ṭūsī analyzes with the sure hand of the phenomenologist. Here is its conclusion: "To come into this world" and into the time of this world, should not be confused with corporeal presence in the world of existence: it is above all a mode of understanding this existence. To come into this world, as we said a moment ago, can have no significance other than to convert its metaphoric reality (*majāz*) into its True Reality (*ḥaqīqat*).[103] Our author makes it clear that there can be beings who, although they have in appearance come into this world, since they are *there*, have in fact never come into it.[104] Inversely—and here the analysis becomes most striking—there are men whom we can visually discern to have left this world. They are dead, they are no longer there. We say: "They have departed." No,

101 Cf. *Taṣawwurāt*, p. 138 (94 of the text). G. Messina, *I Magi a Betlemme* (Rome, 1934), pp. 59ff.; it is curious to note that the term *al-monba'ith al-thālith* (= the Qā'im, *Texte*, IV, 3) is a literal parallel to the Tertius Legatus of the Manichaean soteriology. Cf. n. 74, above.

102 *Taṣawwurāt*, p. 94 (65 of the text). Cf. n. 98 above and nn. 76–80 of Part 1. Cf. also the motif of the celestial *houris* in Naṣīr Ṭūsī, *Āghāz o Anjām* (lith., Teheran, 1320 A.H.), p. 24. There are abundant exemplifications of the archetype; cf. the motif of the robe in *Acta Thomae*, etc.

103 *Taṣawwurāt*, pp. 91–92 (63 of the text). It is to accomplish (and undergo) the metamorphosis of the *ta'wīl;* cf. above, n. 86, and Nāṣir-e Khosraw, *Jāmi' al-Ḥikmatain*, ch. 14, pp. 163, 166 (to be on the Earth of Tomorrow, which it is said will be illumined by the Light of its Lord, whereas today this Earth still holds us shrouded in Night).

104 *Taṣawwurāt*, p. 91.

actually they have never left this world and they will never leave it. For to leave this world it does not suffice to die. One can die and remain in it for ever. One must be living to leave it. Or rather, to be living is just this.[105] Can we distinguish in the winter, as Nāṣir-e Khosraw says, between a living tree and a dead tree? Both, it is true, are materially there. But in one the sap flows secretly. In the other the sap does not flow, because its roots are dead. When the spring comes—that is, the Imām of Resurrection—only the first will be covered with flowers and savorous fruits at his call.[106] It is no indulgence in a mere literary reminiscence if the image of the Iranian philosopher suggests this thought of Balzac: "Resurrection is accomplished by the wind of heaven that sweeps the worlds. The Angel carried by the wind does not say: Arise ye dead! He says: Let the living arise!"[107]

105 Ibid., p. 92 (63 of the text, end).
106 In *Six Chapters*, ed. Ivanow, pp. 85–86 of the translation.
107 In *Louis Lambert* (Paris, 1902), p. 151.

Mircea Eliade

Time and Eternity in Indian Thought

THE FUNCTION OF THE MYTHS

Indian myths are *myths* before they are *Indian*—that is to say, they belong to a particular category of archaic man's spiritual creations; consequently, they can be compared to any other groups of traditional myths. Before presenting the Indian mythology of time, we might say a word about the close connection between myth, as an original form of culture, and time. For aside from its specific functions in archaic society, which need not concern us here, myth is significant for the light it throws on the structure of time. As most modern thinkers agree, myth relates events which took place *in principio*, at the beginnings, in a primordial, atemporal moment, a *sacred time*. This mythical or sacred time is qualitatively different from profane time, from the continuous and irreversible time of our everyday, desacralized existence. In narrating a myth, we reactualize, as it were, the sacred time in which occurred the events of which we are speaking. (And that is why, in traditional societies, myths cannot be related at any time or in any manner one chooses: one can recount them only during holy seasons, in the woods at night, or around the fire before or after the rituals, etc.) In a word, myth is supposed to take place in an intemporal time, if we may be pardoned the term, in a moment without duration, as certain mystics and philosophers conceive of eternity.

This observation is important, for it follows that the narration of myths has profound consequences both for him who narrates and for them who listen. By the simple fact of a myth's narration, profane time is—symbolically at least—abolished: narrator and audience are projected into a sacred, mythical time. We have elsewhere attempted to show that the abolition of profane time by the imitation of exemplary models and the reactualization of mythical events constitutes a specific mark of all traditional societies, and that this in itself suffices to distinguish the archaic world from our modern societies.[1] In the traditional societies men endeavored consciously and voluntarily to abolish time at periodic intervals, to efface the past and to regenerate time by a series of rituals which in a sense reactualize the cosmogony. Here we need not go into details which would take us too far from our subject. It may suffice to recall that a myth tears man away from his own time, from his individual, chronological, "historical" time—and projects him, symbolically at least, into the Great Time, into a paradoxical moment that cannot be measured because it has no duration. Which amounts to saying that myth implies a breach in time and the surrounding world; it opens up a passage to the sacred Great Time.

Merely by listening to a myth, man forgets his profane condition, his "historical situation," as it is nowadays called. A man need not necessarily belong to a historical civilization to justify us in saying that he is in a "historical situation." The Australian who feeds on insects and roots is also in a "historical situation"—that is to say, in a situation that is delimited, expressed in a certain ideology, and sustained by a certain type of social and economic organization; specifically, the existence of the Australian very probably represents a variant of the historical situation of paleolithic man. For "historical situation" does not necessarily imply "history" in the major sense of the term: it implies only the human condition as such—that is to say, a condition governed by a certain set of attitudes. And in listening to a myth an Australian, as well as an individual belonging to a far more highly developed civilization—a Chinese, for example, or a Hindu or a European peasant—forgets, as it were, his particular situation and is projected into another world, into a universe which is no longer his poor little every-day universe.

It must be recalled that for all these individuals, for the Australian as well as the Chinese, the Hindu, and the European peasant, myths are *true*, because they are *sacred*—they speak of sacred beings and events. Consequently, in narrating or listening to a myth, one resumes contact with the sacred and with reality and in so doing transcends the profane condition, the historical situation. In other words, one transcends the temporal and the obtuse self-sufficiency which is the lot of all men because all men are "ignorant"—that is, because they identify the real with their own particular

1 Cf. Eliade, *The Myth of the Eternal Return*, tr. W. R. Trask (New York and London, 1954), pp. 51ff.

situation. For ignorance is primarily that false identification of the real with what each one among us seems to be or seems to possess. A politician believes that the sole and true reality is political power, a millionaire is convinced that wealth alone is real, a scholar has the same belief with regard to his studies, his books, his laboratories, and so on. The same tendency is also found among the less civilized, among primitive peoples and savages, but with this difference: here myths are still alive to prevent them from identifying themselves fully and continuously with nonreality. The periodic recitation of myths breaks through the walls erected by the illusions of profane existence. Myth continuously reactualizes the Great Time and in so doing transfers its audience to a superhuman and suprahistorical plane, which, among other things, enables it to approach a reality that is inaccessible on the plane of individual, profane existence.

INDIAN MYTHS OF TIME

This capital function of "breaking through" individual, historical time and of actualizing the mythical Great Time is strikingly illustrated by certain Indian myths. We shall give a famous example, drawn from the *Brahmavaivarta Purāṇa*, which the late Heinrich Zimmer summed up and commented upon in his book *Myths and Symbols in Indian Art and Civilization.*[2] This text has the particular advantage of starting right in with Great Time as an instrument of knowledge and hence of deliverance from the bonds of Māyā.

After his victory over the dragon Vṛtra, Indra decides to rebuild and embellish the residence of the gods. Viśvakarman, the divine architect, labors for a year and succeeds in constructing a magnificent palace. But Indra is not satisfied: he wishes to make it still larger and more splendid, without its equal in the world. Exhausted with his effort, Viśvakarman complains to Brahmā, the Creator God. Brahmā promises to help him and intervenes with Viṣṇu, the Supreme Being, of whom Brahmā himself is only a simple instrument. Viṣṇu undertakes to bring Indra back to his senses.

One fine day Indra in his palace receives the visit of a ragged boy. It is Viṣṇu himself, who has assumed this aspect to humiliate the King of the Gods. Without immediately revealing his identity, he calls Indra "my child,"

2 Ed. Joseph Campbell (New York and London, 1946), pp. 3ff.

and speaks to him of the innumerable Indras who have inhabited innumerable universes up to this time.

> The life and kingship of an Indra endure seventy-one eons [a cycle, a *mahāyuga*, consists of 12,000 divine years or 4,320,000 years!], and when twenty-eight Indras have expired, one day and night of Brahmā have elapsed. But the existence of one Brahmā, measured in such Brahmā days and nights, is only one hundred and eight years. Brahmā follows Brahmā; one sinks, the next arises; the endless series cannot be told. There is no end to the number of those Brahmās—to say nothing of Indras.
>
> But the universes side by side at any given moment, each harboring a Brahmā and an Indra: who will estimate the number of these? Beyond the farthest vision, crowding outer space, the universes come and go, an innumerable host. Like delicate boats they float on the fathomless, pure waters that form the body of Viṣṇu. Out of every hair-pore of that body a universe bubbles and breaks. Will you presume to count them? Will you number the gods in all those worlds—the worlds present and the worlds past?

As the boy speaks, a procession of ants has made its appearance in the great hall of the palace. Drawn up in a column four yards wide, they parade across the floor. The boy perceives them, pauses, and then, seized with amazement, breaks out in a sudden laugh. "Why do you laugh?" Indra asks him.

And the boy replies: "I saw the ants, O Indra, filing in long parade. Each was once an Indra. Like you, each by virtue of pious deeds once ascended to the rank of a king of gods. But now, through many rebirths, each has become again an ant. This army is an army of former Indras . . . "

This revelation brings home to Indra the vanity of his pride and ambitions. He recalls the admirable architect Viśvakarman, rewards him royally, and abandons forever his project of enlarging the palace of the gods.

The intention of this myth is transparent. The dizzy evocation of the innumerable universes rising and vanishing from the body of Viṣṇu suffices to awaken Indra; it compels him to transcend the limited and strictly contingent horizon of his situation as King of the Gods, we might even be tempted to add, of his *historical* situation, for Indra happens to be the Great Warrior Chieftain of the gods in a certain historical moment, at a certain stage of the grandiose cosmic drama. And from Viṣṇu's very mouth Indra hears a *true story:* the true story of the eternal creation and destruction of the worlds, beside which his own history, his own innumerable heroic adventures culminating in his victory over Vṛtra, seem indeed to be "false," that is, events without transcendent significance. The *true story* reveals to him Great Time, mythical time, which is the true source of all cosmic beings and events. It is because he is enabled to transcend his historically conditioned situation and to rend the illusory veil created by profane time—that is to say, by his own "history"—that Indra is cured of his pride and ignorance; in Christian terms, he is "saved." And this redeeming function of myth operates not only for Indra but also for every human being who hears the story of his adventure. To transcend profane time, to recover the mythical Great Time, is equivalent to a revelation of ultimate reality. And this is a strictly metaphysical reality, accessible only through myths and symbols.

This myth has a sequel, to which we shall return. For the moment it need only be remarked that the conception of a cyclical, infinite Time, presented so strikingly by Viṣṇu, is the pan-Indian conception of cosmic cycles. The belief in the periodic creation and destruction of the universe is already as early as the *Atharva-Veda* (X, 8, 39–40). And as a matter of fact it belongs to the *Weltanschauung* of all archaic societies.

THE DOCTRINE OF THE YUGAS

India developed a doctrine of cosmic cycles which expands the periodic creations and destructions of the universe into staggering proportions. The smallest unit of measurement is the *yuga*, or "age." Each yuga is preceded by a "dawn" and followed by a "dusk," which constitute the transition between them. A complete cycle, or *mahāyuga*, consists of four "ages" of unequal length, the longest occurring at the beginning of the cycle and the shortest at its end. The names of these yugas are borrowed from the names for the "throws" in the game of dice. Kṛta Yuga (from the verb *kṛ*, "to make, accomplish") means the "perfect age," from four, the winning throw in the game of dice. For in the Indian tradition, the number four symbolizes totality, plenitude, and perfection. The Kṛta Yuga is also called Satya Yuga—that is, the "real," true, authentic age. From every point of view, it is the golden age, the beatific epoch of justice, happiness, prosperity. During the Kṛta Yuga the moral order of the universe, the Dharma, is respected in its entirety. Moreover, it is observed by all men spontaneously and without constraint, for during the Kṛta Yuga, the Dharma is in a sense identified with human existence. The perfect man of the Kṛta Yuga incarnates the cosmic and consequently the moral norm. His existence is exemplary, archetypal. In other, non-Indian traditions, this golden age is equivalent to the primordial, paradisiacal epoch.

The following age, the Tretā Yuga, the triad, so named from the three-pointed die, marks a regression. Now men observe only three-quarters of the Dharma. Labor, suffering, and death are now the human lot. Duty is no longer spontaneous, but must be learned. The modes of life pertaining to the four castes begin to be vitiated. With the Dvāpara Yuga (the "age" characterized by "two") only half of the Dharma subsists on earth. The vices and evil increase, human life becomes still shorter. In the Kali Yuga, the "evil age," only one quarter of the Dharma remains. The term *kali* signifies the die marked by a single point, consequently the losing throw (personified moreover by an evil genius); *kali* also signifies dispute, discord, and in general the worst of a group of men or objects. In the Kali Yuga man and society attain the supreme point of disintegration. According to the *Viṣṇu Purāṇa* (IV, 24) the syndrome of the Kali Yuga is recognized by the fact that during this epoch property alone confers social rank, wealth becomes the sole criterion of virtue, passion and lewdness the sole bonds between mates, falsehood the sole condition of success in life, sexuality the sole means of enjoyment, and an outward, purely ritualistic religion is confounded with spirituality. For several thousand years, it goes without saying, we have been living in the Kali Yuga.

The figures 4, 3, 2, and 1 denote both the decreasing length of the yugas and the progressive diminution of the Dharma prevailing in them. Correspondingly the span of human life grows shorter, morality becomes increasingly lax, and human intelligence declines. Certain Hindu schools, the Pāñcarātra for example, establish a connection between the "decline of knowledge" (*jñāna bhraṃśa*) and the theory of cycles.

The relative duration of each of these four yugas may be reckoned in various ways: everything depends on the value accorded to the years, which may be considered as human years or as divine years, each of which embraces 360 human years. According to certain sources,[3] the Kṛta Yuga measures 4,000 years plus 400 years each of dawn and of dusk; then follow the Tretā Yuga, measuring 3,000 years, the Dvāpara, measuring 2,000 years, and the Kali Yuga, of 1,000 (plus the corresponding dawns and dusks, of course). A complete cycle, a mahāyuga, consequently comprises 12,000 years. The

3 *Manu*, I, 69ff.; *Mahābhārata*, III, 12, 826.

passage from one yuga to another occurs in the course of a dusk, marking a decrescendo within each yuga, which always ends with a stage of darkness. As we approach the end of the cycle—that is, the fourth and last yuga—the darkness thickens. The last yuga, in which we now find ourselves, is regarded as the "age of darkness" par excellence, for by a play on words it is associated with the goddess Kālī, the "Black." Kālī is one of the numerous names of the Great Goddess, of Śakti, consort of the god Śiva. This name for the Great Goddess has been related to the Sanskrit word *kāla*, "time": Kālī according to this etymology is not only "the Black One" but also the personification of Time.[4] But regardless of the etymology, the association of *kāla*, Time, with the goddess Kālī and Kali Yuga is structurally justified: Time is black because it is irrational, hard, pitiless; and Kālī, like all the other Great Goddesses, is the mistress of Time, of the destinies she forges and accomplishes.

A complete cycle, a mahāyuga, ends in a "dissolution," a *pralaya*, which is repeated more radically (*mahāpralaya*, the "Great Dissolution") at the end of the thousandth cycle. For later speculation has amplified the primordial rhythm of "creation-destruction-creation" *ad infinitum*, projecting the unity of measure, the yuga, into vaster and vaster cycles. The 12,000 years of a mahāyuga have been considered as "divine years," each comprising 360 years; this would yield a total of 4,320,000 years for a single cosmic cycle. A thousand such mahāyugas constitute a *kalpa* ("form"); 14 kalpas make up a *manvantāra* (so called because each manvantāra is held to be governed by a Manu, or mythical ancestor-king). One kalpa is equivalent to a day in the life of Brahmā; another kalpa to a night. A hundred of these "years" of Brahmā, or 311,000 billion human years, constitute the life of the god. But even this considerable life-span of Brahmā does not exhaust Time, for the gods themselves are not eternal and the cosmic creations and destructions go on forever.

The essential element in this avalanche of figures is the cyclical character of cosmic Time. The same phenomenon (creation-destruction-new creation), foreshadowed in each yuga (dawn and dusk) but fully realized in a mahāyuga, is repeated over and over. The life of Brahmā comprises 2,560,000 of these mahāyugas, each one consisting of the same stages (Kṛta, Tretā, Dvāpara, Kali), and ending in a *pralaya*, a *ragnarök*. (A "definitive" de-

4 Cf. J. Przyluski, "From the Great Goddess to Kāla," *Indian Historical Quarterly* (Calcutta), XIV (1938), 267–74.

struction, or total dissolution of the cosmic Egg occurs in the *mahāpralaya* at the end of each kalpa. The mahāpralaya implies a regression of all the "forms," the modes of existences, into the original undifferentiated *prakṛti*. On the mythical plane nothing subsists but the primordial Ocean, on the surface of which sleeps the Great God Viṣṇu.)

The ideas that stand out from this orgy of figures are: (1) a metaphysical depreciation of *human history*, which by the mere fact of its duration provokes an erosion of all *forms*, exhausting their ontological substance;[5] (2) the notion of the *perfection of beginnings*, a universal tradition which is here exemplified in the myth of a paradise which is gradually lost by the simple fact that it is realized, takes form, and exists in time; and above all (3) the eternal repetition of the fundamental *cosmic rhythm*, the periodic destruction and re-creation of the universe. From this cycle without beginning and end, which is the cosmic manifestation of *māyā*, man can save himself only by an act of spiritual freedom (for all Indian soteriological solutions reduce themselves to a previous deliverance from the cosmic illusion, and to spiritual freedom).

The two great heterodoxies, Buddhism and Jainism, accept this same pan-Indian doctrine of cyclical time in its broad outlines and liken it to a wheel with twelve spokes (this image occurs also in the Vedic texts).[6] Buddhism measures the cosmic cycles by the unit of the *kalpa* (Pāli: *kappa*), which is divided into a variable number of what the texts call "incalculables," *asaṃkhyeya* (Pāli: *asaṇkheyya*). The Pāli sources in general speak of 4 asaṇkheyyas and 100,000 kappas.[7] In the Mahāyānic literature the number of incalculables varies between 3, 7, and 33, and they are related to the career of the Bodhisattva in the diverse cosmoses. The progressive decadence of man is marked in the Buddhist tradition by a continuous diminution in his life span. Thus, according to the *Dīgha-Nikāya* (II, 2–7), the length of man's life was 80,000 years at the epoch of the first Buddha, Vipassi, who appeared 91 kappas ago; it was 70,000 years at the epoch of the second Buddha, Sikhi (31 kappas ago), and so on. The seventh Buddha, Gautama, makes his appearance when the human life span amounts to only 100 years, the absolute minimum. (We find the same motif in the Iranian apocalypses.) Yet for Buddhism as for all Indian speculation, time is un-

5 On all this see *The Myth of the Eternal Return*, pp. 130ff. and passim.
6 Cf., for example, *Atharva-Veda*, X, 8, 4; *Ṛg-Veda*, I, 164, 115.
7 Cf., for example, *Jātaka*, I, p. 2.

limited; and the Bodhisattva is incarnated in order to announce the glad tidings of salvation to all men, for ever and ever. The sole possibility of escaping from time, of breaking through the iron ring of existences, is to abolish the human condition and attain to Nirvāṇa. All these innumerable "incalculables" and eons also have a soteriological function: the mere contemplation of them terrorizes man and compels him to realize that he must begin this same evanescent existence over and over again, billions of times, always enduring the same endless sufferings. And the effect of this is to exacerbate his will to escape, to impel him to transcend his condition as an "existent" once and for all.

COSMIC TIME AND HISTORY

Let us for a moment consider this vision of infinite Time, of the endless cycle of creation and destruction, this myth of the eternal return, as an instrument of knowledge and means of liberation. In the perspective of Great Time, all existence is precarious, evanescent, illusory. Considered in the light of the major cosmic rhythms—that is, of the mahāyugas, kalpas, manvantāras—not only do human existence and history, with all their empires, dynasties, revolutions, and counterrevolutions without number, prove to be ephemeral and in a sense unreal, but the universe itself is bereft of reality, for as we have seen, universes are born continuously from the innumerable pores of Viṣṇu and vanish as rapidly as air bubbles bursting on the surface of the waters. Existence *in* Time is ontologically nonexistence, unreality. It is in this sense that we must understand the belief of Indian idealism, and first and foremost of the Vedānta, that the world is illusory, that it lacks reality because its duration is limited, for, seen in the perspective of eternal recurrence, it is nonduration. This table is unreal not because it does not exist in the strict sense of the term, not because it is an illusion of our senses, for it is not an illusion: at this precise moment it exists—rather, this table is illusory because it will no longer exist in ten thousand or one hundred thousand years. The historical world, the societies and civilizations arduously built by the effort of thousands of generations, all this is illusory because, from the standpoint of the cosmic rhythms, the historical world endures for only the space of an instant. In drawing the logical conclusions from the lesson of infinite Time and the Eternal Return, the Vedāntist, the Buddhist, the Ṛṣi, the Yogi, the Sādhu, etc. renounce the world and seek absolute Reality; for only knowledge of the Absolute helps them to deliver themselves from illusion, to rend the veil of Māyā.

But renunciation of the world is not the only consequence which an Indian is justified in drawing from the discovery of infinite, cyclical Time. As we begin to understand today, India has not only known negation and total rejection of the world. Starting from this same dogma of the fundamental unreality of the cosmos, Indian thought also mapped out a road that does not necessarily lead to asceticism and abandonment of the world. An example is the *phalatṛṣṇavairāgya* preached by Kṛṣṇa in the *Bhagavad-Gītā*, which is to say, "renunciation of the fruits of one's actions," of the profits one might derive from action, but not of action itself.[8] The sequel to the myth of Viṣṇu and Indra recounted above throws light on this principle.

Humiliated by Viṣṇu's revelation, Indra renounces his vocation as warrior god and withdraws to the mountains to practice the harshest asceticism. In other words, he prepares to draw what seems to him the only logical consequence of his discovery of the world's unreality and vanity. He finds himself in the same situation as Prince Siddhartha immediately after abandoning his palace and his wives at Kapilavastu and undertaking his arduous mortifications. But it may be asked whether a king of the gods and a husband had the right to draw such conclusions from a metaphysical revelation, whether his renunciation and asceticism did not imperil the balance of the world. And indeed, his wife, Queen Śacī, desolate at having been forsaken, soon implores the help of their spiritual guide, Bṛhaspati. Bṛhaspati takes her by the hand and leads her to Indra. He speaks to Indra at length, lauding the merits not only of the contemplative life, but also of the active life, the life which finds its fulfillment in this world. Thus Indra receives a second revelation: he now understands that each individual must follow his own path and vocation, or, in the last analysis, do his duty. But since his vocation and duty are to remain Indra, he resumes his identity and pursues his heroic adventures, but without pride and self-conceit, for he has perceived the vanity of all "situations," even that of a king of the gods.

This sequel to the myth restores the balance: the essential is not to renounce one's historical situation, seeking vainly to attain to universal being, but to keep constantly in mind the perspectives of the Great Time, while continuing to fulfill one's duty in historical time. This is precisely the

8 Cf, for example, *Bhagavad-Gītā*, IV, 20; see Eliade, *Techniques du Yoga* (Paris, 1948), pp. 141ff.

lesson which Kṛṣṇa teaches Arjuna in the *Bhagavad-Gītā*. In India, as elsewhere in the archaic world, this access to Great Time gained by the periodic recitation of myths makes possible the indefinite prolongation of a fixed *order* which is at once metaphysical, ethical, and social. This order does not encourage an idolization of history; for the perspective of mythical Time makes any segment of historical time illusory.

As we have just seen, the myth of cyclical Time, by shattering the illusions spun by the minor rhythms of time—that is, by historical time—reveals to us the precariousness and ontological unreality of the universe, and also points a way of deliverance. Actually, we may save ourselves from the trammels of Māyā, either by the contemplative way, by renouncing the world and practicing asceticism and related mystical techniques—or by an active way, by remaining in the world, but ceasing to enjoy the "fruits of our actions" (*phalatṛṣṇavairāgya*). In both cases, the essential is not to believe *exclusively* in the reality of the forms that arise and unfold in time: we must never forget that such forms are "true" only on their own plane of reference, and are ontologically devoid of substance. As we have said, time can become an instrument of knowledge, in the sense that we need only project a thing or an individual upon the plane of cosmic Time in order to become aware of its unreality. The gnoseological and soteriological function of such a change of perspective obtained through access to the major rhythms of time is admirably elucidated by certain myths relating to Viṣṇu's Māyā.

Let us examine one of these myths in the modern, popular variant recorded by Śri Ramakrishna.[9] A famous ascetic named Nārada has gained the favor of Viṣṇu by his innumerable austerities. The god appears to him and promises to grant a wish. "Show me the magical power of thy *māyā*," Nārada asks of him. Viṣṇu consents and beckons the ascetic to follow him. A little later, they find themselves on a deserted path in the blazing sun. Viṣṇu is thirsty and asks Nārada to go on for another few hundred yards, where a village may be seen, and to bring him back some water. Nārada hastens to the village and knocks at the door of the first house. A beautiful girl opens the door. The ascetic gazes upon her at length and forgets why he has come. He enters the house and the girl's parents receive him with the respect due to a saint. Time passes. At length Nārada marries the girl and learns to know the joys of marriage and the hardships

9 *The Sayings of Sri Ramakrishna* (Madras edn., 1938), IV, 22. Cf. another version of this myth according to the *Matsya Purāṇa*, related by Zimmer, *Myths and Symbols*, pp. 27ff.

of a peasant's life. Twelve years pass: now Nārada has three children and at the death of his father-in-law, he has inherited the farm. But in the course of the twelfth year the region is flooded by torrential rains. In one night the herds are drowned and the house collapses. Supporting his wife with one hand, holding his two children with the other, and carrying the smallest child on his shoulder, he struggles through the water. But the burden is too much for him. The smallest child slips into the water. Nārada leaves the other two and tries to recover him, but it is too late, the torrent has swept him away. While he is looking for the little one, the torrent swallows up the two other children and not long after, his wife. Nārada himself falls, and the torrent carries him along unconscious and inert as a piece of wood. When he awakens, he has been cast up on a rock. Remembering his sorrows, he bursts out sobbing. But suddenly he hears a familiar voice: "My child! Where is the water you were to bring? I have been waiting for more than half an hour!" Nārada turns his head and looks. In place of the torrent that had destroyed everything, he sees the deserted sun-baked fields. "And now do you understand the secret of my Māyā?" the God asks him.

Obviously Nārada cannot claim to understand it entirely; but he has learned one essential thing: he knows now that Viṣṇu's cosmic Māyā is manifested through time.

THE "TERROR OF TIME"

The myth of cyclical Time—of the cosmic cycles that repeat themselves *ad infinitum*—is not an innovation of Indian speculation. As we have elsewhere shown,[10] the traditional societies—whose representations of time are so difficult to grasp precisely because they are expressed in symbols and rituals whose profound meaning sometimes remains inaccessible to us—the traditional societies conceive of man's temporal existence not only as an infinite repetition of certain archetypes and exemplary gestures but also as an *eternal renewal*. In symbols and rituals, the world is recreated periodically. The cosmogony is repeated at least once a year—and the cosmogonic myth serves also as a model for a great number of actions: marriage, for example, or healing.

What is the meaning of all these myths and rites? Their central meaning is that the world is born, grows weary, perishes, and is born anew in a precipitate rhythm. Chaos and the cosmogonic act that puts an end to chaos by a

10 Cf. *The Myth of the Eternal Return*, passim.

new creation are periodically reactualized. The year—or what is understood by this term—corresponds to the creation, duration, and destruction of a world, a cosmos. It is highly probable that this conception of the periodic creation and destruction of the world, although reinforced by the spectacle of the periodic death and resurrection of vegetation, is not a creation of agricultural societies. It is found in the myths of pre-agricultural societies and is in all likelihood a lunar conception. For the most evident periodicity is that of the moon, and it was terms relating to the moon which first served to express the measurement of time. The lunar rhythms always mark a "creation" (the new moon) followed by a "growth" (the full moon), and a diminution and "death" (the three moonless nights). It is most probably the image of this eternal birth and death of the moon that helped to crystallize early man's intuitions concerning the periodicity of life and death, and subsequently gave rise to the myth of the periodic creation and destruction of the world. The most ancient myths of the deluge reveal a lunar structure and origin. After each deluge a mythical ancestor gives birth to a new mankind. And most frequently this mythical ancestor takes the form of a lunar animal. (In ethnology, this name is applied to those animals whose life reveals a certain alternation and particularly a periodic appearance and disappearance.)

Thus for "primitive" man, Time is cyclic, the world is periodically created and destroyed, and the lunar symbolism of "birth-death-rebirth" is manifested in a great number of myths and rites. It was on the basis of such an immemorial heritage that the pan-Indian doctrine of the ages of the world and of the cosmic cycles developed. Of course, the archetypal image of the eternal birth, death, and resurrection of the moon was appreciably modified by Indian thought. As for the astronomical aspect of the yugas, it was probably influenced by the cosmological and astrological speculations of the Babylonians. But these possible historical influences of Mesopotamia on India need not concern us here. What we wish to bring out at this point is that with their headlong multiplication of cosmic cycles, the Indians had in mind a soteriological aim. Terrified by the endless births and rebirths of universes, accompanied by an equal number of human births and rebirths governed by the law of karma, the Indian was obliged, as it were, to seek an issue from this cosmic wheel and from these infinite transmigrations. The mystical doctrines and techniques aimed at the deliverance of man from the pain of the infernal cycle of "life-death-rebirth" take over the mythical images of the cosmic cycles, amplify them, and utilize them for purposes of proselytism. For the Indians of the post-Vedic period—that is, for those Indians who had discovered the "suffering of existence"—the eternal return is equivalent to the infinite cycle of transmigration governed by karma. This illusory, ephemeral world, the world of *saṃsāra,* the world of suffering and ignorance, is the world that unfolds in time. Deliverance from this world and attainment of salvation are tantamount to a deliverance from cosmic Time.

INDIAN SYMBOLISM OF THE ABOLITION OF TIME

In Sanskrit the term *kāla* is employed both for indefinite periods of time and for definite moments—as in the European languages. For example: "What *time* is it *now?*" The most ancient texts stress the temporal character of all possible universes and existences: "Time has engendered everything that has been and will be."[11] In the Upaniṣads, Brahman, the Universal Spirit, the Absolute Being, is conceived both as transcending time and as the source and foundation of everything that is manifested in time: "Lord of what has been and will be, he is both today and tomorrow." [12] And Kṛṣṇa, manifesting himself to Arjuna as a cosmic God, declares: "I am the Time which, in progressing, destroys the world."[13]

As we know, the Upaniṣads distinguish two aspects of Brahman, of universal being: "the corporeal and the incorporeal, the mortal and the immortal, the fixed (*sthita*) and the mobile, etc."[14] Which amounts to saying that both the universe in its manifest and nonmanifest aspects and the spirit in its conditioned and nonconditioned modalities repose in the One, in the Brahman which unites all opposites and all oppositions. And the *Maitri Upaniṣad* (VII, 11, 8), in establishing this bipolarity of universal being on the plane of time, distinguishes two forms (*dve rupe*) of Brahman (that is, the aspects of the "two natures" of a single essence [*tad ekam*]), as "Time and Without-Time" (*kālaś-cākalaś-ca*). In other words, Time and eternity are the two aspects of the same principle: in Brahman, the *nunc fluens* and the *nunc stans* (a term by which Boethius defined eternity) coincide. The *Maitri Upaniṣad* continues: "What precedes the Sun is Without-Time (*akāla*) and undivided (*akala*); but what begins with the Sun is Time which has parts (*sakala*) and its form is the Year . . ."

11 *Atharva-Veda,* XIX, 54, 3.

12 *Kena Upaniṣad,* IV, 13.

13 *Bhagavad-Gītā,* XI, 32.

14 *Bṛhadāraṇyaka Upaniṣad,* II, 3, 1.

The expression "What precedes the Sun" may be interpreted cosmologically as relating to the epoch which preceded the Creation—for in the intervals between the mahāyugas or kalpas, during the Great Cosmic Nights, time no longer exists—but its application is above all metaphysical and soteriological: it refers to the paradoxical situation of him who obtains illumination, who becomes a *jīvan-mukta*, who is "delivered in this life," and thereby transcends time in the sense that he no longer participates in it. Thus the *Chāndogya Upaniṣad* (III, 11) declares that for the sage, the illumined one, the sun remains motionless. "But after having risen to the zenith it (the Sun) will never rise or set again. It will remain alone in the Center (*ekala eva madhye sthātā*). Whence this verse: 'There (in the transcendent world of *brahman*) it has never set and never risen . . .' It neither rises nor sets; for him who knows the doctrine of *brahman* it is in the heavens once and for all (*sakṛt*)."

Here, of course, we have a concrete image of transcendence: at the zenith, that is, at the summit of the celestial vault, at the "center of the world"—where a cutting-across the planes, a communication between the three cosmic zones, is possible—the sun (= time) remains immobile for "him who knows"; the *nunc fluens* is paradoxically transformed into a *nunc stans*. Illumination, understanding, accomplishes the miracle of an escape from time. In the Vedic texts and Upaniṣads the paradoxical instant of illumination is likened to the lightning flash. Brahman is understood suddenly, like a lightning flash.[15] "In a lightning flash the truth."[16] (In both Greek metaphysics and Christian mysticism we find the same image used to denote spiritual illumination.)

Let us pause for a moment to consider this mythical image: the zenith which is at once the summit of the world and the "center" par excellence, the infinitesimal point through which passes the cosmic axis (*Axis Mundi*). In our last year's lecture we showed the importance of this symbolism for archaic thought.[17] A "center" represents an ideal point belonging not to profane, geometric space, but to sacred space, a point in which communication with heaven or hell may be realized; in other words, a center is the paradoxical place that cuts across the planes; it is a place where the sensuous world may be transcended. But by transcending the Universe, the created

15 *Kena Upaniṣad*, IV, 4, 5. 16 *Kauṣitaki Upaniṣad*, IV, 2.

17 Cf. Eliade, "Psychologie et histoire des religions: à propos du symbolisme du 'centre,'" *EJ 1950*, pp. 247–82.

world, one also transcends time and achieves stasis, the eternal intemporal present.

The relation between the acts of transcending space and of transcending the temporal flux is elucidated by a myth relating to the nativity of the Buddha. The *Majjhima-Nikāya* (III, p. 123) relates that "as soon as he was born, the Bodhisattva set his feet flat on the ground and turning toward the north, took seven steps, sheltered by a white parasol. He contemplated all the regions round about him and said with the voice of a bull: 'I am the highest in the world, I am the best in the world, I am the oldest in the world; this is my last birth; for me there will never again be a new existence.'" This mythical picture of the Buddha's birth is carried over with certain variations into the subsequent literature of the *Nikāya-Āgamas*, the *Vinaya*, and the biographies of the Buddha.[18] The *sapta padāni*, seven steps which carry the Buddha to the summit of the world, also play a part in Buddhist art and iconography. The symbolism of these seven steps is quite transparent.[19] The phrase "I am the highest in the world" (*aggo'ham asmi lokassa*) signifies the spatial transcendence of the Buddha. For he attained to the "summit of the world" (*lokkagge*) by traversing the seven cosmic stories, which, as we know, correspond to the seven planetary heavens. But in so doing he likewise transcends Time, for in the Indian cosmology, the creation begins at the summit, which is therefore the "oldest" point. That is why the Buddha cries out: "I am the oldest in the world" (*jettho'ham asmi lokassa*). For in attaining to the cosmic summit, the Buddha becomes contemporaneous with the beginning of the world. He has magically abolished time and creation, and finds himself in the atemporal instant preceding the cosmogony. The irreversibility of cosmic time, a terrible law for all those who live in illusion, no longer counts for the Buddha. For him time is reversible, and can even be anticipated: for he knows not only the past but also the future. In addition to abolishing time, the Buddha can pass through it backward (*patiloman*, Skr. *pratiloman*, "against the fur"), and this will be equally true for the Buddhist monks and the yogis who, before obtaining their Nirvāṇa or their *samādhi*, effect a "return backward," which enables them to know their previous existences.

18 In a long note to his translation of the *Mahāprajñāpāramitaśastra* of Nāgārjuna, Etienne Lamotte has collected and arranged the most important of these; cf. *Le Traité de la grande vertu de sagesse de Nāgārjuna*, Book I (Louvain, 1944). pp. 6ff.

19 Cf. Eliade, "Les Sept Pas du Bouddha," in *Pro Regno, pro Sanctuario, Hommage Van der Leeuw* (Nijkerk, 1950), pp. 169–75.

THE "BROKEN EGG"

Side by side with this image of the Buddha transcending space and time by cutting across the seven cosmic planes to the "center" of the world and simultaneously returning to the atemporal moment which precedes the creation of the world, we have another image which felicitously combines the symbolisms of space and time. In a remarkable article, Paul Mus calls attention to this text from the *Suttavibhaṅga:*[20]

> When a hen has laid eggs, says the Buddha, eight or ten or twelve of them, and she has sat upon them and kept them warm for a sufficient time; and when the first chick breaks through the shell with his toe or beak and issues happily from the egg, what shall we call this chick, the oldest or the youngest?—We shall call him the oldest, venerable Gautama, for he is the firstborn among them.—So likewise, O Brāhman, I alone among the men who live in ignorance and are as though enclosed and imprisoned in an egg have burst this shell of ignorance, and I alone in all the world have obtained the beatific universal dignity of the Buddha. Thus, O Brāhman, I am the oldest, the noblest among men.

As Paul Mus says, this imagery is "deceptively simple. To understand it correctly, we must remember that the Brāhmanic initiation was regarded as a second birth. The most common name for the initiates was *dvija:* 'twice-born.' But the birds, snakes, etc. were also given this name, inasmuch as they were born of eggs. The laying of the egg was likened to the 'first birth'—that is, the natural birth of man. The hatching out corresponded to the supernatural birth of initiation. Moreover, the Brāhmanic codes establish the principle that the initiate is socially superior, 'older' than the uninitiated, whatever may be their relations of physical age or kinship."[21]

But this is not all. "It was scarcely possible to liken the supernatural birth of the Buddha to the breaking of the egg containing in germ the 'first-born' (*jyeshta*) of the universe without reminding the listeners of the 'cosmic egg' of Brāhmanic traditions, whence at the dawn of time there issued the primordial God of creation, variously named the Golden Embryo (Hiraṇyagarbha), the Father or Master of Creatures (Prajāpati), Agni (God of the

20 *Suttavibhaṅga, Pārājika* I, 1, 4; cf. H. Oldenberg, *The Buddha*, tr. Wm. Hoey (London, 1928), p. 325; Paul Mus, *La Notion du temps reversible dans la mythologie bouddhique* (Extrait de l'Annuaire de l'École Pratique des Hautes Études, section des sciences religieuses, 1938–39; Melun, 1939), p. 13.

21 Mus, pp. 13–14.

fire, and ritual Fire), or *brahman* (sacrificial principle, 'prayer,' deified text of the hymns, etc.)."[22] And the "cosmic egg" was "definitely identified with the year, the symbolic expression for cosmic Time: so that *saṃsāra*, another image of cyclical Time reduced to its causes, corresponds exactly to the mythical egg."[23]

Thus the action of transcending time is formulated in a symbolism that is both cosmological and spatial. To break the envelope of the egg is equivalent in the Buddha's parable to breaking through *saṃsāra*, the wheel of existences—in other words, to *transcending both cosmic Space and cyclical Time*. In this case, too, the Buddha makes use of images similar to those of the Vedas and Upaniṣads. The motionless sun at the zenith in the *Chāndogya Upaniṣad* is a spatial symbol which expresses the paradoxical act of escape from the cosmos with the same force as the Buddhist image of the broken egg. In describing certain aspects of Tantric Yoga, we shall encounter further archetypal images of this sort, employed to symbolize transcendence.

THE PHILOSOPHY OF TIME IN BUDDHISM

The symbolism of the seven steps of Buddha and of the cosmic egg implies the *reversibility of time*, and we shall have occasion to say more of this paradoxical process. But first we must present the broad outlines of the philosophy of time elaborated by Buddhism and particularly Mahāyāna Buddhism.[24] For the Buddhist, too, time consists of a continuous flux (*saṃtāna*), and this fluidity of time suffices to make every "form" that is manifested in time not only perishable but also ontologically unreal. The philosophers of the Mahāyāna have written copiously on what might be called the instantaneity of time—that is, the fluidity and hence unreality of the present instant which is continuously transformed into past and nonbeing. For the Buddhist philosopher, says Stcherbatsky, "existence and non-existence are not different appurtenances of a thing, they are the thing itself." As Śantarakṣita writes, "the nature of anything is its own momentary stasis and destruction."[25] The destruction to which Śantarakṣita alludes is not em-

22 Ibid., p. 14. 23 Ibid., p. 14, n. 1.

24 The elements of this philosophy will be found in the two volumes of T. Stcherbatsky's *Buddhist Logic* (Bibliotheca Buddhica, XXVI; Leningrad, 1930–32), and in Louis de la Vallée Poussin's valuable *Documents d'Abhidarma: La Controverse du temps* (Mélanges chinois et bouddhiques, V; Brussels, 1937), pp. 1–158. See also S. Schayer, *Contributions to the Problem of Time in Indian Philosophy* (Cracow, 1938) and Ananda K. Coomaraswamy, *Time and Eternity* (Ascona, 1947), pp. 30ff.

25 Stcherbatsky, *Buddhist Logic*, I, pp. 94ff.; *Tattvasangraha*, p. 137.

pirical destruction—for example, that of a vase which breaks when it falls to the ground—but the intrinsic and continuous annihilation of every existent that is involved in time. It is in this sense that Vasubandhu writes: "Because of immediate destruction, there is no (real) motion."[26] Movement and consequently time as such are pragmatic postulates, just as for Buddhism the ego is a pragmatic postulate; but the concept of motion corresponds to no outward reality, for it is "something" constructed by ourselves. Mahāyāna Buddhism expresses the unreality of the temporal world chiefly in terms of its fluidity and instantaneity, its continuous annihilation. From the Mahāyānic conception of time some writers have concluded that for the philosophers of the Greater Vehicle motion is discontinuous, that "motion consists of a series of immobilities" (Stcherbatsky). But as Coomaraswamy remarks, a line is not made up of an infinite series of points but presents itself as a continuum.[27] Vasubandhu himself said as much: "The arising of instants is uninterrupted" (*nirantara-kṣaṇa-utpāda*). Etymologically the term *saṃtāna*, which Stcherbatsky translated by "series," means "continuum."

There is nothing new in all this. The logicians and metaphysicians of the Greater Vehicle did no more than derive the ultimate conclusions from the pan-Indian intuitions concerning the ontological unreality of everything existing in time. Fluidity conceals unreality. The only hope and path of salvation is the Buddha, who has revealed the Dharma (absolute reality) and disclosed the road to Nirvāṇa. Indefatigably he repeats the central theme of his message: all that is contingent is unreal; but he never forgets to add: "this is not I" (*na me so attā*). For he, the Buddha, is identical with the Dharma, and consequently he is "simple, noncomposite" (*asaṃkhata*) and "atemporal, timeless" (*ākaliko*, as the *Aṅguttara-Nikāya* puts it, IV, 359–406). Over and over the Buddha repeats that he "transcends the eons" (*kappātito . . . vipamutto*), that he "is not a man of the eons" (*akkapiyo*), which is to say that he is not really involved in the cyclical flux of time, that he has transcended cosmic Time.[28] For him, according to the *Saṃyutta-Nikāya* (I, 141) "there exists neither past nor future" (*na tassa paccha na purattham atthi*). For the Buddha all times are made present

26 *Abhidharmakośa*, IV, 1, quoted by Coomaraswamy, p. 58. Cf. the translation with commentary by Louis de la Vallée Poussin, *L'Abhidharmakoça de Vasubandhu* (5 vols., Paris, 1923–31).

27 Coomaraswamy, p. 60.

28 *Sutta Nipāta*, 373, 860ff.; and other texts collected by Coomaraswamy, pp. 40ff.

(*Viṣuddhi Magga*, 411); in other words, he has abolished the irreversibility of time.

The total present, the eternal present of the mystics, is stasis, nonduration. Translated into spatial symbolism: nonduration, the eternal present, is immobility. And indeed, to indicate the unconditioned state of the Buddha or the *jīvan-mukta*, Buddhism—like Yoga—makes use of terms relating to immobility, stasis. "He whose thought is stable" (*ṭhita-citto*),[29] "he whose spirit is stable" (*ṭhit'attā*), etc.[30] It should not be forgotten that the first and simplest definition of Yoga is given by Patañjali himself at the beginning of his *Yoga-Sūtras* (I, 2): *yogaḥ cittavṛttinirodhaḥ*, "yoga is the suppression of the states of consciousness." But this suppression is only the final goal. The yogi begins by "halting," by "immobilizing" his states of consciousness, his psychomental flux. (The most usual sense of *nirodha* is "restriction or obstruction," the act of enclosing, etc.). We shall come back to the consequences of this "stoppage," this "immobilization" of the states of consciousness, for the yogi's experience of time.

He "whose thought is stable" and for whom time no longer flows lives in an eternal present, in the *nunc stans*. The present moment, the *nunc*, is called *kṣaṇa* in Sanskrit and *khaṇa* in Pali.[31] It is by the *kṣaṇa*, the "moment," that time is measured. But this term also has the meaning of "favorable moment, opportunity," and for the Buddha it is through the mediation of such a moment that one can escape from time. The Buddha exhorts his adepts "not to lose the moment," for "those who lose the moment will lament." He congratulates those monks who have "seized the moment" (*khaṇo vo paṭiladdho*); and he pities those "for whom the moment is passed" (*khaṇātītā*).[32] This means that after the long road traveled in cosmic Time, through innumerable existences, the illumination is instantaneous (*ekakṣana*). "The instantaneous illumination" (*ekakṣaṇābhisambodhi*), as the Mahāyānic authors call it, means that the comprehension of reality occurs suddenly, like a lightning flash—a metaphor which we have already encountered in the Upaniṣads. Any moment, any *kṣaṇa*, may become the "favorable moment," the paradoxical instant which suspends time and projects the Buddhist monk into the *nunc stans*, an eternal

29 *Dīgha-Nikāya*, II, 157.

30 Ibid., I, 57.

31 See Louis de la Vallée Poussin, "Notes sur le 'moment' ou *kṣaṇa* des bouddhistes," *Rocznik Orientalistczny* (Lwow), VIII (1931), 1–13; Coomaraswamy, pp. 56ff.

32 *Saṃyutta-Nikāya*, IV, 126.

present. This eternal present is no longer part of time; it is qualitatively different from our profane "present," from this precarious present which stands out feebly between two nonentities—the past and the future—and which will cease with our death. The "favorable moment" of illumination may be compared to the lightning flash which communicates revelation, or to the mystical ecstasy which is paradoxically prolonged beyond time.

IMAGES AND PARADOXES

It should be noted that all these images through which the Indians endeavored to express the paradoxical act of escape from time also serve to express *the passage from ignorance to illumination* (or, in other words, from "death" to "life," from the contingent to the absolute, etc.). We may group them roughly into three classes: (1) the images which suggest the abolition of time and hence illumination by a cutting across the planes (the "broken egg," the lightning flash, the seven steps of the Buddha); (2) those which refer to an inconceivable situation (the immobility of the sun at the zenith, the cessation of the flux of the states of consciousness, total cessation of respiration in the practice of Yoga, etc.); and (3) the contradictory image of the "favorable moment," a temporal fragment transfigured into an "instant of illumination." The two last images also suggest a cutting across the planes, for they denote a paradoxical passage from a normal state in the profane sense (the movement of the sun, the flux of consciousness, etc.) to a paradoxical state (the immobility of the sun etc.), or imply the transubstantiation which takes place within the temporal moment itself. (As we know, the passage from profane time to sacred Time provoked by a ritual also implies a "cutting across planes": liturgical Time does not prolong the profane time in which it is situated, but, paradoxically, continues the time of the last ritual accomplished).[33]

The structure of these images should not surprise us. All symbolism of transcendence is paradoxical and impossible to conceive in profane terms. The most common symbol to express the cutting across the planes and penetration into the "other world," the transcendent world (of the dead or of the gods), is the "difficult passage," the razor edge. "It is hard to pass over the whetted blade of the razor," say the poets to express the arduousness of the road (leading to supreme knowledge).[34] We are reminded of the Gospel

33 Cf. Eliade, *Traité d'histoire des religions* (Paris, 1949), pp. 332ff.
34 *Kaṭha Upaniṣad*, III, 14.

passage: "Strait is the gate and narrow the way, which leadeth unto life, and few there be that find it" (Matthew 7 : 14). The "strait gate," the razor edge, and the narrow, dangerous bridge by no means exhaust the wealth of this symbolism. Other images represent a seemingly hopeless situation. The hero of a tale of initiation must go "where night and day meet"; or find a gate in a wall that discloses none; or ascend to heaven by a passage which half opens for the barest instant; or pass between two millstones in continual movement, between two cliffs that touch continuously, or between the jaws of a monster, etc.[35] All these mythical images express the necessity of transcending the contraries, of abolishing the polarity which characterizes the human state, in order to accede to ultimate reality. As Coomaraswamy says, "whoever would transfer from this to the Otherworld, or return, must do so through the undimensioned and timeless 'interval' that divides related but contrary forces, between which, if one is to pass at all, it must be 'instantly.' "[36]

For Indian thought, the human state is defined by the existence of the contraries; deliverance (that is, abolition of the human condition) is equivalent to an unconditional state which transcends the contraries, or, what amounts to the same thing, a state in which the contraries coincide. We are reminded that the *Maitri Upaniṣad*, in speaking of the manifest and unmanifest aspects of being, distinguishes two forms of *brahman* as "Time and Timeless." For the sage, *brahman* plays the part of an exemplary model; deliverance is an "imitation of *brahman*." Thus for "him who knows" there ceases to be an opposition between "time" and the "timeless"; they cease to be distinct from each other; the pairs of opposites are done away with. To illustrate this paradoxical situation Indian thought, like that of other archaic peoples, makes use of images which contain contradiction in their very structure (images such as finding a door in a wall which reveals none).

The coincidence of opposites is still better elucidated by the image of the "instant" (*kṣana*) which is transformed into a "favorable moment." Apparently nothing distinguishes any fragment of profane time from the intem-

35 On these motifs see A. B. Cook, *Zeus* (Cambridge, 1940), III, 2, appendix P: "Floating Islands," pp. 975–1016; Coomaraswamy, "Symplegades," *Studies and Essays in the History of Science and Learning Offered in Homage to George Sarton* (New York, 1947), pp. 463–88; Eliade, *Le Chamanisme et les techniques archaïques de l'extase* (Paris, 1951), pp. 419ff. and passim.

36 Coomaraswamy, "Symplegades," p. 486.

poral instant obtained by illumination. To understand fully the structure and function of such an image, we must recall the dialectic of the holy: any object at all may paradoxically become a hierophany, a receptacle of the sacred, while still continuing to participate in its cosmic environment. (A holy stone for all its holiness still remains a *stone* along with other stones, etc.[37] From this point of view the image of the "favorable moment" expresses the paradox of the coincidence of opposites even more forcefully than do the images of contradictory situations, immobility of the Sun, etc.)

TECHNIQUES OF ESCAPE FROM TIME

Instantaneous illumination, the paradoxical leap outside of time, is obtained in consequence of a long discipline which implies a philosophy as well as a mystical technique. Let us consider a few techniques aimed at halting the temporal flux. The most common of them, which is truly pan-Indian, is the *prāṇāyāma*, the rhythmization of breathing. In this connection it should be noted that although its ultimate aim is to transcend the human state, the practice of Yoga starts out by ameliorating this same human state, by giving it a fullness and a majesty which seem inaccessible to the profane. We are not thinking immediately of Haṭha Yoga, whose express aim is an absolute mastery of the human body and psyche. All forms of Yoga imply a previous transformation of profane man—this feeble, dispersed slave of his body, incapable of a true mental effort—into a glorious Man: possessed of perfect physical health, absolute master of his body and his psychomental life, capable of concentration, conscious of himself. What Yoga seeks ultimately to transcend is a perfect man of this sort, and not merely a profane, everyday man.

In cosmological terms (and to penetrate Indian thought we must always use this key), Yoga starts from a *perfect cosmos* in order to transcend the *cosmic condition as such*—it does not start from a chaos. The physiology and psychomental life of the profane man resemble a chaos. Yoga practice begins by organizing this chaos, by "cosmifying" it. Little by little *prāṇāyāma*, the rhythmization of breathing, forms the yogi into a cosmos: breathing is no longer arhythmic, thought is no longer dispersed, the circulation of the psychomental forces is no longer anarchic.[38] But in thus working on the

37 On the dialectic of the holy, see Eliade, *Traité d'histoire des religions*, pp. 15ff.

38 Cf. Eliade, "Cosmical Homology and Yoga," *Journal of the Indian Society of Oriental Art* (Calcutta), V (1937), pp. 188–203. On the *prāṇāyāma*, see Eliade, *Techniques du Yoga*, pp. 75ff.; *Yoga: Immortality and Liberty* (New York, in press), passim.

respiration, the yogi works directly on lived time. And there is no adept of Yoga who, in the course of these breathing exercises, has not experienced another quality of time. Attempts have been made to describe this experience of lived time during the *prāṇāyāma;* it has been compared to the beatific time of one listening to good music, to the raptures of love, to the serenity or plenitude of prayer. But all these comparisons are inadequate. What is certain is that in progressively decelerating the rhythm of breathing, in prolonging the expiration and inspiration, and increasing the interval between these two elements of respiration, the yogi experiences a time different from ours.[39]

It seems to us that the practice of *prāṇāyāma* presents two essential points: (1) the yogi starts out by "cosmifying" his body and psychomental life; (2) by *prāṇāyāma* the yogi succeeds in integrating himself at will with the diverse rhythms of lived time. In his extremely concise manner, Patañjali recommends "the control of the moments and of their continuity.[40] The later Yogic-Tantric treatises give more details regarding this "control" of time. The *Kālacakra Tantra*, for example, goes so far as to relate inspiration and expiration with day and night, then with fortnights, months, years, arriving finally at the great cosmic cycles.[41]

In other words the yogi by his own respiratory rhythm may be said to repeat Great Cosmic Time, the periodic creations and destructions of the universe. The purpose of this exercise is twofold: on the one hand the yogi

39 It is even possible that the rhythmization of breathing has considerable effects on the physiology of the yogi. I have no competence in this field, but I was struck, at Rishikesh and elsewhere in the Himalayas, by the admirable physical condition of the yogis, although they took scarcely any food. One of the neighbors of my *kutiar* at Rishikesh was a *naga*, a naked ascetic who spent nearly the whole night in practicing the *prāṇāyāma*, and never ate anything more than a handful of rice. He had the body of a perfect athlete, showed no signs of undernourishment or fatigue. I wondered how it came about that he was never hungry. "I live only in the daytime," he replied. "At night I reduce the number of my respirations by one-tenth." I am not entirely sure of having understood what he meant, but perhaps it was simply that since vital time is measured by the number of inspirations and expirations, he lived in ten hours only a tenth part of our time, namely one hour, by virtue of the fact that during the night he reduced his breathings to one-tenth of the normal rhythm. Counted in respiratory hours, a day of twenty-four solar hours only had a length of twelve to thirteen hours for him: thus he ate a handful of rice not every twenty-four hours, but every twelve or thirteen hours. This is only a hypothesis and I do not insist. But, as far as I know, there has still been no satisfactory explanation for the surprising youthfulness of the yogis.

40 *Yoga-Sūtra* III, 52.

41 *Kālacakra Tantra*, quoted by Mario E. Carelli in his edition of Sekoddeśatīkā: *Sekoddeśatīkā of Naḍapāda (Nāropā), Being a Commentary of the Sekoddeśa Section of the Kālacakra Tantra* (Gaekwad Oriental Series, XC; Baroda, 1941), preface, pp. 16ff.

is led to identify his own respiratory moments with the rhythms of Great Cosmic Time, and in so doing realizes the relativity and ultimate unreality of time. But on the other hand, he obtains the reversibility of the temporal flux (*sāra*): he returns backward, relives his previous existences and, as the texts put it, "burns" the consequences of his former acts; he annuls these acts in order to escape from their karmic consequences.

In such an exercise of *prāṇāyāma* we discern a will to relive the rhythms of the Great Cosmic Time: the experience is similar to that of Nārada related above; but here it is obtained voluntarily and consciously. Proof that this is so may be found in the assimilation of the two "mystical veins," *iḍa* and *piṅgala*, to the moon and the sun.[42] In the mystical physiology of Yoga, *iḍa* and *piṅgala* are, as we know, the two canals through which psychovital energy circulates within the human body. The assimilation of these two mystical veins to the sun and the moon completes the operation that we have called the cosmification of the yogi. His mystical body becomes a microcosm. His inspiration corresponds to the course of the sun—that is, to the day; and his expiration to the moon—that is, the night. Thus the breathing rhythm of the yogi ultimately enters into the rhythm of Great Cosmic Time.

But this entrance into Great Cosmic Time does not abolish time as such; only its rhythms have changed. The yogi lives a cosmic Time, but he nevertheless continues to live in time. Yet his ultimate purpose is to issue from time. And this is what happens when the yogi succeeds in unifying the two currents of psychic energy that circulate through *iḍa* and *piṅgala*. By a process that is too difficult to explain in a few words, the yogi stops his respiration and, by unifying the two currents, concentrates them and forces them to circulate through the third "vein," *suṣumnā*, the vein situated at the "center." And according to the *Haṭhayoga-pradīpikā* (IV, 16–17), "*Suṣumnā* devours Time." This paradoxical unification of the two mystical veins *iḍa* and *piṅgala*, the two polar currents, is equivalent to the unification of the sun and the moon—that is, the abolition of the cosmos, the reunion of contraries, which amounts to saying that the yogi transcends both the created universe and the time that governs it. We recall the mythical image of the egg whose shell is broken by the Buddha. Thus it happens to the

42 See the texts collected by P. C. Bagchi, "Some Technical Terms of the Tantras," *Calcutta Oriental Journal*, I : 2 (November, 1934), 75–78, especially pp. 82ff.; and Shashibhusan Dasgupta, *Obscure Religious Texts* (Calcutta, 1946), pp. 274ff.

yogi who "concentrates" his breath in *suṣumnā*: he breaks the shell of his microcosm, he transcends the contingent world which exists in time. A considerable number of Tantric texts allude to this absolute, intemporal state in which there exists neither day nor night, "in which there is neither sickness nor old age"—naïve and approximative formulas for the "escape from time." To transcend day and night means to *transcend the contraries*, which corresponds on the temporal plane to the passage through the "strait gate" on the spatial plane. This experience of Tantric Yoga prepares the way for *samādhi*, the state which is usually translated as "ecstasy" but which we prefer to call "enstasis." The yogi ultimately becomes a *jīvan-mukta*, one who is "delivered in this life." We cannot conceive of his existence, for it is paradoxical. The *jīvan-mukta* is said to live no longer in time, in our time—but in an eternal present, in the *nunc stans*.

But these processes of Tantric Yoga do not exhaust the Indian techniques of "escape from time." From a certain point of view one might even say that Yoga as such aims at deliverance from temporal servitude. All Yoga exercises of concentration or meditation isolate the adept, remove him from the flux of psychomental life, and consequently reduce the pressure of time. Moreover, the yogi aims at a destruction of the subconscious, at a combustion of the *vāsanās*. Yoga, as we know, attaches a considerable importance to the subliminal life designated by the term *vāsanās*. "The *vāsanās* have their origin in memory," writes Vyāsa in his commentary on *Yoga-Sūtra* IV, 9. But more is involved than the individual memory, which for the Hindu includes not only the recollection of actual existence but the karmic residues of innumerable previous existences. The *vāsanās* also represent the entire collective memory transmitted through language and traditions: in a sense, they are equivalent to Professor Jung's collective unconscious.

In seeking to modify the subconscious and finally to "purify," to "burn" and to "destroy" it,[43] the yogi endeavors to deliver himself from memory—that is, to abolish the work of time. And this is no specialty of the Indian techniques. A mystic of the stature of Meister Eckhart never ceases to repeat that "there is no greater obstacle to union with God than time," that time prevents man from knowing God, etc. And in this connection it is not with-

43 Such a presumption will probably seem vain if not dangerous to the Western psychologist. Though claiming no right to intervene in this debate, I should like to remind the reader of the extraordinary psychological science of the yogis and the Hindu ascetics, and on the other hand, of the ignorance of Western scientists in regard to the psychological reality of the Yogic experiences.

out interest to recall that archaic societies periodically "destroy" the world in order to remake it and consequently to live in a new universe without "sin"—that is, without history, without memory. A great number of periodic rituals also aim at a collective wiping away of sin (public confessions, the scapegoat, etc.), amounting ultimately to an abolition of the past. All this, it seems to me, proves that there is no breach in continuity between the man of the archaic societies and the mystic belonging to the great historic religions: both fight with the same energy, though with different means, against memory and time.

But this metaphysical deprecation of time and this struggle against "memory" do not exhaust the attitude of Indian spirituality toward time and history. Let us recall the lesson of the myths of Indra and Nārada: Māyā is manifested through time, but Māyā itself is only the creative force and above all the cosmogonic force of the absolute Being (Śiva, Viṣṇu); and that means that the *Great Cosmic Illusion is ultimately a hierophany*. This truth, revealed in myths by a series of images and stories, is expounded more systematically by the Upaniṣads,[44] and the later philosophers who state explicitly that the ultimate foundation of things, the *Ground*, is constituted *both by Māyā and by the Absolute Spirit*, by Illusion and Reality, by Time and Eternity. In placing all the contraries in one and the same universal void (*Śūnya*), certain Mahāyānic philosophers (for example, Nāgārjuna), and above all the various Tantric schools both Buddhist (Vajrayāna) and Hindu, have come to similar conclusions. In all this there is nothing to surprise us, for we know the eagerness of Indian spirituality to transcend the contraries and polar tensions, to unify the real, to return to the primordial One. If time as Māyā is also a manifestation of the godhead, to live in time is not in itself a "bad action"; *the bad action consists in believing that there exists nothing else, nothing outside of time.* One is devoured by time, *not* because one lives in time, but because one believes in the *reality* of time and hence forgets or despises eternity.

This conclusion is not without importance; we tend too much to reduce Indian spirituality to its extreme positions, which are intensely specialized and hence accessible only to the sages and mystics, and to forget the pan-Indian attitudes, illustrated above all by the myths. Indeed, the "escape from time" obtained by the *jīvan-mukta* amounts to an enstasis or an ecstasy inaccessible to most men. But if the escape from time remains the royal

44 See above, pp. 186f.

road of deliverance (let us recall the symbols of instantaneous illumination etc.), this does not mean that all those who have not obtained it are inexorably condemned to ignorance and servitude. As the myths of Indra and Nārada show, to be delivered from illusion it is sufficient to achieve consciousness of the ontological unreality of time and to "realize" the rhythms of Great Cosmic Time.

Thus, to recapitulate, India is not limited to two possible situations with respect to time: that of the ignorant who live solely in time and illusion—and that of the sage or yogi who endeavors to "issue from time"; there is also a third, intermediate, situation: the situation of him who, while continuing to live in his own time (historic time), preserves an opening toward Great Time, never losing his awareness of the unreality of historic time. This situation, illustrated by Indra after his second revelation, is amply elucidated in the *Bhagavad-Gītā*. It is expounded above all in the Indian spiritual literature for the use of laymen, and by the spiritual masters of modern India. It is not without interest to observe that this last Indian position is in a certain sense a continuation of primitive man's attitude toward time.

C. G. Jung

On Synchronicity[1]

It might seem appropriate to begin my exposition by defining the concept with which it deals. But I would rather approach the subject the other way and first give you a brief description of the facts which the concept of synchronicity is intended to cover. As its etymology shows, this term has something to do with time or, to be more accurate, with a kind of simultaneity. We can also use for simultaneity the concept of a *meaningful coincidence* of two or more events when something other than the probability of chance is involved. A statistical—that is, a probable—concurrence of events, such as the "duplication of cases" found in hospitals, falls within the category of chance. Groupings of this kind can consist of any number of terms and still remain within the framework of the probable and rationally possible. Thus, for instance, it may happen that someone chances to notice the number on his streetcar ticket. On arriving home he receives a telephone call during which the same number is mentioned. In the evening he buys a theater ticket that again has the same number. The three events form a chance grouping that, although not likely to occur often, nevertheless lies well within the framework of probability owing to the frequency of each of its terms. I would like to recount from my own experience the following chance grouping, made up of no fewer than six terms:

On April 1, 1949, I made a note in the morning of an inscription containing a figure that was half man and half fish. There was fish for lunch. Somebody mentioned the custom of making an "April fish" of someone. In the afternoon, a former patient of mine, whom I had not seen in months, showed me some

1 [The German original of this brief essay was later much expanded by Professor Jung as "Synchronizität als ein Prinzip akausaler Zusammenhänge," in *Naturerklärung und Psyche* (Studien aus dem C. G. Jung-Institut, IV; Zurich, 1952). Tr. R. F. C. Hull as "Synchronicity: An Acausal Connecting Principle," in *The Interpretation of Nature and the Psyche* (New York and London, 1955).—Ed.]

impressive pictures of fish. In the evening, I was shown a piece of embroidery with sea monsters and fishes in it. The next morning, I saw a former patient, who was visiting me for the first time in ten years. She had dreamed of a large fish the night before. A few months later, when I was using this series for a larger work and had just finished writing it down, I walked over to a spot by the lake in front of the house where I had already been several times that morning. This time a fish a foot long lay on the sea wall. Since no one else was present, I have no idea how the fish could have got there.

When coincidences pile up in this way one cannot help being impressed by them—for the greater the number of terms in such a series, or the more unusual its character, the more improbable it becomes. For reasons that I have mentioned elsewhere and will not discuss now, I assume that this was a chance grouping. It must be admitted, though, that it is more improbable than a mere duplication.

In the above-mentioned case of the streetcar ticket, I said that the observer "chanced" to notice the number and retain it in his memory, which ordinarily he would never have done. This formed the basis for the series of chance events, but I do not know what caused him to notice the number. It seems to me that in judging such a series a factor of uncertainty enters in at this point and requires attention. I have observed something similar in other cases, without, however, being able to draw any reliable conclusions. But it is sometimes difficult to avoid the impression that there is a sort of foreknowledge of the coming series of events. This feeling becomes irresistible when, as so frequently happens, one thinks one is about to meet an old friend in the street, only to find to one's disappointment that it is a stranger. On turning the next corner one then runs into him in person. Cases of this kind occur in every conceivable form and by no means infrequently, but after the first momentary astonishment they are as a rule quickly forgotten.

Now, the more the foreseen details of an event pile up, the more definite is the impression of an existing foreknowledge, and the more improbable does chance become. I remember the story of a student friend whose father had promised him a trip to Spain if he passed his final examinations satisfactorily. My friend thereupon dreamed that he was walking through a Spanish city. The street led to a square, where there was a Gothic cathedral. He then turned right, around a corner, into another street. There he was met by an elegant carriage drawn by two cream-colored horses. Then he woke up. He told us about the dream as we were sitting round a table drinking beer.

Shortly afterward, having successfully passed his examinations, he went to Spain, and there, in one of the streets, he recognized the city of his dream. He found the square and the cathedral, which exactly corresponded to the dream image. He wanted to go straight to the cathedral, but then remembered that in the dream he had turned right, at the corner, into another street. He was curious to find out whether his dream would be corroborated further. Hardly had he turned the corner when he saw in reality the carriage with the two cream-colored horses.

The *sentiment du déjà-vu* is based, as I have found in a number of cases, on a foreknowledge in dreams, but we see that this foreknowledge can also occur in the waking state. In such cases mere chance becomes highly improbable, since the coincidence is known in advance. It thus loses its chance character not only psychologically and subjectively, but objectively too, since the accumulation of details that coincide immeasurably increases the improbability of chance as a determining factor. (For correct precognitions of death, Dariex and Flammarion have computed probabilities ranging from 1 in 4,000,000 to 1 in 8,000,000.)[2] So in these cases it would be incongruous to speak of "chance" happenings. It is rather a question of meaningful coincidences. Usually they are explained by precognition—in other words, foreknowledge. People also talk of clairvoyance, telepathy, etc., without, however, being able to explain what these faculties consist of or what means of transmission they use in order to render events distant in space and time accessible to our perception. All these ideas are mere names; they are not scientific concepts which we may assume to be statements of principle, for no one has yet succeeded in constructing a causal bridge between the elements making up a meaningful coincidence.

Great credit is due to J. B. Rhine for having established a reliable basis for work in the vast field of these phenomena by his experiments in extrasensory perception, or ESP. He used a pack of 25 cards divided into 5 groups of 5, each with its special sign (star, square, circle, cross, two wavy lines). The experiment was carried out as follows: In each series of experiments the pack is laid out 800 times, in such a way that the subject cannot see the cards. He is then asked to guess the cards as they are turned up. The probability of a correct answer is 1 in 5. The result, computed from very high figures, showed an average of 6.5 hits. The probability of a chance deviation of 1.5 amounts to only 1 in 250,000. Some individuals scored more than twice

2 [For documentation, see "Synchronicity: An Acausal Connecting Principle," p. 20.]

the probable number of hits. On one occasion all 25 cards were guessed correctly, which gives a probability of 1 in 298,023,223,876,953,125. The spatial distance between experimenter and subject was increased from a few yards to about 4,000 miles, with no effect on the result.

A second type of experiment consisted in asking the subject to guess a series of cards that was still to be laid out in the near or more distant future. The time factor was increased from a few minutes to two weeks. The result of these experiments showed a probability of 1 in 400,000.

In a third type of experiment, the subject had to try to influence the fall of mechanically thrown dice by wishing for a certain number. The results of this so-called psychokinetic (PK) experiment were the more positive the more dice were used at a time.

The result of the spatial experiment proves with tolerable certainty that the psyche can, to some extent, eliminate the space factor. The time experiment proves that the time factor (at any rate, in the dimension of the future) can become psychically relative. The experiment with dice proves that moving bodies too can be influenced psychically—a result that could have been predicted from the psychic relativity of space and time.

The energy postulate shows itself to be inapplicable to the Rhine experiments, and thus rules out all ideas about the transmission of force. Equally, the law of causality does not hold—a fact that I pointed out thirty years ago. For we cannot conceive how a future event could bring about an event in the present. Since for the time being there is no possibility whatever of a causal explanation, we must assume provisionally that improbable accidents of an acausal nature—that is, meaningful coincidences—have entered the picture.

In considering these remarkable results we must take into account a fact discovered by Rhine, namely that in each series of experiments the first attempts yielded a better result than the later ones. The falling off in the number of hits scored was connected with the mood of the subject. An initial mood of faith and optimism makes for good results. Skepticism and resistance have the opposite effect, that is, they create an unfavorable disposition. As the energic, and hence also the causal, approach to these experiments has shown itself to be inapplicable, it follows that the affective factor has the significance simply of a *condition* which makes it possible for the phenomenon to occur, though it need not. According to Rhine's results, we may nevertheless expect 6.5 hits instead of only 5. But it cannot be predicted in advance when the hit will come. Could we do so, we would be dealing with a law, and this would contradict the entire nature of the phenomenon. It has, as said, the improbable character of a "lucky hit" or accident that occurs with a more than merely probable frequency and is as a rule dependent on a certain state of affectivity.

This observation has been thoroughly confirmed and suggests that the psychic factor which modifies or even eliminates the principles underlying the physicist's picture of the world is connected with the affective state of the subject. Although the phenomenology of the ESP and PK experiments could be considerably enriched by further experiments of the kind described above, deeper investigation of its bases will have to concern itself with the nature of the affectivity involved. I have therefore directed my attention to certain observations and experiences which, I can fairly say, have forced themselves upon me during the course of my long medical practice. They have to do with spontaneous, meaningful coincidences of so high a degree of improbability as to appear flatly unbelievable. I shall therefore describe to you only one case of this kind, simply to give an example characteristic of a whole category of phenomena. It makes no difference whether you refuse to believe this particular case or whether you dispose of it with an *ad hoc* explanation. I could tell you a great many such stories, which are in principle no more surprising or incredible than the irrefutable results arrived at by Rhine, and you would soon see that almost every case calls for its own explanation. But the causal explanation, the only possible one from the standpoint of natural science, breaks down owing to the psychic relativization of space and time, which together form the indispensable presuppositions for the cause-and-effect relationship.

My example concerns a young woman patient who, in spite of efforts made on both sides, proved to be psychologically inaccessible. The difficulty lay in the fact that she always knew better about everything. Her excellent education had provided her with a weapon ideally suited to this purpose, namely a highly polished Cartesian rationalism with an impeccably "geometrical" [3] idea of reality. After several fruitless attempts to sweeten her rationalism with a somewhat more human understanding, I had to confine myself to the hope that something unexpected and irrational would turn up, something that would burst the intellectual retort into which she had sealed herself. Well, I was sitting opposite her one day, with my back to

3 [Descartes demonstrated his propositions by the "Geometrical Method."—Ed.]

the window, listening to her flow of rhetoric. She had had an impressive dream the night before, in which someone had given her a golden scarab—a costly piece of jewelry. While she was still telling me this dream, I heard something behind me gently tapping on the window. I turned round and saw that it was a fairly large flying insect that was knocking against the window pane from outside in the obvious effort to get into the dark room. This seemed to me very strange. I opened the window immediately and caught the insect in the air as it flew in. It was a scarabaeid beetle, or common rosechafer (*Cetonia aurata*), whose gold-green color most nearly resembles that of a golden scarab. I handed the beetle to my patient with the words, "Here is your scarab." This experience punctured the desired hole in her rationalism and broke the ice of her intellectual resistance. The treatment could now be continued with satisfactory results.

This story is meant only as a paradigm of the innumerable cases of meaningful coincidence that have been observed not only by me but by many others, and recorded in large collections. They include everything that goes by the name of clairvoyance, telepathy, etc., from Swedenborg's well-attested vision of the great fire in Stockholm to the recent report by Air Marshal Sir Victor Goddard about the dream of an unknown officer, which predicted a subsequent accident to Goddard's plane.[4]

All the phenomena I have mentioned can be grouped under three categories:

1. The coincidence of a psychic state in the observer with a simultaneous, objective, external event that corresponds to the psychic state or content (e.g., the scarab), where there is no evidence of a causal connection between the psychic state and the external event, and where, considering the psychic relativity of space and time, such a connection is not even conceivable.

2. The coincidence of a psychic state with a corresponding (more or less simultaneous) external event taking place outside the observer's field of perception, i.e., at a distance, and only verifiable afterward (e.g., the Stockholm fire).

3. The coincidence of a psychic state with a corresponding, not yet existent future event that is distant in time and can likewise only be verified afterward.

In groups 2 and 3 the coinciding events are not yet present in the observer's field of perception, but have been anticipated in time in so far as

4 [This was the subject of a recent English film, *The Night My Number Came Up*.—ED.]

they can only be verified afterward. For this reason I call such events *synchronistic*, which is not to be confused with *synchronous*.

Our survey of this wide field of experience would be incomplete did we not also take into account the so-called mantic methods. Manticism lays claim, if not actually to producing synchronistic events, then at least to making them serve its ends. An example of this is the oracle method of the *I Ching*,[5] which Dr. Hellmut Wilhelm has described in detail at this meeting. The *I Ching* presupposes that there is a synchronistic correspondence between the psychic state of the questioner and the answering hexagram. The hexagram is formed either by the random division of the 49 yarrow stalks or by the equally random throw of three coins. The result of this method is, incontestably, very interesting, but so far as I can see it does not provide any tool for an objective determination of the facts, that is to say a statistical evaluation, since the psychic state in question is much too indefinite and indefinable. The same holds true of the geomantic experiment, which is based on similar principles.

We are in a somewhat more favorable situation when we turn to the astrological method, as it presupposes a meaningful coincidence of planetary aspects and positions with the character or the existing psychic state of the questioner. In the light of the most recent astrophysical research, astrological correspondence is probably not a matter of synchronicity but, very largely, of a causal relationship. As Professor Knoll has demonstrated at this meeting,[6] the solar proton radiation is influenced to such a degree by planetary conjunctions, oppositions, and quartile aspects that the appearance of magnetic storms can be predicted with a fair amount of probability. Relationships can be established between the curve of the earth's magnetic disturbances and the mortality rate that confirm the unfavorable influence of conjunctions, oppositions, and quartile aspects and the favorable influence of trine and sextile aspects. So it is probably a question here of a causal relationship, i.e., of a natural law that excludes synchronicity or restricts it. At the same time, the zodiacal qualification of the houses, which plays a large part in the horoscope, creates a complication in that the astrological zodiac, although agreeing with the calendar, does not coincide with

5 The *I Ching, or Book of Changes*, tr. Cary F. Baynes from the German tr. of Richard Wilhelm (New York and London, 1950). [See H. Wilhelm's paper in this volume, pp. 212ff.—ED.]

6 [See his paper, pp. 264ff.]

the actual constellations themselves. These have shifted their positions by almost a whole platonic month as a result of the precession of the equinoxes since the time when the spring point was in zero Aries, about the beginning of our era. Therefore, anyone born in Aries today (according to the calendar) is actually born in Pisces. It is simply that his birth took place at a time which, for approximately 2,000 years, has been called "Aries." Astrology presupposes that this time has a determining quality. It is possible that this quality, like the disturbances in the earth's magnetic field, is connected with the seasonal fluctuations to which solar proton radiation is subject. It is therefore not beyond the realm of possibility that the zodiacal positions may also represent a causal factor.

Although the psychological interpretation of horoscopes is still a very uncertain matter, there is nevertheless some prospect today of a causal explanation in conformity with natural law. Consequently, we are no longer justified in describing astrology as a mantic method. Astrology is in the process of becoming a science. But as there are still large areas of uncertainty, I decided some time ago to make a test and find out how far an accepted astrological tradition would stand up to statistical investigation. For this purpose it was necessary to select a definite and indisputable fact. My choice fell on marriage. Since antiquity the traditional belief in regard to marriage has been that there is a conjunction of sun and moon in the horoscope of the marriage partners, that is, ☉ (sun) with an orbit of 8 degrees in the case of one partner, in ☌ (conjunction) with ☾ (moon) in the case of the other. A second, equally old, tradition takes ☾☌☾ as another marriage characteristic. Of like importance are the conjunctions of the ascendent (*Asc.*) with the large luminaries.

Together with my co-worker, Mrs. Liliane Frey-Rohn, I first proceeded to collect 180 marriages, that is to say, 360 horoscopes,[7] and compared the 50 most important aspects that might possibly be characteristic of marriage, namely the conjunctions and oppositions of ☉ ☾ ♂ (Mars) ♀ (Venus) *Asc.* and *Desc.* This resulted in a maximum of 10 per cent for ☉☌☾. As Professor Markus Fierz, of Basel, who kindly went to the trouble of computing the probability of my result, informed me, my figure has a probability of 1 : 10,000. The opinion of several mathematical physicists whom

7 This material stemmed from different sources. They were simply horoscopes of married people. There was no selection of any kind. We took at random all the marriage horoscopes we could lay hands on.

I consulted about the significance of this figure is divided: some find it considerable, others find it of questionable value. Our figure is inconclusive inasmuch as a total of 360 horoscopes is far too small from a statistical point of view.

While the aspects of these 180 marriages were being worked out statistically, our collection was enlarged, and when we had collected 220 more marriages, this batch was subjected to separate investigation. As on the first occasion, the material was evaluated just as it came in. It was not selected from any special point of view and was drawn from the most varied sources. Evaluation of this second batch yielded a maximum figure of 10.9 per cent for ☾☌☾. The probability of this figure is also about 1 : 10,000.

Finally, 83 more marriages arrived, and these in turn were investigated separately. The result was a maximum figure of 9.6 per cent for ☾☌*Asc.* The probability of this figure is approximately 1 : 3,000.[8]

One is immediately struck by the fact that the conjunctions are all *moon conjunctions*, which is in accord with astrological expectations. But the strange thing is that what has turned up here are the three basic positions of the horoscope, ☉ ☾ and *Asc.* The probability of a concurrence of ☉☌☾ and ☾☌☾ amounts to 1 : 100,000,000. The concurrence of the three moon conjunctions with ☉ ☾ *Asc.* has a probability of 1 : 3×10^{11}; in other words, the improbability of its being due to mere chance is so enormous that we are forced to take into account the existence of some factor responsible for it. The three batches were so small that little or no theoretical significance can be attached to the individual probabilities of 1 : 10,000 and 1 : 3,000. Their concurrence, however, is so improbable that one cannot help assuming the existence of an impelling factor that produced this result.

The possibility of there being a scientifically valid connection between astrological data and proton radiation cannot be held responsible for this, since the individual probabilities of 1 : 10,000 and 1 : 3,000 are too great for us to be able, with any degree of certainty, to view our result as other than mere chance. Besides, the maxima cancel each other out as soon as one divides up the marriages into a larger number of batches. It would require hundreds of thousands of marriage horoscopes to establish the statistical regularity of occurrences like the sun, moon, and ascendent conjunctions, and even then the result would be questionable. That anything so improb-

8 [These and the following figures were later revised by Professor Fierz and considerably reduced.—Ed.]

able as the turning up of the three classical moon conjunctions should occur at all, however, can only be explained either as the result of an intentional or unintentional fraud, or else as precisely such a meaningful coincidence, that is, as synchronicity.

Although I was obliged to express doubt, earlier, about the mantic character of astrology, I am now forced as a result of my astrological experiment to recognize it again. The chance arrangement of the marriage horoscopes, which were simply piled on top of one another as they came in from the most diverse sources, and the equally fortuitous way they were divided into three unequal batches, suited the sanguine expectations of the research workers and produced an over-all picture that could scarcely have been improved upon from the standpoint of the astrological hypothesis. The success of the experiment is entirely in accord with Rhine's ESP results, which were also favorably affected by expectation, hope, and faith. However, there was no definite expectation of any one result. Our selection of 50 aspects is proof of this. After we got the result of the first batch, a slight expectation did exist that the ☉☌☾ would be confirmed. But we were disappointed. The second time, we made up a larger batch from the newly added horoscopes in order to increase the element of certainty. But the result was ☾☌☾. With the third batch, there was only a faint expectation that ☾☌☾ would be confirmed, but again this was not the case.

What happened in this case was admittedly a curiosity, apparently a unique instance of meaningful coincidence. If one is impressed by such things, one could call it a minor miracle. Today, however, we are obliged to view the miraculous in a somewhat different light. The Rhine experiments have demonstrated that space and time, and hence causality, are factors that can be eliminated, with the result that acausal phenomena, otherwise called miracles, appear possible. All natural phenomena of this kind are unique and exceedingly curious combinations of chance, held together by the common meaning of their parts to form an unmistakable whole. Although meaningful coincidences are infinitely various in their phenomenology, as acausal events they nevertheless form an element that is part of the scientific picture of the world. Causality is the way we explain the link between two successive events. Synchronicity designates the parallelism of time and meaning between psychic and psychophysical events which scientific knowledge so far has been unable to reduce to a common principle. The term explains nothing, it simply formulates the occurrence of meaningful coincidences which, in themselves, are chance happenings, but are so improbable that we must assume them to be based on some kind of principle, or on some property of the empirical world. No reciprocal causal connection can be shown to obtain between parallel events, which is just what gives them their chance character. The only recognizable and demonstrable link between them is a common meaning, or equivalence. The old theory of correspondence was based on the experience of such connections—a theory that reached its culminating point and also its provisional end in Leibniz' idea of pre-established harmony, and was then replaced by causality. Synchronicity is the modern differentiation of the obsolete concept of correspondence, sympathy, and harmony. It is based not on philosophical assumptions but on empirical experience and experimentation.

Synchronistic phenomena prove the simultaneous occurrence of meaningful equivalences in heterogeneous, causally unrelated processes; in other words, they prove that a content perceived by an observer can, at the same time, be represented by an outside event, without any causal connection. From this it follows either that the psyche cannot be localized in space, or that space is relative to the psyche. The same applies to the temporal determination of the psyche and the psychic relativity of time. I do not need to emphasize that the verification of these findings must have far-reaching consequences.

In the short space of a lecture I cannot, unfortunately, do more than give a very cursory sketch of the vast problem of synchronicity. For those of you who would care to go into this question more deeply, I would mention that a more extensive work of mine is soon to appear under the title "Synchronicity: An Acausal Connecting Principle." It will be published together with a work by Professor W. Pauli in a book called *The Interpretation of Nature and the Psyche.*[9]

9 [See n. 1, above.—Ed.]

Hellmut Wilhelm

The Concept of Time in the Book of Changes

I

The system of existence and events underlying the Book of Changes (*I Ching*) [1] lays claim to completeness. The book attempts a correlation of the situations of life in all strata, personal and collective, and in all dimensions. An added feature of the system are the trends of development latent within the various situations and their reciprocal relations. The implications of this second aspect of the book—which reveal, among other things, that none of the sixty-four situations given can be conceived altogether statically—have been so stressed that we have grown accustomed to understand the word *I* of the title as meaning "change." Though this translation certainly comes very close to the meaning of the word both in a logical and an empirical sense, we must not forget that the concept *I* as such connotes not only the dynamic aspect of life but also what is firm, reliable, and irrevocable in the system of coordinates it covers. An early apocryphon states as much in the paradoxical definition: "Change: that is the unchangeable." [2]

We need to focus for once on this logical aspect of the system if we wish to discover the laws that govern it. The book lends itself readily to such speculation. This was the aspect that again and again occupied the minds of the commentators during times when China's stage of social development inclined toward rigidity, as in the days of the Han, and especially during the

1 *The I Ching or Book of Changes*, tr. from the German of Richard Wilhelm by Cary F. Baynes (New York, 1950; London, 1951; 2 vols.). [Abbr. as Baynes/Wilhelm.] [The author has revised this paper in English, with the assistance of Mrs. Baynes and of Ximena de Angulo.—Ed.]

2 It is not even certain that we are justified in retaining the derivation of the character *I* from the picture of the lizard as a mobile, changing animal; studies of recently discovered material suggest that the word is derived from the concept of the fixed and straight, hence also of the directional. I am indebted to my colleague Erwin Reifler for this reference.

Sung Dynasty, when justification for the systematization of social dependencies was sought in the Book of Changes. The early masters of Sung philosophy, who all based their systems on this book, uniformly stressed the elements that persist even in change. Chou Tun-i, for example, the founder of this new philosophical trend, even sees the development inherent within the concept *I* in terms of hierarchical images whose temporal sequence is paralleled by a systematic scale of values; from the supreme pole the two basic powers of yang and yin emanate, from their interaction the five states of change result, and the relations between these five in turn give rise to the world of existence.[3] Here, then, change is seen in a temporal schema which not only is unilinear but also incorporates a rigid hierarchical scale. Such an image is not unimpressive: it could be applied to systems of dependencies outside philosophy, and could be brought to bear on social relations as well as on intellectual life; and this fact contributed to the dominant position of Sung philosophy in subsequent Chinese history.

Thus it is evident that the emphasis on the uniform and the regular in the process of change in time represents a danger. The projection of change into the "unchangeable" finds expression here in spatial images of the relation between above and below. Thus the conception rests on a mixture of two categories, time and space. An attempt is made to understand the temporal in spatial terms. Thinking influenced by hierarchical feeling superimposes one dimension of space on that of time. The origin of this fallacy is easy to grasp: the logic of an order easily established in space leads to the wish for an analogous mastery of time that is much more difficult to order—and it was thought that this could be accomplished through borrowing from spatial modes of thought.

Clearly, the concept of change itself does not lend itself to systematic interpretation; but the world conception set forth in the sixty-four images of the *I Ching* remains open to such an approach, and indeed calls for it. The idea on which this book is based—that questions at the dark gate are to be answered not by the intuition of an oracular priest or priestess, however well equipped, but by a collection of written texts—is valid only if these texts form a self-contained, exhaustive whole: in other words, only if every questioner may find a correspondent answer for every question. This idea is still relatively easy to apprehend if one expects nothing more from the answers

3 Georg von der Gabelentz, *Thai-kih-thu des Tscheu Tse, Tafel des Urprinzips mit Tschu Hi's Commentare* (Dresden, 1876).

than a guide within a definite culture at a definite epoch. After all, it was the creators of this culture, or at least groups close to them, who formulated these texts. But the *I Ching* is not merely a handbook of possible situations and a guide to possible behavior for the early Chou period: it has been used successfully both in other periods and in other cultures. This opens up an aspect of the book which can no longer be explained by saying that the creator of a culture is in a position to ordain the proper form of behavior within the culture. It is striking, for example, that although the *I Ching* contains memories of exemplary situations from the early history of the Chou Dynasty, we find no passages which draw rigid inferences from the typical feudalistic structure of early Chou society. On the contrary, the situations are always raised above temporal manifestations into a realm where they bear an archetypal character; historical recollections are used to illustrate the archetype but never to tie it to a particular manifestation. Thus the system of the texts appears timeless, or above time.

Of course this does not answer the question of how it was possible to create a system of archetypes that can lay claim to completeness. Probably we shall not be able to provide an answer here. It would be necessary to take up in detail the early history of the Chou, who at the time the early strata of the book took form were still close to the dazzling starlight of the high steppes, though their economy had recently shifted to an emphasis on agriculture, under circumstances in which a trusting reliance on nature had to be complemented by artificial, communally directed irrigation projects. Such experiences produced a mind open to the primary questions of human existence. This openness of mind meant a freedom from prejudice toward answers which came from other spheres, for example from the culturally far superior Shang Empire, which the Chou were soon to subjugate, or—perhaps still more important—from their southwestern neighbors in present-day Tibet.[4]

Another of the old masters of Sung philosophy, Shao Yung, who is usually regarded as the father of the idealistic school in this philosophy, made the system of archetypes of the *I Ching*, embodied in the sixty-four hexagrams a subject of his speculation. He was attracted by the step-by-step progres-

4 Wolfram Eberhard was the first to call attention to these influences in the Book of Changes. See his *Lokalkulturen im alten China*, Vol. I (Leiden, 1942), pp. 290–94. His argument there perhaps requires to be worked out in greater detail. Nonetheless his thesis remains extremely suggestive.

sion of the situation within the hexagram, expressed by successive whole or divided lines; and he attempted, by a systematization of this progression within the individual hexagram, to create a new "natural" system of all sixty-four. The essential element of his analysis was the whole and broken—yang and yin—lines, from which, viewing them at first in a strictly graphic sense, he constructed the individual hexagram and with it his new system of the hexagrams.

Starting with the two primary lines, yang and yin, he obtains the fundamental line of the individual hexagram and a twofold division of the whole system:

Then he adds above each of the two a yang line and a yin line. With this the individual sign gains in complexity, and the total system is divided into four:

At first merely graphic images, these four line-complexes also suggest an analysis from the standpoint of content; they are called the big yang, the little yang, the little yin and the big yin—the lowest line in each case determines their character. To each line-complex is now added a yang line and, again, a yin line: an eightfold division is obtained, consisting of trigrams in the following new arrangement:

Through the addition once again of a yang line and a yin line, the following picture results:

+ 8
= 16

The addition for the fifth time of a yang and a yin line yields the following:

+ 24
= 32

And when the simultaneous progression arrives at the last line, the sixty-four hexagrams stand in this new order:

the last eight being:

Shao Yung arranged this new system in various ways. To the linear order beginning with *Ch'ien* and ending with *K'un* he added a square order in which eight rows, each of eight hexagrams, are placed one above the other so that the ninth, seventeenth, twenty-fifth, etc. stand over the first hexagram; the tenth, eighteenth, twenty-sixth, etc. over the second hexagram; etc. It then develops that the horizontal rows always have the lower trigram in common, while the vertical rows have the upper one in common. Finally, he arranged them in a circular form; here, if the second half of his series is stood on its head, a correspondence results with the so-called "Earlier Heaven" order of the eight trigrams.[5]

This restructuring and resystematization of the hexagrams appear to have grown out of a speculation on graphic images. However, it is worth noting that this artificial construction facilitates insights into the locus of a situation characterized by the hexagram (that is to say, into the place of the situation within the system), into the significance of the individual line, and into affinities between the various hexagrams.

It was this aspect of the system that Leibniz happened upon. In the course of his correspondence with Father Bouvet, one of the group of Jesuits who were then active at the court in Peking, Bouvet sent him a chart bearing the square as well as the circular arrangement of Shao Yung. The contemplation of this table led Leibniz to establish a correspondence disclosing one of the most amazing parallelisms between Eastern and Western thought. Some years earlier Leibniz had made use of a new numerical system that was meant to facilitate the computation of tangential magnitudes. This so-called binary system corresponds in principle to the usual decimal system but

5 Cf. Baynes/Wilhelm, I, p. 285.

makes use of only two figures, 1 and 0. The numerical sequence of the binary system would look as follows:

1, 10, 11, 100, 101, 110, 111, 1000, etc.

For Leibniz this system had a significance beyond that of a mathematical aid. He did not regard the events of life and the categories of thought as exhausted by time, space, and causality but apprehended all existence also from the standpoint of pre-established harmony: for his wide-ranging mind, number and the numerical system therefore had more than an abstract meaning; they were expressive of connotative associations which have long since fallen into oblivion. Of course we, too, make use of numbers and numerical formulas in order to express laws in the physical world—the orbit of the moon, for example, or the organization of a flower. But Leibniz attempted more; with the help of numbers he attempted to trace the laws of spiritual truths as well. Spiritual realities, he argued, can become convincing beyond question only if represented in numbers. His pre-established harmony provided the foundation that enabled him without hesitation to associate number with concepts that extend beyond the physical world. In his binary system the number 1 stood for the creative unity (*unité*), whose highest expression is God, and 0 for the nothingness of unformed chaos.

In Leibniz' mind the equation of Shao Yung's arrangement of the sixty-four hexagrams with his own system was immediately consummated. He took the broken line for a 0 and the unbroken line for a 1 and, by disregarding any zeros preceding 1, arrived at a perfect correspondence between the two series. But this correspondence presents two anomalies. First, Leibniz was compelled to draw in the 0 and set it at the beginning of his system, even before the 1. The order would then be: 0, 1, 10, 11, 100, 101, etc. This means that the "nothingness of unformed chaos," which in Leibniz' system occurs not by itself but only in relation to the "creative unity," had to be absolutized and placed before the unity. Thus posited, it gains decisive importance. The second anomaly is that the correspondence is inverse rather than direct. Shao Yung's last sign occupies the first place in Leibniz' system, and his first sign occupies last place. Leibniz himself does not seem to have been aware of this; Father Bouvet's chart did not enable him to distinguish which was the beginning and which the end in the Chinese system. But to us the inversion of the correspondence seems characteristic of the relation between Western and Eastern thinking.[6]

Leibniz' discovery could be said to imply that the hexagrams, as differentiations of a harmonious and systematic whole, are not posited at random but occupy consequent loci. This would mean that they are not chance lots drawn from a grab bag but dispositions in a meaningful complex.

Leibniz himself was well aware of the significance of such conclusions. He assumed that the meaningful character of the position of the hexagram must be manifested in its name and content. (The textual meaning of the hexagrams is indeed entirely in accord with their line structure.) It is doubtful whether he ever obtained corroboration of these assumptions, and his discovery therefore remained in the nature of an episode; but it throws a clear light on the system of the Book of Changes, which in this aspect is a system developing in time, progressing step by step. It might be added that this temporally unilinear progression is predicated on the speculation of a Shao Yung, who transposed the book's *a posteriori* order (the "Order of Later Heaven") into an *a priori* order (the "Order of Earlier Heaven"). In the (*a posteriori*, empirical) Order of Later Heaven the relation in time of hexagram to hexagram is more obscure than in the (*a priori*, logical) Order of Earlier Heaven. And this characterizes the difference between immediately experienced time (of sense perception) and abstract time (of mathematics). The latter is also included in the Book of Changes, though in veiled form; the oracle seeker, however, prefers to leave this aspect of time to logical speculation and to concentrate on the experienced situation manifested in the sign he has drawn.

Indeed, the problem of how an oracle actually comes into being, of how a question becomes coordinated with the correct answer from the text of the book, can be solved only if a system is presupposed. Without a system, the synchronicity [7] of answer and question would seem if not wholly the play of chance at least dimly defined. The oracle seeker may be content with a vague harmony if only the answer applies to his question; but the institution of the oracle requires a firmer foundation. Where this order is sought is less important than the fact of its existence. One may find it in the Leibnizian

6 Leibniz published his discovery of this correspondence in a memorial of the Paris Academy (1703, Vol. III, pp. 85ff.). I discussed the correspondence between Leibniz and Father Bouvet in "Leibniz and the I-ching," *Collectanea Commissionis Synodalis* (Peking), XVI (1943), pp. 205–19.

7 [Cf. Professor Jung's lecture in the present volume.—Ed.]

category of pre-established harmony, in which the harmonious and parallel order of events is assumed to be fixed, or one may accept his idea that laws expressible in numbers underlie all truths and not merely those of the physical world.

Wang Fu-chih (1619–92) has given us a theory of the oracle more in keeping with the second possibility. His premise is an ordered continuum of existence, which is governed by laws and is all embracing. This continuum "lacks appearance"—that is, it is not immediately accessible to sense perception. But through the dynamism inherent in existence, images are differentiated out of the continuum which by their structure and position partake of the laws of the continuum; they are, in a sense, individuations of this continuum. On the one hand, these images—that is, the sixty-four situations of the Book of Changes—can be perceived and experienced; on the other hand, as embodiments of the law and therefore governed by it, they are open to theoretical speculation. With this they enter into the field of numbers and may be numerically structured and ordered as objects of theory governed by law. Thus each situation can be apprehended in two ways: through direct experience as a consequence of the dynamism of existence, and through theoretical speculation as a consequence of the continuousness of existence and its government by laws. The oracle serves to bring the two aspects into harmony with each other, to co-ordinate a question resulting from immediate, differentiated experience, with the theoretically correct—and the only correct—answer. The questioner thus obtains access to the theoretically-established aspect of his own situation, and by reference to the texts set forth under this aspect in the Book of Changes he obtains counsel and guidance from the experience of former generations and the insights of the great masters. Thus the synchronicity disclosed by the oracle is merely the apprehension of two different modes of experiencing the same state of affairs.

This explanation—here somewhat expanded—by Wang Fu-chih has been pretty generally accepted in China, but various things in it may disturb us. First of all, it may trouble us that this explanation was not thought out until some two thousand years after the completion of the Book of Changes. Yet in this connection we might recall a word of Confucius when someone asked him for an explanation of the Grand Sacrifice: " 'I cannot give one. Any person who would know how to explain it would have the world right here.' And he pointed to the palm of his hand." [8] The evidently very complicated

8 *Analects*, 3, 11; in James R. Ware, *The Best of Confucius* (Garden City, 1950), p. 33.

Grand Sacrifice existed, and in the opinion of Confucius had a meaning which, if known, would have elucidated the world order. And yet this meaning was not known. For if anyone had known it, it would have been Confucius, who was more concerned with the form and significance of rites than anyone else in his day. Similar examples might be adduced from other cultures. It would seem that social institutions rise and grow and fulfill their function, although the meaning of this function is not necessarily known and the institution not necessarily devised on the basis of this meaning. Hence it need not trouble us if such a meaning is not distilled from the form and function of the institution until a much later period.

But this does not help us over another difficulty: how is it possible that numbers and numerical formulas arrived at by a throwing of coins or a manipulation of yarrow stalks should disclose a relation that establishes a man's own fate in time and accounts for its development? That it should be a toss of the coins or a division of a bundle of yarrow stalks through which such a result is achieved seems to us to relegate the oracle to the realm of coincidence. For us in the West it is hard to see how a genuine synchronicity could be arrived at by so seemingly mechanical a means.

Obviously Wang Fu-chih was also aware of the rational difficulty back of this doubt. For him number and numerical formulas were tools, and the manner in which they were obtained was method. Of course this method, if incorrectly applied, is just as likely to obscure the law as to reveal it. Something more is needed to put one in a position to make proper use of the tools and the method. It is not something that can be rationally induced at will; it is an attitude, through which alone the tools and the method can be brought to bear effectively. Indeed, modern psychology also has noted the existence of a particular attitude through which synchronicity can be apprehended; there must be an openness to such connections. Unlike the psychologists, however, Wang Fu-chih designates the requisite attitude "integrity." "Only a man of the highest integrity," he says, "can understand this law; basing himself on its revelation he can grasp the symbols, and observing its small expressions he can understand the auguries." [9]

Thus the law is revealed only to the man of integrity; he alone can grasp the connection existing between experience and the meaning of what has been experienced; to him alone is it given to apply the method in such a

9 My *Die Wandlung* (Peking, 1944), pp. 147–48 (tr. in preparation by Cary F. Baynes, *Change*, ch. VIII, sec. 3).

way as to read the tendencies of events from small manifestations. For this no special wisdom is needed and no special experience; it is not the prerogative of a privileged or specially trained group; no priest is made into the administrator or interpreter of human destiny; no mystical immersion is the bridge to a mysterious vision. All that is needed is integrity, a willingness to see things as they are, the attitude of one who does not fool himself or others and does not hide behind conventional or sophisticated rationalizations. Given this intense awareness and openness to the reality of events, the tools and the method become a means of bringing experience into harmony with meaning, present with future.

Of course this does not mean it is advisable to disregard tools and method. As we have said, a number is that manifestation of any law by which it can be apprehended. The sixty-four hexagrams are built up of lines that have numerical values, and the method of drawing the hexagrams by lot is based on the use of numbers. The method itself incorporates certain fundamental insights into the nature of existence and development, and these insights in turn are expressed by numbers and by the frequency of a possible numerical combination. Both of the methods employed, the throwing of coins and the manipulation of yarrow stalks, contain these insights; the former embodies them in a somewhat crude, the latter in a far more differentiated, form. A compilation of the possible results of the toss of the three coins (as we know, the side with the inscription on it is counted as two and the other side as three) makes this clear. The eight possibilities that can emerge from a toss of the coins are distributed among the line numbers as follows:

one possible occurrence of a "six" (changing yin-line)
three possible occurrences of a "seven" (resting yang-line)
three possible occurrences of an "eight" (resting yin-line)
one possible occurrence of a "nine" (changing yang-line)

These possibilities embody certain trends of probability. The probability of throwing a resting line rather than a changing line is three to one. The probability of throwing a yin-line rather than a yang-line is one to one.

But a more greatly differentiated law of probability is operative in the yarrow stalk method. Here the possible results for a line are not eight but sixty-four, which are distributed among the line numbers as follows:

four possible occurrences of a "six"
twenty possible occurrences of a "seven"
twenty-eight possible occurrences of an "eight"
twelve possible occurrences of a "nine"

Here, too, the probability of a yang-line (20 + 12) and of a yin-line (28 + 4) is one to one, and the relation of the resting line (20 + 28) to the changing (4 + 12) line is three to one; but a further probability is incorporated in this method, namely that rest and change are diversely distributed between yin and yang, so that the yang is more inclined (3 : 5) toward change than is the yin (1 : 7).

II

As an introduction to the way in which the aspect of time is expressed in the texts of the Book of Changes, and to the part played by time in the situations described, we select two quotations which throw light on the special nature of the time element. The first is taken from the fourth hexagram, *Mêng*, Youthful Folly:

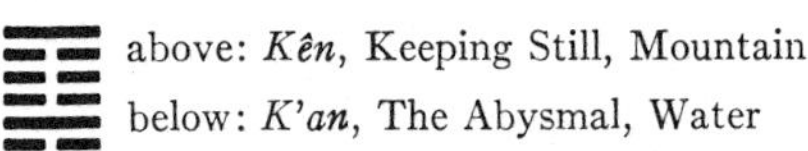
above: *Kên*, Keeping Still, Mountain
below: *K'an*, The Abysmal, Water

Here, much to the dismay of the aged and the wise, the Judgment says:
[I, 21] "Youthful folly has success." The Commentary on the Decision explains
[Cf. II, 41] this statement with the words: "That he succeeds in his action is due to his hitting time (in the bull's-eye)." [10]

Thus the success of the young fool's actions is attributed here to the fact that he is more in harmony with time than the old and wise, whose experience and dogmas may hinder them in this respect. The spontaneous, unreflecting attitude of the young fool enables him to maintain himself in the heart (center) of time. And the time element of this situation is so strong a factor in its unfolding that even the folly of youth cannot obstruct it. (The texts of this hexagram make it perfectly clear that we are concerned here not with a youthful genius but truly with a fool.)

10 In general I follow my father's translation. But I have sharpened it where necessary to bring out the points here discussed. [Citations to the Baynes/Wilhelm version of the *I Ching* are given marginally, by volume and page. Where Hellmut Wilhelm has modified the rendering, "cf." is used.—Ed.]

The second quotation is taken from the sixty-third hexagram, *Chi Chi*, After Completion:

above: *K'an*, The Abysmal, Water
below: *Li*, The Clinging, Fire

Here, under nine in the fifth place, a situation is described which occurs also in the religions of other cultures: the neighbor in the east, who slaughters an ox, does not attain as much real happiness as the neighbor in the west with his small offering. The Commentary on the Images to this text says: "The [II, 366]
eastern neighbor, who slaughters an ox, is not as much in harmony with the time as the western neighbor."[11] This explanation is surprising. The difference in the outcome of the sacrifice depends not on the attitude of the sacrificer, as one might expect, but on the timing [*Zeitgemässheit*] of the sacrifice. This throws light not only on the institution of sacrifice in itself and on the attitude of the sacrificer, but again on the time factor in a given situation.

The conception of time that we encounter in these quotations is very concrete. Here time is immediately experienced and perceived. It does not represent merely a principle of abstract progression but is fulfilled in each of its segments; an effective agent not only in which reality is enacted, but which in turn acts on reality and brings it to completion. Just as space appears to the concrete mind not merely as a schema of extension but as something filled with hills, lakes, and plains—in each of its parts open to different possibilities—so time is here taken as something filled, pregnant with possibilities, which vary with its different moments and which, magically as it were, induce and confirm events. Time here is provided with attributes to which events stand in a relation of right or wrong, favorable or unfavorable.

A more abstract concept of time was not unknown in the China of that period. At the time of the later strata of the Book of Changes, to which the commentaries we have just quoted belong, we find evidence of a mathematical-astronomical concept of time which served as a foundation for a highly developed science of the calendar; and we also have the record of a space-time schema, in which time was regarded as one of the coordinates of extension.[12] But the Book of Changes eschews such theoretical concepts of

11 Wilhelm/Baynes, Vol. II, p. 366. Cf. p. 5, n. 5.

12 See Eduard Erkes, "Antithetische Komposition und Dekomposition im Chinesischen," *Sinologica* (Basel), II (1950), 132 n. A similar passage is found in Shih-tzu, who lived in the 4th century B.C.; see Sun Hsing-yen's edn., ch. 2, fr. 50.

time, operating with the word *shih*, "time," in a manner that is much closer to its derivation. The word meant originally "sowing time," then "season" in general (cf. Fr. *saison*, Lat. *satio*). In its early form it was composed of the character for "sole of the foot" (Lat. *planta*) above that for a unit of measurement.[13] In China, too, the sole of the foot is related semantically to planting; thus the word means a section of time set apart for a certain activity. Thence its meaning was extended to the four seasons, all of which are correspondingly filled with certain activities; and only then to time in general. The word is often used in the Book of Changes in the meaning of season, and many of the characteristic attributes of time can be traced to this heritage.

Thus it is often said that the seasons do not err [14] and that therefore the
[II, 106, great man takes them as a model for his consistent behavior.[15] They derive
125, 15] two of their most important characteristics from the ordered revolution of
heaven and earth.[16] From it they derive their unremitting change as well as
their consistent continuity. In the Great Treatise this is expressed as fol-
[I, 343] lows: "There is nothing that has more movement or greater cohesion than
[Cf. II, 324] the four seasons." And "The changes and continuity correspond to (literally
"are correlated with") the four seasons." Change is not only something that
happens to them or in them, but also something that influences the happening: "The four seasons change and transform, and thus can forever bring
[II, 190] to completion." [17]

Time in its relation to the formative process is then discussed in detail in
[II, 135] the Commentary on the Decision, hexagram 22, *Pi*, Grace: "This is the
form of heaven.[18] Having form, clear and still (literally "capable of holding back"): this is the form of men. If the form of heaven is contemplated, the changes of time can be discovered. If the forms of men are contemplated, one can shape the world."

Highly illuminating is the passage, likewise in the Commentary on the

13 I am again indebted to Erwin Reifler for this information.

14 Commentary on the Decision: hexagram 16, Enthusiasm, and hexagram 20, Contemplation.

15 Commentary on the Words of the Text: hexagram 1, The Creative.

16 Commentary on the Decision: hexagram 49, Revolution: "Heaven and earth bring about revolution, and the four seasons complete themselves thereby." And hexagram 60, Limitation: "Heaven and earth have their order, and the four seasons of the year arise therefrom." Baynes/Wilhelm, Vol. II, p. 285; cf. p. 346.

17 Commentary on the Decision: hexagram 32, Duration.

18 The sentence relating what the form of heaven is has been lost. Wang Pi fills in "The firm and the yielding unite alternately."

Words of the Text, on nine in the fifth place of the first hexagram, describing the relation of the great man to heaven (nature) and time: "When he (the [II, 15]
great man) acts in advance (*hsien-t'ien*, in the *a priori*, theoretical sense) of heaven, heaven does not contradict him. When he follows heaven (*hou-t'ien*, in the *a posteriori*, empirical sense), he adapts himself to the time of heaven (literally "receives time from heaven")."

These passages clearly show how the concept of time is naturally conditioned; time retains its inner cohesion amid unremitting change. They also disclose the concrete and formative character of time, the way in which it is in tune with certain situations and induces them.

To be sure, all these quotations are taken from the later strata of the Book of Changes. This concept of time is contained implicitly in the earlier strata, but here the word "time" is used only once and is nowhere explicitly defined.

The only use of the word in the earlier strata occurs in the fifty-fourth hexagram, *Kuei Mei*, The Marrying Maiden, a hexagram remarkably full of traps and pitfalls:

☳ above: *Chên*, The Arousing, Thunder [I, 222ff.]
☱ below: *Tui*, The Joyous, Lake

The Judgment on this situation runs strangely: "Undertakings bring misfortune. Nothing that would further." And the text of the Image runs: "Thus the superior man understands the transitory in the light of the eternity of the end."

The lines of this text also point to many discouraging aspects. The intellectual independence of the authors of this book may be seen from the fact that they did not formulate their texts in accordance with the requirements of the social institutions of their time but represented a situation as it actually is, in disregard of the rules of propriety of a given period. The only note of cheer in this hexagram occurs in nine in the fourth place, which deals with the maiden who arrives late at her marriage: "The marrying maiden draws out the allotted time. A late marriage comes in due course (literally "has its proper time")." We may congratulate this independent person who does not wish to enter into a marriage merely because it is in keeping with custom, preferring to wait until the "proper time" provides the basis for a real marriage.[19]

19 Cf. also the Commentary on the Images for this line, and my father's remarks, Baynes/Wilhelm, Vol. II, p. 318. The commentary has also been handed down in another

To this line text we might add two more Image texts which, though of later date, come very close in their wording to the original situation. The first is hexagram 25, *Wu Wang*, Innocence:

above: *Ch'ien*, The Creative, Heaven
below: *Chên*, The Arousing, Thunder

The Image: "The kings of old nourished all beings, equaling the times in
[Cf. I, 108] abundance."

The explanation of this sentence is probably to be sought in the notion that the state of naïve innocence has something two-edged about it, since it can be so easily lost.[20] Thus the Commentary on the Decision says, among
[II, 151] other things: "When innocence is gone, where can one go? When the will of heaven does not protect one, can one do anything?" And the Commentary
[Cf. II, 150] known as Miscellaneous Notes on the Hexagrams adds: "Innocence is a catastrophe." For so frail a creature as man it is evidently no easy matter to maintain himself in the unstable situation of innocence. He whose position requires it can apparently only preserve his innocence by abundantly nourishing all beings, the wicked along with the righteous, just as the times in their blindness show no one favor or disfavor.

Another Image text that places the concept of time in a new light may be found in the forty-ninth hexagram, *Ko*, Revolution:

above: *Tui*, The Joyous, Lake
below: *Li*, The Clinging, Fire

[I, 201ff.] This hexagram contains many recollections of the rise to power of the Chou Dynasty. The hexagram states that it is salutary to change the form of government (nine in the fourth place), and that in such a situation it is not even necessary to wait for the oracle (nine in the fifth place).[21] The Image

version, which might be translated: "Resolved to let slip the allotted time, she will go only when the right time is at hand." As for the meaning of the word *shih*, "time," it is characteristic that here, and in one version of another passage (hexagram 39, Obstruction, Commentary on the Images, six at the beginning), it seems to be interchangeable with the word *tai*, "to wait."

20 This is made particularly clear by the line text on six in the third place, where someone in all innocence filches a cow tethered by someone else also in all innocence. The line text calls this "undeserved misfortune." Here again we see the author free from the bourgeois morality of ownership. It continues: "The wanderer's gain is the citizen's loss." (I, 109.)

21 There is actually a tradition that the omens were unfavorable when King Wu went into the great battle that gave him command of the empire. Another tradition has it

for this hexagram runs: "Thus the superior man sets the calendar in order and makes the seasons clear."

Here, then, the natural concept of time is coupled with the mathematical-astronomical concept. In this way time can be handed down to the people—that is, a political use can be made of this formative function of natural time.

In the sixty-four situations of the Book of Changes the time element is not always given equal emphasis. Although it is always present and significant, there are situations in which other factors are so dominant that no mention is made of time. But in other situations, the time element is so essential as to determine the total constellation. In these cases the Commentary on the Decision says that the time of a certain situation is great; and it can happen that the situation as such may be great or significant. However, a glance at the hexagrams in question shows that this is not necessarily so, but that these remarks stress the weight of the time category in a situation. We find such a remark in connection with hexagrams 27, *I*, Nourishment; 28, *Ta Kuo*, Preponderance of the Great; 40, *Hsieh*, Deliverance; and 49, *Ko*, Revolution.

In other instances the Commentary on the Decision stresses a particular aspect of the time concept. Often the meaning of the time of a given situation is called great. The word *I*, here rendered as "meaning," refers not so much to meaning in general as to the normative significance. Here time has the force of a verdict by which certain relations are decided, so that it binds like a law. Such a statement is found in hexagrams 17, *Sui*, Following; 33, *Tun*, Retreat; 44, *Kou*, Coming to Meet; and 56, *Lü*, The Wanderer—all situations in which, for better or worse, "the father's house has been forsaken."

Then reference is made to the practical effect of time, and this is called great, especially in certain—but not all—unfavorable circumstances, as in hexagrams 29, *K'an*, The Abysmal, Danger; 38, *K'uei*, Opposition; and 39, *Chien*, Obstruction.

A man's relation to time, understood thus, may be taken as a task or as foreordained destiny. In some situations one can assume a correct or a wrong attitude toward time, while in others one must accept the time as fate. The most advantageous relation to time is naturally that of harmony. In the

that the tortoise oracle advised against the battle, but that the yarrow stalk oracle was favorable.

situations where one is in harmony with time, the maxims of action are a matter of course, or at least they are easy to follow. We have already noted examples of the man who is within the time or "has" the right time (as though in his possession). In these cases success comes of itself, or in any event it is not difficult "to go with time," "to act in keeping with time," "to act in a timely [*zeitgemäss*] way." The classic example of these situations is contained in the Commentary on the Words of the Text, on the second hexagram, *K'un*, The Receptive: "The way of the Receptive—how devoted
[II, 26] it is! It receives heaven into itself and acts in its own time."

Equally simple is the situation in the cases of hexagrams 41 and 42, *Sun* and *I*, Decrease and Increase, where the Commentary on the Decision runs:
[II, 237] "In decreasing and increasing, in being full and being empty, one must go
[II, 245] with the time," and "The way of Increase everywhere proceeds in harmony with the time." [22]

Somewhat more personal initiative is required in the case of the fourteenth hexagram, *Ta Yu*, Possession in Great Measure. This, too, is a situation blessed by time, but one which can be fully exploited only by the attitude one assumes. Here the Commentary on the Decision says: "(His
[II, 95] character) finds correspondence in heaven and moves with the time; hence the words, 'Supreme Success.' "

Even less promising situations can be influenced through their time element and by a correct timely [*zeitgemäss*] attitude, so that good fortune, or even great good fortune, may result. This is the case, for example, in the sixty-second hexagram, *Hsiao Kuo*, Preponderance of the Small. Here we have a transitional situation brought about by little things (mortar and pestle); the situation is characterized as follows in the Judgment: "The
[I, 256] flying bird brings the message: It is not well to strive upward, it is well to remain below. Great good fortune." On which the Commentary on the
[Cf. II, 357] Decision remarks: "To be furthered in transition by perseverance is the result of going with the time."

Even situations that outwardly seem still more unfavorable may be turned to success with the help of the time element, as for example in hexagram 33, *Tun*, Retreat, where the Judgment promises success despite contrary circumstances. The Commentary on the Decision explains this as follows:

22 Here much is retained of the seasonal character of the word "time." But see the preceding passage: "'Two small bowls' (used for offerings) is in accord with the time" (literally, "have their right time"). And: "There is a time for decreasing the firm and a time for increasing the yielding." (II, 237.)

"The firm is in the appropriate place and finds correspondence. This means [II, 195] that one is in accord with the time."

But to keep in accord with the time often requires greater exertions. Twice the first hexagram, *Ch'ien*, The Creative, describes a situation in which this harmony can be preserved or induced only if all energies are brought to bear. In nine in the third place, the time of the first action of the creative man, the line text runs: "All day long the superior man is creatively ac- [I, 7] tive. At nightfall his mind is still beset with cares. Danger. No blame." On which a passage in the Commentary on the Words of the Text remarks: "All day long he is creatively active in order to act in harmony with the [Cf. II, 14] time." These nights beset with worry show a consciousness of responsibility, an awareness that in all such situations even a creative genius can act only in accord with the time.

In the succeeding stage of the same hexagram, the line text runs: "Waver- [I, 7] ing flight over the depths. No blame." Here the time factor is still extremely significant, and strenuous endeavor is needed to keep step with the time. To be sure, an effort of a different kind is called for. Whereas nine in the third place called for outward action, here work on oneself is required. On this line the Commentary on the Words of the Text says: "The superior [Cf. II, 14] man fosters his character and labors at his task, in order to keep pace with the time." In these two line-texts the desired harmony with time is expressed in different ways. In the first case action must be in tune with an existing harmony with time; in the second case, man requires every effort even to keep pace with the time.

Finally, a remark in the Great Treatise throws light on still another highly dramatic case of timely action. The reference is to six at the top in hexagram 40, *Hsieh*, Deliverance:

above: *Chen*, The Arousing, Thunder
below: *K'an*, The Abysmal, Water

The text runs: "The prince shoots at a hawk on a high wall. He kills it. [I, 168] Everything serves to further." On this archetype of the supreme and ultimate deliverance the Great Treatise remarks: "The superior man contains the means in his own person. He bides his time and then acts." Here the superior man must await the exact time in which alone the act of deliverance can be effected. "Too early" or "too late" will deflect the arrow from its target (deliverance, not the slaying of the hawk). Having to await the proper time in a tense situation of this sort may be more difficult than the active participation required in the situations of *Ch'ien*, The Creative.

Of course, this harmony with time is not something that is present or can be induced in all cases. The Book of Changes also contains some situations in which it is not possible, or is not attained, because of either fate or a man's own fault. Consider for example the tragic six at the beginning of hexagram 48, *Ching*, The Well:

above: *K'an*, The Abysmal, Water
below: *Sun*, The Gentle, Wind, Wood

[I, 199] "One does not drink the mud of the well. No animals come to an old
[Cf. II, 281] well." And the Commentary on the Images: "Time has rejected it." The situation speaks for itself. Suddenly the well's function of supplying life-giving water can no longer be fulfilled. And no personal exertion can do anything about it.

Another situation is perhaps still more tragic, namely the nine in the second place, again of the first hexagram, where the Creative first appears but cannot rise over the field, hence remains without success and response.
[Cf. II, 13] Here again the Commentary on the Words of the Text says: "Time has rejected him." [23] Here it is not the exhausted old man but the creative young man whom time passes by. He must subordinate himself, and it is not given him to rise above the community of men. This situation, too, is the consequence not of his own failure but of fate.[24]

In one case the Commentary on the Images attributes lack of harmony with the time to personal failing and speaks of "missing the time." The underlying situation is to be found in hexagram 60, *Chieh*, Limitation:

above: *K'an*, The Abysmal, Water
below: *Tui*, The Joyous, Lake

This is one of those signs under which inconveniences are overcome with relative ease, or at least borne without great disadvantage,[25] since it is provided that the limitation should be accepted without bitterness. Only two

23 My father's translation, "The reason is that he is not needed as yet," is euphemistic.

24 Cf. the passage in Shih-tzu (Sun's edn., ch. 2, fr. 174): "The wild duck is called Fu, the domestic duck Wu. Its wings are unsuited to flying. Like a common man it guards the fields and nothing more."

25 A line in the Commentary on the Decision runs: "Where limitation is applied in the creation of (political) institutions, property is not encroached upon, and people are not harmed." (II, 346.)

of the limited, i.e., restricted, lines are really unfortunate: six at the top, which carries the restriction beyond necessity to the point of bitterness, and nine in the second place, where the line text runs: "Not going out of the gate and the courtyard brings misfortune." On this line the Commentary on the Images says: "Such a missing of the (right) time is really the limit!" [I, 248] [Cf. II, 348]

Actually, the gate stands open to this line; the line itself is strong and presses for activity. If we still practice limitation here, it really looks as if we do not understand the time. But the amusing dissatisfaction of the commentary should not be taken too seriously, for a glance at the sign as a whole shows us what we would come to if we should accede to the urge for motion and gaily pass through the gate: we would come to the abyss. Here the commentary seems guilty of a certain shortsightedness in condemning the man who accepts the drawbacks of restriction in order to avoid being carried away by the vortex of the abyss. From the standpoint of the line's position alone the commentary is right. But here it takes the time in too personal a sense.[26] And many who have succumbed to the lure of an open gate have learned this to their grief.

We have mentioned a number of cases in which time was basic to or formative of the situation of the hexagram as a whole, or played a part in one of its stages. In all these situations time is one element among many. But among the sixty-four hexagrams there is one which, according to the Miscellaneous Notes on the Hexagrams, rests entirely on time. This is hexagram 26, *Ta Ch'u*, The Taming Power of the Great:

☶ above: *Kên*, Keeping Still, Mountain
☰ below: *Ch'ien*, The Creative, Heaven

The archetypal situation from which this sign starts is the taming of the domestic animals, the ox and the pig—that is, the herd animal and the animal of the lower individualism, which wallows in its own muck. Untamed, both animals signify a danger to life and limb; tamed, they are extremely useful and indispensable aids in the building of material civilization. The ox draws the plow and pulls loads, the pig fertilizes the fields and serves for food.

The danger presented by these animals running around untamed is clearly expressed in the first three strong lines of the sign. Awareness of the danger

26 This is clear, too, from the contradiction between the sign's nuclear trigrams: *Chên*, The Arousing, or Movement, whose first line this is, is opposed by *Kên*, Keeping Still.

(fear) is so great as to encourage "armed defense."[27] However, despite all their masculine power it is not given to any of the three yang-lines to exorcise the danger and tame the animals. They find it advantageous to stand aside, they even fall into situations of helplessness (the axletrees are taken from the wagon), or prefer to seek an escape. It is the two yin-lines in the fourth and fifth place that accomplish the task of taming. The way in which they do this varies. To take his wildness from the bull is relatively easy. In this situation one acts even before the wildness appears. A headboard attached to the young bull keeps his horns from growing dangerously. With the boar a stronger kind of intervention is necessary. Gelding deprives the boar of his savagery (that is, his nature is changed). Both operations are wholly successful solely because of their timeliness, and thus make room for nine at
[II, 160] the top, the way of heaven,[28] the time when again "truth works in the great":

[Cf. II, 26] The way of the Receptive—how successful it is! It receives heaven into itself and acts in accord with its own time.

27 This is the only occurrence of the word *wei*—"armed defense"—in the Book of Changes. One reading of this passage runs: "Seclude yourself and practice chariot driving and armed defense."

28 Here "way" is not *tao* but the path of natural development.

Helmuth Plessner

On the Relation of Time to Death

I

Two years ago, when the late Gerardus van der Leeuw [1] spoke in this circle about primordial time and final time [*Urzeit und Endzeit*] and distinguished between the eschatological history-producing consciousness and the primitive consciousness to which history is alien, he touched upon a theme that now concerns us again. At that time he said:

> Here we approach the great cleavage in the self-consciousness of mankind. On the one side, time takes a cyclical course, on the other it has a beginning before which there was nothing and an end with which it stops. On the one side, every sunrise is a victory over chaos, every festival a cosmic beginning, every sowing a new creation, every holy place a foundation of the cosmos, every historical event a rise or fall according to the regular course of the world, and even the law that sustains society is nothing other than the rule of the sun's course. . . . On the other side, everything is exactly the same except that at a certain point in the cycle someone appears who proclaims a definitive event, the day of Yahweh, the last judgment, the ultimate salvation, or the final conflict as in Iran. The images used are all borrowed from the course of nature: day and night, summer and winter. But the ethos has changed; a hiatus has been made, a *tempus* in the strict sense, which changes everything. . . . This final time revolutionizes the course of the world.[2]

By contrast, the primordial time of myth does not actually signify one particular phase of the cycle—that is, a time when things began; what it signifies is that the revolution of time is a closed circuit, a cycle. Before the

1 [Died 1950. See below, pp. 324ff.—Ed.]

2 See below, pp. 338f.

eschatological consciousness arises, there is no real beginning to time. Primordial time is as much alive today as it was yesterday, an eternal beginning. And as there is no beginning there is also no end. The myth finds no conclusion; time revolves.

> "What happens now is what happened long ago." Primitive man—that is, the man who still lives close to the womb, in an unsplit world, who has objectified neither his own life nor that of the world—lives in circles, in an eternal today. The patriarchs and what they did are today as much alive as they were then. A real past exists no more than a real future. When scholars seek to explain this state of affairs, they say that primitive man is lacking in historical consciousness—for the most part without suspecting that this merely suggests the problem, but does not clarify it from an anthropological point of view.[3]

What would be the nature of such an anthropological clarification? Would it be ethnological or psychological? The ethnological material gives us only an intimation of the vast diversity of things human, and consequently the help of depth psychology is as indispensable here as in the other cultural sciences. But the difficulties in the way of an interpretation do not reside merely in the facts. I have no desire to indulge in polemics, and I can accept the definition of primitive man as a man who lives close to the maternal in an unsplit world, even though I have my misgivings about the formulation that he has objectified neither his own life nor the world. Why then does he live in circles, in sacred cycles, in myths and rites? He, too, is a man, and surely he, too, can have a kind of objectivity, a conception of himself and the world, different though it may be from the one familiar to us. But without any objectivization whatever man is not merely primitive—he is no man at all. The influence of the evolutionary theory, with its tendency to think in terms of "not yet," has caused primitive man to be regarded as a precursor, a prehuman or primordial human being who has scarcely grown away from unconscious animal life—a being who had to undergo a development of consciousness before he could overcome his primitiveness. Is this not in itself a definite anthropological theory? Does it not interpret what we know from the ontogenesis of individual consciousness as the struggle of the ego with the self, of consciousness with the unconscious, in the light of a phylogenesis of mankind's consciousness, forgetting the while that this

3 See below, p. 337.

phylogenesis itself is a mere hypothesis? It is possible, I will not deny, that past modes of existence and consciousness have been preserved in the substrate of our present existence and consciousness, but even if this is so I venture to assert that it is not possible for our present consciousness to deduce from the supporting function of the deposits in the substrate anything regarding the nature of the past functions. We must reckon with functional changes of the early strata, otherwise our perspectives become distorted. The Romantics did not always avoid this error, and it seems to me that one of the tasks of anthropological clarification is to point out this danger inherent in any retrospective interpretation.

Let me try to explain myself more clearly: Even if prehuman and primordial human experiences influenced our psychic and spiritual ontogenesis much as primordial human physical development roughly determines the structure, function, and ontogenesis of our bodies; even if (with the necessary reservations, of course) we are justified in thinking of such a fundamental psychogenetic law—still the functional transformation of the old in the new and for the new would have to be expressly considered in any interpretation of the past. The biologist and historian are familiar with this notion, and the depth psychologist will have to take it into account. From our point of view, what has become unconscious in the depth stratum seems to be closer to the womb and to the unsplit world. But was it *then* in and for itself? Of course not, one will say, man was not sufficiently removed from himself in time, nor because of his very primitivity could he look at himself and the world from a sufficient intellectual distance. But are we not thus presupposing what was to be determined? To determine the facts, neither historical nor psychological statements suffice; above all, we require a philosophical inquiry concerning the limits within which we may speak of the specifically human.

*

My present topic, the relation of time to death, does not permit me to go any more deeply than this into the question of the aim and method of a philosophical anthropology. But I had to mention it in order to throw light on the sense in which I mean to treat of my theme. I am not a historian of religion and not a psychologist who has worked in the field pioneered by Professor Jung. I am a guest on his ground. From me you may expect no analyses of myth; in my work—for such is the situation of the philosopher—

I use material worked out by others, in order to provide examples for certain structural laws of anthropology. Accordingly I beg your indulgence and patience, of which philosophical disquisitions are more in need than are investigations of concrete experience.

We shall start with a discussion of the mythical consciousness of time. A cyclically ordered world knows death only as an organic phenomenon. In a culture where the "chain" does not break off, or more precisely, where transience is subject to the law of recurrence, the significance of individual death remains limited and veiled, so to speak. It is only with the transformation of the mythical consciousness of time from its cyclical to its eschatological form that a vision opens on the "nevermore" and a separation arises between past, present, and future. This transformation of the nascent historical feeling of time would seem to correspond to an increasing individualization both of groups and of the individuals who form them. It is at this point that peoples enter into history. The emergence of death as a problem begins to be discernible in the spiritualized forms of myth and cult—which, however, still have incontestable answers to all questions.

With Christianity a new development sets in which goes beyond the eschatology achieved by other religions and leads to a demythicization of the temporal consciousness. Since it culminates in our present situation, I shall attempt to give a brief picture of this decline of myth—a decline that in the end led to a shattering of the world of Christian revelation. The progressive profanization or secularization of history is accompanied by a corresponding rationalization of the concept of time. Natural time and historical time become separate, but the rational chronology of natural time forms the basis of historical time. Thus the problem of the rational relation between time and death arises. This we shall consider in the second part of our lecture, which will take up questions of organic life and its stages, questions of an ontological character, since man, limited in his historicity, is a physical being and as such is subject to the laws of death that apply to the other organisms, regardless of the fact that he alone knows of them. Thus the last part of my lecture will deal with the experience and certainty of death, a question involving man's relation to the ultimate form of time, "historicity." With this, to be sure, we move away from psychological research in myth but hope to contribute toward an anthropological clarification of the basis on which it too must operate; and in the long run such a clarification is indispensable.

*

Primordial time, the immemorial "once upon a time" which lays down the prototypes for all happenings, does not narrow down into a "time of beginning" until there is a corresponding "time of the end." This transition from a world without beginning and end to a world of extreme limitations is clearly connected with a release of man from "nature," which for us, the heirs of this process of emancipation, has the sense of an awakening, a liberation. Thus the discovery of the linear time that makes possible a directed consciousness of limits and plunges everything into the light of the unique and unrepeatable raises man's conceptions to a new plane. World and man become worthy of being remembered in tradition, monuments, and documents. Past, present, and future become distinct. The more deeply this temporal consciousness takes hold of a living community, the more it will be drawn into the individualization of its members and feel death as a threat, whose gravity depends on the mode and measure of the individual's delimitation against the world and the chain of the generations. Thus the growth of ego-consciousness, the development of death as a problem, and the actualization of the linear time that unfolds in past, present, and future belong together. Although many of the ancient cultures realized the transition to an eschatological view of time potentially contained in the cyclical consciousness of time, they were unable to take the last step. Israel accomplished it with the idea of a *creatio ex nihilo*.

This was the source of the Christian view of the world and, in conjunction with Greek causal thinking, the source of the eventual unfolding of the historical consciousness. Here alone has a myth, a mythical revelation, developed powers which led to demythicization. The extreme consequences of this, however, our consciousness cannot bear, even though it has itself conjured them up. The progressive demythicization of time, which I have elsewhere described (in a study of the stages in the decline of the Christian consciousness of time)[4] as a metamorphosis and dissolution of the historically conceived picture of the world, leads ultimately to the discovery of a time totally bereft of meaning. This empty time is nothing more than a locus of possible changes, related to chronological modes. Today the concept of time has undergone a fragmentation. Each scientific discipline, human dimension,

4 *Das Schicksal des deutschen Geistes im Ausgang seiner bürgerlichen Epoche* (Zurich, 1935).

and cultural sphere has its own time; there is a physical, a biological, a psychological, and a historical time; there is an experienced and an imagined time; an economic, a religious, an artistic, and a political time. All this betokens the total neutralization of our temporal consciousness. Before I go into the genesis of this temporal consciousness of ours with the intention of clearing the way for our theme, the relation between time and death, I should like to turn back once again and attempt to delineate the mythical consciousness of time.

What is mythical time? Let us consider an answer given by Thomas Mann:

> What concerns us here is not calculable time. Rather it is time's abrogation and dissolution in the alternation of tradition and prophecy, which lends to the phrase "once upon a time" its double sense of past and future and therewith its burden of potential present. Here the idea of reincarnation has its roots. The kings of Babel and the two Egypts, that curly-bearded Kurigalzu as well as Horus in the palace at Thebes, called Amun-is-satisfied, and all their predecessors and successors, *were* manifestations in the flesh of the sun god, that is to say the myth became in them a *mysterium*, and there was no distinction left between being and meaning. It was not until three thousand years later that men began disputing as to whether the Eucharist "was" or only "signified" the body of the Sacrifice; but even such highly supererogatory discussions as these cannot alter the fact that the essence of the mystery is and remains the timeless present. Such is the meaning of ritual, of the feast. Every Christmas the world-saving Babe is born anew and lies in the cradle, destined to suffer, to die and to arise again.[5]

The mythical intuition of time, which like that of space grows out of the simple process of orientation, is qualitative and concrete. "For myth," says Cassirer, "there is no time 'as such,' no perpetual duration and no regular occurrence or succession; there are only configurations of particular content which in turn reveal a certain temporal *Gestalt*, a coming and going, a rhythmical being and becoming." [6] We may also reverse Cassirer's words and say that without ritual, time does not pass. Mythical time is enacted time, a celebration of a change in the position of the sun, the moon, and the

5 Thomas Mann, *The Tales of Jacob* [*Joseph and His Brothers*], tr. H. T. Lowe-Porter (New York, 1934), pp. 29–30.

6 Ernst Cassirer, *The Philosophy of Symbolic Forms*, tr. Ralph Manheim (New Haven, 1955), Vol. II, p. 108.

stars, of the change of the seasons. This time is not objective or subjective, physical or historical (since these distinctions are alien to mythical man's attitude toward the world), but is experienced and thought in terms of cosmic correspondences between man, earth, and heaven. Even so, it contains potentialities of formalization, which result in the universal cyclical order of the cosmos, an extremely abstract conception and at the same time a powerful image. A turn from the individual concrete event to the general rule, from particular rhythms and periods to numbers and dates, marks the progress to spiritualized myth. It can be followed clearly in the birthplace of all "astral" religion: Babylonia and Assyria. The regularity of the astronomical process becomes the basic phenomenon underlying the divine order of the cosmos. Where sun and moon are taken as measures of time, "thought rises to the idea of the temporal order as a universal order of destiny, dominating all being and change," to a truly cosmic power that binds all things, men, demons, and gods.

In this cosmic power are embedded oppositions which religious thinkers have often sensed and formulated in contradictory ways; these are the oppositions between the fateful and the creative aspect of time. Time is the year and unity in the recurrence of the seasons; it is change and unity in change; it is the evanescent and the enduring, *sempiternitas* and *aeternitas*. Myth itself thus tends toward a differentiation between the great and the little year, for which it employs two different calculations. As man's power to survey the chain of the years increases, the little year loses its cyclical character. Where urban culture integrates large groups of men and creates fine differentiations in their lives, consciousness breaks away from its roots in the little things. For man's own lifetime as it passes from year to year, the notion of repetition recedes in favor of the additive series; the sequence of the years, prefigured from time immemorial in the irreversible process of growing old, begins to extend in a straight line and gradually takes on a different character from that of the great cosmic year. The great year begins and ends when it leads back to its beginning, and this is the lifetime of a cosmos, which the Babylonians called *adu*, the Persians *hazara*, the Hebrews *olam*, the Greeks *aion*, the Romans *aevum*, and the early Germans *ewa*.

The computation of its curvature is the work of the peoples of Mesopotamia and starts from the discovery of the "precession," the advance of the vernal equinoxes along the zodiac—and this, we might say in passing, indicates that the objectivizing ratio can be very highly developed in the mythical consciousness, though it need not take a direction corresponding to our scientific thinking. "This memorable discovery," says Leopold Ziegler in his richly documented book *Überlieferung* ("Tradition"),

> provides the mathematic foundation for the idea of the Platonic or Great Year, which increasingly assimilates to it the idea of the recurrence of the eternal, but in such a way that after a complete rotation of the vernal point along the zodiac, time, in a manner of speaking, ceases to advance, but begins again: and with it a "new heaven and a new earth." For after exactly 25,920 solar years, the "son" will be born again in the same position of the same constellation in the same zodiac, and thus rejuvenate and renew the universe—and this figure is the Babylonian measure for the duration of a real cosmic period, for the unfolding and fulfillment of an aeon. To be sure, every time reckoning, even the historical-biographical or simply chronological reckoning of the civil calendar, is based on the orbits of regularly moving celestial bodies. But while the little year increasingly casts off and disregards the notion of the original "curvature" of all measured time, the great year retains it in its strictest sense. In the end the circular form of the normal calendar year emerges only with the most important annual festivals, in which the calendar remembers its hieratic origin. But whereas an individual human life lines up inexorably passing time as on a suspended string, the god retains the unquestioned prerogative of moving himself and his world in pace with the circling vernal point and of achieving rejuvenation in the cycle.[7]

Yet where the world is conceived as strictly separate from God, as in Old Testament Yahwism, the aeonic conception of the cosmos can have only a secondary importance. That ancient oriental heritage has indeed left traces, and perhaps the days of the creation, perhaps the prophets' hopes of return and fears of doom, preserve a memory of it. But the doctrine that the world was created from nothingness establishes an absolute beginning and so puts an end to the image of the cosmic cycle. The great year makes place for a linear chronology which has its source in a divine plan and provides the framework for history. And one thing is indisputable: the Messianic promise, "the promised return of the kingdom, enhanced for all time in Isaiah to a return of the Golden Age, indeed of the glory of paradise, could easily be related to the other Asiatic traditions." [8] Yet the birth of the Lamb—at the time when the vernal point traveling along the zodiac left the

7 Leopold Ziegler, *Überlieferung* (Leipzig, 1936), p. 344.

8 Ibid., p. 355.

sign of Taurus for that of Aries, so becoming a cosmic month younger, as does the Ram in the Lamb—also has a historical, datable significance. The Saviour is a man. Hence this fusion of aeonic-cyclical and historical-chronological time reckoning has come down to us as the story of salvation, in which myth and history form an undifferentiable whole, running from the beginning of creation through the Old and the New Testaments down to the end of time.

This order of salvation has its exact correspondence in a new reply to death in the *theologoumenon* of the Resurrection which, although clad in—and in fact fused with—the mythical Return, is sharply opposed to the idea of immortality. For mythical thinking, with its blurred view of physico-spiritual individuality, reincarnation and the continuity of individual life are not fundamentally distinct. The individual thought of himself as part and parcel of the exemplary past and lived out of it as "an" Abraham, "an" Isaac, or "a" Jacob. This is illustrated by another passage from Mann's *Tales of Jacob:*

> "Woe, alas, for the lord!" That had often been cried over Yitzchak the rescued sacrifice and many a time and oft had he lived again in his tales, telling them in the first person, as was right, partly because his ego faded out and back into the archetype, partly because what had been had now become the present in his flesh and might have repeated itself conformably to the foundation. In this sense had Jacob and the rest heard and understood it when dying he spoke again of the averted scarifice; heard as it were with a double ear yet understood in a single sense—just as we, in fact, hear with two ears and see with two eyes, yet grasp the thing heard and seen as one.[9]

And in a passage just preceding, Mann wrote significantly: "Together they sewed up Yitzchak in a ram-skin, with his knees under his chin, and thus they gave him to time to devour, to time which devours his children that they may not set themselves over him, but must choke them up again to live in the same old stories as the same children." [10]

In the sphere of Christian revelation and soteriology, however, death is taken in a profounder sense as destruction, and at the same time transcended in the mystery of resurrection. The *creatio ex nihilo* implies the possibility of dissolution into nothingness, which in turn corresponds to the individ-

9 Tr. Lowe-Porter, p. 203. 10 Ibid.

uality of the person, an individuality, moreover, which is not simply given by nature, but which confirms itself in an act of hope and faith. When Buddhism negates life in favor of the reality of death, it presupposes the Brāhmanic faith in the ineluctable chain of birth and death, the eternal cycle. Christ promises rebirth into an eternal life removed from earthly change, a life on which death as an event originating in the fall from grace, hence a unique event, can have no hold. Similarly the Jewish faith invokes the divine grace that can overcome sin and death. As Landsberg writes: "Christ promises a birth which shall be followed by no death. Buddha promises a death which shall be followed by no birth, and thus by no further death."[11] Birth through the transcendent, personal, and imageless God, who creates out of nothingness, brings with it the discovery of linear, eschatologically limited time. It has the aeon in it, but over it lies eternity in total otherness. Originating in nothingness, it leads from promise to fulfillment and ends in eternity.

Thus the power of the negative is not, as in Buddhism, restricted to inhibiting the cycle of existence by voluntary mortification, concentration, and contemplation, or as in Greek philosophy, to the dialectical opposition to existence. As nowhere else, it is seen as that which cannot be transcended by natural means, because Judeo-Christian thinking has recognized that time and temporality have been created out of nothingness. Without this nihilism embedded in the foundation of the Judeo-Christian faith, we can understand neither its conception of a history of salvation nor its doctrine of resurrection. And without it we cannot understand the most surprising phenomenon of all, namely that this revelation was able in the course of time to cast off its mythical elements and to secularize itself into views of the world that are no longer transcendent and no longer bound to tradition.

Essentially the specific and utterly novel achievement of Europe consists in the release of free scientific investigation; and Judeo-Christian thought, side by side with Greek thought, has always been recognized as one of the roots of this Western rationalism. But despite their early amalgamation the two traditions—on the one hand, Greek ontology and causal thinking; on the other, Christian faith—stand to one another in a relation of irremediable tension. For the ontological concept of the world and the nihilist-creative concept—the idea of cosmic immanence and that of absolute

11 Paul Ludwig Landsberg, *The Experience of Death; The Moral Problem of Suicide,* tr. Cynthia Rowland (London, 1953), p. 9.

transcendence by grace—are incompatible, despite all attempts made by Christian theology to reconcile them. This incompatibility constitutes the creative unrest of the Western spirit, its driving force, the germ of its striving toward the open formulation of problems—that is, toward enlightenment and free scientific inquiry. The discovery of an understanding of nature and history, emancipated from God and divine revelation, is ultimately its work, and this we see time and time again in the fact that all radical questioning is exposed to the danger of nihilism—that is, of the uninterpreted, unreconciled, and thus disastrous power of the negative.

It was Nietzsche who perceived these matters and recognized in European nihilism the heritage of the Christian idea of transcendence, and in his theory of eternal return he dared to draw the consequence of his insight. If faith in the revealed meaning of the eschatological order of time succumbs to doubt, if the transcendent meaning of the rectilinear course of the world is lost, time becomes barren, a "low-grade" infinity [12] of succession without beginning and end. It becomes formalized as a mere dimension of measurement and chronology; its original values are lost and a new myth is required, a new profession of faith in pure being, if man, who is always in need of meaning, is to gain a substitute for his lost faith.

When the belief in ultimate things loses weight, the equilibrium between eschatological-linear time and mythical-cyclic time is disturbed. Christian faith is overbalanced by myth, and this dialectic dominates the history of postmedieval enlightenment, which simply cannot free itself from its innate duality. The decline of the belief that salvation will come in history is characterized by a disenchantment of heaven and of time, which calls forth an incursion of Nothingness. This situation must be dealt with, and it was dealt with according to a schema related to eschatology as long as that was possible. Thus in the eighteenth and nineteenth centuries we encounter the historical constructions (whose aftereffects are still with us) of Hegel and Marx. The element of salvational promise in these theories is clearly recognizable. The personal act of faith has been replaced by reason and practical decision; transcendent redemption has given way to the self-reconciliation of the human spirit, the humanization of man who has become alienated from his own nature. But as scientific critique progresses, these constructions also lose their cogency. Causal and relativizing thought, brought to the fore by the empirical sciences of nature and history, gains the upper

12 "*Schlechte Unendlichkeit*" (Hegel).

hand, with the result that theory and practice are no longer subordinated to a common directive. Thought and action are related no longer continuously but only from instance to instance in the sense of a mandate and its execution, though the belief in progress—that last pale memory of an eschatological concept of time—may tend to obscure this fact.

Another quasi-eschatology arose from the linking of scientific and historical factors in Darwinism. It strove to base a faith in infinite perfectibility on the facts of biological development; today this assumption has been unmasked by biology, history, and sociology as an unwarranted construction. It has lost its magic, for the liberal order of society, which it served to justify, no longer exists. Since then there has been a continuous search for new interpretations and *ersatz* religions which strive to extract a promise of salvation from the material of experience, a promise that may provide a common directive for thought and action. As we can see from Nietzsche's theory of eternal return, there is something violent about these directives. In order to exorcise the fatal meaninglessness of the empty future, they must inhibit criticism—that is, set themselves up as dogma. The ideology of National Socialism was a product of such fear. Its regressive mythology banished collective historical fear and also the individual fear of death as life grown meaningless. If the individual is nothing and the nation is everything (though possessing value only because of its racial quality), the practical survival of the individual in the nation guarantees the fulfillment of his existence and prescribes his political line. The same, with appropriate transpositions, is true of the mythology of class struggle.

Thus for the secularized consciousness the political myth has become one answer to the problem of our epoch's relation to death—an answer arising from the distorted relation to the meaning of life of a consciousness at one and the same time deprived of faith but intensified in its sense of individuality by its position with the atomized mass. The other answer is to be found in the various forms of existential philosophy, whose call for a free acceptance of death relates them to Stoicism. Both can say: "In order not to fear death, bear it always in mind." Yet for our time, when we no longer, as in antiquity, believe in a cosmos, the *virtus moriendi*, the study of how to die, has taken on a new meaning. It signifies the making of one's peace with the meaninglessness of life, learning not to despair at the absence of naturally or historically given directives, relying with radical freedom on the nullity of this same freedom, and striking roots in the moment. Since no directive for a qualitatively determined future can now be derived from the past, the relation between the two aspects of time is reversed; the hegemony passes to the future with its indefiniteness. Under the pressure of the formalization of time—that is, the relativization of the past and the indirection of the future—the moment becomes the only temporal modality in which meaning is still possible. But the creation of meaning by decision in concrete situations is a formula that fits both individual and collective subjects, and this pure decisionism can neither summon them to responsibility nor stifle them.

In invoking the disintegration of God-ordained authority, the decay not only of Christian revelation but also of the whole body of metaphysical and ethical thinking molded by it, decisionism takes the line of the Enlightenment and makes unlimited use of reason, though, to be sure, without the slightest tendency to deify it. The man who has a purely instrumental relation to his own critical faculty, without a vestige of the religious respect for reason which still animated the great Enlighteners, has taken upon himself a consciousness without myth and therefore without security. In such a situation there is no longer any Romantic yearning for death, no Tristan-Schopenhauerian Romanticism of death the redeemer. Epochs such as the nineteenth century that still felt protected can hope for something from death. It threatens us all, but individually, and the individual must make his peace with it. Yet today it menaces us in still another way, as the barrenness of a time that has lost its meaning.

Apparently even enlightened man cannot bear to face a boundless emptiness without the protective covering of some sort of cosmic order. "Low-grade" infinity kills him. He needs simultaneity and, as van der Leeuw says, "This relation of simultaneity has from time immemorial been related to the image of the circle. For the relation between space and time is the same as that between the straight line and the circle. The problem of the squaring of the circle is not a whim, but a problem rooted in our innermost being." [13] Why then is it not a whim, a prejudice? Or in other words: Is the idea of an absolute meaning one of man's vital needs? Can he exist only in a directed time, once it has dawned on him that time is essentially alien to space? Can he cast off the heritage of eschatological thinking? Can he cease to ask after a meaning, aim, or purpose, without confronting death as nothingness? Are we reduced to the alternative of a renewal of Christian

13 Cf. below, p. 326.

transcendence—that is, the eschatological picture of time—or of the flight from time into a mythical view of eternal recurrence?

I am convinced that this question contains within it the whole difficult relationship between world and environment. Erich Neumann once said: "The malaise of culture is in reality the malaise of life in a world bereft of myth." [14] But this radical loss of myth occurred only when the last interpretations of the world originating in the tradition of the Enlightenment were unmasked as *ersatz* forms of once binding religions and so lost their authority; at the same time a discrepancy between the world and the human environment became perceptible. The destruction of the cosmos—that is, of a meaningfully ordered structure of being which possesses a natural relation to human existence and which despite repeated upheavals reaches back through the long Christian tradition to the dawn of Greek thought—the destruction of this meaningful order is the work of rational science and the technical revolution that came in its train. If the discrepancy between world and environment which remained latent, or at least did not become virulent between the emergence of mathematical science in the Renaissance and the period of Goethe, became intensified into a crisis in the succeeding century, this can only be attributed to the effect of modern science and technology. Philosophers anticipated at an early day that once mathematics had seen through it, the world of heaven and earth in which men live would lose its traditionally respected proportions and become relativized. Today this insight has become living everyday experience and we have drawn its technological consequences. Utopia has become reality, but the *topoi* appropriate to man have been lost.

And yet it would be a mistake to regard the conquest of space and time in their atomic and interstellar aspects as something absolutely contrary to man's nature. Even under the most primitive conditions man never had an absolutely self-contained environment like that of the animals; never did he possess the natural shelter of an environment attuned to his organs and drives. His field has always been the world; his openness to the world has always been disproportionate to his physical possibilities, and at all times this situation has called for artificial correctives. Man has been compelled to mold his environment into a second nature. And for this reason the technological revolution, even in its present form, contains nothing specifically new. What is unprecedented in it is only the magnitude and urgency

14 "Die mythische Welt und der Einzelne," *EJ 1949*, p. 222.

of the threat emanating from the now complete limitlessness and formalization of space and time. With the total transformation of the cosmos into fields of possible action the world has lost its face. The actual threat of death with which the growth of power confronts mankind is only the manifest expression of this loss.

II

From time immemorial the image of the hourglass has served to symbolize the relation between formalized time and death. When the measure is full, the corresponding time interval has lapsed and the end is at hand. And this instrument discloses the dialectic of the end, for it can be reversed, so that the sand begins to flow again toward a new end and a new beginning. If the act of reversal is not taken as part of the picture, the possibility of an endless playing with the image of the sand running down opens up a perspective on the unbounded barrenness of the simple, irreversible succession which time, as a pure condition without relation to any concrete reality, has become for us. But if the reversal is taken into account, the image recalls the cosmic concept of time, whose fundamental form is the circle, symbol of recurrence, rebirth, and eternal life. Human thought cannot evade these two symbolizations of time when it encounters the problem of death, which always involves the problem of its meaning and of how to transcend it. Our clocks, it is true, have cast off this symbolism, for what we are concerned with measuring is unmeasured or abstract time, and no longer commensurate time. In the seventeenth-century clocks ornamented with moving figures, the twelve hours—represented as the apostles or as the figures of a dance of death—enter into a relation to that which is above time; at the sight of their naïvely sublime melancholy we are seized with the dread of death and eternity. And the tolling of the bells arouses a grief which may find some solace in these words of Ludwig Feuerbach:

> Every moment of life is fulfilled being, infinitely significant for its own sake, self-appointed and self-satisfied—an unlimited affirmation of itself; each moment drains the beaker of infinity, which like Oberon's magic cup is forever filled anew. Fools say that life is nothing but an empty sound, that it passes like smoke and is wafted away like wind. No, life is music; each moment is melody or a full, soulful tone. . . . The tones of music also pass, but each tone has meaning as a tone; in the presence of this innermost meaning and soul of the tone, transience vanishes into insignificance.[15]

15 *Gedanken über Tod und Unsterblichkeit*, in *Sämmtliche Werke*, III (Leipzig, 1847).

*

At first sight it may seem self-evident that in a world without becoming and passing away there can be neither time nor death; that although the order of mere becoming and passing away is projected in time, it need not for this reason imply death, so that if we consider the relation between time and death as something more than external and formal, the concepts are not simply interchangeable; and that the two must be considered within a circumscribed horizon, namely that of human life. But all this is not so self-evident as it may seem. For today there is a pronounced tendency to endow time and death with an exclusively existential meaning—that is, to consider them solely in terms of human decision; and this tendency threatens to distort our inquiry from the start. To be sure, the increasingly complex relation between death and time is disclosed only in experiences restricted to us humans, but time and death extend beyond the human dimension and give this dimension its place in the encompassing structure of the world, which may not be interpreted merely as man's environment and dwelling place.

From the point of view of time as the locus of transience, death is the modality of the end of all living things. The inanimate passes, wears out, vanishes; it can disintegrate and be destroyed, but of itself it does not end unless an end is administered to it. Only what moves of itself, what grows and develops—life—can die (and must die when it has reached a certain degree of differentiation); only life can come to an end—whether a natural or a violent death—in and through itself, by virtue of a certain frailty which is evidently inherent in the living substance. To know this is the privilege and fatality of man. Plants fade, animals expire, only man dies, because he knows his finite nature. That he must end is evident to him, so that his life is shaped by death as its antithesis and destiny. For his life is related to death as to a constant threat under which it takes place. Man, who has the privilege of having to conduct his life, is confronted by his finiteness; he lives from out of death toward death—that is to say, he gives it some place in the order of things. He alone of living creatures conceives his death as a must in the full double sense that it is inevitable and without exception: there is no reason why it might not *not* be, although it always is. Or, to envisage this situation in its acutest form: death belongs only conditionally and factually to the nature of man. Its exceptionless "must" conveys no inner necessity. If it did, we should have to regard the phenomena of rebellion against it, or of acceptance and pious resignation, as irrelevant and meaningless in view of the allegation of the simple finiteness of human existence. If it were so, death would be natural, even self-evident to man, a *vérité éternelle* and not a *vérité de fait*, a material *a priori* of genuine essential necessity, and not a *factum brutum*, a *tremendum*. The fact that all living creatures must die, which we men know—though only from experience—is not compatible with the contention that human existence is essentially finite. Man's knowledge of this fact as a fact raises him above mere finiteness; which thus comes to his consciousness as a fatality, as something contrary to his essence, an accident, despite its naturalness and matter-of-courseness.

The distinction between violent death and normal, natural death from old age does not affect the issue, and similarly the difference between sickness and health becomes irrelevant in the light of death. As Gottfried Benn has written:

> A normal life, a normal death,
> these are nothing. A normal life
> also leads to a sick death. Altogether death
> has nothing to do with health and sickness,
> it uses them for its ends.
> What do you mean by "death has nothing to do with sickness?"
> I mean this: many fall sick without dying,
> so something more must be involved,
> a fragment of the questionable,
> a factor of uncertainty;
> it is not so clearly outlined,
> and it has no scythe,
> it observes, looks round the corner, and even holds back,
> and it is musical in another melody.[16]

Of course, the notion that death is musical in another melody is true for man, who lives with death as a constant threat, but not for plants and animals—that is, for organic life as such, which merely succumbs to it through frailty. In the organic world, death simply equals the end of the processes necessary for the manifestations of life: for example, respiration, metabolism, generation, and regeneration. Expiration here is the countermotion inherent in the life process, the contrary to all differentiation, develop-

16 "Restaurant," from "Fragmente," in *Neue Gedichte* (Wiesbaden, 1951).

ment, and reproduction. Here death is simply the price which the living substance pays for all the expenditures through which and in which it lives. To this melody, if you will, dying is not alien; it belongs in it as counterpoint or as the simple contradiction to aliveness as such. Here death and life form a dialectical unity; death is the antithesis of a purposive self-fulfilling finite process. But for man (because he knows of it) it is this only in so far as man is also a living creature. It would be easy to come to an understanding regarding this "in so far" and "also" if we wished to characterize the transition to the dimension of the soul and the spirit. But for the moment all this would tell us is that the knowledge of having-to-die divides and detaches man from his own finiteness. This detachment, to be sure, does not make the finiteness illusory, it does not take away death's sting; indeed, it gives death its sting and lends a fragmentary aspect to man's own finiteness. That is to say, man's finiteness remains, but as a fact which can only be justified from the standpoint of the organic and which is imposed as a fatality on him who knows of it. Death is not immanent in man as it is in animals and plants, but transgredient, not only something running counter to livingness, inherent in it and belonging to its essence, but also something that comes to his humanity from outside.

It is this finiteness, rendered questionable by our awareness of death, that first enables us to grasp the relation of death to time. Finiteness is synonymous with temporality, and is so in a precise sense which is exemplified in varying degrees only by living creatures. Not only are living creatures datable in time like lifeless material phenomena; they also require time in order to live. They all need time in order to be, they all develop and age, they all possess potencies and lose them. Animal forms, moreover, manifest their connection with time in the anticipations of instinctive actions and the recapitulations of memory, achievements which do not occur in the vegetable world. On the human level, finally, we have planning and memory, actualizations of the future and the past both lacking in the animals, which consequently do not know the three aspects of temporality. Where actualization is not possible, past and future do not emerge—actualization and objectivization are fundamentally one and the same act—so that only man can think of time and death in an objective form.

The vegetable, animal, and human stages of organic life represent three distinctly separate modes of temporality or finiteness, only the last and highest of which discloses the relation of time to death. But—and here I cite a passage from a book of mine that appeared in 1928—"the essential anticipation immanent in all living being, the character of anticipating itself, is not to be confused with a relation to the future. Living being as such does not relate itself to the future—neither animals nor plants can do this, but only man; rather, each individual, each potential totality, is related to the sphere of its not-yet-being-so as to an opposite and counterpart of itself. Living being is grounded in the future, not related to the future."[17] I repeat that only man has this possibility of relatedness to the future, only man, who from the necessity of his aliveness makes a virtue of living into the future, of bold anticipation, of adventure or formative planning. "But in living through a becoming, a becoming-something, a development in this relation to the future, the individual moves toward his death."[18] He grows old and life replies to this irreversible descent into old age by reproduction, in which it is rejuvenated.

> It is not because life is eternal and indestructible by nature that rejuvenation and increase exist, and it is not because the individual cannot hold the fullness of life and merely acts as a narrow channel through which the stream of life flows that individuals succeed one another in the chain of generation; what conditions renewal is rather the limited character of [individual] life and its decline into old age. Rejuvenation compensates for old age but does not negate or transcend it. No artificial rejuvenation that prolongs the life of an individual or a species can compensate for destiny itself, for the decline of the life line as a whole. If the rejuvenation process could present a true opposition to the process of growing old, life would take on a stationary character.[19]
>
> Compensatory renewal can only be effected in such a way as to preserve the process of development as a whole. If it is directed toward the living individual, he dies of it. Thus among unicellular animals, renewal coincides under certain conditions with death. The cell splits: this is the type of reproduction from which Weismann derived the concept of the "potential immortality" of the unicellular animals. In multiple-celled organisms the compensatory renewal is effected by the formation of germ cells which, in relation to the total body, contain a maximum of undeveloped potentialities. . . . Thus the individual is rejuvenated in *another* individual. . . . In the individual the development moves with inner necessity toward death; hence there must be a chain of individuals.[20]

17 *Die Stufen des Organischen und der Mensch* (Berlin and Leipzig, 1928), pp. 212, 213.
18 Ibid. 19 Ibid. 20 Ibid.

Every living individual, whether animal, vegetable, or human, is—as a finite, that is, temporal, being—exposed to having-to-end, with the qualification of a possible survival through reproduction in other germs of its own type. Death and reproduction stand together as manifestations of a finite being interwoven with time; only their form and relation to one another are modified at different stages of organic formation. Man, too, as a vital system, is subject to this structural law of living being. His knowledge of it, his life in the face of death, avails him nothing. But his having laid bare his own finiteness means a confrontation with it, which limits it for him, which makes it questionable and fragmentary. The knowledge of his finiteness reveals the contrary possibility, and now in a sense other than the survival discernible in the reproduction that compensates for the death of the individual. Only now does finiteness in the three phases of temporality—past, present, and future—stand out from the background of an all-encompassing time, in which everything comes and remains and passes but which does not itself come and go. Duration becomes visible and death becomes visible. Just as the duration of the one time now relativizes the modes of temporality into aspects of a finite being, so death limits and transcends finite being, and confronts man.

Time and death, as we said at the start, are not simply interchangeable concepts; that is to say, time forms the foundation of death but does not necessarily include it, though both rise together on the same horizon for man, and for man alone simultaneously. Plants and animals also die, but they lack the relation to death, they undergo the end without suffering from it; they are finite but they do not know it. Although the complex inner relation between death and time can thus be disclosed only to man, the relation itself extends to the extrahuman dimensions of organic life and belongs to those orders of the world which encompass human existence. It is for this reason only that myths speak of it. If on the contrary we follow the existentialist vision and isolate finiteness as temporality from the extrahuman sphere—as Heidegger, for example, has attempted to do—the relation between time and death gains in depth, but at the expense of its cosmic dimension.

Because the experience of death, or rather the knowledge that it cannot be experienced, is reserved for man, the question concerning it falls back on the asker himself, although it deals with something that not only befalls man but is laid down for all living creatures on the basis of their finiteness.

Though this finiteness discloses itself to man alone as a specific involvement in and with time, it constitutes more than mere human existence. For temporality is the fundamental mode of living and fulfilling time—that is, of germinating, developing, maturing, aging, and finally dying—a mode which varies according to the vegetable, animal, and human stage and which is altogether distinct from mere lifeless "being there." Where biology speaks its own language in characterizing this basic mode and does not sidestep the issue by using the language of physics and chemistry, with which it can apprehend the conditions of life but not the phenomenon of each living creature as an individual whole, it must use the Aristotelian concepts of potency and act, *dynamis*, energy, and entelechy, which impart the inner relatedness of living things to time. If for these words that have become ambiguous we wish to substitute neutral terms, we arrive at formulations that seem to be coined for us men and which we tend to elucidate by the example of our human behavior. But the Aristotelian terms aim beyond it and aspire to designate attributes of all living things.

Perhaps a second quotation from my own work will show how the relation between time and death is rooted in the nature of organic life: "Only to the living being are the modes of time essential, for it constitutes itself by means of time in so far as it is a being that anticipates itself." The germ contains the fully developed organism embedded in itself, and the fact that we do not yet know how this comes about need not concern us in this connection. For even if we should know some day, our statements about attributes of living being would not be invalidated. Organic "being shows a foundation of a temporal character, determined by the direction from the future. . . . Anticipation is the mode of living being, anticipation not of something determinate that is still . . . to come, but anticipation of itself as something determinate. . . . Thus living being implies its self-fulfillment. This assures the living thing of what is given to no lifeless thing: actuality." [21]

To be actual—I say this only to avoid misunderstanding—does not mean to actualize or to make something present. Actuality contains only this *possibility*, which is first released for man. "Therefore," I continue,

> the living body, by implication that which succeeds itself, has a past. It does not simply pass away and lose in what it is that which it was, or preserve it as a mountain preserves what it was as that which it is, but preserves it in its having-beenness. . . . As that

21 Ibid., pp. 179–80.

> which succeeds itself, it is all past. To this extent one may speak of memory . . . as a universal function of living matter . . . an entity which, through the mediation [but this mediation, be it said for the benefit of ears trained in the school of existentialism, is not yet a relationship] of the image of the endless cycle or the tranquil flame, signifies continuous transition from one to another mode of time and the unity of the transition, that is to say, the present.[22]

In this light, a clarification of the relation between death and temporality becomes significant for that other relation (which does not coincide with it) between death and time, and for that relation's character of necessity. The insight into the finiteness of living being does indeed suggest the thought that decay and ultimate dissolution are a part of life; that is, it suggests the immanence of death. But the inference is not compelling, quite aside from the fact that for man this immanence surely does not apply. Finiteness means primarily the orientation of the germ toward the fully developed organism and not toward the succeeding phase of decline. The summit is the *telos*, not death. It seems to be Christian thinking that first brought this distortion to the ancient conception.

In any case there are two main possibilities. The first is that aging and death are alien and external to life, and subordinate living individuals to their law only through the secretion of waste products and chemical attrition—however inevitable these processes may be. In this case life as such would be endless and would incur exhaustion only through certain inadequacies of the body. Then one might simply say that the proteins were not able to keep up the pace. "Life in its pure state would have to be conceived as a mere tangent to the parabola of youth, maturity, old age." The fragmentary life of plants, animals, and men would announce a perpetual life.

The second possibility is that old age and death are essential to life as such. "The actual development would consist only of a struggle, grounded in life itself, between two conflicting tendencies, one of which, the rising, positive tendency, would have the upper hand at first, while the other, the negative declining tendency, would gain preponderance in the end; and in the middle there would be a necessary transitional phase in which the two tendencies would be evenly balanced."[23] Thus life would be an interweaving of two conflicting tendencies, neither of which is wholly realized; or else it

22 Ibid., p. 180. 23 Ibid., p. 147.

would consist of its own involvement with death, its opposite—a view which is very close to that of Simmel.[24]

In my opinion neither of these interpretations strikes at the actual essence of finiteness. For this finiteness comprises a tendency toward both rectilinear progression and circular self-containment. Thus for man with his faculty of actualization, the two tendencies constitute the double meaning of time: irreversible succession and cycle. The synthesis of the two is the spiral, symbolized in the curve of youth, maturity, and old age—the parabolic curve with the rising arc, apogee, and descending arc. The development provides the foundation for old age and death, but life by itself cannot effect the border crossing into death. This only man can do, because he can detach himself from his livingness. In plants, animals, and men, life ages toward death, but it cannot make death into its end (not even in suicide). It inclines toward death, but it must still be overpowered by death. Plants fade away without any abrupt transition, although here, too, a violent end is possible. In the case of animals with their higher degree of differentiation, the breach is sharper; the animal expires. Man, finally, dies and suffers death.

*

Up until now we have emphasized the phenomenon of natural death, death in its more conciliatory form, which seems almost to merge with life. But the certainty of having-to-die springs from a fundamental susceptibility, which is something more than the frailty of the organic substance, than sickness and old age. The proximity of death, the feeling that in the midst of life we are surrounded by death, quite apart from sickness and health, accentuates our uncertainty as to the moment of its coming. We know only *that* we will die; we do not know when, and we do not know what our death will be; and the crucial point is that this "when" can be any moment, that this "what" is fundamentally beyond our knowledge. Man's death is situated in a twilight between knowledge and nonknowledge. Thus if we wish to grasp the nature of man's certainty of death, the only authority to which we can turn is the modality of death as a datum and of man's encounter with it. The certain expectation of death makes it actual to us, *praesens de futuris expectatio.*

Whence the certainty? According to the strict principle of induction, the experience that no man has yet escaped death constitutes an extreme prob-

24 Georg Simmel, *Lebensanschauung: Vier metaphysische Kapitel* (Munich, 1918).

ability but no certainty. Yet if the "must" is based not on experience but on insight, it expresses no fatality but an antithesis of an *a priori* character. Simmel, borrowing from Hegel, elucidates the relation between life and death by the situation of men on shipboard, moving in a direction opposite to that of the ship's course: "As they walk southward, the ground on which they do so is carried northward with them." [25] The difficulty, here disclosed, of not falsifying the certainty of having-to-die by the either-or of *a priori-a posteriori*, but of considering its own intrinsic character that possesses something of both, has been treated at length by three representatives of the phenomenological school, Scheler, Heidegger, and Landsberg.

Scheler attempts to assimilate the human experience of death to the experience of growing old, which according to him is experienced as an increase in the pressure of the past and a decrease in the number of possibilities.[26] In this perspective, death is the limit toward which man moves, and in it he encounters an extreme relation between pressure of the past and loss of freedom; this relation is equivalent to a loss of self. Thus the certainty of death retains a character of experience—of self-experience in fact; seen more closely, it is the experience of gradual suffocation and extinction. The vector is provided by the increase or decrease of two reactions toward the past and the future.

In opposition to this, Landsberg points out that the human experience of death comprises something entirely different from the idea of an extreme limit to individual biological development. Death, which we await and infer as the immanent future for our own life, can be experienced only through our fellow man, who usually passes away before his time and does not attain his natural end. The certainty that one must not only pass away at some time but that one is close to death at every moment is the reverse side of a fundamental ignorance, and

> not merely the result of a lacuna in biology, but also of my ignorance of my destiny, and even this "ignorance" is an act in which there is a presence as well as an absence of death. *Mors certa, hora incerta.* The dialectic of death is secret. It is an absent presence. Thus the problem of the human experience of the necessity of death reaches beyond biology, just as it reaches beyond the data provided by the feeling of growing old.[27]

25 Ibid.
26 Max Scheler, "Tod und Fortleben," *Schriften aus dem Nachlass* (Berlin, 1933).
27 Landsberg, *The Experience of Death*, p. 6.

When we approach a deathbed, we experience the dead as absent in presence. The dialectic has reversed itself.

Landsberg has pointed out quite correctly that such an experience strikes at the "we"—at the community in which we live with all others and eminently with those who were close to us.

The transformation of the person we knew into a corpse from which precisely this person has departed is the basis of the double phenomenon of absence in presence. Since in a certain sense this community with him is and was myself, "death penetrates the center of my own existence and thus becomes immediately discernible." In the experience of my dead fellow man, through our broken bond, I experience the connection between being a person and being mortal. "The general necessity here is not of a logical but rather of a symbolic nature. The *other* represents in reality all the others. He is Everyman, and this Everyman dies each time in the death of the man we know, who dies his own death." [28]

A case of death, then, is a case of thoroughgoing necessity only because the individual person, regardless of his individuality, can stand for every other person. This above all gives meaning to Luther's words of warning, which indeed spring from a very definite conception of the relation between man and God: "We are all called upon to die, and no one will die for another." The experienced fragility of physical persons is thus recognizable as a genuine essential experience, as a material *a priori* of personal being, not reaching beyond it but wholly limited to definite potentialities of human being, and within them susceptible of increase and diminution. Clearly then, the certainty of death is related to the differentiation of human consciousness. This notion has been stated by Simmel and is supported by many of the findings of ethnology.

Landsberg's essay provides an answer to certain propositions of Heidegger, whose analysis of death is devoted to preparing the way for an analysis of temporality and merely touches on the way in which death itself is given. We do not experience death but are merely present at it; it takes place in that noncommittal sphere to which we belong with others and in which we are not ourself committed. In the certainty that "one dies," our potential being is changed into a being-toward-our-own-death. Here there is only a passing away, an incurring of death; it stands between the expiring of the animals and the authentic dying that can be achieved only by man, dying

28 Ibid., p. 15.

as being-toward-death, toward-the-end of this existence. The nature of death is not disclosed in the observation of others or in any observation at all, but in an act of subjectivization, of making death into one's own task. This is not done by life with other men but only by our taking of our own end upon ourselves. "In anticipative resolution man has the courage for fear, because being-toward-death is essentially fear. Thus being-there [*Dasein*] does not have an end in which it merely ceases, expires, passes away; rather, it exists finitely, that is to say, in a relation to the end. By withstanding this threat, it has won the freedom for death, it has freely surrendered itself to death itself in an inherited, but nevertheless chosen possibility."

This "heroism of finiteness," representing itself as fundamental ontology, is an ethic deriving from Kierkegaard's call for subjectivization, though it deliberately sacrifices the latter's religious meaning and content. Be what you are out of your own self, take your destiny on yourself. Accept the possibility of the impossibility of your being, for only in this way will you be authentic and only in this way will you understand what being actually means and is. By contrast, Landsberg's accentuation of man as Everyman retains a Christian meaning. He is my neighbor, he is the other, he is I, I am he. What happens to him happens to me, and conversely. Heidegger's philosophy reveals the signature of Protestantism secularized and formalized; in Landsberg we hear the voice of Catholic piety.

For Heidegger, the way in which death—by definition not experienceable but nonetheless certain—is given is anticipatory decision. "To anticipate one's extreme and ownest possibility is an understanding return to one's ownest having-been." And this letting-come-toward-one is the phenomenon of the future [*Zukunft*]—that is, the coming [*Kunft*] in which existence, in which man, comes to himself. It is itself his future, just as in coming-to-himself in his having-beenness it is his past, both by virtue of the actualization in which, as present, it emerges from itself or matures. This unitary phenomenon of a having-been and actualizing future we call temporality, and in its maturations the fundamental possibilities of existence, authenticity, and inauthenticity are grounded. Under the eyes of death (which we do not see, but which we know sees us) man's being is disclosed to him as temporality. In this extreme readiness for confrontation with the nothingness of our existence, what for classical philosophy still counted as the indestructible core of our being—reason, the ego, the will, life, or individuality—vanishes into thin air. What remains is pure ecstatic temporality in the unity of actualization, letting-come-toward-oneself, and having-beenness—that is, of perspectives according to which men lead and interpret their lives, assume their destiny, and have a history.

Let us not become bewildered by the power of language in this twilight region of ethics and ontology. If I were to attempt to sum up the purpose and the fruits of this philosophical endeavor, I should have to start from the relativization of the Christian view of the world and of history, a view preserved, though secularized almost beyond recognition, down into the era of faith in progress. My point of departure would be this total relativization of a single historical chain of time. It dissolves the metaphor of epochs and phases and reduces it in each case to different conditions of human existence—different attitudes, evaluations, and conceptions. On the one hand we have this relativization, which does not stop at "human" nature but leaves interpretations of the world and the self; on the other, an extreme and sublime science, working with all the means of rational discovery but no longer believing in *ratio* itself, a science which unbinds everything and transposes everything into functions. Heidegger's theory of temporality is an answer to this dissolution of the human situation. With the decline of Christianity, time has more and more lost its meaning. The formalization of the concept of time, to which primordial time and eschatological time have succumbed, has brought about a fragmentation of time into diverse concepts corresponding to the various sciences: into physical, biological, psychological, and historical time. Their horizons do not encompass one another and they cannot be articulated into one cosmic time but are engaged in a competition that can no longer be resolved (the rate of disintegration of radium, for example, is useful for physical dating but meaningless for the qualitative determination of psychic or spiritual time—the perspectives are at cross purposes). Consequently nothing remains of "time" but temporality, just as nothing remains of history but historicity.

Heidegger in his philosophy transcends historicity in the limited sector of human finiteness. In so doing, he has undertaken by way of the concept of temporality (first formulated, we may note in passing, in the *Confessions* of St. Augustine) an interpretation of the relation of time to death which divests both time and death of meaning. For time and death are nothing without eternity, in the light of which alone they are what they are. Kant made time formal and subjective, and opposed to it the eternity of the Ideas; true, he lifted time out of the realm of possible experience, but he held fast to it as a transcendent factor. But Heidegger's formal destruction with its radical turn to the immanence of being-there deprives time of its duration and death of its threat. Death is a real threat only where it is set against continuity of life or rebirth, otherwise it is reduced to a marginal phenomenon; only on a foundation of *aeternitas* can there be *sempiternitas*, the succession and the modes of fulfilled time. Landsberg puts this as follows: "The anguish of death, and not only the pain of dying, would be incomprehensible if the fundamental structure of our being did not include the existential postulate of something beyond." [29] In the actualization of the endowment that each man has been given for his life, man (by actualizing!) escapes from time: he enters into its order, but in so doing has broken through it. To actualize means to objectivize, and objectivity means removal from time, detachment from time.

The empty forms of time, space, self, and death have in common the fact that they presuppose a detaching act of objectivization; they can be attained only by the type of human being who has become conscious of his individuation. By contrast, children and primitive peoples meet death, and indeed the phenomenon of disappearance as such, unselfconsciously and without much wonder. Here death does not strike the individual so deeply that another within the group cannot replace him, taking over his function, his name, his power. To the chain of births corresponds a chain of deaths, and often a child born in the death hour of a member of the group is regarded as a new embodiment of his released power. Thus it seems plausible to draw a line of development and couple the deepening of the consciousness of death with a deepening of self-consciousness. The more pronounced the personal consciousness becomes and the more differentiated and also fragile the social structure, the more profoundly this consciousness feels the horror of death and of time. The epochs of disintegration and social transformation, the Hellenistic period or the late Middle Ages, show this distinctly.

But never does death threaten the existence that accepts its finiteness. Existence must insist on its infiniteness if it wishes to arrive at that fear, open to which is the imperative of existential philosophy. Death must put the continuity of individual life in question; otherwise it is a full stop and no more. It is in this struggle to secure or avoid continuation of life that religious thought has always gained its form and depth, and consequently it loses its resonance once consciousness accustoms itself to nothingness as the

29 Ibid., p. 23.

limit and other shore of existence. Such an indifference, even though disguised by a heroic gesture, is manifested, it seems to me, in Heidegger's unhesitating detachment of man from his bond with nature in his analysis of the relation of temporality to death.

The existential analysis which appears so realistic by contrast with all thinking that finds man's center of gravity in his "consciousness" or "spirit" has preserved the inward orientation that came to it from idealism. Thanks to their phenomenological method, existentialist thinkers can preserve an open eye for their fellow man, for bodily existence, and even in a certain sense for material data; yet nature apart from man, particularly in its biological aspects, does not enter their regard. It is considered extraneous. But how, we ask, can the depth of death be maintained if the continuity it endangers is not anchored in the dimension of life which sustains not man alone but also the animals, and is common to them both? If it is not recognized that temporality (which to be sure is realized by man in a special way)—that the attitude toward future, past, and present which is reserved for him alone—is grounded in a very real sense in those preliminary stages revealed to us by plants and animals? Even though the special privilege of so-called existence may be the relation to a relationship, and even though special possibilities for a relation to death may thus be derived, nevertheless death gains its ontological weight only from its evident involvement with aliveness.

Equally dubious, it seems to me, is the existentialists' disregard of another evident involvement of living forms with time. As has often been remarked, time passes in youth more slowly than in old age; a day or a year seems far longer to a child than to a mature or aged man, while a time interval that was long and tedious for us while we were passing through it seems in retrospect to have vanished in a twinkling. Conversely, time abundantly filled flies as we experience it but seems long in retrospect. Thus our experience of duration is determined by the order and meaning of its content.

This brings us to the intricate relation between duration and measured time, *temps durée* and *temps cadran*, which I should like to illustrate with two passages from the chapter entitled "By the Ocean of Time" in *The Magic Mountain.* The first passage is a variation on an idea which has occupied such biologists as K. E. von Baer and J. von Üxküll:

> It would not be hard to imagine the existence of creatures, perhaps upon smaller planets than ours, practicing a miniature time-economy in whose brief span the brisk tripping gait of our second

> hand would possess the tenacious spatial economy of our hand that marks the hours. And contrariwise, one can conceive of a world so spacious that its time system too has a majestic stride, and the distinctions between "still," "in a little while," "yesterday," "tomorrow," are, in its economy, possessed of hugely extended significance.[30]

The other passage is concerned with the reciprocal relation between the content of time and the experience of duration:

> The time element in music is single. Into a section of mortal time music pours itself, thereby inexpressibly enhancing and ennobling what it fills. But a narrative must have two kinds of time: first, its own, like music, actual time, conditioning its presentation and course; and second, the time of its content, which is relative, so extremely relative that the imaginary time of the narrative can either coincide nearly or completely with the actual, or musical time, or can be a world away. A piece of music called "A Five-Minute Waltz" lasts five minutes, and this is its sole relation to the time element. But a narrative which concerned itself with the events of five minutes, might, by extraordinary conscientiousness in the telling, take up a thousand times five minutes, and even then seem very short, though long in its relation to its imaginary time. On the other hand, the contentual time of a story can shrink from its actual time out of all measure. We put it in this way on purpose, in order to suggest another element, an illusory, even, to speak plainly, a morbid element, which is quite definitely a factor in the situation. I am speaking of cases where the story practises a hermetical magic, a temporal distortion of perspective reminding one of certain abnormal and transcendental experiences in actual life. We have records of opium dreams in which the dreamer, during a brief narcotic sleep, had experiences stretching over a period of ten, thirty, sixty years, or even passing the extreme limit of man's temporal capacity for experience; dreams whose contentual time was enormously greater than their actual or musical time, and in which there obtained an incredible foreshortening of events; the images pressing upon one another with such rapidity that it was as though "something had been taken away, like the spring of a broken watch" from the brain of the sleeper. Such is the description of a hashish eater.[31]

The fact that experienced time obviously depends on lived time is a strong argument for the illusory character of time as a whole. We can minimize this

30 Tr. Lowe-Porter (New York, 1927), p. 689.

31 Ibid., pp. 683–84.

illusoriness, as does Kant, who sees a distinction between appearance and phenomenon and who posits time as one of the conditions of the phenomenal world a subject must fulfill if—but only if—it wishes to arrive at an objective order of nature. Or we can regard the dependency of time on subjectivity, consciousness, and life as so essential that the distinction between appearance and phenomenon seems mere play if contrasted with the wholeness of authentic being. But in either case, time's nearness to the transition into the dimension other than the world—that is, time's nearness to death—becomes plain once again. Behind the reality of experienced time and lived time, behind temporality fulfilled by organisms, plants, animals, and men, and behind temporality made into "time" by animals and men, pure time looms as the background against which they all are relative. Similarly, religious and philosophical speculation reveals an extratemporal and supratemporal depth to time: the eternal, that neither endures nor passes, the *nunc stans*, the paradoxical unity of Always and Now, without past or future. To gain a vision of it or to partake of it in some other way has from time immemorial been the supreme mandate of mystical experience and its interpretation of death. He whose life receives the seal of this moment has conquered not only time but also death.

Max Knoll

Transformations of Science in Our Age[1]

When we compare the present state of science with that of a few decades ago, we gain the impression that it has grown in something more than scope: the very structure has changed. Most of the significant work done in recent years has not been in the main disciplines, but in their borderline fields. Disciplines which used to be strictly separate or even opposed, as, for example, medicine and psychology, have so knit together at their borders that they can no longer be sharply distinguished from one another.[1a] In general, a new perspective on the relationship between the various disciplines seems to be opening. An outward sign of this new co-ordination is the fact that all over the world, not only in Ascona at the Eranos meetings but also in other places, scholars in such diverse fields as theology and biology or psychology and physics are coming together and are beginning once again to unite their special disciplines into a *universitas*, into a new whole. On the inward plane, there must lie back of this phenomenon a new awareness; that is to say, within the individual branches of learning a process of becoming aware of forgotten psychological contents must be taking place, and it is this process and its manifestation with particular respect to the concept of time which we shall here attempt to describe.

1 [This paper has been revised in English by the author. Professor Knoll has augmented and substituted material (1957) to bring in later scientific publications—ED.]

1a Cf., for example, Franz Alexander, *Psychosomatic Medicine* (New York, 1950). A different matter is the coalescence of closely related and not fundamentally antithetical fields as, for example, in biology: "The most diversive phenomena which occur in living matter can be regarded as expressions of fundamental processes which are similar throughout the living world. The divisions of biology, such as botany, zoology, bacteriology, embryology, and biochemistry, are accordingly breaking down."—A. Buzzati-Traverso, "The State of Genetics," *Scientific American* (New York), CLXXXV (Oct., 1951), 22. The same process of assimilation has also taken place in the case of physics and chemistry. But this kind of structural change in the sciences is not our concern here.

It is clear that contemporary natural science itself arose from a great process of becoming conscious—from the nineteenth-century striving for ever more exact and "impersonal" cognition of the surrounding world with the development of the *ratio*[2] as the dominant (psychological) function. This process naturally entailed a limitation of the human cognitive faculties to what can be "objectively" or causally apprehended and predicted in a system of physical space and time, and even now this trend does not seem to have reached its extreme. True, the logical and causal linking of phenomena that could be measured or counted made possible an apparent consistency in the scientific conception of the world. But by the beginning of the twentieth century it was already obvious that this picture of the world must be one-sided. For example, it provided means for describing living processes, including psychological ones, in such a space-time ("dimensional") system, but not for describing them according to their dynamic content. Moreover, the very trend toward increasing objectivization made considerable breaches in the coherence of such a rationalistic[3] world view; logicians found gaps in the rational cognitive faculty,[4] and physicists found relations between conjugate energy and position values of elementary particles which intrinsically exclude an accurate determination of both at the same time.

Nonetheless there are positivists who still believe that in the not too distant future an extension of the classical physical picture of the world will enable us to describe and predict accurately all the phenomena around us, including living processes, in the dimensional and quantitative form. There

2 Here we understand by *ratio* the "thinking function," one of the perceptive (cognitive) functions as defined by C. G. Jung. This function may be related to Grey Walter's P-type (*The Living Brain*, London, 1954, p. 2), which is based on cortical encephalograms (persistent α-rhythm).

3 In connection with philosophical systems, the word "rationalistic" is often used in a very broad sense which even includes systems of the Platonic type; cf., e.g., H. Reichenbach, *The Rise of Scientific Philosophy* (Los Angeles, 1951), p. 32. As mentioned in n. 2, we prefer to use the concept "rational" in the sense of a psychological, empirically established cognitive function that excludes "ideas" and *a priori* assumptions (cf. Part I, sec. A of our paper), in accordance with the traditional philosophic definition of rationalism as a tendency to use reason as the only source of cognition and organization of life (Alois Dempf, "Metaphysik des Mittelalters," p. 7, in A. Baeumler and M. Schröter, *Handbuch der Philosophie*, 4 vols., Munich and Berlin, 1934, Vol. I). The Platonic world view can certainly not be designated as "rationalistic" in this sense.

4 Cf. Kurt Goedel, "Über formal unterscheidbare Sätze der *Principia mathematica* und verwandter Systeme," *Monatshefte für Mathematik und Physik* (Vienna), XXXVIII (1931), 173. It is possible that any one of these gaps is only temporary, but such gaps are always present.

is, however, sufficient reason to doubt this—not only because for a long time science has made no discernible progress in this direction, but also because the findings of quantum physics and the psychology of the unconscious make a complete, homogeneous description of the world in terms of exactly predictable causes and effects appear inherently unattainable.

As Bohr has shown,[5] quantum physics necessarily contains "fragments of aspects[6] and causal chains that can no longer be fitted together to create a model of a nature that exists independently of the observer."[7] Only now, after the recognition of these "irrational" connections between complementary theories ("aspects") and complementary determinants of elementary particles has taken place, may we speak of a new unification of physical theories. It seems paradoxical that the abandonment of an accurate determination of certain atomic properties should have appreciably increased the scientific value of the exact discipline of microphysics. At first this state of affairs, which one might be less surprised to find in psychology, seems very strange in a field dealing with mechanical systems. It appears at present, however, that departure from a logically (or causally) consistent system in favor of a "pair of aspects" system, though frequently thought to be inconsistent, not only did not interfere with the scientific description of matter as a "whole," but was even necessary for a general "unified theory."

A considerable literature has already come into existence concerning this structural change in physics and its philosophical consequences.[8] An at-

5 See the following works by Niels Bohr: *Atomtheorie und Naturbeschreibung* (Berlin, 1931); "Can Quantum-mechanical Description of Physical Relativity Be Considered Complete?", *Physikalische Revue* (Stuttgart), XLVIII (1935), 696; *New Theories of Physics* (Paris, 1939), p. 11; "On the Notions of Causality and Complementarity," *Science* (Cambridge, Mass.), CXI (Jan., 1950), 51; "Kausalität und Komplementarität," *Erkenntnis* (Leipzig), VI (1936), 293.

6 In this paper the word "aspect" will be used in the sense of the German *Anschauung*, i.e., the description of an object by an observer according to his chosen "point of view," or his manifest psychological function. About such points of view see, e.g., Table 2.

7 C. F. von Weizsäcker, *Zum Weltbild der Physik* (Stuttgart, 1949), p. 86.

8 Bohr, works in n. 5; Louis de Broglie, *Die Elementarteilchen* (Hamburg, 1946); H. Dolch, *Theologie und Physik* (Freiburg i. B., 1950); P. von Handel, *Physik und Metaphysik* (Bergen, 1947); Werner Heisenberg, "Recent Changes in the Foundation of Exact Science," in *Philosophic Problems of Nuclear Science* (London and New York, 1952), pp. 11–26; K. von Neergard, *Untergang im Relativismus?* (Zurich, 1946); H. Conrad-Martius, *Naturwissenschaftlich-metaphysische Perspektiven* (Hamburg, 1948); Pascual Jordan: *Die Physik und das Geheimnis des organischen Lebens* (Brunswick, 1947), *Verdrängung und Komplementarität* (Hamburg, 1947), and *Die Physik des 20. Jahrhunderts* (Brunswick, 1938).

tempt will be made below to show that a similar structural change (the formation of "pairs of aspects") is taking place in other sciences, especially in psychology.[9] We will start, however, with modern physics, because its precisely formulated and tested findings[10] reflect most clearly the nature of the new structure as it appears in the description of matter.

Then, later, in line with the principal subject of this volume, we shall demonstrate in particular how our scientific concept of time is also subject to this structural change. Using examples of effects of the solar cycle on man, we shall show that "biological time" and "psychological time," familiar to us from psychology and mythology, can form a complement to physical time and that together they make up a pair of aspects in the scientific sense.

1. Growing Awareness of Typical Pairs of Aspects in Physics, Psychology, and Other Sciences

A. NATURE OF THE HUMAN PERCEPTIVE FACULTY: COMPLEMENTARITY OF THE PERCEPTIVE FUNCTION AND OF THE "OBSERVABLE" WORLD

Since physics is made by men, its general structure cannot be "objective," but must in principle be of a subjective nature, dependent on the anatomical and psychological structure of the human faculty of perception. This was already true of classical physics. For a closer description of this perceptive faculty, we shall use some empirical findings of psychology as a point of departure.

In his study of psychological types,[11] C. G. Jung, using material from history and the data gathered in his practice, considered four main types of

9 Cf., e.g., Bohr, in *Erkenntnis*, VI (1936), 302; Jordan, *Verdrängung und Komplementarität;* G. Heyer, *Vom Kraftfeld der Seele* (Stuttgart, 1949); C. A. Meier, "Moderne Physik—Moderne Psychologie," in *Die kulturelle Bedeutung der komplexen Psychologie* (Berlin, 1935), pp. 349–62; Bohr, in *Naturwissenschaften* (Berlin), XVI (1928), 245, and XVII (1929), 483; C. G. Jung, "The Spirit of Psychology," PEY, 1, pp. 385ff.; Markus Fierz, "Zur physikalischen Erkenntnis," *EJ 1948*, pp. 433ff.; and the following works of Jordan: *Die Physik des 20. Jahrhunderts;* "Positivistische Bemerkungen über die parapsychischen Erscheinungen," *Zentralblatt für Psychotherapie* (Leipzig), IX (1936), 3; *Anschauliche Quantentheorie* (Berlin, 1936), p. 271; *Die Physik und das Geheimnis des organischen Lebens*, p. 114; "Quantenphysikalische Bemerkungen zur Biologie und Psychologie," *Erkenntnis*, IV (1934), 3 and 215.

10 With the exception of present-day nuclear physics.

11 *Psychological Types* (New York and London, 1923). On the significance of this typology for human ways of expression, especially in art, and its correlations with other typologies, cf. Herbert Read, *Education through Art* (London and New York, 1945)

individual human perception or cognition, namely, thinking, sensation,[12] intuition, and feeling. He accordingly defined four different human types (thinking type, sensation type, etc.[13]), in each of which one of the forms of perception is dominant. The intentional limitation of this typology to perceptive functions that also come into play in science, in contrast to typologies concerning themselves with other strata of the psyche, such as drives,[14] is of great importance for our subject.

In general, two each of the perceptive functions described by Jung (thought/feeling, intuition/sensation) complement each other to form a typological pair of opposites; the functions compensate for one another in the sense that the more one perceptive function is prominent in consciousness, the more its opposite function disappears into the unconscious (or is seen less precisely from the standpoint of consciousness) and conversely.[15] This is true with respect to structure both of a personality (its perceptive "character") and of single elementary perceptive reactions. In physics today we call a similar reciprocal relation between the latitudes with which two variables (for example, energy and time) can be fixed in single elementary reactions a complementary one. Thus we find the same general concept of complementarity in psychology (including a "relation of uncertainty" for the conscious and unconscious components of the same elementary psychological reaction) as the one developed later by the physicists for a description of properties of individual atoms.[16] It is probable that this psychological (subjective) complementarity is introduced by the anatomy of the human nervous system, which may evaluate the same information independently and simultaneously in a cortical and in a subcortical (possibly thalamic)

12 According to Jung's definition, this concept includes perception by the outward sense organs, hence, for example, observation of the physical world.

13 If we take into account the fact that each type may have an introverted or extraverted attitude, eight different types result. Of course, we must not forget that these are abstractions that cannot have complete precision—but yet are precise enough to serve as a basis for practical work.

14 Cf. Lipot Szondi: *Schicksalsanalyse* (Basel, 1944), *Experimentelle Triebdiagnostik* (Bern, 1947), *Triebpathologie*, Vol. I (Bern, 1952), *Ichanalyse* (Bern, 1956). For the question to what degree the cognitive functions may be derived from a possible "cognitive drive," see n. 25, below. [See also Szondi, *Experimental Diagnostics of Drives* (New York, 1952); Susan Deri, *Introduction to the Szondi Test* (New York, 1949); and Molly Harrower, *Appraising Personality* (New York, 1952).—Ed.]

15 Jung, *Psychological Types*, p. 515; cf. also Jolande Jacobi, *The Psychology of C. G. Jung* (New Haven, 1951), p. 68.

16 Heisenberg, *The Physical Principles of the Quantum Theory*, tr. Carl Eckart and Frank C. Hoyt (Chicago, 1930); and Bohr, works cited in n. 5, above.

perceptive network [17] or in two different cortical or two different subcortical perceptive networks.

From the existence of these diverse perceptive functions we must infer a corresponding order in the perceived ("observable") world. If we assume that Jung's typology also applies to scientists, it follows that in each science there must exist fundamentally different aspects or theories, which nonetheless complement one another. Jung drew this inference in 1920 for psychology. He writes:

> I can, therefore, explain one and the same psychic process by two antagonistic and mutually exclusive theories, concerning neither of which am I in a position to maintain that it is wrong. . . .
>
> I believe that other equally "true" explanations of the psychic process can still be advanced, just as many in fact as there are types.
>
> In view of their existence [i.e., types], every theory of the psychic processes must submit to be valued in its turn as a psychic process, and, moreover, as the expression of an existing and recognized type of human psychology. Only from such typical presentations can the materials be gathered whose *co-operation* shall bring about the possibility of a higher synthesis.[18]

According to these sentences, in connection with the complementarity of the perceptive functions, this idea of different yet complementary aspects may also be used to describe one and the same process in other scientific systems.

In conformity with the definition of complementarity in quantum physics, we here designate such theories as "complementary" pairs of aspects only when, as in quantum physics, there exists a "relation of uncertainty" between them.[19] As we shall later show, there are other systems derived from perceptive functions which also represent pairs of aspects, but without this relation of uncertainty. These we shall call "simple pairs of aspects." In general, according to this psychologically oriented view, the "completeness" of a science will depend on the degree to which appropriate perceptive functions have been admitted to develop it.

First we shall examine the various types of scientific perception in physics.

17 Cf. A. Bachem: "Complementarity of Matter and Mind," *Acta Psychologica* (The Hague), VIII (1952), 322; "Heisenberg's Indeterminacy Principle and Life," *Philosophy of Science* (Baltimore), XIX (1952), 261.

18 Jung, *Types*, pp. 625f., 628.

19 As, for example, between the corpuscular theory and the wave theory of light and matter. Cf. W. Pauli, "Die philosophische Bedeutung der Theorie der Komplementarität," *Experientia* (Basel), VI (1950), 72.

B. PERCEPTIVE FUNCTIONS NECESSARY FOR PHYSICISTS

The existence of "rational" and of "observing" perception (cognition) in physics is evident. What is not so universally recognized (though often postulated) is the existence of a special "intuitive" function, a "faculty of inner vision," which one might designate somewhat more accurately as a non-sensory perception of pre-existent "ideas" in the Platonic sense, or of inherited archetypes in the Jungian sense, or of a previously unconscious content.

Particularly in quantum physics, however, the fact that an idea (for example, an atomic model) suddenly emerges full-blown does call for the existence of such a special intuitive function. The content of this idea is best described in qualitative, subjective, timeless, nonspatial and dynamic terms, in contrast to its subsequent systematic development by the thinking function, which is best presented in the form of quantitative, objective, and space-time terms, e.g., calculations or rational deductions. Always unmistakable are the suddenness and activity of the intuitive event, and its tendency to occur in a state of relaxation, and after a protracted "period of meditation." [20] A further characteristic (contrasting with the logical act which merely "deduces," but analogous to the act of observation) is the "simultaneous" recognition of relatively complex, composite structures as a meaningful whole. This accords with Lorenz's definition, derived from observations in animal behavior, of intuition as a "Gestalt perception," [21] which cannot be attributed, as by Helmholtz, to higher thinking functions.

Plato's theory that intuitive knowledge has its source in a common order inherent both in nature and mind has not yet been superseded. Pauli remarks: "The process of understanding nature as well as the happiness that man feels in understanding, that is, in the conscious realization of new knowledge, seems thus to be based on a correspondence, a 'matching' of

20 Cf., for example, Pauli; Broglie, *Die Elementarteilchen*, p. 87; and A. Kondo, "Intuition in Zen Buddhism," *American Journal of Psychoanalysis* (New York), XII (1952), 10.

21 Konrad Z. Lorenz, "The Role of Gestalt Perception in Animal and Human Behaviour," in Lancelot Law Whyte, ed., *Aspects of Form* (London, 1951), and "Die angeborenen Formen möglicher Erfahrung," *Zeitschrift für Tierpsychologie* (Berlin and Hamburg), V (1943), 235, 323. See also the distinction between "intuitive" and "logical" mathematicians, discussed by J. Hadamard, "Á propos de la psychologie de l'invention," *Acta Psychologica*, VIII (1951), 147.

inner images pre-existent in the human psyche with external objects and their behavior."[22]

In agreement with Jung's corresponding perceptive functions, we thus distinguish three different types of scientific knowledge:

1. Intuitive perception ("non-sensory"). This is connected with the conception of new (scientific) ideas.

2. Observational perception (by the senses). This is utilized in experimentation or observation.

3. Rational perception, or cognition (with the help of the thinking function). This kind of cognition is mostly used to clear up contradictions between 1 and 2, or to amplify the results of intuitive or observational knowledge by logical processes.

The missing fourth of the Jungian typology, the feeling function, actually would not be expected to contribute anything to scientific findings. But on closer scrutiny we find that its influence cannot be neglected even in physics. As an evaluating function, complementary to the rational function, it determines the acceptance or rejection by the physicist of a given problem in research. Thus, we often observe, among physicists as among other scientists, a distinct unwillingness to concern themselves either theoretically or experimentally with new findings which seem at first sight to contradict what is known, and a distinct preference for problems which fit into the old system.[23] This is frequently due to a conditioning of the physicist's individual unconscious by the scientific environment. In other cases, such as Goethe's well-known attack on Newton's theory of light, it is a question not of a conditioned response but of a disparagement, more or less affective, of the way the opposite type views things.[24]

Today we find this "selective" attitude chiefly among such physicists as may be assigned to the rational (thinking) type in Jung's typology, in which the function of feeling is preponderantly unconscious. The feeling function, then, is also an important perceptive function. While it does not affect the structure of physics directly, it influences it through the selection of problems

22 Pauli, "The Influence of Archetypal Ideas on the Scientific Theories of Kepler," in *The Interpretation of Nature and the Psyche*, by C. G. Jung and W. Pauli (New York and London, 1955), p. 152.

23 Cf. Fierz, "Zur physikalischen Erkenntnis," p. 440.

24 Here, in line with Jung's typology, the feeling function is presented as an organ of the individual psyche. But in addition there are archetypal aspects stemming from the collective unconscious, such as the "causalistic" or the "bipolar" view, and these exist for all perceptive functions. Cf. the end of Part 1, sec. G.

to be tested by observation, albeit the motivating factor is frequently obscured by a screen of apparently logical explanations ("rationalizations").

A structure analogous to Jung's four perceptive functions is suggested by Szondi in his theory of drives.[25]

When we consider the momentary perceptive reactions arising from the first three functions (all equally necessary for the complete knowledge of a thing), it appears certain that intuitive and observational knowledge cannot arise simultaneously, when the physicist's attention is concentrated on the object in question. Even if a physicist possessed an equally great faculty for both intuitive and observational perception, he could, at any moment, apply *only* the intuitive *or* the observational faculty (but within certain limits he might exercise either one simultaneously with the rational faculty). If, for example, he is concerned with the mechanism of excitation of a certain atom, either he will be able at any given moment to gain a complete, intuitive idea (model) of it, in which case his sense perception will be very largely impaired; or else he will accurately observe the light emitted by the excited atoms, in almost total disregard of the intuitive model. Here, then, we find a pair of aspects of perceptive reactions, whose components stand in a complementary relation to one another which is different from the complementary relation of each of them to the rational function. For either component the admission of the rational function is less disturbing than an intrusion of the opposite nonrational function.

In theoretical physics it is chiefly the intuitive and the rational functions that are exercised; in experimental physics chiefly the sensational (observational) and, again, the rational function. Thus the two main fields of physics have arisen from a "pair of aspects" of perception. The one was produced by a "non-sensory" (intuitive) function, the other by a "sensory" (observational) function; the rational function serves solely to amplify and logically verify the intuitively found ideas or the observed phenomena.[26] Although

25 Cf. n. 14, above. Szondi considers Jung's four perceptive (cognitive) functions as a result of four elementary functions of the "ego drives": $+ p$ = intuitive; $- p$ = observational, projective; $+ k$ = rational; $- k$ = critically evaluating form (oral communication). [In Szondi's system, k = catatonic factor, p = paranoid factor.—Ed.]

26 The fact that even the results of these different perceptions with respect to the same object are not rationally connected, but also form a pair of aspects, is frequently overlooked. For example, a stone thrown into the earth's gravitational field may be observed to follow a parabolic course; or a theoretical physicist may arrive at the same parabolic course by intuition and calculation. A possible explanation—which, however, is not always sufficient for the subconscious formation of new ideas in science—seems to be a common order that underlies both matter and the psyche and

rational cognition in physics thus seems to be more or less subordinated to the other two types of perception, serving only to develop details of the physical picture, it should not be forgotten that we owe the quantitative aspect of this picture to the thinking function alone, for accuracy is not present in the two other types of perception.

C. PAIRS OF ASPECTS IN PHYSICAL KNOWLEDGE
(Table I, sec. III)

With respect to perception, there are as we know only two main divisions in physics, although three or even four types of perceptive functions have been used in building them: theoretical physics and experimental physics.[27] The reason for this is that the findings of physics can be meaningfully described only if they are grouped around ideas (models), which are arrived at intuitively, or around typical observations or experiences acquired by sensory perception. Table I shows the two main groups resulting from this dichotomy. We limit ourselves (with a view to a later structural comparison with psychology) to the physics of moving bodies, i.e., mechanics, and find in each member of this main group two additional sets of paired aspects (IV and V; see Sec. D, below).

The diagram shows, at top, the three types of perception: on the left, the intuitive, on the right, the observational. Intuitive perception produces an idea (model) which may provide the basis of a theory or branch in theoretical physics. The feeling function (F, usually unconscious) decides whether the idea will be accepted or rejected by the physicist. The idea in itself still has something vague and indefinite about it; rational perception is required to develop the desired systematic theory from it by calculation or by logical operations. This may occur in several stages. When, for example, at a given point calculation seems to lead no further, new ideas are needed in order to find new ways for the theory.

On the right side we find the analogous development of a branch in experimental physics. In the physical experiment, observation produces an "impression" of an "effect," which in turn may be favored or rejected by feeling (F). *Rational* perception is called in to provide systematic measure-

may be based on inherited experiences. Without such a common "Platonic" order there would be no intuitive knowledge. It is from this situation that Descartes derived his postulate that God had created the structure of the world.

27 We find similar main divisions in all natural sciences.

TABLE 1. PERCEPTIVE FUNCTIONS AND PAIRS OF ASPECTS IN PHYSICS

Perceptive Functions

I	(Intuitive Perception) ↓	(Rational Perception) Calculation ← ┘ └ → Measurement	(Observational Perception) ↓
II	Idea (Phys. Model) → F →		Impression (Effect) ↓ F ↓
III	Theoretical physics		Experimental physics

A. Material bodies (with "continuously variable" properties)

IV	1. Cont. var. energetic determinants, calculated	Cont. var. energetic determinants, measured
	2. Cont. var. space-time determinants, calculated	Cont. var. space-time determinants, measured

B. Individual atoms (with "sudden variable" properties)

V	1. Instantaneous energetic determinants, calculated	Instantaneous energetic determinants, measured
	2. Instantaneous space-time determinants, calculated	Instantaneous space-time determinants, measured

↑——Identical inherent structure of theory and of observed matter——↑

Pairs of Aspects

I *Complementary, in the "perceptive character" of physicists, e.g.:*

Predominant conscious function:	Complementary unconscious function:
intuitive	observational
observational	intuitive
rational (thinking)	evaluating (feeling)

II *Complementary, in single perceptive reactions of individual physicists:*

Instantaneous intuitive reaction	Instantaneous observing reaction

III *In physical knowledge*

Theoretical physics	Experimental physics

IV *In macroscopic events (statistics of atomic events), e.g.:*

Continuously variable energy quantities	Continuously variable space-time quantities

↑——in the description of material bodies——↑

V *Complementary, in single atomic events, e.g.:*

Instantaneous energy quantities	Instantaneous space-time quantities

↑——in the description of individual atoms——↑

ments and so create a system of empirical observations free from contradiction. Finally, such a system becomes a part of experimental physics.

D. PAIRS OF ASPECTS IN THE DESCRIPTION OF MACROSCOPIC EVENTS (Table I, sec. IV)

Other typical pairs of aspects, which occur analogously both in theoretical and experimental physics, have long been known in the description of moving bodies in macrophysics. In mechanics, for example, the "behavior" of a body is described on one hand in "kinematic" theory by its movements only. This requires the knowledge of its "positional quantities" (space-time quantities), i.e., its co-ordinates X, Y, Z, as a function of time. Another aspect of the body is given by description of its energetical quantities in "physical dynamics." This requires in addition the knowledge of forces, mass, etc. Both groups occur in theoretical physics, where they can be calculated, as well as in experimental physics, where they can be measured. Since we are here always dealing with bodies consisting of a great number of atoms, we shall designate these quantities as "continuously variable," as distinguished from the same quantities when they relate to a single atom and vary suddenly in an exchange of energy with other atoms. According to our definition, we do not call such simple aspect pairs (IV in Table I) of energetic or positional quantities complementary, because there is no relation of uncertainty between their components and both can be measured or calculated "simultaneously" with adequate accuracy within the required precision of the measurement.

E. COMPLEMENTARY PAIRS OF ASPECTS IN THE DESCRIPTION OF A SINGLE ATOM (Table I, sec. V)

We find, however, a "true" complementary system in the physical sense when we consider the individual atoms. Here the energetic quantities and the space-time quantities are suddenly variable. If, for example, one wishes to calculate the impulse and the position of a free atom for one and the same moment in time (this is essential for the following argument), it has been shown that only one of these two properties can be determined with accuracy, while the other remains inaccurate to the degree of magnitude of Planck's constant. Or both calculated quantities may be equally inaccurate. The "relation of uncertainty," formulated by Heisenberg[28] for this case, states only that "the product of the average errors of two such mechanical variables (canonically conjugated) must be larger than the quantum of action (the Planckian constant h)," or, in the language of Bohr, "there always will be a reciprocal relation $\Delta q \cdot \Delta p \cdot = h$ between the latitudes Δq and Δp with which these variables can be fixed."[29]

We find a similar situation in *experimental* quantum physics: Only one of two properties ascribed to a particle, either an energetic one such as its impulse, or a space-time property such as its position, can be measured exactly at one time.[30] The reason for this is that such measurements can be undertaken only with the help of additional particles or light quanta, and that a reaction between the "observing" and the observed particle cannot be avoided. Thus even experimentally, in the exact *measurement* of instantaneous energy and space-time quantities, an analogous condition of uncertainty also appears. Here, then, we have a relation between the properties of elementary particles which is similar to the complementarity of the perceptive functions found by Jung.

In conclusion, we find in the branch of physics under consideration three different structures (cf. Table 1):

(1) the simple aspect pairs of physical knowledge (III);

(2) the simple aspect pairs of the energetic and space-time quantities in the description of macroscopic events (IV); and

(3) the complementary aspect pairs of energetic and space-time quantities in the description of individual atoms (V).

F. ANALOGOUS PAIRS OF ASPECTS IN PHYSICS AND PSYCHOLOGY

The existence of complementary pairs of aspects in psychology has been presumed not only by Jung[31] and Szondi but also by Bohr, Jordan, and Pauli,[32] mostly in connection with specific conscious-or-unconscious functional activities.

We now come to the question of whether there exist in psychology pairs

28 See n. 8, above. Though "irrational" and "amechanic," this statistically determined relationship is not considered by all authors to be an "acausal" one; cf. A. Mittasch, in *Physikalische Blätter* (Baden), IX (1953), 254.

29 "On the Notions of Science and Complementarity," *Science*, CXI (1950), 51.

30 Heisenberg, as in n. 8.

31 See also Jung, "The Spirit of Psychology," p. 439.

32 Cf. nn. 5 and 14. Also Jordan, *Die Physik und das Geheimnis organischen Lebens*, and "Reflections on Parapsychology, Psychoanalysis, and Atomic Physics," *American Journal of Parapsychology* (Durham, N.C.), XV (Dec., 1951), 278; Pauli, "The

of aspects analogous to those in physics shown in Table 1. It seems reasonable to look for such analogous pairs of aspects in the description of personality and of personal complex reactions. As we know, here psychologists use the concept of "psychic energy" or "libido" [33] or "psychic activity" of a function or complex as a working hypothesis, applying this term to *both* the conscious and the unconscious parts of the psyche, and especially in cases of the transition of psychic activities between two states. Thus, we may consider psychic activity in psychology to be an aspect analogous to energy in physics. In psychology, activity cannot be separated from its structure, pattern, form, or Gestalt; [34] likewise, potential energy in atomic physics cannot be separated from atomic structure—for instance, atoms with electrons in certain orbits. However, whereas different atomic structures in physics indicate in general different energy contents of the system, different excited network structures in neuropsychology do not necessarily indicate different amounts of activities of the functions involved. But, analogously to physics, in psychology the activity patterns or space-time patterns of a personality, observed by an onlooking subject, may be experienced by the observer's intuitive or sensation function or thought about by his thinking function. Like properties referring to patterns of psychic energy, space-time properties in psychology may also contain both conscious and unconscious components.

In conclusion, we find that as one regards a single autonomous function in a personality system, both its activity-pattern (e.g., as visualized or measured dynamically) and its space-time pattern (e.g., as visualized or measured in space-time co-ordinates) are equally necessary for a complete description of it.[35]

Influence of Archetypal Ideas on Kepler," and as Jung cites him in "The Spirit of Psychology," p. 439, n. 126.

33 Jung, "On Psychical Energy," in *Contributions to Analytical Psychology* (London and New York, 1928), p. 31. Cf. also the publications of Freud and such other authors as Otto Fenichel.

34 We define *Gestalt* as "invariant of perception," in agreement with the term known in psychology. On this definition cf. also Max Born, "Physical Reality," *Philosophical Quarterly* (St. Andrews), III (1953), 139, and "Physikalische Wirklichkeit," *Physikalische Blätter*, X (1954), 49. For a logical analysis of the Gestalt concept, see K. Grelling and P. Oppenheim, "Der Gestaltbegriff im Lichte der neuen Logik," *Erkenntnis*, VII (1937), 211.

I am indebted to Dr. Erich Neumann and Dr. Erwin Zippert for stimulating discussions on these psychological pairs of aspects.

35 The events of nature mentioned above, which are to be described in physics or psychology, are obviously undivided. From this it follows that such "pairs of aspects"

A comparison of such analogous pairs of aspects in physics and psychology is shown schematically in Table 2. To the left we find the aspect pairs for material bodies and for atoms; to the right the analogous aspect pairs for drives or functions in personality structures and for various unconscious complex reactions. To certain continuously variable pairs in the description of *matter* in physical systems of material bodies (namely, the energy and the space-time determinants) correspond continuously variable pairs in the description of *psychic* properties of the personality (namely, the activity and the space-time determinants of the "character"). For our purpose, it is not necessary to define more accurately the nature of the psychic activity patterns here, as this is done in the "objective" electroencephalographic and projective test methods.

The pair of aspects of activity-pattern and space-time relationship may be more easily understood with the help of the Szondi test: In this test the subject to be analyzed is confronted with forty-eight photographs of psychiatrically well-defined individuals, who represent, according to Szondi's theory, a set of eight particular "drive types" (catatonic, paranoid, manic, etc.). From his attitude of rejection, acceptance, or indifference towards them is determined the subject's "drive profile," that is, the frequency of his momentary reactions towards each of the eight types shown to him. Thus, in numerous (at least six) series the space-time pattern and the relative activity of the subject's "characteristical" drives (in this particular drive set) can be statistically determined. Such "character components," therefore, represent an example of continuously variable "pairs of properties" within a personality (A 1, 2 in Table 2).

To the pairs of properties in the *sudden variable* quantized elementary processes of physics correspond the well-known, sudden variable properties of the psyche, as they appear in individual autonomous *complex* reactions, such as emotional reactions.[36] Here, in analogy to the elementary particles of physics, we presume a relation of "subjective complementarity" between the activity determinants and the space-time determinants of the reacting function. For it seems impossible for one observer to determine both the

are only a neuropsychological or anatomical postulate of our present description and are not postulated by the events themselves.

36 In view of the frequent quantum-like transitions of activity within the same function (unconscious-conscious) or between different functions, the term "quantum psychology" seems justified for the psychology of sudden, autonomous psychic reactions as observed, for example, in the Szondi test, or in animal behavior.

TABLE 2. ANALOGY OF "ENERGETIC" AND "SPACE-TIME" ASPECTS IN PHYSICS AND PSYCHOLOGY

Physics	*Psychology*
A. Continuously variable properties of matter (in systems of material bodies).	A′. Continuously variable properties of the mind (in function systems of personality).
1. Determinants of potential or kinetic energy (e.g., mass, force, impulse, or energy).	1. Determinants of potential or actual activity patterns (e.g., intensity or frequency character of a drive).
2. Space-time determinants (e.g., position or time).	2. Space-time ("descriptive") determinants (e.g., Gestalt, type, definition or form of a drive).
B. Sudden variable properties of matter (in individual atoms).	B′. Sudden variable properties of the mind (in personal, unconscious autonomous reactions.)
1. Determinants of potential or kinetic energy (e.g., mass, force, impulse, or energy).	1. Determinants of a potential or actual activity pattern (e.g., intensity of an autonomous reaction).
2. Space-time determinants (e.g., position or time).	2. Space-time ("descriptive") determinants (e.g., Gestalt, type, definition or form of an autonomous reaction).

Pairs of Aspects:

I, II } *As in Table 1.*

III *In scientific knowledge:*

Theoretical physics	Experimental physics
Theoretical psychology	Experimental psychology

IV *In the description of characteristic physical or psychological events (statistics of elementary events), e.g.,* A *and* A′ *(continuously variable systems).*

These pairs of aspects may be "exactly" defined independently of one another (no relation of uncertainty). The energy or the activity pattern is of a potential nature (e.g., material bodies at rest, or potential drives) or kinetic (moving material bodies, or actual drives) and continuously variable. An "exact" prediction of the course of an event or a measurement of two conjugate determinants A 1 and A 2, or A′ 1 and A′ 2, is possible, e.g., by "simultaneous" determination of the frequency or type of a drive (as in statistic projective tests).

V *In the description of single elementary events, e.g.,* B *and* B′ *(sudden variable and complementary properties).*

The probable values of the determinants of each pair of aspects are established (in physics and presumably also in psychology) on the basis of a relation of uncertainty. The physical energy or the psychic activity is of a potential or kinetic (dynamic) nature; their sudden transitions can be described as jumps of quanta. An exact prediction of such dynamic events is impossible. A "simultaneous" observation of two conjugate determinants B 1 and B 2 or B′1 and B′2 is impossible, either in quantum physics or in the psychology of individual autonomous reactions. * However, in contrast to complementarity in physics, complementarity in psychology does not exist if, instead of one, several observers or several recorders are used, and their interference with the subject is excluded.

* Cf. n. 36.

activity patterns and the space-time appearance of a single autonomous reaction "simultaneously" with maximum accuracy. Furthermore, the very act of observing frequently modifies the original activity or the original space-time pattern of the reaction by interference in a way that cannot be predicted. Similar considerations apply also to single instantaneous perceptive reactions.[37] A noncomplementary situation exists, however, if (instead of one observer) several noninterfering observers or noninterfering recorders of activity and space-time patterns are used.

In concluding, we may say that analogous pairs of aspects (energy patterns and space-time patterns) occur in the description of "character" structures and single complex reactions in psychology and in the description of material bodies and elementary processes in physics. This meaningful connection between physics and psychology carries us back to our central theme, the transformation of the sciences, for the essence of the transformation that has occurred in both these disciplines is to be sought in a conception of such pairs of aspects as a new scientific order, over against the classical "continuous" order. This is made even clearer by a glance at the structure of psychology before the introduction of the energetic concept of the libido by Freud and Jung, which can be compared with the structure of physics before the introduction of the concept of physical energy by Robert Mayer. To set aside activity (libido) as a component of psychology (in Table 2) would be very much the same as attempting to describe the properties of material bodies or elementary particles of physics solely on the basis of their position or movement in the space-time system, without reference to their "dynamic" qualities, i.e., the production of their velocity or impulse by the forces to which they are exposed. In either case, our "scientific" description would become one-sided and therefore unscientific.

G. FURTHER PAIRS OF ASPECTS IN VARIOUS SCIENCES AND IN ANCIENT AND MODERN PHILOSOPHY

The existence of systems of pairs of aspects in physics and in psychology is not restricted to the groups of determinants thus far discussed, but extends

37 Obviously, the concept of complementarity in physics is of general significance, in the sense that there are no cases in which, e.g., the energetic quantities and the positional quantities of an elementary particle can be exactly defined "simultaneously." A complete proof of this sort has not yet been given for the complex reactions and perceptive reactions of psychology. For attempts in this direction see Weizsäcker's "revolving door" (*Der Gestaltkreis*, 3rd edn., Stuttgart, 1947); Szondi's "revolving stage of the drives," in works cited in n. 14; and Pauli, in "The Influence of Archetypal Ideas on Kepler."

to entire theories: for example, to the wave theory and the particle theory of light in physics. Thus, the wave theory describes properties of light that cannot be explained by the particle theory, and vice versa.[38] In addition, Pauli has shown [39] that these theories are also complementary. Here the pairs of aspects refer to the description of the elementary particles themselves, not only to their determinants as in Tables 1 and 2.

In psychology, situations similar to those in physics exist for the human personality, particularly the neurotic personality, where, as we know, a function in its unconscious (complex) state can never be described by the same theory as in its conscious state. The phenomenon of agoraphobia, for example, cannot satisfactorily be described in terms of the subject's behavior in space and time, but requires also a description in terms of activity patterns which may reflect unconscious imprints of conditioning situations in childhood.

Jordan [40] finds a relation of complementarity in the case of the "split personality": "In such a personality, Mr. A and Mr. B are two different persons, each with his own memory, his own desires and aims; each of the two belongs entirely to the unconscious part of the other personality. In order to observe Mr. A we must remove Mr. B from the sphere of observation—for example, by hypnotic suggestion; for we can never observe Mr. A and Mr. B at once."

Likewise, the concept of "Vordergänger" and "Hintergänger" in Szondi's "revolving stage of the drives" seems to be of a complementary nature.[40a]

Bohr, to whom we owe the formulation of the concept of complementarity in physics and suggestions for its extension to other sciences and to philosophy,[41] as well as other authors, has pointed out that pairs of aspects of

38 Cf. Broglie, as in n. 8, above.

39 "Die philosophische Bedeutung der Komplementarität," p. 72. Cf. also E. Buchwald, *Das Doppelbild von Licht und Stoff* (Berlin, 1947).

40 Jordan (as in n. 32, above), p. 278.

40a ["Vordergänger," as Dr. Susan Deri has explained in a communication, refers to what is more integrated in the surface personality, "Hintergänger" to what is more deeply hidden in the further depths of the unconscious.—Ed.]

41 In many complementary concepts suggested by Bohr and in many concepts of a philosophical character put forward below, the components do not stand in a relation of uncertainty to one another. In view of the fact that the original term "complementary" as used in classical physics does not contain the relation of uncertainty, it is open to discussion whether, as many believe, such simple pairs of aspects should not also be designated as complementary (or as complementary of a second order). Such a distinction in terminology is not essential for our present considerations; but it would be necessary in clarifying the problem of a complementary relationship between

determinants and theories exist (more or less explicitly, or else indirectly discernible) in other sciences also. There, because of their apparently contradictory nature, they have often led to contention between different "schools of thought" or have been regarded as mere temporary expedients.

To this category belong the vitalistic and mechanistic theories of biology;[42] the sense and meaning of words in linguistics;[43] the relation between "body" and "soul" in psychology;[44] sensory and clinical psychology; "form and process" in evolutionary theory;[45] "matter" and "form," "psyche" and "body" in medicine; mystical and scholastical systems in theology; and many other pairs of aspects which, before the discovery of the concepts of physical energy and psychic activity, did not seem to fit together into any consistent scientific view of the world.

What distinguishes such "alogical" pairs of aspects from mere antinomies[46] is that both are necessary for a complete description of one and the same "object." Their polarity expresses itself not only in antithesis, but also in the continuous co-operation of the two poles, which by their simultaneous existence produce a new structure with typical properties.[47]

This structure is particularly apparent in Jung's definition of a genuine symbol as a bipolar totality resulting from the union of the opposites: "meaning" (= the integrating component of the thinking and form-giving conscious) and "image" (= the content, the raw material, of the creative

---

physics and psychology, or matter and mind. (Bachem, as in n. 17, p. 322; Meier, as in n. 9, p. 362; Fierz, in *EJ 1949*, p. 455; Jung, "The Spirit of Psychology," p. 442.)

42 Cf. E. W. Sinnott, *Cell and Psyche, The Biology of Purpose* (Chapel Hill, 1950). Sinnott proposes the aspect pair of organization/energy. Also A. C. Moulyn, "The Limitations of Mechanistic Methods in the Biological Sciences," *Scientific Monthly* (New York), LXXI (July, 1950), 44.

43 Cf. G. Freys, "Über Sinn und Bedeutung," *Zeitschrift für Philosophie und philosophische Kritik* (Leipzig), C (1892), and the translation, "On Sense and Nominatum," in H. Feigl and W. Sellars, *Readings in Philosophical Analysis* (New York, 1949).

44 Cf. G. Heyer, *Vom Kraftfeld der Seele* (Stuttgart, 1949), pp. 23, 64; H. Prinzhorn, *Leib—Seele—Einheit* (Zurich, 1927), and the works of Goethe, Carus, Nietzsche, and Klages on this subject that he discusses.

45 Lancelot Law Whyte, *The Next Development in Man* (New York, 1949).

46 Cf. F. Seifert, in Baeumler and Schröter (eds.), *Handbuch der Philosophie*, Vol. III, F, p. 39. Polar pairs of aspects are essential components of the philosophy of Goethe and Schelling but (according to Seifert, p. 42) contrast with the purely antinomic, dialectical pairs of contradictories of Hegel. This view is supported by Dolch (see n. 8, above), the opposite view by M. Wundt in "Hegels Logik und die moderne Physik," *Universitas* (Stuttgart), I (1946), 547, 703.

47 Cf. Thomas Aquinas, "*ipsae res contrariae non habent contrarietatem in anima, quia unum est ratio cognoscendi alterum*" (*Summa Theol.*, I–II, q. 64, a. 3, ad 3).

unconscious).[48] Jacobi describes the transformation of the symbol (in dreams or fantasies during analysis or in works of art) if one of the two opposites is completely lacking:

> Translated into the psychological reality of an individual this means one of two things: either the symbol utterly loses its unconscious overtone of ineffability, mystery, and intimations of the unknown, that is to say, its meaning is fully known and understood, and it becomes a mere intellectual content, a mere sign; or else it is cut off from the conscious power that lends meaning, and degenerates into a psychotic symptom. Hence a symbol is alive only as long as it is pregnant with meaning, i.e., as long as it unites the opposites—form and the image raw material—into a meaningful totality.[49]

Thus a relation of complementarity exists between the two in such measure as either the meaning (structural) or the image (active) component in "genuine" symbols can predominate without the disappearance of the opposite component. This holds for any situation in which the symbol is exposed to a single subject.

As Dolch [50] has pointed out, the bipolar pairs of aspects are analogous in structure to the electric or magnetic dipoles in physics. In philosophy, this bipolar structure of pairs of aspects is found in Heraclitus,[51] Aristotle, Nicholas of Cusa, Goethe, Schelling,[52] Guardini,[53] Whitehead,[54] Hartmann,[55] Bell,[56] Nink,[57] Schopenhauer, and others. It occurs also in the Chinese Yin and Yang, which unite to form *t'ai chi*,[58] the concept of the absolute, and in

48 Jung, *Psychological Types*, pp. 601ff.

49 Jolande Jacobi, "Komplex, Archetypus, Symbol," *Schweizerische Zeitschrift für Psychologie* (Bern), IV (1945), 304.

50 Cf. Dolch's remarks on a "dipolar structure" of our concepts, p. 46.

51 Cf. Stenzel, in Baeumler and Schröter (eds.), *Handbuch der Philosophie*, Vol. I, D, p. 56.

52 Cf. n. 46, above.

53 R. Guardini, *Der Gegensatz, Versuche zu einer Philosophie des Lebendig-Konkreten* (Mainz, 1925).

54 A. N. Whitehead, *Science and the Modern World* (New York, 1925).

55 Nicolai Hartmann, *Der Aufbau der realen Welt* (Berlin, 1946), Parts 2 and 3, p. 171.

56 C. Bell, "Towards a New Organic," *Common Cause* (Chicago), IV (June, 1951), 588.

57 C. Nink, *Sein und Erkennen* (Leipzig, 1938), and "Sein, Einheit und Gegensatz," *Scholastik* (Freiburg i. B.), XVII (1942), 504. Cf. also Nink's pair of aspects "act and potency" within the determinants of activity.

58 Cf. *The I Ching or Book of Changes*, tr. Cary F. Baynes from the Richard Wilhelm tr. (New York and London, 1950), Vol. I, p. xxvv; and Lily Abegg, *The Mind of East Asia*, tr. A. J. Crick and E. L. Thomas (London and New York, 1952), especially p. 75.

the relation between the Hindu deities Shiva and Shakti.[59] This bipolar structure also appears characteristic of the ancient Egyptian view of the world; it is expressed not only in the twofold nature of the Pharaoh, who embodies the opposing divine principles, Horus and Set, in a state of equilibrium, but also in the mystery plays, religion, and the state.[60] The Chinese and the Hindus impute a divine character to the bipolar totality manifested in the "*coincidentia oppositorum*," and Nicholas of Cusa says of it:

> It is a great thing to hold fast to the conjunction of opposites. For even if we know that this should be done, we often err when we return to discursive thinking, and do our utmost to find rational grounds for a vision which bears in itself total certainty and is above all reason. And thence we descend from the divine to the human and adduce rational considerations that are unstable and ephemeral.[61]

Considering in general what pairs of aspects are likely to provide analogous elements for a unitary scientific view of nature and humanities, we find that (in line with the analogy between physics and psychology as presented in Table 2) the pairs of activity-pattern aspects and space-time aspects seem, more than any others, to be common to many sciences.[62]

Corresponding notions in philosophy are Thomas Aquinas' *essentia* and *esse,* Guardini's "enantiological series," Bell's "New Organic," Moulyn's "act and quantitative attitude,"[63] or the Existentialists' "essence and existence." Here we make the astonishing discovery that the very same bipolar pairs of aspects, which in other "double aspect philosophies" are evaluated as symbols of harmony,[64] are regarded by many existentialists

59 Cf. Heinrich Zimmer, *Myths and Symbols in Indian Art and Civilization,* ed. Joseph Campbell (New York and London, 1946), index *s.v.* "Shiva-Shakti."

60 Cf. Henri Frankfort, *Kingship and the Gods* (Chicago, 1948), pp. 19–23 and especially n. 12, p. 350. Particularly impressive in connection with our discussion of theories as pairs of aspects is the name of the hall for the judgment of the dead: "The hall of the two truths" (n. 13, p. 350).

61 *De Beryllo,* XXI; tr. after Karl Fleischmann (*Philosophische Bibliothek,* 217, Leipzig, 1938, ed. Ernst Hoffmann), quoted in A. Petzelt, *Nikolaus von Cues* (Stuttgart, 1948).

62 This statement is not necessarily in disagreement with L. L. Whyte's choice of "form and process" as the pair of aspects essential to his "system of unitary thought" (see n. 45, above). By "process" Whyte means not a "dynamic process" but a development of form, defined by a decrease in the asymmetry of the system. Whyte's "unitary system" is essentially a theory of evolution.

63 A. C. Moulyn, "Reflections on the Problem of Time in Relation to Neurophysiology and Psychology," *Philosophy of Science* (Baltimore), XIX (1952), 33.

64 Cf. H. Weston, "The Philosophy of Complementarism," *Proteus Quarterly* (Spring Valley, N.Y.), II (1951): 1, p. 29; and n. 56, above.

as intolerably disharmonious. Like the sense of disharmony which the quantum theory has evoked in many physicists, this feeling usually goes hand in hand with a preference for a homogeneous, nonpolar, purely logical picture of the world. Here we are probably dealing with variant archetypal attitudes arising from the unconscious, similar to the prescientific notions of trinity or quaternity.[65]

2. *Astrobiological, Astropsychological, and Physical Time*

The increasing significance of the "dynamic" (as compared to the "dimensional") aspects in the modern sciences and humanities expresses itself also in a transformation of the concept of time. Side by side with the abstraction of astronomical time that is used in physics,[66] a "biological time,"[67] a "psychological time,"[68] and a "cosmic time" have been postulated.

In our civilization, the marks of physical time are mainly restricted to periodically recurrent events, for example, the passing of pointers on scales which as such do not convey meaningful information to the observer.[68a] In contrast to this, the scale marks of psychological time are a chain of single meaningful experiences, which are identical with the excitation of inherited, imprinted, or learned networks[69] within the human nervous system. This

65 Cf. the discussions between Kepler and Fludd in Pauli, pp. 190ff. (see n. 22, above). To Kepler, the essential symbol of a cosmic order appeared to be the trinity, to Fludd the quaternity. On analogous "styles" in modern physics, see Max Born, "The Conceptual Situation in Physics and the Prospects of Its Future Development," *Proceedings of the Physical Society* (London), Sec. A, LXVI (1953), 501, and "Die begriffliche Situation in der Physik," *Physikalische Blätter*, X (1954), 193.

66 L. L. Whyte has recently suggested ("Fundamental Physical Theory," *British Journal for the Philosophy of Science*, Edinburgh, I : 4, 1951, p. 303) that in certain physical systems time should be eliminated as an independent variable and replaced by a special time correıated with these systems.

67 Cf. Pierre Lecomte du Noüy, *Biological Time* (London, 1936), and the newer concepts of the "inner clock" in animal behavior; cf., e. g., C. S. P ttendrigh, "Clock System Controlling Emergence Time in Drosophila," *Proceedings of the National Academy of Sciences* (Washington), XL (Oct., 1954), 1018; and H. Kalmus, "The Sun Navigation of Animals," *Scientific American*, CXCI (Oct., 1954), 74.

68 H. A. Dobbs, "The Relation between the Time of Psychology and the Time of Physics," *British Journal for the Philosophy of Science*, II (Aug., 1951), 122. Cf. also C. D. Broad, "A Logistic Analysis of the Twofold Time Theory of the Specious Present," ibid., p. 137; and Carol Baumann, "Reflections on Time and Tao," *Spring* (New York; mimeographed), 1951.

68a Except for conditioned reflexes of an observer bound to certain scale marks.

69 The word *engram* (R. W. Semon, *The Mneme*, tr. L. Simon, London and New York, 1921) is sometimes used for imprinted or learned networks.

excitation may be conveyed by the sense organs or may take place "spontaneously."

The scale marks of physical time are always experienced as extremely short, and progressing in one direction only, running from the past into the future. In contrast to this, each scale mark of psychological time is experienced as a duration, which contains besides the present all earlier and possible future excitations of the same nervous network area. Many experiences of this psychological time never become conscious to the human personality.

The course of this "inner," nondirectional psychological time, because it is a series of single excitations, is always discontinuous, that is, it proceeds in quanta. It seems to form a complementary pair of aspects together with the one-directional, continuous physical time, measured in seconds, of which D. H. Lawrence writes: "Time went on as the clock does, half-past eight instead of half-past seven." [70] On the nature of man's inner, psychological time, on the other hand, Herbert Read says: "But now Oliver had lost all consciousness of terrestrial time, and judged all things by their inherent duration." [71]

We find a notion of psychological time among the ancient Egyptians, who divided the nights into twelve hours each of which increased or decreased in duration with the seasons.[72] In this astropsychological time, the experience "night" was considered to be a constant unit, independent of its duration in terms of (water-) clock time.

In addition to the events of psychological time that are inherent in biological time, there is another kind of biological time which does not seem necessarily to depend on the existence of a nervous system. The "inner clock" of this time is conditioned by the sun's cycle. It not only impresses astrophysical rhythms on behavior patterns, as in the emergence time of Drosophila,[73] but also makes possible the skywise—i.e., by the light of the sun—navigation of insects and crabs.[74]

The significance attached to the "inner" time in modern biology and psy-

70 D. H. Lawrence, *Lady Chatterley's Lover* (New York, 1932), p. 18.

71 Herbert Read, *The Green Child* (New York, 1950), p. 191.

72 Cf. Siegfried Schott, "Die Altägyptischen Dekane," in W. Gundel, *Dekane und Dekansternbilder* (Studien der Bibliothek Warburg; Hamburg, 1936), p. 12.

73 Cf. n. 67, above, and Knoll, "Endogene Rhythmen und biologische Zeit," *EJ 1956*, 433.

74 See Karl Buhler, "The Skywise and Neighborwise Navigation of Ants and Bees," *Acta Psychologica*, VIII (1951/2), 225–63.

chology shows that the concept of time has undergone a structural change similar to that which we have noted for other scientific concepts in Part 1. But in view of the abundant literature [75] on the subject, we will here discuss only the concept of astrobiological time. In doing so, we shall attempt to clarify whether such events in the physical environment as are caused singly or in periodical sequences by the sun may, according to the present state of our knowledge, constitute a biological or psychological time for the human personality.[76]

It is obvious that in psychological time, time marks (events) will happen periodically (referred to in seconds) only within or after a periodically changing environment. In our case, therefore, it may occur that an astropsychological time scale is identical with or closely related to the scale of *physical* time. For example, such a coincidence in time scales may exist for the experience of day and night, summer and winter, new and full moon, and high and low tide. In general, therefore, the astrobiological time, which is induced in the human personality by such astrophysical events, must be distinguished clearly (as usually is done in biological experiment) from physical time as perceived from "outer" clocks in the visual cortex.

A. PHYSICAL EFFECTS OF SOLAR RADIATIONS

(1) *Solar phenomena: sunspots, prominences, and the corona*

As we all know, *dark spots* appear on the sun at irregular intervals. It is only during the last few decades that we have learned something in regard to their nature. We know that they are vortices rising from the interior of the sun, but thus far we do not know what causes them. These vortices are accompanied by powerful magnetic fields and send out proton or calcium-ion "clouds" in beams more or less perpendicular to the sun's surface. The sunspots appear mostly in a zone above and below the solar equator, and their frequency follows roughly an eleven-year period. There is still disagreement as to the cause of this variation in frequency. Most scientists suggest

75 The various events which constitute the experience of "psychological time" are called "precious present" by Moulyn (cf. n. 63), "specious present" or "experiential present" by Dobbs (cf. n. 68). Cf. the "absolute present" and the "unity of consciousness" as elements of time in Zen Buddhism. D. T. Suzuki, "The Philosophy of Zen," *Philosophy of East and West* (Honolulu), I (July, 1951), 3.

76 In analogy to the "geopsychical phenomena" described by W. Hellpach, we might speak here of "astropsychical phenomena." Actually Hellpach's well-known book *Geopsyche* (Leipzig, 1939) contains many interesting contributions to our subject, including some of an astrophysical nature.

an internal mechanism in the sun.[77] A few believe that the sunspots are caused by changing configurations of the planets,[78] in which case the sun itself would provide the necessary energy and Jupiter, with its period of somewhat less than 11.3 years, approximating the length of the sunspot cycle, would play a leading role.

Since the sunspots emit particles some of which reach the earth, where they provoke magnetic storms and climatic changes, their frequency was already being noted in ancient times. Hirayama,[79] the Japanese astronomer, has collected such notations going back to the second century A.D. in China and drawn up a statistical table (Table 3) showing sunspot frequency in

TABLE 3

Pentads in all centuries	Number of notations in the pentad	Pentads in all centuries	Number of notations in the pentad
00–04	13	50–54	1
05–09	2	55–59	2
10–14	2	60–64	1
15–19	4	65–69	1
20–24	7	70–74	19
25–29	3	75–79	11
30–34	2	80–84	3
35–39	9	85–89	6
40–44	2	90–94	2
45–49	2	95–99	3

Greatest frequency of sunspot notations in the pentads 00–04, 35–39, and 70–74 of each century in China (A.D. 138–1870)

former times. Starting from the assumption that notations were made only when the sunspot frequency was particularly great, he lists the number of notations for each five-year period down the centuries.

As we see, he finds the most notations in the pentads 00–04, 35–39, and 70–74 of each century. Thus sunspot frequency discloses a thirty-three-year period along with its eleven-year period. This period of roughly thirty-three

77 Cf. B. S. Chapman and J. Bartels, *Geomagnetism* (Oxford, 1940); and H. Alfvén, *Cosmical Electrodynamics* (Oxford, 1950).

78 Cf. E. Huntington, *Sun and Earth* (New Haven, 1923); H. H. Clayton, *Solar Relations* (Clayton Weather Service; Canton, Mass., 1943).

79 See S. Hirayama, "On Supposed Sun Spots Observed with the Naked Eye," *Observatory* (London), XII (1889), 217.

years is also known to us from more exact measurements made in the last hundred years. To be precise, it is thirty-three and one-third years, so that the maxima, as in the Chinese notations, seem to recur exactly every hundred years. This may be taken as a late justification of the "hundred-year" or secular calendar,[80] if we assume that the influence on our "world weather" of proton "beam clouds" emanating from the sunspots is a function of the sunspot frequency, though apparently this parallelism is not as universal as was once supposed.

Another striking solar phenomenon is to be found in the so-called *prominences*. We know them as arcs of light which appear on the edge of the sun during solar eclipses; but they are also present, though invisible to us, on the rest of the sun's surface. Measurements have shown that these prominences also emit proton "clouds," which reach the earth. But their velocity is only roughly 300 kilometers (186 miles) per second, whereas that of the sunspot radiations is approximately 1,000 kilometers (620 miles) per second. Seen from the earth, the prominences are long threadlike formations ("filaments") which move slowly from the eastern to the western edge of the sun in correspondence to the sun's rotation round its axis in a period of approximately 27 days. The proton radiations they emit move through the ecliptic with them. As a rule the prominences last for several rotations of the sun, or several months. Nothing definitive is known about how they originate;[81] it merely seems established that in their vicinity fine particles of matter originating in outer space reach the sun's surface.

In the normal light of the sun it is impossible to find the emission source of the prominences on the side of the sun that is turned toward us. But they may be photographed with the help of a spectroheliograph in the light of a hydrogen line and they then become visible by an effect analogous to that which produces the dark Fraunhofer lines in the sun's spectrum (Plate I).

The sun's *corona* likewise is visible only during a solar eclipse and has a more or less starlike form. This form changes. For reasons thus far unexplained, it is relatively symmetrical during periods of a minimum frequency of sunspots, and becomes wholly asymmetrical in periods of a sunspot maxi-

80 Calendar with weather predictions recurring every hundred years; for example the "Hundertjährige Kalender" in Germany.

81 Cf., however, the theory of K. O. Kiepenheuer, "Über die Verdampfung der Sonnenkorona," *Naturwissenschaften* (Berlin), XXXVIII (June, 1951).

mum (Plate II). Possibly it is the visible manifestation of slow proton and calcium beams leaving the sun.

(2) *Effects of solar ion "beam clouds" on the earth*

Ordinarily, the ion "beam clouds" emitted by the prominences or sunspots reach the earth a few days after their emission. Their diameter is almost always considerably larger than that of the earth, so that the earth remains within them for several days.

The earth has a magnetic field whose poles are not far from its rotational poles. A part of the arriving ion rays are diverted toward the magnetic poles and penetrate the atmosphere near them. In the Arctic Zone we can consequently observe this ion radiation and its secondary effects in the form of northern lights. Some of the ions are caught in the earth's magnetic field and encircle the earth. This "ring current" often continues longer than the ion beam that caused it, and produces the more or less rapid changes in the earth's magnetic field and in the earth's electric currents known to us as "magnetic storms."

All this makes it understandable that sunspot frequency, prominence frequency, the earth's magnetic field and its electric currents, northern lights, and ionospherical disturbances of radio waves exhibit corresponding periods. The proton beams entering the earth's atmosphere also influence "world weather," general temperatures, the potential gradients of atmospheric electricity (Fig. 1),[82] and the atmospheric pressure over areas of a certain size.[83] In addition, astrophysical events produce a periodicity in plant growth. The growth of trees is accelerated during sunspot maxima;[84] thus,

82 Cf. R. Reiter, "Elektrische Feldänderungen als Vermittler meteorotroper und solarer Witterungen," *Grenzgebiete der Medizin* (Munich), 1948, No. 6, p. 233. The main character of the curves in Fig. 1 seems to depend on world-wide thunderstorm activity.

83 Cf. H. Koppe, "Sonnenaktivität, Grosswetter und wetterbezogene Reaktionen," *Annalen der Meteorologie* (Hamburg), IV (1951), 87.

84 A. D. Douglass, in *Climatic Cycles and Tree-growth: A Study of the Annual Rings of Trees in Relation to Climate and Solar Activity* (Carnegie Institution, Publications, 289, Vol. III; Washington, 1936), attributes this to the increased rainfall during sunspot maxima. Another conceivable explanation is a corresponding influence of the sun's electromagnetic radiation (which is increased during sunspot maxima) w thin the 0.1-to-100-m.c. band. A considerable influence of meter waves on the growth of plants by cell division has been demonstrated by K. O. Kiepenheuer, F. Brauer, and C. Harte (*Naturwissenschaften*, XXXVI, 1949, p. 27). In their experiments, a very small electrical gradient (10^{-6} to 10^{-2} volt/cm) was sufficient to produce a 30-per-cent increase or decrease in the division frequency. The gradients produced on the earth by solar activity sometimes approach these values.

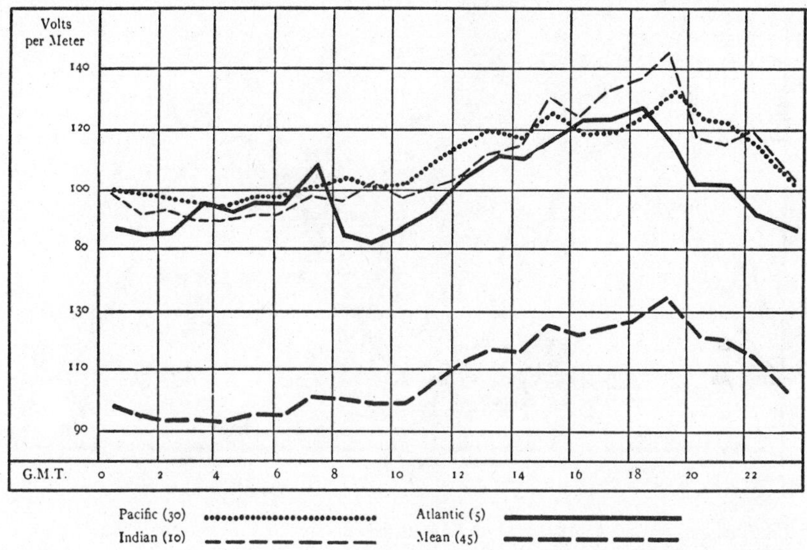

Fig. 1. Mean daily course of the potential gradient of atmospheric electricity above the Pacific, Indian, and Atlantic Oceans as a function of Greenwich Time (observations on board the ship *Carnegie*)

the eleven-year sunspot cycle is reflected in the increasing and decreasing width of the annual rings of trees (Plate III). This effect is so reliable that archaeologists use it to date the establishment of ancient settlements.

Measurements of the intensity of the earth's magnetic field show not only a diurnal period, but also a 27-day period of low- and medium-level magnetic storms, and a 30-day period of intense magnetic storms. In addition, there are anomalous magnetic storms without recognizable periodicity; these are almost always intense. This diversity stems from the different rotation times of the sun's surface: seen from a star, this rotation time is 25 days at the solar equator, 26 days at latitude 20 degrees, 32 days at latitude 75 degrees. Seen from the rotating earth, the sun's rotation time is 1.5 to 2 days longer and amounts to 27.2 days on the average for the sunspot zone.

Further, there are seasonal periodicities of magnetic storms, possibly caused by the oblique position of the sun's axis (Fig. 2).[85] The number of

85 After H. B. Marvis, "Seasonal Variations in Magnetic Storms," *Physical Review* (Ithaca, N.Y.), XXXIX (1932), p. 504. Cf. also Chapman and Bartels, *Geomagnetism*.

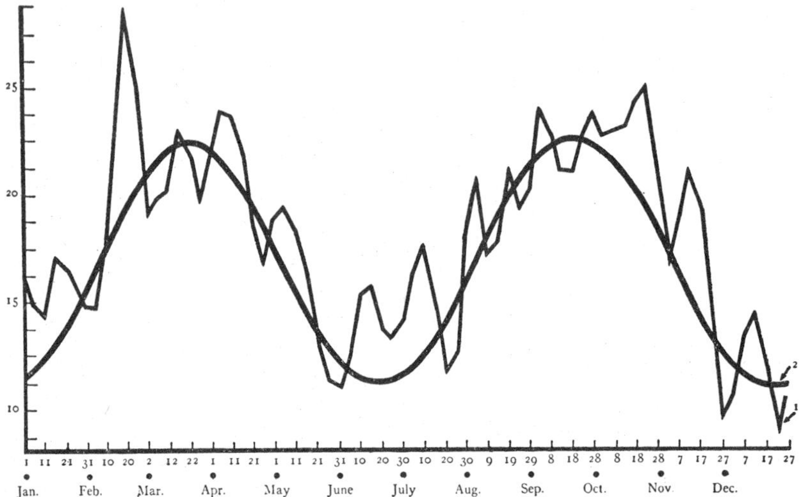

Fig. 2. Frequency of magnetic storms as a function of the seasons (1839–1930)

magnetic storms in the early spring and early fall, i.e., at the equinoxes, is roughly double the number in summer and winter. The irregular curve of the storms observed over a period of many years also shows a number of annually recurring peaks corresponding to a 27-to-30-day period; such a period, however, cannot be directly derived from periods of the sun's rotation. The sine curve in Fig. 1 is the median curve over these observed peaks.

(3) *Possibility of planetary effects on the sun and the earth*

As we have mentioned, some scientists believe that sunspot frequency is influenced by the planets, particularly Jupiter, though no details of this mechanism are known. This theory invokes not only periods of the planetary cycle (e.g., the recurrence of a planet's aphelion or perihelion), but also periods belonging to typical configurations of planets, such as conjunction (0 degrees heliocentric longitude), opposition (180 degrees), and quadrature (90 degrees). Relationships between these configurations and sunspot frequencies have indeed been reported;[86] yet it seems certain that this

86 Cf., for example, Fernando Sanford, *Influence of Planetary Configurations upon the Frequency of Visible Sunspots* (Smithsonian Institution, Collections, No. 95; Washington, 1936); C. A. Mills, "Some Possible Relationships of Planetary Configurations and Sunspots to World Weather," *Bulletin of the American Meteorological Society* (Easton, Pa.), XXII (1941), 167.

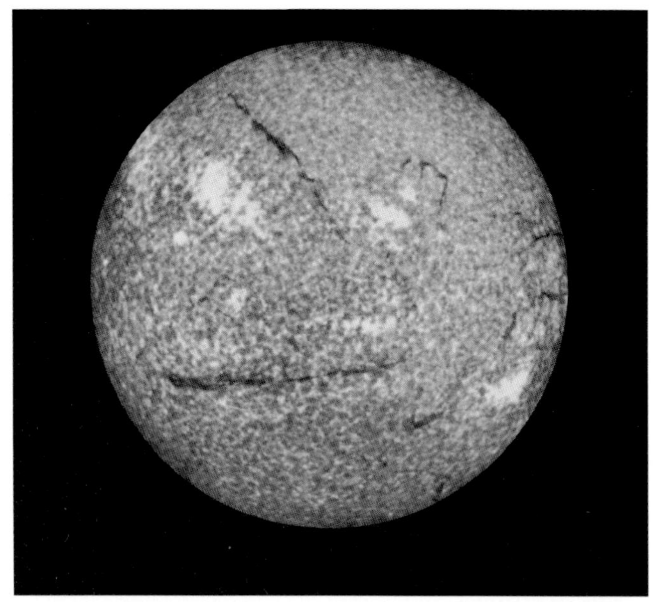

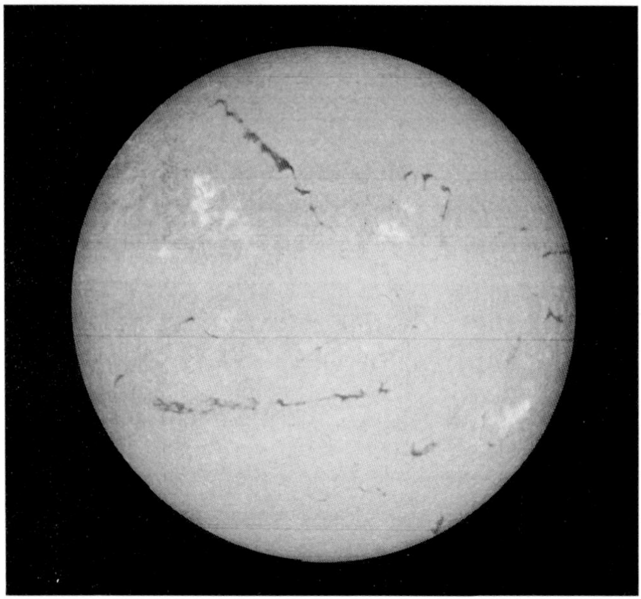

Spectroheliographic pictures of the sun (May 26, 1930) in respect of calcium (above) and hydrogen (below). The black filaments correspond to prominences

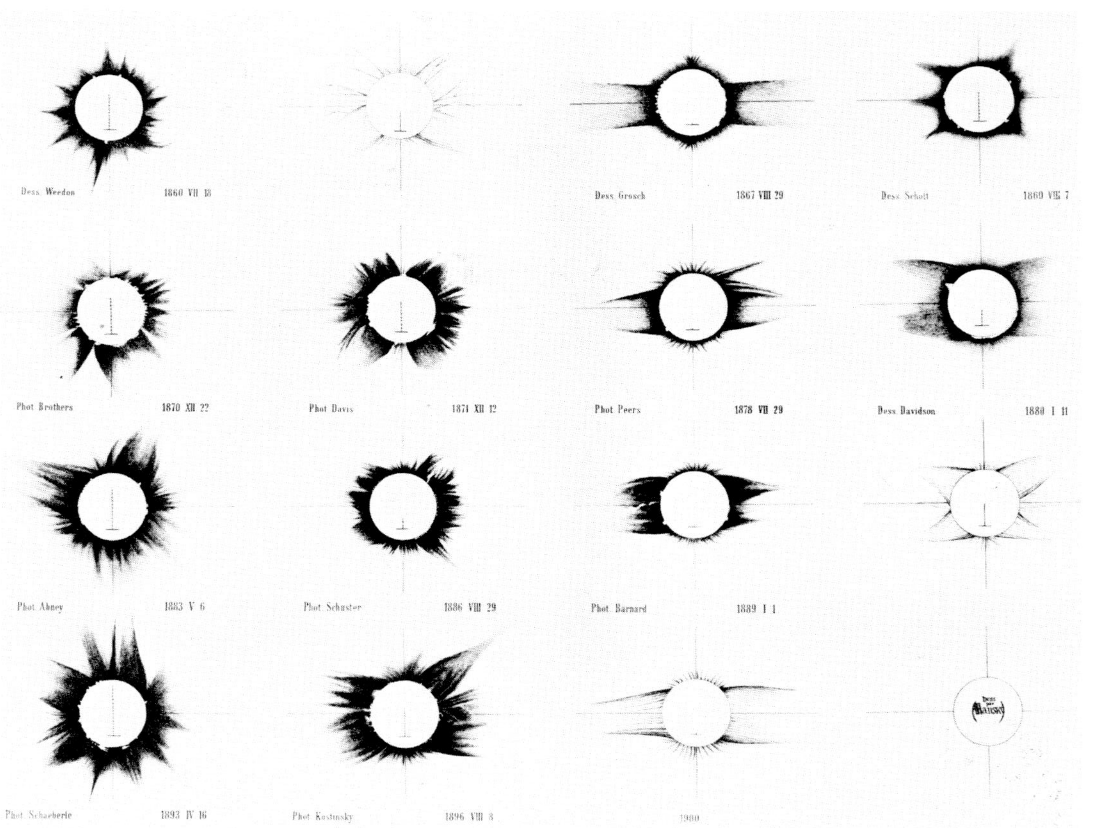

Various shapes of the sun's corona (1860–96)

II

Pine-tree section, with heavier annual rings corresponding to the sunspot maxima

III

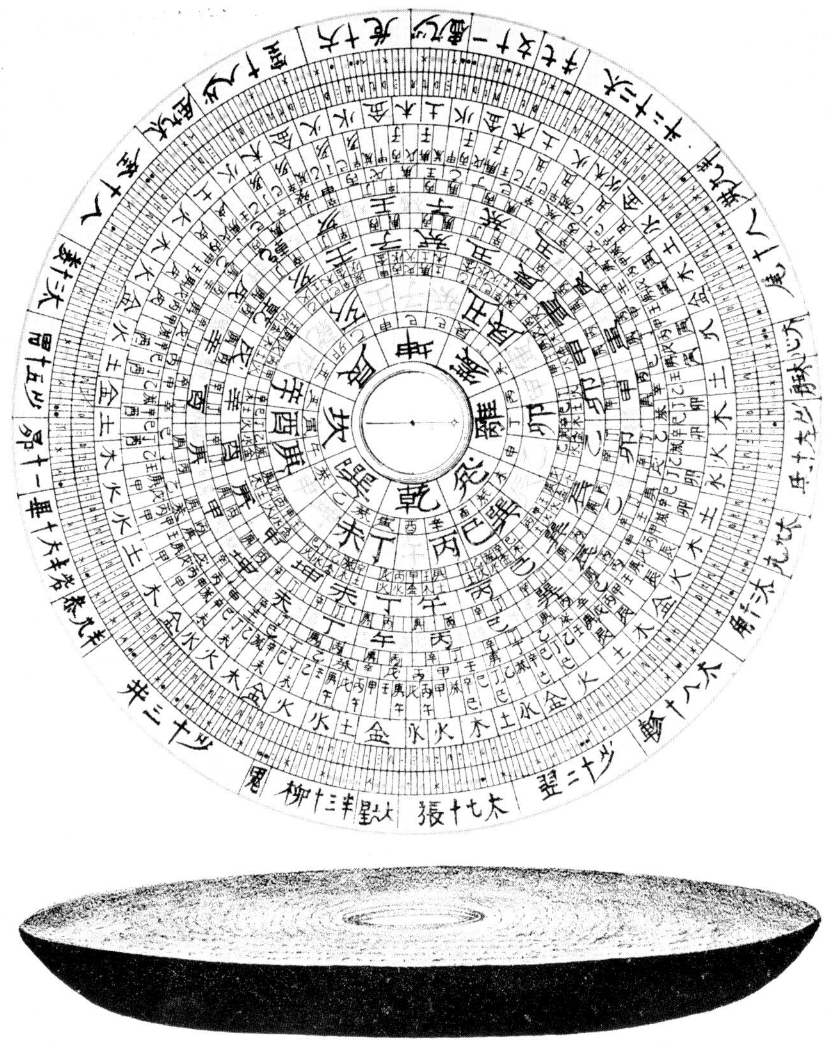

Chinese geomantic compass

planetary influence is small and is by no means the only factor in determining periodic sunspot frequency.

This seems to contradict the findings of Nelson,[87] who connects many of the well-known interruptions of transatlantic shortwave-radio propagation (transmission) lasting hours or days with the planetary configurations we have mentioned, and finds considerable effects *unrelated* to sunspot frequency. He has studied reports of radio disturbances before and after a configuration and found that a disturbing influence became noticeable one or two days before the actual day of the configuration and that the maximum disturbance appeared shortly after this day. On the basis of such correlations, Nelson has been able to predict the "radio weather" correctly from planetary positions for 80 per cent of the eight-hour periods investigated in transatlantic propagation by him for many years. Whether this fact has more of an astrophysical or more of a psychological significance is still uncertain.[88]

If Nelson's conclusions should be confirmed by a statistically significant number of observations, we might discuss the hypothesis of an existence of planetary tidal effects in the ionosphere similar to the tidal effect of the sun (and the moon) on the F_2 layer found by Martyn [89] which causes the high velocity ionospheric winds. At present, however, the quantitative theoretical consideration involved in such a hypothesis does not seem to be satisfactory. Since in many cases of "planetary" propagation disturbances Nelson has established a coincidence with magnetic storms, we should, on the other hand, have to look for corresponding components in earth currents, northern light frequency, and world weather. Another possible effect to be considered would then be that planetary magnetic fields may change the density or frequency (of occurrence) of solar ion beams (before they strike the iono-

87 J. H. Nelson, "Shortwave Radio Propagation Correlation with Planetary Positions," *R.C.A. Review* (New York), XII (March, 1951), 26. See also *Journal of the American Institute of Electrical Engineers* (New York), May, 1952, p. 421, and *Transactions of the Institute of Radio Engineers*, Vol. CS II : 1 (Jan., 1954), 19.

88 Because thus far it hardly seems possible to correlate *all* constellations of the planets which may be significant with *all* the magnetic and ionospheric storms that occur. Such a correlation is difficult because of the relatively large number of such configurations (over 100 a year, unequally distributed).

89 D. F. Martyn, "Atmospheric Tides in the Ionosphere," *Proceedings of the Royal Society* (London), A, CLXXXIX (1947), 241; CXC (1947), 273; CXCIV (1948), 429 and 455; T. Shimazaki, "The Effect of Solar Tides on the F_2 Layer," *Journal of Geomagnetism and Geoelectricity of Japan* (Kyoto), VI (1954), p. 68.

sphere) by reflecting or deflecting them.[90] But so long as the actual shape and intensity of these fields is still unknown the probability of this effect causing ionospheric disturbances cannot yet be estimated.

B. SOME ASTROBIOLOGICAL PHENOMENA

Now let us turn to some biological [91] or pathological phenomena which seem to disclose an appreciable relation to the sun cycle. We shall first consider the work of B. and T. Duell.[92] These authors found correlations between the 27-day period of the sun, the frequency of magnetic storms and of northern lights, the death rate, and the rate of incidence of certain diseases. Particulars are shown in Fig. 3. The statistics cover several hundred thousand cases; the 27-day period was virtually the same for Zurich and for Copenhagen.

90 Such a theory might start from the fact, recently observed, that the magnetic field of the sun is considerably smaller than was formerly supposed, and from the assumption that all the planets possess magnetic dipolar fields oriented in the same direction, with intensities proportional to the volume of the planet. Employing as a second assumption electron-optic laws (in a space-charge-free medium), it can be shown that the existence of such dipolar fields may result in a deflection or reflection toward the earth of the corpuscular beams emitted by the sun, the amount of reflection being such that accumulations of planets at approximately equal heliocentric longitudes would under certain conditions correspond with maximum ion radiation towards the earth.

Not knowing, however, how far both assumptions are true, uncertainty prevails not only with regard to the actual intensity of the planetary magnetic fields, but also about their range as the planets move within the "ecliptic plasma." The propagation of these fields is probably very much reduced by the conductivity of the electronic and ionic space charge within the ecliptic. Owing to this space charge, distortions of the ecliptical magnetic field will occur, particularly in the vicinity of the sun, which are difficult to compute. On the other hand, two factors would favor such a theory: the reported frequent occurrence of ionospheric disturbances when planets pass through the ecliptic, and the fact that they often occur when there is no possibility of correlating them with definite sunspot groups (and even when there is no sunspot group visible on the side of the sun turned toward the earth). Many more observations have to be made, however, before the action of these "frozen" magnetic fields will be classified.

91 A general and detailed survey of astrobiological periodicities in nature is given by H. Caspers, "Rhythmische Erscheinungen in der Fortpflanzung von Clunio marinus," *Archiv für Hydrobiologie*, Suppl. (Stuttgart), XVIII (1951), 415–594.

92 B. and T. Duell, "Über die Abhängigkeit des Gesundheitszustandes von plötzlichen Eruptionen auf der Sonne und die Existenz einer 27-tägigen Periode in den Sterbefallen," *Virchows Archiv für pathologische Anatomie* (Berlin), CCXCIII (1934), 272–319. This is the source of Fig. 3.

Cf. B. De Rudder, "Über sogenannte 'kosmische' Rhythmen beim Menschen," *Zentralblatt für Gynäkologie* (Leipzig), I (1937), p. 44; and E. Bach and L. Schluck, "Untersuchung über den Einfluss von meteorologischen, ionosphärischen und solaren Faktoren sowie der Mondphasen auf die Auslösung von Eklampsie und Praeklampsie," ibid., IV (1942), 196.

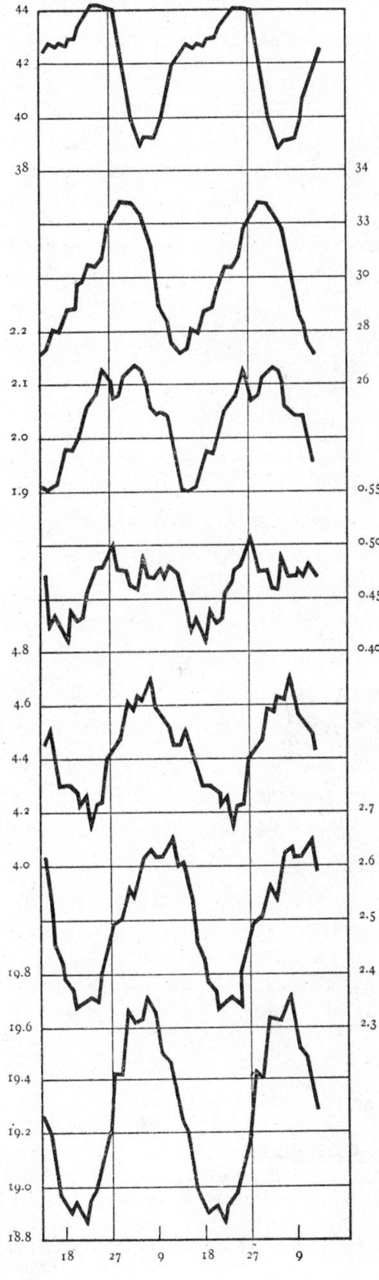

Fig. 3. Correlations between relative sunspot numbers, magnetic character, and deaths during an average 27-day rotation of the sun

First Curve: Relative sunspot numbers over an average 27-day rotation of the sun. (Average of the 68 rotations during the period from Jan. 1, 1928, to Dec. 31, 1932.) Computed according to the M-method.

Second Curve: Magnetic "character" (world total) during an average 27-day rotation of the sun.

Third Curve: Deaths from diseases of the nervous system and sense organs and mental diseases in Copenhagen during an average 27-day rotation of the sun. This figure is based on 3,720 deaths.

Fourth Curve: Deaths from suicide in Copenhagen during an average 27-day rotation of the sun. This curve is based on 849 deaths.

Fifth Curve: Deaths from circulatory diseases and *marasmus senilis* in Copenhagen during an average 27-day rotation of the sun. This curve is based on 8,099 deaths.

Sixth Curve: Deaths from respiratory diseases in Copenhagen during an average 27-day rotation of the sun. This figure is based on 4,579 deaths.

Seventh Curve: Deaths from all causes except homicide in Copenhagen during an average 27-day rotation of the sun. This curve is based on 35,244 deaths.

Duell's hypothesis is that death or sickness is set off only in persons who were already close to death or physically weakened. The most likely causes, in the light of our present knowledge, are climatic phenomena caused by solar ion radiation. When Duell (with R. Rösli) infers from his findings that perhaps in the not too distant future surgical operations will have to be performed on suitable days and examinations held on "irritation-free" days, we are reminded of the ancient calendar astrology; but we should not forget that the amplitudes of the periods shown in Fig. 3 are relatively small, so that the periodic fluctuations concern only a small percentage of all the cases. That is, there is a distinct effect (in view of the large number of cases), but (in cities, at least) the probability of its occurrence is low.

In another paper,[93] B. Duell shows that the human reaction time to optical and acoustic signals constitutes a useful measure for influences of the environment, particularly those of a meteorological nature. Among other things, he finds a seasonal factor: the reaction time during autumn may be up to 10 per cent shorter than during summer and winter (spring was not investigated). He points to a parallelism of this effect to the great fluctuations in atmospheric pressure of the northern hemisphere,[94] the suicide rate,[95] the conception rate of epileptics,[96] and the frequency of manic-depressive attacks[97] and of eclampsia.[98] All these phenomena disclose a double annual cycle with maxima at the solstices and equinoxes. Furthermore, Duell finds a correlation between large area weather (i.e., the frequency of coastal storms and the atmospheric depression character in central Europe) and reaction time, which exhibit irregular periods of from 5 to 28 days duration. Similar changes in reaction time as a function of meteorological disturbances have been reported by Dirnagl.[99]

A possible explanation for the phenomena observed by B. and T. Duell may be a fluctuation in the air's concentration of ozone or oxygen ions,[100]

93 B. Duell, *Wetter und Gesundheit* (Dresden, 1941).

94 H. Landsberg, *Gerlachs Beiträge zur Geophysik* (Leipzig), XL (1933), 238.

95 Cf. n. 68, above.

96 W. F. Petersen, *The Patient and the Weather* (Ann Arbor, 1934), Vols. II and III.

97 Ibid.

98 H. Eufinger and I. Weikersheimer, *Archiv für Gynäkologie* (Berlin), CLIV (1933), 15.

99 K. Dirnagl, *Archiv für physikalische Therapie* (Leipzig), V (1953), 87.

100 This ion concentration is of the order of 10^2 to 10^4 ions per $cm.^3$ For clinical effects, see F. Dessauer, *Zehn Jahre Forschung auf dem physikalisch-medizinischen Grenzgebiet* (Leipzig, 1931), pp. 111-75. For a chemical method of their measurement, see Manfred Curry, *Bioklimatik* (2 vols., Oldenburg, 1947).

produced by ionization processes in the ionosphere.[101] This would be in agreement with clinical results of Dessauer and Happel,[102] who found distinct psychological and physiological effects—such as changing blood pressure, breathing rate, and ability to solve problems—to be a function of the ion concentration in the air.

Another explanation takes into consideration a direct influence of the earth's magnetic field, based on Hansen's [103] and Magnusson's and Stevens' [104] results in studying irritations of the human nervous system by magnetic fields. However, the field of gradient in their experiments was many orders of magnitude higher than that of the geomagnetic field, so that the probability that magnetic storms release biological phenomena directly is rather small. A third explanation [105] takes into account the well-known electromagnetic atmospheric disturbances ("atmospherics"),[106] the effect of which may be comparable with the phenomenon of nervous irritation observed in persons in short-wave fields.[107] The irritating action of such "transients" on the orientation ability of pigeons is known.[108]

Changes in the atmospheric ion concentration [109] caused by the sun's

101 H. K. Paetzoldt, "Ozonschicht und Luftbewegungen in der Stratosphäre," *Naturwissenschaften*, XLI (1954), 318.

102 Cf. n. 100, above. (P. Happel, "Physiologische und klinische Anwendung unipolar beladener Luft," pp. 111–75 in the Dessauer vol.)

103 K. H. Hansen, "Studies Made for the End of Finding an Objective Influence of Magnetism on Man, and of Ascertaining whether This Influence Is Carried by way of the Autonomic Nervous System," *Acta Medica Scandinavica* (Stockholm), CXXXV (1949), 448. Cf. also C. Henschen, "Über den Einfluss der Sonnentätigkeit auf meteorologisch-pathologische Zustände des Menschen ('Solarpathologie')," *Helvetica Medica Acta* (Basel), 1943, nos. 3 and 4, p. 409.

104 C. E. Magnusson and H. C. Stevens, "Visual Sensations Caused by Changes in the Strength of a Magnetic Field," *American Journal of Physiology* (Boston), XXIX (1911), 124.

105 Cf. n. 93, above.

106 W. O. Schumann, "Über die Ausbreitung langer elektrischer Wellen um die Erde und einige Anwendungen auf Senderinterferenzen und Blitzsignale," *Zeitschrift für angewandte Physik* (Munich), VI (1954), 346.

107 Cf. n. 84, above.

108 H. Knieriem, "Voraussetzungen für schnelles Heimfinden der Brieftauben," *Zeitschrift für Tierpsychologie* (Berlin and Hamburg), V (1943), 131 and 139. How far this effect may be due to an increase of ion concentration in the atmosphere by the sources of "atmospherics," we will not discuss here.

109 Cf. L. R. Koller, "Ionization of the Atmosphere and Its Biological Effects," *Journal of the Franklin Institute* (Philadelphia), CCXIV (Nov., 1932), 543. Also, Cf. also A. L. Chizhevski, "Electric Factors of the External Environment, and Micro-organisms," *Bulletin de l'Association des diplômés de microbiologie, Faculté de Pharmacie, Université de Nancy*, No. 16 (1938), pp. 30–62. Chizhevski reports a correlation between bacterial diseases and the ionization of the atmosphere caused by the sun (51 bibliographical

ultraviolet radiation and its ionization products may possibly also explain the daily variations in the diameter of the human blood cells which have been observed by Price-Jones and Pijper.[110]

C. REPORTS AND HYPOTHESES ON THE INDUCTION OF TYPICAL BEHAVIOR PATTERNS BY METEOROLOGICAL FACTORS

Hellpach [111] has raised the question whether there exist human types conditioned by environmental factors that in turn are influenced by the sun. Thus far no satisfactory answer has been given, but there is a considerable body of data that argues in the affirmative. If we take account of the recently discovered correlations between world weather and solar activity,[112] a positive reply to our question would follow from the theory of Petersen,[113] who attributes to meteorological influences a permanent "imprinting" of certain population groups as well as passing physical and psychic states.

Petersen believes that changing air-pressure fronts bring about changes in the active oxygen content of the atmosphere (through air currents coming from the stratosphere or out of cavities in the soil), and that the resulting excess or deficiency of active oxygen noticeably disturbs the balance of the autonomous nervous system of certain population groups.[114] According to his observations, the "meteorologically stigmatized" (Bergmann) [115] group

references). On clinical applications of unipolar ionized air, see Dessauer (n. 100); and D. Silverman and I. H Kornblueh, "The Effect of Artificial Ionization of the Air on the Encephalogram," *Amer. Jnl. of Physical Medicine* (Baltimore), Aug., 1957.

110 Cf. Otto Glasser et al., *Medical Physics* (Chicago, 1944), p. 1201; Cecil Price-Jones, "Diurnal Variation in Sizes of Red Blood Cells," *Journal of Pathology and Bacteriology* (Cambridge, Edinburgh), XXIII (1920), 371–83, and "The Diameters of Red Blood Cells," ibid., XXV (1922), 487–504.

111 Hellpach, *Geopsyche*, p. 190.

112 Cf. Koppe, as in n. 83, and his references.

113 Cf. n. 96, above.

114 Cf. R. A. Farland, *The Psychological Effects of Oxygen Deprivation on Human Behavior* (New York, 1932). See also Curry, *Bioklimatik*.

115 I am indebted to Professor A. Portmann for a reference to the vegetatively stigmatized type in the European population: Gustav Bergmann, "Die vegetativ Stigmatisierten," *Zeitschrift für klinische Medizin* (Berlin), CVIII (1928), 90; and "Die vegetativ Stigmatisierten," *Medizinische Klinik* (Berlin), XXIV (1928), 813. This type seems to be concentrated chiefly in the cities, while the diffuse opposite type is found for the most part among those who have remained behind in the country. It would be interesting to find out whether the birth statistics of the former type also do show seasonal fluctuations like the ones discussed below. For additional observations regarding this type, and its later definition as "thyreoidical constitution," see Bergmann, "Klinische funktionelle Pathologie des vegetativen Nervensystems," in A. Bethe et al., eds., *Handbuch der normalen und pathologischen Physiologie* (Berlin), XVI (1930), 1025.

includes not only the familiar clinical cases of sensitivity to weather, but also psychotics and healthy persons. The healthy members of the group tend to be uncommonly gifted, but are highly sensitive to weather fluctuations.[116] The "imprinting process" is explained by Petersen as follows: During the early period of pregnancy, a meteorologically induced disturbance in the oxygen balance of the air exerts a lasting influence on the developing cells and organs; this influence may take the form of a stimulation (among the gifted) or of an impairment (in the mentally disordered) of the cerebral tissues. Thus if we accept the correlation between world-weather (or ion-concentration) fluctuations and solar activity,[117] including recent observations on fluctuations of ozone concentration near sea level as a function of down winds from the stratosphere [118] and, in addition, Dessauer's and Happel's findings,[119] we may hypothetically regard Bergmann's "stigmatized" group predominantly as an "ion conditioned" type, imprinted in its embryonic stage by extreme environmental conditions. As Dessauer and Happel have shown, negative and positive ions mostly produce opposite physiological effects. It may be possible, therefore, that besides the diffuse, non-imprinted Bergmann type [120] *two* different "ion conditioned" types exist.

To prove Petersen's hypothesis it would be necessary to correlate solar events of short duration or daily changes of the earth's magnetic field with typical reactions of one particular individual; this would naturally be difficult. We should possibly be able to find, however, an influence of the sun's rotational period or at least of the seasonal fluctuations of the geomagnetic and ionospheric storms (with maxima at the equinoxes; Fig. 2), and possibly also of seasonal fluctuations in the intensity of the sunlight (with a maximum and minimum at the solstices). These phenomena should also be the most readily accessible to statistical treatment.

The seasonal fluctuations of conception, according to statistics from Germany and France,[121] show a maximum (approximately ten per cent over the average) from April to June and a smaller maximum in December. More recent statistics covering the entire American population [122] show similar but

116 "It is the most sensitive minds which suffer most from the weather" (Goethe).

117 Cf. n. 83, above. 118 Cf. n. 101, above. 119 Cf. nn. 100, 102, above.

120 Cf. n. 115, above.

121 Cf. Hellpach, pp. 301ff. These statistics were composed for Germany in 1872–88, for France in 1827–69.

122 *Statistics on Birth Rates in the U. S. 1932–1936 (Referred to Conception Dates)* (U.S. Department of Commerce; Washington, 1936).

slighter fluctuations. Such annually recurrent maxima must obviously be regarded as effects of the sun's periodically changing light intensity on adult behavior [123] and seem to be important for our discussion only because they are superimposed on any possible frequency curve of Bergmann's [124] "stigmatized" type.

As the effective [125] atmospheric ion concentration varies not only in intensity but also in sign, a typology based on ion conditioning would have to take at least two groups into account. One of these, the "unconditioned group," should disclose diffuse characteristics,[126] whereas the other (or the two other groups) should represent a distinctive type depending on the effects of the conditioning with positive or with negative ions. By definition, the psychological activity and the conception distribution of such groups, if any, should correspond to known periodicities induced by the sun.

In his extensive investigations of "meteorologically stigmatized" population groups,[127] Petersen actually finds not only, as mentioned above, an increased irritability at the onset of cold or warm fronts, but also unusual seasonal fluctuations of conception frequency (up to ± 35 per cent), superimposed on the constant "normal" conception frequency.

For the conception fluctuations of the particularly gifted (the only group which we are discussing here) Petersen finds in a European sampling (5,261 names from *Wer ist's*) two regular maxima (mid-April to mid-July and mid-October to the end of January) and two regular minima (February to mid-April and mid-July to mid-October). In an American sampling (1,000 prominent names from *American Men of Science*) these two minima also occur, and also, superimposed, a distinct concentration in the first half of

123 In regard to Hellpach's hypothesis of a connection between solar activity and conspicuous examples of mass psychosis, cf. the reference of S. M. Shirokogorov, in the *Psychomental Complex of the Tungus* (London, 1935), p. 261, to Svidalsky's correlation of mental diseases with sunspot frequency in the Russian Arctic. Shirokogorov himself finds no such effect among the Tungus. On the other hand, a great nervous epidemic among the Yukaghirs in 1900, reported by V. I. Jochelson (according to Åke Ohlmarks, *Studien zum Problem des Schamanismus*, Lund, 1939), occurred during one of the secular sunspot maxima. Cf. Table 3.

Reports on Arctic mass psychoses are given by M. A. Czaplicka, *Aboriginal Siberia* (Oxford, 1914), p. 312; U. Knoll-Greiling, "Die sozial-psychologische Funktion des Schamanen," in *Beiträge zur Gesellungs- und Völkerwissenschaft* (Berlin, 1950), and Ohlmarks. Rasmussen reports that psychoses among the polar Eskimos usually occur in the fall; thus in all probability they are induced neither by the abundant ultraviolet radiation in summer nor by the vitamin deficiency of the polar night, as some authorities have supposed.

124 Cf. n. 115, above.

125 Cf. n. 100, above.

126 Cf. n. 115, above.

127 Cf. n. 96, above.

the year. The conception frequency of the presidents of the United States, also cited by Petersen, shows the same concentration in the first half of the year, but at the same time a distinct minimum from August to October and a distinct maximum from May to July, manifested particularly in the frequency of personalities designated as "outstanding." Of a total of ten such persons,[128] six, namely Washington, Lincoln, Madison, Cleveland, Jefferson, and Monroe were conceived from May to July. Common to all samplings are the maximum from mid-April to July, and the minimum from August to October. This minimum was also found by Pintner and Forlano in intelligence tests of 17,500 persons (cited by Petersen).

A comparison of these findings with solar periods shows that a correlation exists both with the seasonal changes in the frequency of magnetic storms and with the seasonal changes in light intensity. The latter is more pronounced in the American examples, the former in the European example.

From these correlations, however, an environmental imprint at the conception date appears improbable in view of the nine-month phase difference between the seasonal solar periodicities and the seasonal conception frequency. For example, the maximal frequency of magnetic storms occurs at the equinoxes, but it is at this period that we note a minimum in the conception statistics for talented Europeans. Hence, if we assume that increasing oxygen formation or other factors related to magnetic storms exert a decisive influence on the formation of an ion-conditioned type, we must look on birth rather than conception as the most probable period of imprinting.

Table 4 shows another attempt to determine the existence and the season of a possible ion-imprint period by taking a stricter view of the concept of talent. Here the Nobel Prize winners in physics and chemistry are arranged according to the seasons of their birth dates.[129] As can be seen, sixty-seven per cent of the persons in question were born within a three-month period around the equinoxes and only thirty-three per cent within such a period around the solstices. If we assume the existence of an "ion-conditioned" type, this result would support again the theory that conditioning occurs close to the time of birth rather than in the early embryonic period as assumed by Petersen. In general, the existence of meteorological imprinting

128 According to Herbert Agar, *The People's Choice* (New York, 1933).

129 Birth dates from Flora Kaplan, *Nobel Prize Winners: Charts–Indexes–Sketches* (2nd edn., Chicago, 1941). I am indebted to Professor Kurt Goedel (Princeton) for stimulating discussions on this subject.

processes would not contradict earlier anthropological,[130] biological, and sociological[131] observations on other imprinting processes occurring in children and young animals.

The distribution of birth frequencies in Table 4 also shows a correspondence to Duell's measurements of reaction time.[132] There seems to be no correlation with the monthly or daily curve of relative sunspot numbers,[133] but there is instead a five- to twenty-eight-day irregular periodicity, overlaying the principal period and similar to the periodicity of Duell's reaction-time curve.

Because of the small number of Nobel Prize winners, this example does not permit general conclusions, and provides only a modest probability that the frequency distribution in this case is not accidental. On the other hand, the probability of ion-conditioned fluctuations in the birth frequency of certain population groups (and hence of the existence of an ion- or sun-conditioned type) is considerably higher in Petersen's observations, which include many thousands of persons.

D. TRACES OF ASTROBIOLOGICAL TIME IN ANCIENT CIVILIZATIONS

It is known that in the prescientific period not only the daily, monthly, and seasonal rhythms, but other cyclic manifestations of the solar system as well, played a significant role in the consciousness of almost all peoples and were regarded as an expression of a time "inherent in nature." Our present scientific knowledge points to actual solar effects on the psychological state of

130 Concerning the susceptibility of immigrant children in America to imprinting, cf. Franz Boas, "Changes in Bodily Form of Descendants of Immigrants," in *Race, Language, and Culture* (New York, 1940); "Anthropometry of Porto Rico," *American Journal of Physical Anthropology* (Washington), III (1920), 247–53. Cf. also E. Fischer, "Anthropologie," in Paul Hinneberg, ed., *Die Kultur der Gegenwart*, Part 3, Sec. 5 (Berlin and Leipzig, 1923), p. 122; and Hellpach (as in n. 76, above), p. 209.

131 On the imprinting of newborn animals and children by environmental factors, cf. Portmann, *Biologische Fragmente zu einer Lehre vom Menschen* (Basel, 1944); Konrad Lorenz, *Und er redete mit dem Vieh* (Vienna, 1950) (experiments in imprinting newborn animals), and work cited in n. 21, above; E. Kaila, "Die Reaktionen des Säuglings auf das menschliche Gesicht, "*Annales Universitatis Aboensis* (Turku), Series B, XVII (1932); R. Spitz and K. M. Wolff, *The Smiling Response* (New York, 1946); G. Bally, "Lächeln, Spiel und Maske," *Psyche* (Stuttgart), V (April, 1951), 18.

132 Cf. also n. 93, above.

133 Professor K. O. Kiepenheuer (Fraunhofer Institut, Freiburg i. B.) has been kind enough to compare the birth dates of the Nobel Prize winners with the monthly and annual periods of relative sunspot numbers (1835–1901). According to his findings, there is no noteworthy correlation, although the small number of birth dates (here 84) is not a sufficient basis for definite conclusions.

TABLE 4

DISTRIBUTION OF THE BIRTH DATES OF NOBEL PRIZE WINNERS IN PHYSICS AND CHEMISTRY, 1901–1939

Before and after vernal equinox (Feb. 5–May 6)	*Before and after autumnal equinox (Aug. 7–Nov. 7)*	*Before and after the summer solstice (May 7–Aug. 6)*	*Before and after the winter solstice (Nov. 8–Feb. 4)*
Arrhenius	Anderson	Barkla	Becquerel
W. L. Bragg	Aston	W. H. Bragg	Dalén
Butenandt	Baeyer	Braun	Haber
Debye	Bergius	Buchner	Heisenberg
Einstein	Bohr	P. Curie	Langmuir
Von Euler-Chelpin	Bosch	H. Fischer	Michelson
Grignard	L. de Broglie	Hertz	Rayleigh
Guillaume	Chadwick	Hess	Richards
Haworth	A. H. Compton	Lenard	Siegbahn
F. Joliot-Curie	M. Curie	Lorentz	J. J. Thomson
Karrer	Davisson	Nernst	Werner
Marconi	Dirac	Wieland	Wien
Millikan	Fermi	Zeeman	Windaus
Planck	E. Fischer		Van der Waals
Richardson	J. Franck		
Roentgen	Harden		
Stark	I. Joliot-Curie		
G. P. Thomson	Kamerlingh-Onnes		
Urey	Von Laue		
Wallach	Lawrence		
Wilson	Lippmann		
Zsigmondy	Moissan		
	Ostwald		
	Perrin		
	Pregl		
	Raman		
	Ramsay		
	Rutherford		
	Ruzicka		
	Sabatier		
	Schrödinger		
	Soddy		
	Svedberg		
	Van't Hoff		
	Willstätter		
TOTAL 22	TOTAL 35	TOTAL 13	TOTAL 14
			GRAND TOTAL 84

Summary: Born before and after the equinoxes: 22 + 35 = 57 or 68% of 84.
Born before and after the solstices: 13 + 14 = 27 or 32% of 84.

man; but they scarcely penetrate man's consciousness in Western civilization. Even the pronounced effects of the daily and seasonal changes in light intensity and temperature tend to pass unnoticed in our hermetically sealed, windowless plants and factories, with their "daylight" illumination, day and night shifts, and automatic air conditioning.

Early civilizations were closer to nature and consequently imputed greater importance to the sun cycle; so it is with many primitive peoples today. It is psychologically understandable—for no better system of reference was available—that the observation even of small effects should have given rise to the inference that the entire earthly and celestial world is governed by the cycles of the solar system and constellations.

Thus the solar "cosmic systems" of ancient civilizations and the early astrology that formed a part of them should be regarded neither as mere superstition nor purely as psychological projection or theological symbolism, but must be interpreted in part as a speculative attempt to derive the whole structure of the material and psychic world from comparatively small solar effects on man and nature. Some of these early systems have a far more real and empirical character than the later, largely astrological, cosmologies. Here we shall be able to consider only a few of the many cases which suggest a knowledge of the sun's effects.

(1) *Elements of astrobiological time in China*

In the opinion of the Chinese rural population the sun, moon, planets, and stars bring about climatic changes which influence the moral conduct and fate of the individual. Thus one must make no change in the landscape, such as the laying out of a garden or the building of a house, without consulting a geomancer. The forms of the hills, the contours of the water courses, and other peculiarities of the landscape affect the *Ch'i*, the great breath of the universe. It is the task of the geomancer to select dwellings for the living and the dead that will accord with the two local currents of the cosmic breath, the "dragon" and the "tiger." [134]

It is surprising how close this picture comes to our own geophysical view, if we interpret the "cosmic breath" as the ion radiations that periodically strike the earth's atmosphere and bear in mind the contrary cyclical effects, including earth currents, that they induce. But what seems most remarkable is that the geomancers have observed (and still observe) field anomalies

134 Cf., e.g., J. Dyer Ball, *Things Chinese* (Shanghai, 1925), pp. 55, 269.

with the help of magnetic needles, the very same instruments that we use today to detect magnetic storms and anomalies in the geomagnetic field. Plate IV shows such an instrument (*lo pan*), which uses as a scale a large terra-cotta disk.[135] The magnetic needle is placed in the center of a design consisting of many concentric circles, configuring the ancient views of the natural energies and their cosmic harmony, of the planets and the quarters of heaven. The sixth circle contains the twenty-four climatic periods of the sun cycle, which are of particular interest here, because they show a certain similarity to the annual frequency of magnetic storms (Fig. 2).

The art of geomancy is passed down from father to son by word of mouth, and thus far no systematic study of the way in which the magnetic needle was used for this purpose seems to be known. For the magnetic needle may serve not only for determination of direction and magnetic declination and horizontal and vertical intensity of the geomagnetic field, but also for qualitative observation of magnetic storms, particularly in places with high magnetic-field gradients.[136]

At a very early period the Chinese developed an astrology[137] based on planetary positions; but its orientation was again chiefly "climatic," and the significance of the hour of birth seems to have been introduced from Western astrological systems at a later date.[138]

(2) *Astrobiological and physical time in ancient Egypt*

The component of astrobiological time connected only with the sun's rotation (and not with assumed planetary influences) is impressively symbolized in some pictures from the late period of the Old Kingdom in Egypt, showing the functions of the time gods ("decans"), each of whom presides over one of the celestial sphere's thirty-six ten-day sections. We have here the "emergence" of physical time and its tieup with astrobiological time to form

135 From J. J. M. De Groot, *The Religious System of China* (6 vols., Leiden, 1892–1910), Vol. III, p. 959; and *Universismus* (Berlin, 1918). Cf. also Samuel Couling, *Encyclopedia Sinica* (London, 1917), p. 315; and P. Carus, *Chinese Thought* (Chicago, 1907), p. 58. I am indebted to Professor T. Yiu (Princeton) for valuable suggestions.

136 There are, for example, places of this kind near Ascona [site of the Eranos lectures—ED.]. Cf. E. K. Weber, F. Gassmann, E. Niggli, and H. Röthlisberger, "Die magnetische Anomalie westlich von Locarno," *Schweizerische mineralogische und petrographische Mitteilungen* (Frauenfeld), XXIX (1949), 492. The maximal deviations from the "normal" geomagnetic intensity here are of the order of ± 25 per cent.

137 Cf. Couling, *Encyclopedia Sinica*.

138 Not before the Sung Period (A.D. 960–1127). Cf. Shu Hsin-ch'êng et al., *Tz'u-hai, A Dictionary of Chinese* (Shanghai, 1948), p. 320.

a pair of aspects, where "the time gods enter into a role which had previously been reserved for the local gods." [139] Not until later did planets and signs of the zodiac acquire an influence over this heavenly sphere.

In pictorial works that have come down to us from Saft el-Hena, "the souls of the decade gods, in the form of stars in Heaven, govern the growth of the crops, by means of wind and rain." The field representing each decade contains three superimposed beings who, according to the inscriptions, represent the three manifestations of the time gods: one brings storms, sickness and (sudden) death; the second brings life; and the third represents the soul of the godhead.

In correspondence with the hypothesis of astrophysical conditioning discussed above, one could interpret the first and second beings as manifestations of two opposite atmospheric conditions, which set the marks of astrobiological time; the third figure could represent the unity aspect of this "pair of opposites." Like their effects, however, the threefold manifestations of the time gods are present in *all* the decade fields, thus indicating the forcing of the irregular astrobiological time marks into the continuous scale of physical time.

Above and beside each time god is written:

> He stands in this picture as a star, Lord of Doom,
> He issues from the temple of Saft el-Hena in his decade
> To serve as a messenger [140] in the land.
> It is he who gives sudden death.

Above all the time gods is written:

> Heaven, earth, and underworld are subject to their plans,
> They rise and go down to their houses of Saft el-Hena,
> It is they who bring the storms,
> It is they who sweep the heavens and drive away the clouds,
> They pass day and night (protecting Saft el-Hena)

Their power is praised in these words:

> . . . They who circle daily on his (the sun god's) path
> As living soul of the gods.
> They who serve the sun god
> As messengers in the cities and countries.[141]

139 Schott (as in n. 72), p. 14.
140 Messengers of the gods bring sicknesses, plagues, and (sudden) death.
141 Schott, pp. 15, 16.

*

Returning to our starting point, the process of the transformation of science, we may summarize our survey as follows:

In the sciences, the tendency to seek a logically or causally homogeneous description of nature and things (designed after the pattern of mathematics) is on the decline. It is giving way to a trend, originating in philosophy, psychology, and atomic physics, to stress the bipolar character of the phenomenal world and of time. This new trend is changing the structure of the sciences. Foreshadowed in Nicholas of Cusa's "*coincidentia oppositorum*," and similar conceptions in Eastern and Western philosophy, this description, though logically not homogeneous, is only apparently contradictory; it is bipolar, that is, it expresses simultaneously two views which, though different, are both requisite to our picture of an "object." This transformation of science, because of its archetypal character, may lead to a new correspondence between the sciences and humanities based on a dual (dynamic and dimensional) description of nature.

Adolf Portmann

Time in the Life of the Organism

Our theme—time in the life of the organism—has many aspects and we shall be able to touch on only a few of them. First we shall take up a question that has been mentioned in some of the preceding lectures, namely the age of the earth—a subject that carries us far beyond human measurements and our brief human life-span.

With our limited mental powers we wrest particulars from the illimitable unknown; from the dark remoteness of the universe we strive unremittingly to detach more familiar figures. In the preceding lectures, expert guides have unfolded the archaic endeavors to express the experience of time in words. We have been led through the cyclical and rectilinear concepts of time; we have encountered the dizzying time perspectives of India, calculated to prepare the mind for the experience of the timeless by comparison with the transience of human time. Some reference has been made to geological time, and of this we shall now have to speak in somewhat greater detail.

Geology seeks among other things to investigate those formative processes by which a part of the cosmos became our earth with its characteristic transformations. It was only after stormy spiritual struggles that Western thought overcame the Old Testament time reckoning, grounded in popular thinking, and established a new conception of the earth's history. And it should not be forgotten that the first glimpses of Eastern cosmology played an important part in turning the Western mind toward new ideas about the earth's history. We have seen in the course of our conference how fruitful this Eastern influence was for Leibniz, and the same influence was at work in the middle of the eighteenth century when Buffon, in his history of the earth,[1] boldly put forward the figure of 75,000 years as the extent of the earth's history, in place of the Biblical 6,000 years. From then on our no-

1 [*Théorie de la terre,* part of his *Histoire naturelle* (44 vols., 1749–1804).—Ed.]

tions developed rapidly, and by 1830 Charles Lyell calculated that the geological stratification of the earth had required 230 million years. Strange as it may seem to the modern observer, it was the physicists, of all people, who at that time rejected these computations as exaggerated. Both Helmholtz and Lord Kelvin held that the process could not have taken more than ten to twenty million years. But in the newest computations based on the radioactivity of rock, it is the physicists who have accustomed our minds to new figures far exceeding Lyell's boldest conceptions: according to these new calculations, 1,100 million years have passed since unquestionable traces of life first appeared on the earth, while the oldest datable minerals were formed 1,900 million years ago. Still higher figures have been put forward, but these belong to the realm of scientific controversy: to the realm where even the scientist is surrounded by the total darkness of all thinking about origins, where even the sober-minded student of nature can create a picture only with the help of that drive toward completion that is innate in man. It is not without significance that the statements of modern cosmology have come to resemble the primordial myths of the creation, the sagas of cycles and aeons.

All the computations of genuine science which confer some degree of certainty in a small segment of reality refer to "understood" time—arrived at through our intellect. Numbers take on meaning for us only through images, and even then our conception remains inadequate. By and large, Western science communicates no more with such astronomical figures than what Vishnu communicated in his lesson to Indra: the impression that the time of our life, compared with the infinite history of the earth, is only a brief dream. In this sense the situation of the modern scientist remains as archaic as ever. And in this connection it may be well to recall that one of the paramount needs of our day is to achieve a new balance between our experience of the earthly time allotted to us and our reasoned conception of the earth's lifetime. To strive for such a balance is one of the main psychotherapeutic labors to be performed by science.

While some scientists seek to determine the chronology of the earth's history, others investigate man's inner experience of time and, as far as possible, that of animals. Let us also for one moment consider the study of this cyclically experienced time, the observation of the subject living here and now, who experiences the days and years in the particular rhythm allotted to his species. Thus far the scientific endeavor to determine the laws of this experience of time, to explain how the experience of succession came into being, has yielded little certainty. However, let us take a look at some of its relatively secure findings.

Differentiated experiences presuppose a change of impressions distinct in space or time. An instrument for measuring temporal impressions must therefore be capable of producing impulses in rapid succession. There must be a minimum duration and intensity of stimulus that leaves an impression in our experience. Let us designate this element of experience as a "moment."

A word about our efforts to measure the duration of an "impression." For events in our brain cortex, neurologists have ascertained a minimal time of $\frac{1}{14}$ second (70 milliseconds). A study of the visual sense shows that a series of 16 to 18 images a second produces the impression of a flowing, uninterrupted process, provided that each image is presented at rest for $\frac{1}{16}$ to $\frac{1}{18}$ of a second.

In connection with the auditory sense, we find that where the stimuli are presented at a rate of less than 18 a second, only separate air waves are registered. Beginning with 18 stimuli, an entirely new form of sensation occurs: we hear tones. Here again, 18 stimuli a second is an important threshold.

Investigations of the tactile sense also show that the character of sensation changes at approximately 18 stimuli a second: where there are less than 18, we note clearly differentiated tactile impressions; where there are more, we experience the new sensation of vibration. The striking constancy of this threshold of 18 stimuli suggests that a central apparatus governs our experience of temporal succession and that it operates at a rhythm of roughly eighteen "beats" a second. The use of drugs, either stimulants or sedatives, changes the rhythm: the duration of a moment is increased to roughly $\frac{1}{12}$ of a second. This duration of a "human moment" plays a decisive role in our whole experience of the world. Consequently, scientists have long speculated about forms of life in which an entirely different moment would produce an entirely different experience of the world. Plessner has reminded us [2] of the example mentioned by Thomas Mann in *The Magic Mountain*, and assuredly suggested by the ideas of Karl Ernst von Baer. What the poet seeks in his fantasy, the scientist strives to establish objectively by painstaking investigation. Here we cannot go into all the fascinating and complicated stratagems that have been employed to determine the length of a moment

2 See pp. 261f., above.

for the various animal species. Suffice to say that such experiments disclose a moment similar to ours for the dog, while the moment of the snail amounts to roughly $\frac{1}{4}$ second and that of the fighting fish to approximately $\frac{1}{30}$ second. Thus in the snail the unit of time contains many fewer impressions than in man, while in the fighting fish it contains many more.[3]

It is hard to say what consequences such differences in the duration of the moment have for the animal's subjective experience and the structure of its world, and the scientist will do well not to say too much about the inner world of the snail or fighting fish—that is, the nature of their experience. Still, these animal experiments are of great value in that they show us once again how dependent our experience of the world is on our structure, and how significant a question it is whether this structure is adequate to the apperception of hidden reality. The infinite variety we may expect to find in this realm of "relations with time" is suggested by motion pictures of hummingbirds in flight. In the space of $\frac{1}{8}$ second these tiny creatures, while remaining in one place, effect a complete revolution on their longitudinal axis and another on their transverse axis; at the same time they complete four wing beats. From this we may infer an amazing reaction velocity, which must in turn be reflected in the nature of the hummingbird's experience.[4]

Now let us turn to another scientific attempt to penetrate the temporal experience of an animal organism: let us consider the astonishing results obtained by Karl von Frisch in his ingenious experiments with bees. Just as bees can be conditioned to a particular color, so that in the end they will seek food only when stimulated by the color in question, they can be trained to search for food only at a particular time of day. Of course the success of these experiments required great knowledge and experience, as may be seen from von Frisch's own fascinating account of them. Here we can merely summarize the findings. Von Frisch demonstrated that the bees of a hive can be habituated equally well to one, two, or three feeding times a day. The training is just as successful in an enclosed room with constant light—that is, a room from which the day-night rhythm is totally excluded. The bee's time memory proves to be independent of the changes in sunlight and appears to be much more accurate than that of man. In a highly ingenious

3 Cf. Gerhard A. Brecher, "Die Entstehung und biologische Bedeutung der subjektiven Zeiteinheit,—des Momentes," *Zeitschrift für vergleichende Physiologie* (Berlin), XVIII (1932–33), 204–43.

4 W. Knoll, "Über den Schwirrflug der Kolibris," *Vierteljahrsschrift der Naturforschenden Gesellschaft in Zürich*, XCVI (1951), 162–75.

series of experiments von Frisch succeeded in showing that bees can be trained to react to a specific time only if a 24-hour rhythm is observed. Training to other rhythms, even to a 48-hour interval, produced no results; when such training was attempted, the bees came out to feed every 24 hours. We know nothing of the operations in the nervous system that regulate this behavior, but the decisive role of the 24-hour rhythm indicates that this time memory has an important place in the daily life of the bee. The flowers offer both nectar and pollen more plentifully at certain times of day than at others. A memory for the periodicity of this phenomenon enables the bee to spend the necessary hours of rest in the security of the hive. Thus the time memory must be an important factor in the preservation of the species.[5] How happy we should be to know something about the conscious aspect of this process that von Frisch has revealed in his magnificent experiments. Yet, though in all probability we shall never gain access to the innermost experience of the animal, our investigation of animals opens up broad insights which throw new light on our far more extensive knowledge of our own experience. What we know of animal experience serves to bring out the specific character of our human experience.

II

Every form of life appears to us as a *Gestalt* with a specific development in time as well as space. Living things, like melodies, might be said to be configured time; life manifests itself as configured time. Let us consider the organisms in this light.

In the preceding lectures, much has been said about profane and sacred time; the hallowed character of the lunar animals has also been mentioned in this connection. I shall therefore introduce our discussion of animals as configured time with a reference to one of these sacral lunar animals, namely that strange worm known as the palolo, which plays so important a part in the time reckoning of many of the South Sea Islanders. The natives of Oceania have two different years: the agricultural year, based on the cultivation of yams and beginning in March, and the equally important sacral year, which begins in the autumn and is calculated according to the life cycle of the palolo. This worm (*Eunice viridis;* named palolo by the Samoans) is an inhabitant of the coral reefs. Each year it sloughs off a part of its body, charged with sexual substances, and reproduction takes place in the open sea, where the worm reconstitutes itself. The temporal rhythm of these phe-

5 Von Frisch, *The Dancing Bees*, tr. Dora Ilse (London, 1954; New York, 1955).

nomena is amazingly constant and is related in some way to the phases of the moon. On Atchin (Malekula), where Layard studied it,[5a] the palolo is associated with the twentieth day of the lunar month occurring in October and November. Lesser swarms take place exactly one lunar month earlier and one later. Curiously, the natives look on the flowering of a certain tree with brilliant red blossoms (*Erythrina indica*) as a sign that the day of the palolo is approaching. This tree attracts particular attention in the ever green tropics, because its flowering time is just as strictly regulated as the life of the palolo.

Here we shall not go into the complex network of conceptions which the islanders build around the palolo's lunar regularity. The biologist sees this phenomenon in a broader context, which includes other marine organisms. The reproductive rhythm of the sea urchins of the Egyptian Mediterranean and that of the oyster and scallop in temperate seas follow similar rhythms, showing an evident relation to the phases of the moon. And phenomena reminiscent of the palolo are not unknown to students of marine life in our own latitudes, although they are not nearly so striking as those which enter so deeply into the life of the South Sea Islanders. Indeed, it seems likely that increased knowledge will disclose a lunar influence in the lives of many more animals.

Animal life, as the palolo so strikingly brings home to us, is configured time. The development of animals in time is more than a mere undergoing of the temporal process; it is a resistance to time, a mode of formation provided in the protoplasm of the particular species, which works counter to the merely material processes studied by physics and chemistry. Let us consider those traits which most eminently characterize the organism as configured time. First of all we turn to the phenomenon known as metamorphosis, for it is here that the change of forms in time is most clearly revealed. The transformation of a caterpillar into a butterfly, a common occurrence which most people never give a thought to, casts a bright light on processes characteristic of all organic life. The features manifested in the final transformation to a colored, large-winged butterfly, features secretly prepared in the phase of rest in the cocoon, were built into the caterpillar during its earliest larval periods. In ingenious experiments insect eggs have been subjected to radiations, with the result that subsequent development takes place normally except that in the final stage, known as the imago, certain important and

5a Personal communication.

characteristic organs, such as the wings, legs, or mandibles, are lacking or are abnormally formed. In other words it is possible to alter in the egg an organic predisposition directed exclusively toward the imago. From these experiments we must conclude that the specific formation of the mature organism is prefigured in the egg, though in what way we do not yet know. Even in the larva these organs are physically ascertainable: they consist of little groups of cells that we designate as imaginal disks. Here they lie, all ready to be set in motion in the critical process of metamorphosis and to unfold into their final form. Just as in a well-planned display of fireworks one set piece may bear the next latent within it, so in the life of many insects we find at each stage a prefiguration of new organs, which subsequently unfold in an exactly regulated temporal process.

Unnamed and unknown powers of natural formation make use of the possibilities provided by the dimension of time, the stadial development of each species, to multiply the earth's wealth of phenomena. We have spoken of the insect, but we are all aware that such temporal processes are embedded in our own life. I need scarcely mention the periodicity of women, but perhaps it will be well to consider that such factors as late sexual maturity, the specifically human characteristic of accelerated growth during the period of pubescence, and the special nature of human old age show a certain relationship to the metamorphoses of insects.[6] It need scarcely be stressed that all these configurations of time with their assembly of potentialities lead us into the very center of the problem of "act and potency."

And now I come to one of the most impressive and at the same time puzzling examples of how a living configuration of time can be correlated with the earth's annual cycle. I am speaking of the singular phenomenon of bird migration.

The bird's orientation belongs to the realm of the unconscious, of what need never be learned, hence to a field of experience which is obviously of particular interest to the psychologist. A striking indication of this unconscious character is that in many species the fledglings who undertake the migration for the first time leave the breeding grounds before the parents; experiments with banded birds show that despite this lack of guidance they follow the ancient migratory routes of their species. It is evident that bird migration is related to the annual cycle, to the rotation of the earth around

6 See my *Biologische Fragmente zu einer Lehre vom Menschen* (2nd edn., Basel, 1951).

the sun. Among the manifestations of this annual process there is only one which changes with sufficient regularity to release such a phenomenon: the illumination of the earth, the intensity of which is regulated by the changes in the position of the sun. But how do changes in illumination affect the bird? Experiments carried on over a period of years from the most divergent points of view provide significant indications. There is no doubt that the light acts upon the eye, and thence, by way of the nerves, upon the pituitary gland (although this gland can also be influenced in other ways). The secretions of the pituitary promote organic changes of various sorts, for example in the gonads and the "pitch" of the central nervous system. These combined influences, which cannot here be discussed in detail, create in the bird a general condition involving all those factors which result in migration. This is what is meant by the "migratory instinct," and some of us go so far as to imagine that with this term we have explained a mysterious process, though actually the deceptive simplicity of the term merely obscures the problem.

Thus the built-in organizations of the eyes, the ductless glands, and other organs are prerequisite to the phenomenon of bird migration. Our knowledge of this dependence on light seems to provide a very preliminary and partial explanation for some of the factors that ornithologists have noted. The regularity of the annual changes in the earth's illumination probably accounts within certain limits for the bird's reaction to the position of the sun. We have here a highly complex correlation which has been worked out only in rough approximations. But it has been observed that the time at which many birds arrive in our European countryside and the time at which they leave it are almost exactly the same number of weeks before and after the summer solstice. Table 1 gives a few examples.

TABLE 1

	Weeks before Summer Solstice	*Weeks after Summer Solstice*
Golden oriole	9–6	7–9
Stonechat	17–15	15–16
Bluethroat	14–10	10–14
Stock dove	17–14	15–17

But we should not make too much of such approximate rules—I am interested not in providing hasty solutions but rather in presenting an idea of the complexity of the problem.

The migratory instinct is so strong in the swift that it has been known to let a belated brood starve in the nest and fly off southward when the position of the sun commands. But though the swallow migrates by a similar route, it always waits until such a belated brood is fully fledged; not until the nurturing instinct has abated does the migratory drive assert itself.

The influence of light accounts only in part for the phenomenon of migration. This is evident from the fact that the susceptibility to the influence of light is embedded in all birds, but only certain species of them are migratory; frequently even close relatives of migratory species are sedentary, as Table 2 shows. A single genus may produce very divergent types of behavior in respect to migration. The starlings of the European continent are distinctly migratory, while the English starling winters on his island. Again, among

TABLE 2

Family	*Sedentary Bird*	*Migratory Bird* *
Gallinaceae	partridge	quail
Thrushes	blackbird	song thrush
Titmice	nuthatch	great tit
Finches	greenfinch	goldfinch

the Continental starlings those of Switzerland and East Prussia have a special trait: in early youth they undertake a summer flight which differs considerably in direction from their autumn migration.

The complexity of the factors at work is suggested by another observation: when our native migratory birds cross the equator, they reach areas where the days begin to grow longer. If they are kept captive in our climate and the length of their days is artificially increased, their gonads mature in the middle of the winter and the migratory urge is extinguished. But if the bird is free and undertakes its migration, the increasing length of the day in the spring of the southern hemisphere (our late fall) does not have the same effect as the increase of daily light in the experiment. Here it may be relevant to note that some of our birds spend the winter in the equatorial zone, where there is little or no variation in the length of the days. Yet these birds, too, fly northward in the spring. Thus it is clear that a number of unknown factors, some of which assuredly have nothing to do with the change in the length of the day, must play a part in the rhythm of migration.

For an over-all appreciation of this richly diversified time phenomenon there is still another fact that should be mentioned. The northern halves of

* [This table refers to European birds.—ED.]

the continents are inhabited by two totally different types of migratory birds, which have been formed concomitant with geological development. To the first belong the many species (probably including most of the European migrants) that were driven southward from their original home by the advancing ice cap. Ever since the receding of the glacier these birds, impelled by age-old inherited instincts, have settled every summer in their old breeding grounds, while in the winter they are guided southward by instincts that developed later. Thus their hereditary structure includes a new apparatus which regulates their withdrawal in winter from their original breeding grounds. (How such a new set of instincts becomes embedded in an old structural system we do not yet know.) To this second type of birds belong such species as the swifts, or in North America the hummingbirds, which have their home in warmer zones; only after the last ice age can these birds have extended their breeding grounds to northern zones, where they take new advantage of the long days for breeding. It is after the abatement of the reproductive urge that they fly back to their original home.

We see that in the course of geologic history the main factors which have regulated the migratory process have been combined in very different ways. This historical aspect of the problem should also prevent us from taking too simple a view of the periodicity prevailing in the life of the birds as of the other animals.

I have spoken in some detail of the diversity of bird migration, in order to make it clear that a study of the bird's relation to the changes in the sunlight does not explain everything. Only a careful consideration of many factors can save us from premature generalizations. With all this I have not even touched on the difficult problem of the bird's orientation during migration, and I shall not have time to do so. We must content ourselves with observing that this problem, too, is highly complex. Above all, it should be borne in mind that the direction finding of migratory birds is not identical with that of carrier pigeons in their return to their home. An adequate indication of this is the fact, which we have already mentioned, that many fledglings, in the first summer of their lives, start southward long before their parents and follow the age-old migratory routes established by their species.

Let us now look into the correlation between the life of a bird species and the annual cycle. For this purpose we may select the arctic tern (*Sterna macrura* or *paradisaea*). This delicately built white sea bird, related to the gulls, breeds in the entire Arctic Zone; its most southerly breeding grounds are situated on the German islands of the North Sea. The eggs are set down in the sand, without a nest, and after a hatching period of from 20 to 23 days the chicks slip out. Let us pause to consider for a moment that in this hidden period all the organs required for the bird's migratory habit are built up in the egg by inherited processes: the slender wings, the special character of the nerve centers, the special hormone apparatus—all are achieved by an unconscious process of development. It is not without reason that in this connection some biologists speak of developmental instincts. Just as the adult animal acts "instinctively," so the plasm of the species "instinctively" regulates the temporal sequence of formative processes. The species in its first state as pure plasm builds up all its organs. (We are perfectly well aware that with this simple sentence we have touched on a very complex problem and that such a statement brings us into close contact with those psychologists who claim that a hidden "self" plays a special guiding role in the life process.)

For roughly one month the chick remains in the "nest." Here the young, intensively fed by their parents, grow quickly. At the end of this period the migratory drive awakens in consequence of hereditary processes of development. "A hereditary drive awakens." This is easy to say, but what riddles such a statement creates! It implies an almost inconceivably complex assembly in the organism. We conceive of this assembly primarily as occurring in the embryo of each individual bird, but we must also think of it as an assembly that came into being down through geologic ages in the process of the evolution of the species. This historical process has transformed a sedentary bird into a migratory bird. Concomitantly there must have been corresponding changes in the germ plasm, which in each new generation produce the time-responses of a migratory bird with its annual rhythm. This evolutionary process impresses us with the significance of temporal structures for the organism. And what a powerful drive it is that "awakens" in our tern! Long before the older birds and uninfluenced by them, the fledglings start on their first journey, which is literally a world tour. The Northern European terns cross the Continent and follow the coasts of Africa. In the distant south of Africa they sometimes meet American birds of their species, which may have flown from Labrador, crossed North and Central America, and then traversed the Atlantic. Sometimes the journey continues on into the Antarctic, for these terns have been definitely observed as far south as the sixty-sixth parallel. When they fly away from our latitudes, it is summer; and when they arrive in their "winter quarters," it is again summer with its long days. For a few weeks the terns remain in the southern summer. In the southern autumn, just as our spring is coming on, the unknown urge drives them northward again, where the days have once more begun to grow longer. In the first part of May they are back in the North Sea territory, in their hereditary breeding grounds. Twice a year the little white bird effects this immense flight that carries him almost from pole to pole, from one summer to another, from a life in the long light days of the northern hemisphere to another with equally long and bright days in the southern half of our earth. Experiments with banded birds have shown for certain that this species has a longevity of at least twelve years, but for all we know they may live longer. An aging tern, then, has carried out at least twenty-four flights, each measuring almost the entire length of a meridian. We have little knowledge of the physical performance required by these journeys, and even the biologist surely reflects too little on the extraordinary inward processes of a bird engaged in migration. This transformation of many structures in the course of the interval from breeding time to migration period also belongs to the picture of the bird as a being in whom the dimension of time is extraordinarily filled with varying content, with transformations of structure and action—an extreme example of configured time.

In many respects the tern represents a supreme development of animal life. In all flying birds, the transformation of the reptile's forelimbs into wings has opened up the air as a third dimension; but in addition these migrants, by a complex organization of internal structures, realize the potentiality of variable formation in time to a very high degree. All birds have the faculty of utilizing a change of light as a stimulus to inner changes. But in the migrant this faculty is combined with a special inherited mechanism, as a result of which the bird's life is regulated by a time factor, the earthly light year. Year in, year out, the tern tends in rhythmic alternation toward the zones with the longest duration of daylight. In its travels it is guided not only by the spatial configuration of the continents but also by the temporal change in the position of the sun. When we compare the sedentary bird with this world traveler, we find in both cases a complete flight organization; in both cases the sunlight can affect the pituitary by way of the eye; yet how different is the life of the sedentary bird from that of the migrant! The migratory bird appears to us as a supreme unfolding of potentialities which are implicit in the existence of the bird but which the sedentary bird realizes only in small part.

There is no doubt that bird migrations represent a solution to certain ecological problems, that they enable the bird to exchange unfavorable seasons for more propitious ones. But if we consider all the aspects of these migratory phenomena in their immense variety, it becomes increasingly plain that they surpass elementary practical needs, such as the preservation of the species. All necessity is transcended in these great formative processes, into which tellurian events are integrated as wonderful alarm-signals for the awakening and enrichment of organic life in time. The passage of clock time, meaningless in itself, is employed for the enrichment of life. It need hardly be added that human life is a magnificent configuration of time in this same sense, offering in its successive ages ever new possibilities of development in time and hence of living riches.

None of us knows what living creatures really are. We are forever seeking to learn what we ourselves are amid the totality of earthly forms of life and of the cosmic forms that are unknown to us. And true knowledge only deepens the great mystery of formation; far from disenchanting, it teaches us how really profound is the mystery of origins. The exploration of the unconscious, as part of the boundless exploration of life, is an endless sounding of these same depths. In a very special way, it brings home to us the difficulty and vastness of the problem of origins. In the exploration of the unconscious—and all work in biology is ultimately such an exploration—we seek to transcend the old archaic distinctions of body, soul, and spirit, not because we belittle what they designate but because we see with new eyes the life forms in which these distinctions were formerly made. Indeed, the far-reaching implications of a deepening knowledge of all life processes have led to the inclusion of biology in the Eranos meetings.

But in this collaboration we are not concerned with a mere increase of information, a mere heaping up of interesting findings of biological research. Important as such an increase of knowledge is, we are working here on an entirely different problem, which all of us, speakers as well as listeners—who are more than listeners—are seeking to solve. In the course of a long historical development, we ages ago departed from the phase in which the imagination was dominant in spiritual life and the world of images exerted a paramount influence on thought and feeling. Gravely shaken by modern science and the technology that came in its wake, we are once more seeking a new balance in our altered way of life. Thus our concern is not a mere increase of knowledge. What we are striving for is a new wholeness, an activation of our imaginative powers that now lie fallow, new images which will not contradict the findings of scientific research but will encompass and transcend them. We hope that our contemplation of new fields of research will provide nourishment for new living worlds of the soul. In a previous lecture Erich Neumann [7] has shown to what high degree these curative powers of the spirit are at work in modern art. These saving possibilities also include a more intensive experience of natural forms, a spiritual relation to them, whereby these phenomena will come to play an intimate part in our lives. What we are seeking, in short, is an "imagination" of natural life in the most literal sense of the word. Like the great works of art, the biological forms embody all phases from the beautiful to the terrible; consequently they can release forces which will profoundly affect our inner life.

Among scientists there is much discussion about the need for surpassing the imaginative, prescientific form of thought which operated by images drawn from everyday life and by analogy—a mode of thought eminently exemplified in alchemy. And it is true that Western science with all its great achievements has been made possible only by a continuous surpassing of this form. But it should not be forgotten that this victory of rational science over archaic experience involves a grave threat to humanity. The wholeness of human life is menaced; the imaginative function is dying away; living, creative imagination is in process of atrophy, a profound secret source of creativity—from which even scientific activity ultimately draws its inspiration—is running low. In response to this danger Eranos turns back to archaic man and seeks to understand his manifestations. Archaic man was many-sided in his creativeness; precisely because it accomplishes such great things, the one-sided development of the rational function threatens to destroy a part of our full human potentialities by stultifying essential complementary functions.

Hence the scientist who is concerned with the fate of his fellow men faces a new task today. He must help not only to realize our rational potentialities, but also to nurture the imaginative powers that now lie fallow. A part of this work is performed by Eranos. In our meetings we always endeavor to disclose the whole of spiritual life in all its vastness, to see man's powers in

7 See pp. 3–37, above.

their full scope, and to harness them for the attempt to know the cosmos. This exploration of the cosmos includes the striving to see the true greatness of all living things. For life, after all, is the greatest of earthly creations and consequently has a special power of directing our thoughts toward the cosmos with its inaccessible distances. Hence the biologist also has his place in the study of man, since he seeks to apprehend the hidden inwardness of a biological form in the representative value of its outward configuration.

The richness of all living forms cannot be explained by elementary necessity, by practical needs. It goes far beyond the preservation of the species. We find, potential in their plasm and fully formed in the course of their development, an expression of something far exceeding mere vegetative existence. The diversity of the hidden inner life presents a mysterious correspondence to the richness of the sensuous manifestation, a correspondence which speaks to all our senses. In the dimension of space forms develop which one is tempted to describe in terms drawn from the study of art. And time, too, is a medium of this manifestation of inner life. In song the temporal sequence is utilized to enhance the display characteristic of the bird—in flowering, a change in the plant's inner state is manifested in time; in their changes of garb from childhood to old age the higher animals disclose their innermost transformations; the scarcely perceptible flow of life is punctuated, articulated, enriched. The higher we go in the scale of life, the more *form* becomes an expression of innermost being. The succession of manifestations in time increases the expressiveness of an organism undergoing inner change. Thus the dimension of time serves to enhance and enrich life; empty clock time helps to configure hidden transformations. And thus the solar year with the changes it creates on the earth is integrated with all life. An extreme fullness of life is realized in the migratory bird which travels nearly to the ends of the earth in pursuit of longer days. Here time becomes an essential trait in the life picture.

The aim of this talk has been to illustrate this wealth of temporal expression by examples drawn from the vast realm of biology. We have attempted to show how, in all the higher forms of life, time is filled by diversity. And this vision leads us to the tasks of human existence. All of us seek to broaden our experience and to exercise the creative forces within us. From the mere assimilation of knowledge we strive forward toward the phase of creation and toward a more intense inner experience. We want the experience that comes to us from all sides to continue working within us, weaving the fabric of self-fulfillment that is our inward and outward life. We are not all of us scientists or artists, but we are all human beings, hence creative. Our aim is not to know as much as possible, but by wise love to transform as much knowledge as possible into creative life. This is our own special kind of rite, something akin to the sacrifice to heaven, the meaning of which was unknown even to a Confucius. "Wise love"—that is what I should like to call the driving force which moves us here in our common effort. All of us together are working on a tapestry, a meaningful fabric in which the powers of the imagination and those of the intellect, like warp and woof, serve to realize the whole.

G. van der Leeuw

Primordial Time and Final Time

I

Since 1895, when Hermann Gunkel published his celebrated work on creation and chaos in primordial time and final time,[1] there have been numerous developments in the history of religions and in the related fields of ethnology, philosophical anthropology, and psychology. But his brilliant insight, the conception of primordial time and final time as the two poles of one and the same history, has been confirmed, and is still finding new confirmation with every day that passes.

Many concepts which were simply presupposed in Gunkel's formulation of the problem have become clear in the last thirty years, or else it has been shown that they are not clear at all and require clarification. In Gunkel's day only the barest intimation of the nature of primordial time and eschatology was possible, while the underlying concept of "time" has always been a philosophical stumbling-block.

Since then the discussion of these questions has continued unremittingly; so much so, that shortly after I had finished collecting and organizing the material for this lecture, I was embarrassed to come across two new and extremely important books which anticipated much of what I had to say. These are Karl Löwith's *Meaning in History*[2] and Mircea Eliade's fine study *The Myth of the Eternal Return*.[3]

Under these circumstances there seems to be only one thing for me to do, namely to steer my own course from my own scientific primordial time toward an always unattainable final time, in the hope that many more such new and important ideas as those of Löwith and Eliade will disturb and enrich my own thinking.

1 *Schöpfung und Chaos in Urzeit und Endzeit* (Göttingen, 1895).

2 Chicago, 1949.

3 Tr. W. R. Trask (New York and London, 1954; orig.: Paris, 1949).

TIME

There is a remarkable verse in Hermann Hesse's *Magister Ludi:*

> A magic dwells in each beginning and
> Protecting us it tells us how to live.[4]

The riddle of time is the riddle of the beginning. We know that there can be no true beginning. Something has always gone before. In the beginning lies the whole past. The beginning is the past. Yet we say that we begin something, that we make a new beginning. And we call the long list of such beginnings, time.

We live in time. We live out of the fact that we always begin anew: on awakening in the morning, at the beginning of the year, with every task we undertake, with each move from one place to another. And we do not understand this magic of the new beginning, this eternal transition from past to today, from today to past. The mysterious divide between yesterday and tomorrow, the intangible now, in which and through which we have our existence, is incomprehensible to us.

This is ancient wisdom. We recall the famous words of St. Augustine:

> What then *is* time? If no one asks me, I know; if I want to explain it to a questioner, I do not know. But at any rate this much I dare affirm I know; that if nothing passed there would be no past time; if nothing were approaching, there would be no future time; if nothing were, there would be no present time.
>
> But the two times, past and future, how can they *be*, since the past is no more and the future is not yet? On the other hand, if the present were always present and never flowed away into the past, it would not be time at all, but eternity. But if the present is only time, because it flows away into the past, how can we say that it *is?* For it is, only because it will cease to be. Thus we can affirm that time *is* only in that it tends towards not-being.[5]

That is the riddle of time.

We also remember Bergson's famous distinction between spatial time and purely temporal time. Spatial time, the time of our clocks, is a "hybrid concept, resulting from the incursion of the idea of space into the domain of pure consciousness." It is an experience of time that we have organized

4 Tr. Mervyn Savill (London and New York, 1949), p. 396 (orig.: *Das Glasperlenspiel*, Zurich, 1943).

5 St. Augustine, *Confessions*, XI, 14, tr. F. J. Sheed (London and New York, 1944).

spatially, a homogeneous *temps-cadran*, a sequence of segments. In reality there are no segments. Nor is time homogeneous; one second passes continuously into the next and is likewise inseparable from those that preceded it. Real time is a river, a melody. One can count seconds, because they are not time but space. In *temps-durée* there is no counting, any more than one can dissect a melody into notes. The peculiarity of time is precisely that it passes through our hands like water, that it is intangible, as St. Augustine said. There is no punctual present: either it is already past or still future. When we say it is nine thirty, it is no longer nine thirty, and the telephone operator's voice announcing the time does not speak of time at all, but only of the clock.

And yet time, today's time, is our vital element. We like to imagine that we stand at a fixed point, from which we look comfortably back into the past or expectantly forward into the future. But there is no fixed point; we are carried along by time as though by a torrent. We are temporal—that is to say, we can neither grasp nor hold fast a point in time, can neither grasp nor hold fast our own existence. The man of nine thirty is not the same as the man of nine twenty-five. We *are* time.

Nevertheless we exist and call ourselves "we." We have "our" past and make plans for "our" future. This implies something which Karl Heim called "simultaneity": "If . . . a segment of time is experienced, there must be a relation of simultaneity between the elements of the temporal event side by side with the relation of succession. The notes of a piece of music cannot merely sound successively, they must also merge with one another. The images that a motion-picture projector casts on the screen in swift succession may not simply appear one after the other, they must fuse into one total image."[6]

This relation of simultaneity has from time immemorial been related to the image of the circle. For the relation between space and time is the same as that between the straight line and the circle. The problem of the squaring of the circle is not a whim, but a problem rooted in our innermost being. The circle is not a sequence of infinitesimal straight lines, but precisely a circle. A point on this circle is always at the same time the next point. We can draw a tangent to the circle, yet it will not really touch the circle except in a mathematical sense.

Moreover a flight from time into space can help us only if the continuity

6 Karl Heim, *Glaubensgewissheit* (Leipzig, 1923), p. 70.

of space is established—that is, again, only in a mathematical sense. Originally space itself is not measured space, not a surface that can be subdivided; for such a space exists no more than does the time of the clock. Experienced space is not a continuum but a number of islands between which there is nothing. This is the space I experience when I take a walk or a drive in a car. Here there is a beautiful meadow, there a river, here a village, there a farmhouse. Only when I take part in a race or when I am overtired is it different. Then I only count the miles and move from milestone to milestone. But that is a subhuman process—as though I were to do nothing all day but look at the clock.

But space as well as time is a form of the life that man creates by singling out favored points and intervals. Space is not an abstract magnitude, but a series of "places" where I settle down, so to speak, which I favor; time is a series of temporal points which I distinguish for their values and which, in a sense, I hold fast. These are the "feast days" that I celebrate in cult and which taken together form the calendar. Through them I experience both the progression of time and my own duration. Harvest, sowing time, the rise or fall of a heavenly body are the actual "data," the given, by which I have my life. "*La fête est le chaos retrouvé et façonné à nouveau*," says Caillois.[7]

A certain parallelism is unmistakable between the data without and the data within. The parallelism between the phases of the moon and the menstrual period is particularly evident. Danzel is probably right in saying that "some of the astronomical-cosmic periods first rose to consciousness as a corresponding symbolic expression of human periods."[8] But in general we may say that "time" signifies a life-value. It is time to harvest or time to work or time to sleep. Originally the year was not the astronomical year—which came into being only when the correspondences were noticed—but the season. The Greek *eniautos* is the harvest year, the *horae* bring flowers and fruits, said Jane Harrison. But at the same time they are gods, *daimones*, who renew life over and over again, as our life is renewed. For the year is primarily the "year of the soul"; time is the time of life.

What is to be singled out and favored is of supreme importance for life as soon as correspondence with the outside world gives us a firm basis on which to work out a calendar and fix the *dies fasti* and *nefasti*. We learn to draw the correct dividing lines, to ascertain the time. In ancient Rome the

7 Roger Caillois, *L'Homme et le sacré* (Paris, 1939).
8 T. W. Danzel, *Kultur und Religion des primitiven Menschen* (Stuttgart, 1924).

calendar—that is, the days for sowing, harvest, marriage, etc.—was solemnly proclaimed by the *Rex sacrorum,* the king's successor, at the nones, the first quarter of the moon, after the priests had established it at the calends, the time of the new moon. The Aztecs called the period of fifty-two years after which all fires had to be extinguished and drilled anew the "bundle of the year." Here fire is the measure of the time interval. After a long journey the Aztecs drilled fire in order to express the fact that "their years had joined together in Chapultepec; for they had been unable to drill fire as long as they were surrounded by their enemies." Krickeberg calls this mode of expression "figurative."[8a] But this does not mean that it is secondary. On the contrary, it dominated their entire thinking. If time is not "joined," if the calendar is not proclaimed, both cease to be; everything simply stops, as for the schizophrenic whose time stands still, or for Sleeping Beauty in the castle.

Hamann saw this clearly. Every moment of time, he said, is "perfectly round," each hour independent of the next. The continuity results only from the thread of providence. But man can be his own providence and magically establish time; he can make a beginning.

For once again, everything depends on the beginning which does not exist naturally. As soon as the beginning is at hand, everything can be repeated. But Janus is the first god to make a beginning. There must be one who already exists in order to set time in motion. As in the profound words of Walther von der Vogelweide:

> He who never had a beginning
> And can make a beginning,
> Can surely make an end or can make endlessness.[9]

MYTH

One more poem from Hermann Hesse's *Magister Ludi:*

> 'Tis true the simpletons who nothing dare
> The harvest of our doubts will never reap;
> The world is flat they solemnly declare,
> An old wives' tale the legend of the deep.

8a [Walter Krickeberg, *Märchen der Azteken und Inkaperuaner* (Jena, 1928), pp. 351, 100.—Ed.]

9
> Der anegenge nie gewan
> Und anegenge mac̄hen kan,
> Der kan wol ende machen und ân ende.

For were dimensions to exist as well
As those in which our childish trust we place,
How should a single soul in safety dwell,
How should men live untroubled and at peace?
To safeguard, then, the freedom of our minds
Let us cast one dimension to the winds!
If honest is the ingenuous man's intention,
And is so perilous the mind's declension,
We will make do without a third dimension.[10]

But if we wish to be ingenuous enough to erase time, we require not three but four dimensions. We can reduce time to space, we can make space homogeneous. We can live with clocks, angles, and square feet. And all these are assuredly necessary. Except that we cannot actually *live* by them. When one says space and time, one means one's own life. That is, one means not empty surface, not a chronometer, but myth.

Time is favored time: the dividing lines have been made on the basis of life's experiences. Time is full, and its content is the myths—that is, the forms of life that lie heaped up for all time in the womb of the unconscious. Actually Goethe said all this in *Dauer im Wechsel:*

Hielte diesen frühen Segen,
Ach, nur eine Stunde fest!
Aber vollen Blütenregen
Schüttelt schon der laue West.
Soll ich mich des Grünen freuen,
Dem ich Schatten erst verdankt?
Bald wird Sturm auch das zerstreuen,
Wenn es falb im Herbst geschwankt.

Willst du nach den Früchten greifen,
Eilig nimm dein Teil davon!
Diese fangen an zu reifen,
Und die andern keimen schon;
Gleich mit jedem Regengusse
Ändert sich dein holdes Tal,
Ach, und in demselben Flusse
Schwimmst du nicht zum zweitenmal.

Lass den Anfang mit dem Ende
Sich in eins zusammenziehn!

10 Tr. Savill, pp. 387ff.

Schneller als die Gegenstände
Selber dich vorüberfliehn!
Danke, dass die Gunst der Musen
Unvergängliches verheisst:
Den Gehalt in deinem Busen
Und die Form in deinem Geist.[11]

So much has been written about myth in recent years, by myself among others,[12] that here I can stress only the most essential points. The best and most succinct formulation is that of Raffaele Pettazzoni:

> Myth is not fable, but history, "true history" and not "false history." It is true history by virtue of its content, the narrative of events that really occurred, beginning with those grandiose events of the origins: the origin of the world, of humanity, the origin of life and death, of the animal and vegetable species, the origin of the hunt and of agriculture, the origin of fire, the origin of the cult, the origin of the initiatory rites, of the Shamanistic societies and of their therapeutic powers: events remote in time from which

11 *Constancy in Change*

Could this early bliss but rest
  Constant for one single hour!
But e'en now the humid West
  Scatters many a vernal shower.
Should the verdure give me joy?
  'Tis to it I owe the shade;
Soon will storms its bloom destroy,
  Soon will Autumn bid it fade.

Eagerly thy portion seize,
  If thou wouldst possess the fruit!
Fast begin to ripen these,
  And the rest already shoot.
With each heavy storm of rain,
  Change comes o'er thy valley fair,
Once, alas! but not again,
  Can the same stream hold thee e'er.

Be then the beginning found
  With the end in unison.
Swifter than the forms around
  Are themselves now fleeting on!
Thank the merit in thy breast,
  Thank the mold within thy heart,
That the Muses' favor blest
  Ne'er will perish, ne'er depart.

Tr. E. A. Bowring (London, 1853), p. 121.

12 Most recently in "Die Bedeutung der Mythen," *Festschrift für Alfred Bertholet*, ed. W. Baumgartner et al. (Tübingen, 1950), 287–93.

> present-day life took its beginning and foundation, from which the present structure of society issued and on which it still depends. The divine or supernatural personages that are active in myth, their extraordinary undertakings, their singular adventures, all this marvelous world is a transcendent reality that cannot be placed in doubt because it is the antecedent and condition *sine qua non* of present reality.—Myth is true history because it is sacred history: by virtue not only of its content, but also of the concrete sacral forces that it sets in motion. The recitation of the myths of the origins is incorporated in the cult because it is itself cult and contributes to the aims for which the cult is celebrated, which are the preservation and increase of life. . . . To relate the creation of the world helps to maintain the life of mankind—that is, the community, the tribal group; to relate the origin of the initiatory rites and the Shamanist practices serves to assure their efficacy and duration in time. . . . That is why myths are true histories and cannot be false. Their truth is not of a logical nor of a historical order: it is above all a religious and more specially magical order. The efficacy of myth in serving the ends of the cult, in preserving the world and life, resides in the magic of the word, in the evocative power of the word, of the *mythos*, of the *fabula*, not as fabulous discourse but as an arcane and potent force akin—also according to the etymology—to the power of *fa-tum*.[13]

What Lévy-Bruhl, K. T. Preuss, Malinowski, and many other scholars have shown by numerous examples is here brilliantly summed up in few words. I should like to add a characteristic remark of Malinowski: myth is "not merely a story told, but a reality lived—not an intellectual reaction upon a puzzle, but an explicit act of faith—a statement of primeval reality which still lives in present-day life and a justification by precedent."[14]

The essential for our purposes is this: the existence of the world, whether seen on a small or on a large scale, is not permanently established or given. It must always be begun anew through recourse to myth—that is, through recitation of the myth of the origin and the consequent revival of the primordial events. Myth and the sacral action connected with it guarantee the survival of the world. With Preuss: "The primitive man not only repeats, but represents the initial enactment."[15]

An example: an Old Norse poet finds that his inspiration has run dry.

13 Pettazzoni, *Miti e leggende* (Turin, 1948), Vol. I, p. v.

14 B. Malinowski, *Myth in Primitive Psychology* (London, 1926), pp. 21, 43, 124.

15 K. T. Preuss, *Der religiöse Gehalt der Mythen* (Tübingen, 1933), p. 7.

Accordingly he must recall the myth of how Odin "acquired the scaldic mead. For in the example there is hidden a magical power, which enables the adept to repeat the primary divine action or at least to make an attempt at it."[16] Here we have the idea of primordial time, not as a time very remote in the past, but rather as a prototypical time in which everything already happened which today does not begin anew but is only repeated. Primordial time is creative; it creates what happens today. And this is brought about through the repetition of its myth.

The new conception of myth has the broadest implications. "It yields a world view that is totally different from the usual conceptions. Nothing is fixed, in fact, nothing *is*. Nothing can appear except by being forever newly created, by being activated as myth."[17] But this means that every myth is etiological, not in the old sense that it "explains" a fact, but in the sense that it provides a guarantee for this fact. This applies as much to particulars—such as the poetry of the scald, the craft of an artisan, or a natural phenomenon—as it does to the whole, the creation of the world. It applies, to speak with Pettazzoni, to the *origine*—that is, to the creative source of every event in its actuality.

"In our time this mythical view of the world lives in remnants at most; it is assuredly not dead; every myth lies buried somewhere in our unconscious and can come to life again at any time, as depth psychology amply shows. But in our Western European culture there is one sphere where this mythical consciousness of the world survives unchanged, namely in Christian religion. As a rule theologians have no time for myth, or else they denounce it as 'pagan.' Yet in Christianity it lives on intact, so much so that if it were to vanish, the Christian faith would die with it. The first three chapters of Genesis are a myth κατ' 'εξοχήν, a myth which is still believed and which, like every genuine, living myth, is actually taken as supreme truth. Here the prototype in the existential sense is perfectly clear. As Chesterton put it: 'An apple is eaten and the hope of God is gone.' Every Christian lives in Adam and Eve and his life in its sinfulness is determined by this event in primordial time. Each of us has eaten of the tree and been driven from paradise. This is no 'metaphor,' no analogy. In the events of Genesis our fate was determined once and for all.

16 A. G. van Hamel, "The Conception of Fate in Early Teutonic and Celtic Religion," *Saga-Book of the Viking Society* (Coventry, England), XI (1928–36), 209.

17 Van der Leeuw, in *Festschrift für Bertholet*, p. 291.

"And it is not only the creation and the fall from grace that live on in myth, but also redemption, the second creation. Essentially the rite of the Lord's Supper is simply an activation of the myth of Christ (how far behind us lies the time in which this term could be used as a kind of argument against the historicity of Jesus!). The recitation of the words of the Consecration—'*Qui pridie quam pateretur*,' etc.—is the heart and foundation of every Christian liturgy of the Lord's Supper. Whatever theory of the sacrament we may espouse, the rite remains an activation and actualization of the story of Christ, a transference of the original event from primordial time into the present."[18]

With this the essential has been said. Time and myth belong together. Myth creates time, gives it "content and form." This is still implicit in the calendar: "An III de la République," "in the tenth year of Fascism," "A.D. 1949." Time was determined by an event that emerged from the unconscious at the moment when it was given form, an *αἴτιον*, a primal cause—not external, but situated in the profoundest stratum of our life, in the archetype.

In listing the possessions of primitive man, Goldenweiser mentions not only house, pot, boat, implements, and weapons, but also dances, songs, stories, rites and formulas, and names.[19] All these are forms of myth, handed down from one generation to another. For myth and so-called reality are indissolubly interwoven. When they read the earliest history of certain tribes or peoples, scholars wonder: is it myth or history? mythical usage or real usage? Were the ancient Roman kings real kings or "mere" mythical figures? Are certain demons in which peoples believe represented in the rites of the secret societies, or were they from the very beginning nothing but members of these societies? But the whole question is false. Myth is life and life is myth.

Henri Frankfort speaks of the "mythopoeic thought" of the ancient Egyptians. The configurations of life as such are mythical. The state, for example—which for us, as we suppose, is an institution—is for the Egyptian the figure of the king, a man and a god at once, born of his parents but at the same time from the union of the queen with a god, a living myth, Pharaoh "by whose dealings one lives." Even in his lifetime he appears to belong to the sphere of myth as much as to that of actuality.[20] Isis is

18 Ibid., pp. 292–93.
19 Arthur Goldenweiser, *Anthropology* (New York, 1946), p. 149.
20 Frankfort, *Ancient Egyptian Religion* (New York, 1948), pp. 4, 43ff.

a goddess, but at the same time a seat, a chair, a throne: *is-t*. She is the king's mother, the throne that makes the king, just like the women of certain Negro kings, on whose knees the kings recline when they wish to rest.

Drama is one of the most important forms of the actualization of myth. It is "performed"—that is to say, enacted. But the dividing line between the performer and what he represents is fluid, and the distance between the *αἴτιον* and what is caused sometimes ceases to exist. In Ameland, a Dutch island in the North Sea, the whole male population comes together on December 6 to celebrate the feast of St. Nicholas. The women and children are excluded. Every grown man represents a St. Nicholas or "uncle"; he wears a mask surmounted by a hat that is often a yard high, bears a stick and horn, with which he produces growling sounds. All the doors and windows are closed. The unmarried girls and boys under eighteen are terrorized. Is this a dramatic performance? or a collective celebration of the community? or an age-old magic action, tending to "distinguish" the time? Strictly observed, the rite closely resembles that of the secret societies, of the young men's societies, etc., among primitive peoples. Myth is manifested in life. The men are St. Nicholases, demons, gods for a day. The time is marked off; life can continue.

Experienced time is mythical time, time of the beginning, the middle, and the end appointed by "providence" or ourselves; it is *connected* time. We find the most majestic example of this in the first lines of the *Divine Comedy:*

> Nel mezzo del cammin di nostra vita
> Mi ritrovai per una selva oscura
> Chè la diritta via era smarrita.

In the middle of his life the poet finds himself in darkness; an "unruly beast" threatens to drive him "where the sun is silent." At this point a new beginning must be made, a new myth uttered. And so it is! Antiquity takes him by the hand and all the richness of hell, purgatory, and paradise is poured into his life as a new content. Cleansed and transfigured, he goes his way.

This is an indication that, as Jung has said:

> it would be a serious mistake to suppose that he [the poet] works with materials received at second-hand. The primordial experience is the source of his creativeness; it cannot be fathomed, and there-

> fore requires mythological imagery to give it form. . . . Dante's presentiments are clothed in images that run the gamut of Heaven and Hell; Goethe must bring in the Blocksberg and the infernal regions of Greek antiquity; Wagner needs the whole body of Nordic myth; Nietzsche returns to the hieratic style and recreates the legendary seer of prehistoric times.[21]

The poet and the neurotic—more's the pity—are the only men who experience lived time "normally," and who quench their soul's thirst from the eternal sources of myth. All others have accustomed themselves to the clock and homogeneous space as though they really existed. But deep within us repose the old treasures, the old monsters and the old gods, hell and paradise.

In last year's lecture on mystical man[22] Erich Neumann gave us a brilliant account of how man and mankind first seek the hidden self in "creative nothingness," of how consciousness then bursts forth and how the primordial One is split; how the Great Mother, terrible and devouring, returns, threatens, and lures; how the hero frees the ego with the help of Marduk's spit, Yahweh's word, or the lance of St. George; how the unconscious is walled in; how finally the sacred marriage is celebrated and creative life emanates from cleavage.

Myth, filled time, signifies all this. Everything is already present in the beginning. Even the discoveries of science, even the steps in the growth of consciousness, are present before they come to light, lying, as Louis de Broglie has recently shown, embedded in the scientist's unconscious.[23]

PRIMORDIAL TIME

If all this is so, actually nothing remains but the painful process of becoming conscious. Everything is contained in the primordial age. But in the life of primitive man and ancient man the growth of consciousness is made manifest and real only through the rites that repeat the primordial events. The primordial experience is reproduced, represented anew, and so gains duration and consistency, becoming real "time." Lévy-Bruhl and others have shown at length how the primordial age is the foundation of all present-day happenings, of the social structure of the tribe, of the law, and the behavior of the individual. Everything is predetermined, from time immemorial.

21 "Psychology and Literature," in *Modern Man in Search of a Soul*, tr. W. S. Dell and Cary F. Baynes (Harvest Books edn., New York, 1955), pp. 164f.

22 "Der mystische Mensch," *EJ 1948*.

23 L. de Broglie, *Continu et le discontinu dans la physique moderne* (Paris, 1942).

In his most recent study Eliade has described the bearing of this context on culture as a whole. "Man constructs according to an archetype." Every settlement has a celestial prototype; only the ownerless, uncultivated land sits there just as it is. Settlement itself is an act of creation. Jerusalem was built on chaos (*tehom*), Babylon on the waters of chaos (*apsu*). Every subsequent act is a repetition of an original happening. "Reality is acquired solely through repetition or participation."[23a] Culture, in a manner of speaking, is the fixation and confirmation of the given, the establishment of the cosmos as opposed to chaos.

The confirmation of the act, whether we call it rite or act of culture, is always myth. It "points," as Preuss says, "into the past where the sacral action was first undertaken; in fact, it can sometimes be shown that the primitive does not merely repeat the initial event, but consciously represents its first performance with all the beings who then participated in it." Hence myth is a "necessary ingredient in the cult (and in culture) insofar as a beginning in primordial time is regarded as requisite to its validity."[24] Recited myth is always a story of creation.

Yet even the so-called natural event is not new but a repetition of the beginning. Thus in ancient Egypt every flood that rejuvenates the life of the land is a new creation of the world. And this is also true in the Old Testament myth of the deluge.

The circular course of time impresses itself upon us more and more. There are no new times, no moment that has not yet been attained. There is only primordial time, today as in the past and in the most distant future.

Only one conception of primordial time points in another direction. This is the conception of the Golden Age, the happy primordial past, when heaven and earth had not yet split apart, when male had not yet been separated from female (Japan), when there was no struggle, no injustice (Egypt). True, this primordial age is also repeated, but this repetition is not taken for granted. The Egyptians said that in a good king's reign "the truth remained, the lie was shunned, and the land was as in its primordial age." Here we seem to have a regression, which can partly be explained by the yearning for unsplit, unconscious being, but (as in the case of Egypt) this yearning assuredly stems also from other factors.

But there is still another circumstance that we must take into account:

23a Eliade, *The Myth of the Eternal Return*, pp. 10, 15, 34.
24 Preuss, *Der religiöse Gehalt.*

The concept of the primordial era is no truly eschatological concept; it is not a marginal time, but simply time. This view is supported by the fact that there is seldom a corresponding final time among primitive peoples. Primordial time and final time as eschatological concepts presuppose something that has not yet entered into our discussion: history.

2
ESCHATOLOGY

By eschatology we mean man's utterances in so far as they refer to events at the margin of the world before it was world, and after it has ceased to be world. It includes the glory of the first day but also the horror of the last day, *novissima rerum.*

Now there is here a noteworthy distinction that follows from the changed cultural situation of which I spoke at our preceding conference.[25] The so-called primitive man knows no eschatology in the strict sense. He knows primordial time, which for him dominates all life, which is renewed over and over again in the present-day occurrences that are the guarantee of his life. As long as he performs the rites correctly, he creates his world anew each day, in a manner of *creatio continua.* The creative word of myth renews the world for him.

But primordial time is not a beginning in the strict sense. It is just as much alive today as it was yesterday; it begins each day anew. Consequently there is no end corresponding to it. Primitive myth has little if anything to say of final time. The myth finds no conclusion: according to it, time turns round and round. "What happens now is what happened long ago." Primitive man—that is, the man who still lives close to the womb, in an unsplit world, who has objectified neither his own life nor that of the world—lives in circles, in an eternal today. The patriarchs and what they did are today as much alive as they were then. A real past exists no more than a real future. When scholars seek to explain this state of affairs, they say that primitive man is lacking in historical consciousness—for the most part without suspecting that this merely suggests the problem, but does not clarify it from an anthropological point of view.

It is true, to be sure, that the natives whom Malinowski and Fortune have described count only four generations backward, and that the first of

25 "L'Homme et la civilisation," *EJ 1948.*

these is already coeval with the creation, the primordial age. One might then say that their historical view is limited—but not much more limited than that of most modern men, at least of those who are not burdened with the weight of ruins or patents of nobility, or who do not lean heavily on their schoolbooks (which for most of us represent no living reality at all). What is far more important is that in these four generations (or forty, there is no essential difference) nothing new happens, that time stands still as in the tale of Sleeping Beauty. The end of the story is missing.

But this end is just as problematic as the beginning. In our stories, to be sure, we must content ourselves with the assurance that after the marriage of the prince with the heroine they both lived happily ever after. Marriage is the end, after which nothing more can happen—as is only proper in a good marriage. Just as the beginning ultimately presupposes a primordial beginning, so does every end, every conclusion presuppose a final conclusion, a "last judgment." Primordial time has its correspondence in final time—but only after man has made a considerable advance in his painful awakening to consciousness, and the suffering of human existence has set itself a term either in a supreme terror or an infinite bliss.

The stupendous idea of an end of time is an attempt to negate the eternal stasis, to break the circle. All peoples that have awakened to the suffering and hope of the *condition humaine* have arrived at the idea. The magnificent image of the Norse *ragnarök*, in which the gods die along with men and the world, is perhaps its most radical form. But, each in its own way, the other peoples who have created a world for themselves have also appointed an end to it: Indians, Persians, Greeks, Arabs, and Jews.

Sometimes this end is the conclusion of a slow degeneration, just as the Golden Age was a climax. But much more characteristic is the conception of a final time that irrupts suddenly and puts an end to everything, slashing the fabric of time like a sword. Here it can really become an experience. Its advent is expected shortly, as we know from the New Testament. As late as the second century a Syrian bishop led his whole community, including children, into the desert to meet the Lord.[26]

Here we approach the great cleavage in the self-consciousness of mankind. On the one side, time takes a cyclical course, on the other it has a beginning before which there was nothing and an end with which it stops. On the one

26 Hans Lietzmann, *A History of the Early Church*, Vol. II: *The Founding of the Church Universal*, tr. B. Lee-Woolf (London, 3rd edn., 1953), p. 196.

side, every sunrise is a victory over chaos, every festival a cosmic beginning, every sowing a new creation, every holy place a foundation of the cosmos, every historical event a rise or fall according to the regular course of the world, and even the law that sustains society is nothing other than the rule of the sun's course, as Wensinck has so admirably set forth for the Semitic world,[27] but as is also true of a certain phase in the development of all peoples. On the other side, everything is exactly the same except that at a certain point in the cycle someone appears who proclaims a definitive event, the day of Yahweh, the last judgment, the ultimate salvation, or the final conflict as in Iran. The images used are all borrowed from the course of nature: day and night, summer and winter. But the ethos has changed; a hiatus has been made, a *tempus* in the strict sense, which changes everything. Thus the prophet Zacharias can say that it will be light at eventide. This final time revolutionizes the course of the world.

Here we have the working out of an idea that has always lived. We find it in the so-called "adunata," the jestlike sayings that refer to an impossible moment in time: "That happens on little Neverday, when the calves dance on the ice," or "At Pentecost when the mosquitoes sprinkle and the squirrels bark," or "That will happen in Three Thursday Week, forty days after never." [28] Or to take the moral view with Piers Plowman, it will not happen

> till lads and ladies love the truth,
> till they hate the loose word, to hear it or speak it,

and that, alas, is never. Thus in a thousand variants the impossible is represented, sometimes with popular wit, but sometimes also with deep sorrow or biting irony. Until one day the impossible becomes possible after all:

> Macbeth shall never vanquish'd be until
> Great Birnam wood to high Dunsinane hill
> Shall come against him . . .

And the incredible happens: the wood moves up to judgment against the wicked king. Or conversely, the pope's barren staff sprouts branches, all human justice ceases, and Tannhäuser experiences the impossibility of grace.

27 A.S. Wensinck, "The Semitic Year and the Origin of Eschatology," *Acta Orientalia* (Leiden), I (1922), 158–99.

28 G. van der Leeuw, "Adunata," *Jaarbericht van het Vooraziatisch-Egyptisch Gezelschap "Ex Oriente Lux"* (Leiden), no. 8 (1942), 631–41.

In these adunata there lives eschatology, the myth of the impossible. A tenth-century scaldic song of the Icelander Kormak employs the whole apparatus of the myth of final time, which he must have known from the Völuspa, for a wholly frivolous description of an impossibility: "Stones will float as lightly as grain on the water, the earth will sink, the magnificent great cliffs will sink into the deep sea—before a girl as beautiful as Steingerd will be born." Or, in another scaldic song: "The bright sun will turn black, the earth will sink into the dark sea, the heavy burden of Eystris (the sky) will burst, the whole ocean will flow up along the cliffs—before such a yarl will be born on the islands."[29]

The irruption of a time that is impossible, of an event that falls out of the cycle—we are familiar with this notion, from the fishes that remain hanging on the limbs of the trees in the myth of Deucalion, to the mountain that is transplanted into the sea in the sermon of Jesus.

The transvaluation of all values, the realization of the impossible: what is not possible for man is possible for God. The word "God" has many meanings. But in the strictest sense, the idea of "God" like that of "time" is situated outside of the world, far from man. The eschatological myths are full of what ancient theology called God's *aseitas*, and what I will translate as God's aloneness. When there was nothing, there was God; when there is nothing, there will still be God. God is the first and the last, the alpha and omega, the *eschaton*. Perhaps this is most beautifully expressed in the Christian Germanic poem that we call the "Wessobrunn Prayer":

> This is the greatest of the sciences that I learned among men,
> that the earth was not nor the heavens above,
> nor tree nor mountain
> nor any (star), nor did the sun yet shine
> nor did the moon gleam, nor (was) the glorious sea.
> And when there were no ends or limits,
> there was the one all-powerful God . . .[30]

As has been pointed out, it is no accident that the first Christian poem that has come down to us deals with the beginning of the world.[31] For only in Judaism and Christianity is the idea of the unthinkable, of the beginning

29 A. Olrik, *Ragnarök* (Berlin, 1922), pp. 22ff. ["yarl" = "earl."—Ed.]

30 From a ninth-century MS of the Wessobrunn Monastery. After Gustav Ehrismann's modern German version.

31 T. C. van Stockum and J. van Dam, *Geschichte der deutschen Literatur* (2 vols., Groningen, 1934–35), Vol. I, p. 48.

and the end, fully thought out. But it is everywhere suggested, always in the modality of the specific religious revelation. A few examples from the most diverse regions may make this clear.

From the Enuma Elish, the great Babylonian epic of creation:

> When in the height heaven was not named
> And the earth beneath did not yet bear a name,
> And the primeval Apsū, who begat them,
> And chaos, Tiamat, the mother of them both,—
> Their waters were mingled together,
> And no field was formed, no marsh was to be seen;
> When of the gods none had been called into being,
> And none bore a name, and no destinies were ordained;
> Then were created the gods in the midst of heaven,
> Lahmu and Lahamu were called into being.[32]

The gods are included in the world; at most they provide names, but they themselves must be named. The chaos in its male (Apsū) and female (Tiamat) form is the only thing that was before anything was. The act of creation is the proclaiming word.

In an ancient Egyptian text the king is said to have been born in Nun, the primordial water, "when the earth had not yet come into being, when the two supports [of the sky] had not yet come into being, when unrest had not yet come into being, when fear had not yet come into being."[33] Unrest is the mark of the present state of things, creation is cleavage, as in the myth of Shu who lifts the mother of heaven from the embrace of the earth father (Nut and Keb), makes air, and puts an end to the original unity. And again in one of the so-called Pyramid Texts: "[was born] before there was any anger; [was born] before there was a clamor [lit., voice]; [was born] before there was conflict; [was born] before there was strife; [was born] before the eye of Horus was plucked out; [was born] before the testicles of Set were torn away."[34] Or in a still different variant, the king was born from his father Atum "before the sky came into being, before earth came into being . . . before death came into being."[35] Here again the gods are counted as part of the world. Only the king, the man-god who represents all divine and

32 Enuma Elish, ed. L. W. King, *The Seven Tablets of Creation* (Luzac's Semitic Text and Translation Series; 2 vols., London, 1902), Vol. I, p. 3.

33 From Samuel A. B. Mercer, *The Pyramid Texts in Translation and Commentary* (4 vols., New York, 1952), Vol. I, p. 181.

34 Ibid., p. 237.

35 Ibid., p. 233.

human life, was present before all time, before the foundation of the world, a kind of logos.

And now a narrative of creation from the Popol Vuh of the Maya:

> There was not yet a single man, not a single animal; no birds, no fish, no crayfish, wood, stone, pits or bogs, ravines, grass, or groves of trees; only the heaven existed. The face of the earth was not yet visible. Only the sea was, and all the space of the heavens. There was nothing yet which was solid, nothing which possessed coherence, nothing which swayed or moved or made the least rustling, nothing which made any sound, to be heard in heaven. There was nothing that stood upright; there was only the peaceful water, and the calm sea, alone in its boundaries; nothing existed. There was only immobility and silence in the darkness, in the night. And alone the Creator, the Fashioner, the Dominator, the Serpent Covered with Feathers, Those who Engender, Those who Give Being, are on the water like an increasing light. They are clad in green and blue; that is why their name is Gucumatz.[36]

According to one authority the bisexual godhead named here is a form of Quetzalcoatl; in any case it is what always was, although this version of the Popol Vuh cannot think away the heavens and the sea.

And in the primordial age of Japan heaven and earth were not yet separate, nor were the male and female principle; there was a chaos like a hen's egg, and in this chaos a germ. Here again cleavage is the creative principle, but chaos itself is the primal being.

Finally the Rig-Veda: in the primordial age, "the non-existent was not, the existent was not then; air was not nor the firmament that is beyond. What stirred? Where? Under whose shelter? Was the deep abyss water?

"Death was not, immortality was not then; no distinction was there of night and day. That One breathed, windless, self-dependent. Other than That there was nought beyond."[37] This is not only very impressive but also very characteristic of Indian religious feeling with its affinity to nothingness. From the One, which breathes out of itself, comes everything, including the gods. But the One is neither being nor nonbeing. Concerning it one can speak only in questions. Even the breathing of the One is without breath.

36 "The Popol Vuh," tr. from the French of Brasseur de Bourbourg by Philip A. Malpas, *Theosophical Path* (Point Loma, Cal., 1930), p. 206.

37 Rig-Veda, 10, 129, *Vedic Hymns*, tr. Edward Joseph Thomas (Wisdom of the East Series; London, 1923), p. 127.

Among the myths of primordial time this represents the pole farthest removed from that of the "Wessobrunn Prayer."

CREATION

Among the Hebrews, too, there is a primordial time, *olam.* J. Pedersen writes:

> Primordial time gathers within it the whole content of time, hence it is also the beginning of time; *olam* is history and hence also the world as a concentrated totality. History is borne by the generations, and they are a product of primordial time, concentrated in the fathers in whom the life of the race is lived. Adam is primordial man, at one and the same time the first man and the human species, in which all men are subsumed.[38]

This, then, is the primordial age, just as we have found it in other religious spheres. But in Israel the idea of the caesura and of the noncyclical beginning is much more sharply delimited than elsewhere. Not that the circle and birth are entirely lacking. On the contrary they are the background against which the new concept of time stands out. Genesis I begins with chaos-darkness and cleavage-light. But the principle of cleavage is the word of the speaking God who was always present. The Ninetieth Psalm expresses this thought most beautifully: "Before the mountains were brought forth, or ever thou hadst formed the earth and the world [the myth of birth], even from everlasting [*me-olam ad-olam*],[38a] thou art God." This is the true aloneness of God. Man can never be wholly alone, for he never exists without a world that is his world. But God exists even without a world, *a se.*

Proverbs 8 adds the logos-like figure of wisdom, which was there before all else and which later found its continuation in the New Testament figure of Christ, the intermediary of creation. And Genesis 2 draws man and culture into the picture: "In the day that the Lord God made the earth and the heavens, And every plant of the field before it was in the earth, and every herb of the field before it grew: for the Lord God had not caused it to rain upon the earth, and there was not a man to till the ground." But then *adama,* the fruitful earth belonging to Adam, came into being and with it the world of men.[39]

38 J. Pedersen, *Israel,* Vol. I (Copenhagen, 1920), pp. 384ff.

38a [Or in van der Leeuw's version, "from primordial time to primordial time." TR.]

39 Paul Humbert, *Etudes sur le récit du paradis et de la chute dans la Genèse* (Neuchâtel, 1940), pp. 50ff.

What this means becomes clear to us when we compare the Israelite myth of the creation with the Egyptian myth. In Egypt the world, i.e., the primordial hill, was created; the "high sand" arose over the waters. After that nothing happened. The world is static, as Frankfort says, the creation is the only real event, in which everything else is contained, an eternal equilibrium.[40] In Israel also, to be sure, history is read into God's creative act. Just as Pharaoh slays the enemies of the world in his enemies, so does Yahweh in the Egyptian enemy slay the mighty powers of chaos, Rahab and Leviathan. The Deluge and the Exodus are in a manner of speaking repetitions of the act of creation. Noah and the Israelites pass through the menacing waters, the enemies must drown.[41] But with these events there begins at the same time a whole new world; with the Flodo the world that is governed by Noah's covenant, with the Exodus the historical world that is subordinated to the Law.

True, the idea of equilibrium is also present. For the creation is never a fact established once and for all, never a mere foundation of the world, but a *creatio continua,* and God's act of creation is repeated over and over again. God defends the earth against the primordial waters that always threaten it. A few quotations which refer both to the primordial time and to the present may make this clear.

Psalm 104: "Who laid the foundations of the earth, that it should not be removed for ever. Thou coveredst it with the deep as with a garment; the waters stood above the mountains. At thy rebuke they fled [the separating word!]; at the voice of thy thunder they hasted away. . . . Thou hast set a bound that they may not pass over; that they turn not again to cover the earth."

Or still more plainly in Job 38: "Who shut up the sea with doors, when it brake forth, as if it had issued out of the womb? . . . and set bars and doors, And said, Hitherto shalt thou come, but no further, and here shall thy proud waves be stayed?"

The primordial womb of the mother is there, the Eternal Feminine is not lacking. But it is not said that "*in gremio matris sedet sapientia patris.*" The father, further removed than the mother from the act of birth, is free

40 Frankfort, *Ancient Egyptian Religion,* pp. 50, 88, 91; A. de Buck, *De Egyptische Voorstellingen betreffende den Oerheuvel* (Leiden, 1922); H. Ricke, "Der Hohe Sand in Heliopolis," *Zeitschrift für ägyptische Sprache und Altertumskunde* (Leipzig), LXXI (1935), 107ff.

41 F. M. T. Böhl, *Nieuwjaarsfeest en Koningsdag in Babylon en Israel* (Groningen, 1927).

and independent; he separates and seals off, commands and sets boundaries.

Late, in Manasses' prayer: "Who hast bound the sea by the word of thy commandment; who hast shut up the deep, and sealed it by thy terrible and glorious name."

And Psalm 74: "Thou didst divide the sea by thy strength: thou brakest the heads of the dragons in the waters. Thou brakest the heads of leviathan in pieces. . . ."

Finally, Isaiah 51: "Awake, awake, put on strength, O arm of the Lord; awake, as in the ancient [*olam*-like!] days, in the generations of old. Art thou not it that hath cut Rahab, and wounded the dragon?"

But in primordial time, today, and in final time God is present, *me-olam ad-olam*, from time to time, high above the cyclic renewal of the world. He is a hero figure, but unlike Siegfried or even Marduk he is the solitary One, who does not dissolve in nature but resists nature and the cycle of birth and death. Even the tilling of the *adama* is a punishment, a curse. And actually the whole history of Israel has only one theme: the struggle between the lonely desert god, between Him who, as Buber translates, is nowhere at home, and the baalim, the gods and goddesses of the earth.

Here Israelite-Christian thinking deviates from that of all other peoples, including the Greeks. Of course in considering this fact we must avoid assumptions about the creation as causation and source of the world—notions which may generally be said to be Greek with eighteenth-century trappings. And the archetypal chain, going back from the hero by way of the mother to the original unity, is also only partially helpful. The category of history appears as a *krisis*, as historical time. "Here," says Martin Buber, "there is no nature in the Greek, the Chinese, or the modern occidental sense. What is shown us of Nature, is stamped by History. Even the work of Creation has a historical tone."[42] Culture and history begin, not to be sure in the desert oasis of Eden, but with the tilling of the *adama*. And from then on God's "covenant" with Israel dominates everything. "And God remembered his covenant with Abraham, with Isaac, and with Jacob." Here there is continually something new that breaks through the cycle. For the world is not static, it is always about to be destroyed, both the little spot that human toil has wrested from the desert and the cosmos that God has wrested from chaos. In Milton's fine image, it hangs over the chaos like a drop on a golden chain.

42 Martin Buber, *Moses* (London, 1946), pp. 78ff.

The God who sustains the world is not a static source, but one who is active from *olam* to *olam*. The source is nothingness; God's act of creation is the only reality. God is not contingent on the world, the world is only and always contingent on God. This is expressed in the *theologoumenon* of the *creatio ex nihilo*, which, though supported by only one passage in the Bible (II Macc. 7 : 28), is deeply anchored in the Jewish consciousness. The paradox of a creation from nothingness—not a mere ordering, not even a founding, but a kind of magical evocation, is already inherent in the contrast between the two Biblical terms *bara*, "to create by the word," and *asa*, "to make," "to produce"; and between the two myths of the creation in Genesis. Least of all is the world begotten by God; the Psalmist prefers to leave the business of reproduction to the world itself. Only in one other instance do we find such a turning away from the reproductive process as a beginning—which after all must always suggest an earlier act of generation, a still more initial beginning. The ancient Egyptian creator god Atum engenders the other gods, but without female aid, by masturbation. *Htp dt*, "satisfied in relation to his hand." And among the Indians of Central and South America, Preuss has demonstrated a creation from nothingness by God the great magician.[43]

HISTORY

Here there is a possibility of returning to our general topic of primordial time and final time, as it occurred among the Jews and Christians. This possibility, which we may call gnosis, is illustrated by the following verses from the great modern gnostic, Victor Hugo:

Dieu n'a créé que l'être impondérable,
Il le fit radieux, beau, candide, adorable,
Mais imparfait; sans quoi, sur la même hauteur,
La créature étant égale au créateur,
Cette perfection, dans l'infini perdue,
Se serait avec Dieu mêlée et confondue,
Et la création, à force de clarté,
En lui serait rentrée et n'aurait pas été.
La création sainte où rêve le prophète,
Pour être, ô profondeur! devait être imparfaite.[44]

43 K. T. Preuss, in *Zeitschrift für Missionskunde und Religionswissenschaft* (Berlin) XLVII (1932), 8.

44 Victor Hugo, "Ce que dit la bouche d'ombre," in *Contemplations*.

In a sense this is another formulation of the idea of the *creatio continua*, which can never be separated from that of the *creatio ex nihilo*. But it represents also a shift of accent from God to the world. For the Hebrew mind, the idea that God and even a perfect world might ever become one is unthinkable. Or, in other words it is incompatible with the world of history represented in the Bible that God and man, self and ego, should be twins, one necessary to the other. The flaming sword of the cherub lies between the two.[45]

The unfortunate identification (condemned so frequently by C. G. Jung) of God with the *summum bonum* has caused considerable confusion in this connection. Since God can only be good, His world must be perfect. Indeed, "Yahweh could have taught man a lesson in this respect, if man himself is incapable of realizing his intellectual presumption in limiting God's omnipotence and freedom." God is not good. He is not to be measured by human standards, not unless he is the *Dieu des philosophes* and not the God of history. It is only such terms as freedom and grace which, though inadequate, give at least some intimation of the ineffable. He belongs not to the self-contained circle of nature but to history, which is open to everything that is sublime and everything that is abysmal.

Thus we have a time between beginning and end, a today that is intangible but still a "today of grace," a possibility of human life, because God holds his hand over it to destroy or to save. "In Babylon," writes Buber, "the cult calendar might carry on its eternal cycle above and immune to the vicissitudes of history; in Israel history with its own hand transcribed the calendar into the stupendous signs of the unique."[46] In this connection we may consider the words of Minucius Felix, the Christian apologist, regarding the vanity of the annual cycle of the mysteries of Osiris: "They cease not to lose what they find, or to find what they lose."[47] The Christian calendar, to be sure, is built on the self-contained cycle of nature (like the entire Biblical vision it does not do away with alien forms, but simply cuts through them); yet it starts from a seemingly arbitrary point in history, the *kairos*, the fulfilled time that is historical time.[48] And the credo gives still greater

45 In the Cabala and in Gnosis, Judaism and Christianity, as well as Islam, which derives from them, return to the cyclical type.

46 Buber, *Königtum Gottes* (Berlin, 1932), p. 121.

47 Minucius Felix, XXIII, I (tr. G. H. Rendall, LCL, 1931).

48 Lietzmann, *A History of the Early Church*, Vol. III: *From Constantine to Julian*, tr. B. Lee-Woolf (New York, 1950).

stress to this historical arbitrariness by including the seemingly superfluous but historical Pontius Pilate in its formulation of the supreme truth. This contrasts sharply with Greek feeling, which is fundamentally ahistorical. True, here too there is myth: in Herodotus the history of the gods, in Thucydides the greatness of Athens, in Polybius the greatness of Rome. But always without eschatology, and so closely articulated with nature that nature and history in their rotation are ultimately the same: "The cycle of States is the same as the cycle of nature."

FINAL TIME

It would be tempting to relate some of the myths that various peoples have devised concerning final time. But in view of what has been said this would take us too far, and it is not absolutely necessary. The epistle of Barnabas has a remarkable passage: "The present sabbaths are not acceptable to me [saith the Lord], but that which I have made, in which I will give rest to all things and make the beginning of an eighth day, that is the beginning of another world."[49] This suggests something more than the contrast between the Jewish Sabbath and the Christian day of the Lord. What is meant is the "beginning," the new beginning that fulfills time. The eighth day is the day of the Resurrection. That is final time, but a final time that is a beginning.

Of final time itself we see nothing. There is only God. And concerning it man can only sing, with Dante in the *Paradiso:*

> . . . Gloria . . . riso dell'Universo . . .
> Oh gioia! oh ineffabile allegrezza!
> . . . .
> La 've s'appunta ogni Ubi ed ogni Quando.

Here all dimensions are effaced, including the fourth dimension, of time. But the Biblical concept of eternity is no abstract timelessness, no *aeternitas*, but a *me-olam ad-olam.* Final time begins in the midst of historical time. In the New Testament as elsewhere it is announced to the peoples by omens—adunata and wonders. But it also sets its stamp upon time. In the ancient world, including Egypt, there was an eschatological schema, according to which a time of decline and despair heralded the advent of final time. The

49 *Epistle of Barnabas* 15 : 9. *The Apostolic Fathers,* with a tr. by Kirsopp Lake (LCL, 1914), Vol. I, pp. 395–97.

historical events were read into this schema, as conversely the event that seceded from time was read into history.

There can be scarcely any doubt that Jesus lived according to this schema. The final time was about to begin, the great despair was ready to set in. For *ὁ καιρὸς πεπλήρωται*, the time had grown full; a new creative act of God was about to be fulfilled through him. When nothing seemed to happen, He drew the consequence by seeking a sacrificial death and giving himself over to extreme despair. Then with His death and resurrection the new beginning is at hand, which he calls the kingdom of God. Actually everything is still exactly as in the Old Testament, except that the powers of chaos have given way to the demons, the baalim have given way to the astral powers and principalities, and a "new" creation is replacing the old. "In and with [Jesus] and his working," writes Rudolf Otto in his excellent *Kingdom of God and the Son of Man*, "comes the kingdom, after it has first been realized in heaven by Satan's overthrow, in order that it might now become real 'in earth as it is in heaven.' And it comes chiefly not as claim and decision but as saving *δύναμις*, as redeeming power, to set free a world lying in the clutches of Satan, threatened by the devil and by demons, tormented, possessed, demon-ridden; and to capture the spoil from the strong one." [50]

Here the ideas of Iranian and Jewish eschatology are fulfilled. The kingdom is at hand "in your midst." One day it will be completed. That is God's affair. But the beginning has been made. And in the beginning resides the secret, the mysterium. But ever since then, as Cullmann sets forth, our time has begun at the center, where we stand, looking forward and backward. The *Anno Domini* chronology, which seems to have become definitive only in the eighteenth century, is the ultimate inference from the Christian experience of time: *christiana tempora*.[51]

SACRAMENT

For now, at the end, the problem of simultaneity reappears. We have seen how even primitive peoples require for their existence a relation to primordial time, a myth relating how present institutions were "established" by the patriarchs. And Hamann reminded us that the separate moments, each taken for itself, do not constitute time, that the beads must be strung

50 Tr. F. V. Filson and B. Lee-Woolf (new edn., London, 1943), p. 105.
51 O. Cullmann, *Christus und die Zeit* (Zurich, 1946).

on a thread. This is done by primordial time. But it is no less true of final time. It forms the thread. It performs the miracle of simultaneity, of experienced time. It makes possible all experience of time—in short, life.

The New Testament expresses this by the formula: "Jesus Christ, the same yesterday and today and for ever"—down through the *aion*, the *olam*, primordial time and final time. In the New Testament this is accomplished in the sacrament. Christ enacts his sacrificial death even before the Jews and the Romans compel him to do so. And whenever, at the supper of the new covenant, He sacrifices his body and his blood, "He binds the time."

Ever since then his creative act has always been newly present, forever a new source of life.

CONCLUSION

I have attempted in these lectures to give a picture of the myth of primordial time and final time as it is forever renewed from the archetypal reservoir of mankind, and as it gives its substance to time. And I have attempted to follow the two great trends, the cyclical and the linear: self-contained time and the open time that has a beginning and an end.

In his above-mentioned book, *Meaning in History*, Löwith has demonstrated these two trends in historiography. Nietzsche is the only modern who had drawn the extreme consequence from the cyclical view—in his theory of eternal return. Modern science has not renewed it. Rather, it sees the process of development as linear and unrepeatable, but on principle without eschatology, without meaning and purpose. Outside the confines of our Western culture, nevertheless, many millions of men live by the cyclical idea. In this bicentenary of the birth of Goethe, who doubtless may be regarded as the most convinced modern exponent of the cyclical idea and of mother religion, we are confronted more than ever by a choice. Here I can only suggest this choice as a possibility. It contains the fourth dimension of time, that is apprehended in faith.

That is the dimension of God. For God is not "eternal" in the sense of timeless. He is a Lord of history, past and present, as in every *olam*, every *aion—sicut erat in principio et nunc et in saecula saeculorum.*

APPENDICES

Biographical Notes
(as of 1957)

HENRY CORBIN, Ph.D. Born 1903, Paris. Since 1954, professor of Islamic religion, École des Hautes-Études, Sorbonne. Divides his professional activity between Paris and Teheran. 1939–45, at the Institut français d'archéologie, Istanbul, engaged in research in the mosque libraries. 1946–54, director of the department of Iranic studies, French-Iranian Institute, Teheran. Founder and editor, *Bibliothèque iranienne.* His special field embraces Shi'ism (Iranian Islam), Ismaelism, and Sufism. Principal publications: *Œuvres philosophiques et mystiques de Sohrawardî* (Istanbul, 1945; Teheran and Paris, 1952); *Le Livre des deux sagesses de Nâsir Khosraw: Philosophie grecque et théosophie ismaélienne* (Teheran and Paris, 1953); *Avicenne et le Récit visionnaire* (Teheran and Paris, 1954); *La Qasîda ismaélienne d'Abû'l-Haitham Jorjânî* (Teheran and Paris, 1955). He has lectured at a number of Eranos meetings from 1949 on.

MIRCEA ELIADE, Ph.D. Born 1907, Bucharest. Resident of France since 1945. Engaged in lectures in comparative religion at the École des Hautes-Études, Sorbonne, writing, and research. 1956–57, visiting professor of the history of religion and Haskell Lecturer, University of Chicago. 1928–32, predoctoral studies at the University of Calcutta; studies in the techniques of yoga at Rishikesh. 1933–39, maître de conférences, University of Bucharest. Founder and editor, *Zalmoxis: Revue des études religieuses* (Paris and Bucharest, 1938–42). Special fields: Indian philosophy and comparative religion. Author also of several popular novels. Principal works: *Traité d'histoire des religions* (Paris, 1949; English tr. in preparation); *The Myth of the Eternal Return* (tr., New York and London, 1954); *Le Chamanisme et les techniques archaïques de l'extase* (Paris, 1951); *Images et symboles* (Paris, 1952); *Yoga: Immortality and Liberty* (tr., New York and London, in press; original, Paris, 1954); *Forgerons et alchimistes* (Paris, 1956). Has lectured at all Eranos meetings since 1950.

C. G. JUNG, M.D., L.L.D. (hon., Clark), L.L.D. (hon., Fordham), Sc.D. (hon., Harvard), Litt.D. (hon., Benares), L.L.D. (hon., Allahabad), Sc.D. (hon., Oxford), L.L.D. (hon., Calcutta), Litt.D. (hon., Geneva), Sc.D. (hon., Federal Polytechnic Inst., Zurich). Born 1875, Kesswil, Canton Thurgau, Switzerland. 1905–1909, privatdocent, University of Zurich. 1907–13, associated with Bleuler and with Freud in experimental research. 1933–42, taught at the Federal Polytechnic Institute, Zurich. He was called to the University of Basel in 1944 to occupy the chair of medical psychology, established for him, but was forced to resign owing to illness after only a year. In recent years, he has been engaged in researches in symbolism at his home at Küsnacht, near Zurich. His eightieth birthday, in 1955, was celebrated by a convocation of friends and students from many countries, and the 1955 Eranos meeting was dedicated to him. Jung's collected works, in English, are being published simultaneously in New York and London; of 18 or more projected, the volumes published or in preparation are: 1. *Psychiatric Studies* (1957); 5. *Symbols of Transformation* (1956; superseding *Psychology of the Unconscious*); 7. *Two Essays on Analytical Psychology* (1953); 11. *Psychology and Religion: West and East* (1958; containing *Answer to Job* and other works); 12. *Psychology and Alchemy* (1953); 16. *The Practice of Psychotherapy* (1954); 17. *The Development of Personality* (1954). His publications otherwise—including many earlier translations into English—number over 150. Dr. Jung has lectured at thirteen Eranos meetings, beginning with the first, in 1933; special volumes of the *Eranos-Jahrbuch* were published in honor of his 70th and 75th birthdays.

MAX KNOLL, Dr. Eng. Born 1897, Schlangenbad (Hesse), Germany. Since 1948, professor in the department of electrical engineering, Princeton University; also, since 1956, professor and director of the electronics institute, Technische Hochschule, Munich. Divides his professional work between Princeton and Munich. 1927–31, assistant professor, Technische Hochschule, Berlin. Engaged in research in electron optics; developed the first electron microscope, with assistance of undergraduate students. 1931–45, associate professor, Technische Hochschule, Berlin, and director, electron research laboratory, Telefunken Co. 1945–47, professor and director, electron research institute, University of Munich. Author of some sixty publications on electron optics, electric discharges, high vacuum physics, electron microscopes, and electronic storage. Special interest: the philosophy of science. With representatives of other disciplines—physics, biology, psychology, the arts, and theology—he has organized in the United States and in Europe forums to discuss the problem of a general description of nature, using corresponding functions in the various fields. Lectured at the 1952, 1953, and 1955 Eranos meetings.

GERARDUS VAN DER LEEUW, Ph.D. (Leiden), Ph.D. (hon., Brno). Born 1890, The Hague; died 1950. 1916–18, pastor of the Dutch Reformed Church and teacher of Hebrew in a college. 1918–50, professor of the history of religion, religious phenomenology, general theology, Egyptian language and literature, and liturgy,

Groningen University (1934–35, rector). Member, Royal Netherlands Academy of Sciences, Royal Flemish Academy of Science, Letters and Fine Arts, and Accadèmia dei Lincei. 1945–46, minister of instruction, arts, and sciences in the first cabinet after the liberation of the Netherlands. Travelled in South Africa (1947) and America (1949). 1950, presided over 7th International Congress of the History of Religions (Amsterdam). His numerous publications include: *Einführung in die Phänomenologie der Religion* (tr., Munich, 1925; 2nd edn. in Dutch, 1948); *Mystiek* (Baarn, 1924); *La Structure de la mentalité primitive* (Strasbourg, 1928); *Religion in Essence and Manifestation* (tr., London, 1938); *Bach's Matthaeus-Passion* (Amsterdam, 6th edn., 1948); *L'Homme primitif et la religion* (tr., Paris, 1940); *De Godsdienst van het oude Aegypte* (The Hague, 1944); *Sacramentstheologie* (Nijkerk, 1949). Dr. van der Leeuw lectured at the Eranos meetings of 1948, 1949, and 1950.

Louis Massignon, Ph.D. Born 1883, Nogent-sur-Marne, France. Professor of Islamic studies, Collège de France; professor, École des Hautes-Études, Sorbonne; president, Institut des études iraniennes, Sorbonne; secretary, Comité France-Islam; vice-president, Comité France-Maghreb. Member, royal academies of Afghanistan, Belgium, Denmark, Iran, Iraq, Netherlands, and Sweden, academies of Egypt and Damascus, Royal Asiatic Society (London), Russian Academy of Sciences, and American Oriental Society. Legion of Honor; Croix de Guerre (1914–18). Formerly editor, *Revue du monde musulman*, *Revue des études islamiques*, and *Annuaire du monde musulman*. Resident many years in Arab countries. Of an extensive bibliography the following may be cited: *Essai sur les origines du lexique technique de la mystique musulmane* (new edn., Paris, 1954); *La Passion d'al Hallaj, martyr mystique de l'Islam* (Paris, 1922); *Recueil de textes inédits concernant l'histoire de la mystique en pays d'Islam* (Paris, 1929); *La Syntaxe intérieure des langues sémitiques* (Paris, in press). Professor Massignon has lectured at nine Eranos meetings, 1937–55.

Erich Neumann, Ph.D. Born 1905, Berlin. Studied medicine and completed the examinations in 1933 in Germany. Left Germany in 1933, and has been practicing as an analytical psychologist since 1934 in Tel Aviv, now Israel. Patron and lecturer, C. G. Jung Institute, Zurich; has lectured elsewhere in Switzerland and the Netherlands. Publications: *Tiefenpsychologie und neue Ethik* (Zurich, 1949); *The Origins and History of Consciousness* (tr., New York and London, 1954); *The Great Mother* (tr., New York and London, 1954); *Amor and Psyche: The Psychic Development of the Feminine* (tr., New York and London, 1956); an English tr. of his essays is in preparation (original: *Umkreisung der Mitte*, 3 vols., Zurich, 1953–1954). Dr. Neumann has lectured at all the Eranos meetings from 1948 on.

HELMUTH PLESSNER, Ph.D. (Erlangen). Born 1892, Wiesbaden, Germany. Since 1951, professor of sociology and philosophy, University of Göttingen. From 1920 until 1933, in which year he was removed from his post by the Nazi regime, he taught at the University of Cologne (after 1926, professor of philosophy). 1934–51, professor of sociology and philosophy, University of Groningen, Netherlands. Dismissed by the Reichskommissar for the Netherlands in 1943, reinstated in 1945. Principal works include: *Die Einheit der Sinne: Grundlinien einer Aesthesiologie des Geistes* (Bonn, 1923); *Grenzen der Gemeinschaft* (Bonn, 1924); *Die Stufen des Organischen und der Mensch* (Berlin, 1928); *Das Schicksal deutschen Geistes im Ausgang seiner bürgerlichen Epoche* (Zurich, 1935); *Lachen und Weinen* (Bern, 1950). *Zwischen Philosophie und Gesellschaft* (Bern, 1953). Professor Plessner lectured at the Eranos meeting of 1951.

ADOLF PORTMANN, Ph.D. Born 1897. Since 1931, professor of zoology, University of Basel. Early studies as a painter helped direct his interest to general questions of animal form and pattern and to the comparative morphology of vertebrates. He began his studies in marine biology at laboratories in France and Germany. Principal publications: *Biologische Fragmente zu einer Lehre vom Menschen* (Basel, 1944); *Einführung in die vergleichende Morphologie der Wirbeltiere* (Basel, 1948); *Animal Forms and Pattern* (tr., London, 1952); *Das Tier als soziales Wesen* (Zurich, 1953); and numerous popular works, among them *Vom Ursprung des Menschen* (Basel, 1944). He has spoken at all the Eranos meetings from 1946 on.

HENRI-CHARLES PUECH, Ph.D. Born 1902, Montpellier, France. Since 1929, directeur d'études, École des Hautes-Études, Sorbonne: professor of the history of the early Church and patristic theology and president of the section on comparative religion. Also, since 1952, professor of the history of religion, Collège de France. Captain of a Zouave regiment in the second World War. Chevalier of the Legion of Honor (1951). Editor of the *Revue de l'histoire des religions.* Special fields: history of religion and ancient philosophy; patristics; oriental religions (particularly Gnosticism) in relation to the origin of Christianity. Publications include: with G. Quispel and W. C. van Unnik, *The Jung Codex, A Newly Recovered Gnostic Papyrus: Three Studies* (tr. and ed. Frank Leslie Cross, London, 1955); with A. Vaillant, *Le Traité contre les Bogomiles de Cosmas le Prêtre* (Paris, 1945); *Le Manichéisme: Son fondateur, sa doctrine* (Paris, 1949); and numerous articles in encyclopedias and scholarly journals. Professor Puech lectured at the Eranos meetings of 1936 and 1951.

GILLES QUISPEL, Ph.D. Born 1916, Rotterdam. Since 1952, professor of early Christian literature, University of Utrecht. 1948–49, Bollingen Fellow in Rome;

1951–52, lecturer, C. G. Jung Institute, Zurich. Special interest: Gnosticism. Publications include: *The Jung Codex* (see foregoing note on H.-C. Puech). Other works include *Gli Etruschi nel Vecchio Testamento* (Florence, 1939); *De Bronnen van Tertullianus' "Adversus Marcionem"* (Leiden, 1942); *Gnosis als Weltreligion* (Zurich, 1951). He has lectured at several Eranos meetings from 1947 on.

Hellmut Wilhelm, Ph.D. Born 1905, Tsingtao, China. Since 1948, lecturer in, then professor of, Chinese history and literature at the University of Washington, Seattle. Resided in China until his 14th year, when he went to Germany to complete his education. 1932–37 and 1945–48, instructor, then professor, at the National University of Peking. Spent the period of the Japanese occupation in seclusion, doing research. Left Peking in 1948, before the Communist government took over, and came to the United States. Now an American citizen. Publications include: *Chinas Geschichte* (Peking, 1942); *Die Wandlung* (Peking, 1944); *Gesellschaft und Staat in China* (Peking, 1944); *Deutsch-chinesisches Wörterbuch* (Shanghai, 1945). Professor Wilhelm lectured at the Eranos meetings of 1951 and 1955.

Contents of the *Eranos-Jahrbücher* (through 1956)

The contents of the *Eranos-Jahrbücher*, consisting up to the present time of twenty-five volumes, are here listed, in translation, as a reference aid and an indication of the scope of the Eranos meetings. The lectures were originally delivered in German, with a few exceptions in French, English, and Italian. In the first eight *Jahrbücher*, all of the papers were published in German; in the later volumes, the papers were published respectively in the original language. An index of contributors is at the end.

C. M. VON CAMMERLOHER: The Position of Art in the Psychology of Our Time

Swami YATISWARANANDA: A Brief Survey of Hindu Religious Symbolism in Its Relation to Spiritual Exercises and Higher Development

III: 1935: Spiritual Guidance in the East and the West

C. G. JUNG: Dream Symbols of the Individuation Process

G. R. HEYER: On Getting Along with Oneself

ERWIN ROUSSELLE: Lao-tse's Journey through Soul, History, and World

Mrs. RHYS DAVIDS: Man, the Search, and Nirvana

RUDOLF BERNOULLI: Psychic Development in the Mirror of Alchemy and Related Disciplines

ERNESTO BUONAIUTI: I. Gnostic Initiation and Early Christianity. II. The Exercises of St. Ignatius Loyola

ROBERT EISLER: The Riddle of the Gospel of St. John

J. B. LANG: Pauline and Analytical Spiritual Guidance

IV: 1936: The Shaping of the Idea of Redemption in the East and the West

C. G. JUNG: The Idea of Redemption in Alchemy

PAUL MASSON-OURSEL: I. The Indian Theories of Redemption in the Frame of the Religions of Salvation. II. The Doctrine of Grace in the Religious Thought of India [2]

Mrs. RHYS DAVIDS: Redemption in India's Past and in Our Present

ERNESTO BUONAIUTI: Redemption in the Orphic Mysteries

HENRI-CHARLES PUECH: The Concept of Redemption in Manichaeism

BORIS VYSHESLAWZEFF: Two Ways of Redemption: Redemption as a Solution of the Tragic Contradiction

V: 1937: The Shaping of the Idea of Redemption in the East and the West

C. G. JUNG: Some Observations on the Visions of Zosimos

LOUIS MASSIGNON: The Origins and Significance of Gnosticism in Islam

PAUL MASSON-OURSEL: I. The Indian Conception of Psychology. II. Indian Techniques of Salvation [1]

JEAN PRZYLUSKI: I. Redemption after Death in the Upanishads and in Early Buddhism. II. Redemption in This Lifetime, in Advanced Buddhism

ANDREAS SPEISER: The Concept of Redemption in Plotinus

CHARLOTTE A. BAYNES: The Idea of Redemption in Christian Gnosticism

THEODOR-WILHELM DANZEL: On the Psychology of Aztec Symbolism

JOHN LAYARD: The Myth of the Journey of the Dead in Malekula

ERNESTO BUONAIUTI: Ecclesia Spiritualis [1]

1 Tr. in *Spirit and Nature* (Papers from the Eranos Yearbooks, 1, 1954).
2 Tr. in *The Mysteries* (Papers from the Eranos Yearbooks, 2, 1955).

VI: 1938: The Configuration and Cult of the "Great Mother"

JEAN PRZYLUSKI: I. Origins and Development of the Cult of the Mother Goddess. II. The Mother Goddess as a Link between the Local Gods and the Universal God

CHARLES PICARD: I. The Anatolian Ephesia. II. The Great Mother from Crete to Eleusis

CHARLES VIROLLEAUD: I. Ishtar, Isis, Astarte. II. Anat-Astarte

LOUIS MASSIGNON: The Gnostic Cult of Fatima in Shiite Islam

HEINRICH ZIMMER: The Indian World Mother

V. C. C. COLLUM: The Creative Mother Goddess of the Celtic-speaking Peoples, Her Instrument, the Mystical "Word," Her Cult and Cult Symbols

ERNESTO BUOANIUTI: I. Mary and the Virgin Birth. II. St. Mary Immaculata in the Christian Tradition

C. G. JUNG: Psychological Aspects of the Mother Archetype

G. R. HEYER: The Great Mother in the Psyche of Modern Man

VII: 1939: The Symbolism of Rebirth in the Religious Imagery of Various Times and Peoples

LOUIS MASSIGNON: Resurrection in the Mohammedan World

CHARLES VIROLLEAUD: The Idea of Rebirth among the Phoenicians

PAUL PELLIOT: The Chinese Conception of the Other World

WALTER F. OTTO: The Meaning of the Eleusinian Mysteries [2]

CHARLES R. C. ALLBERRY: Symbols of Death and Rebirth in Manichaeism

HANS LEISEGANG: The Mystery of the Serpent [2]

HEINRICH ZIMMER: Death and Rebirth in the Light of India

ERNESTO BUONAIUTI: Rebirth, Immortality, and Resurrection in Early Christianity

RICHARD THURNWALD: Primitive Rites of Initiation and Rebirth

C. G. JUNG: The Different Aspects of Rebirth

VIII: 1940–41: The Trinity, Christian Symbolism, and Gnosis

ANDREAS SPEISER: The Platonic Doctrine of the Unknown God and the Christian Trinity

C. G. JUNG: A Psychological Approach to the Dogma of the Trinity

C. KERÉNYI: Mythology and Gnosis

C. G. JUNG: Transformation Symbolism in the Mass [2]

ERNESTO BUONAIUTI: Christ and St. Paul

MAX PULVER: Gnostic Experience and Gnostic Life in Early Christianity (from the Sources)

ERNESTO BUONAIUTI: Christology and Ecclesiology in St. Paul

IX: 1942: The Hermetic Principle in Mythology, Gnosis, and Alchemy

C. KERÉNYI: Hermes Guide of Souls: The Mythologem of the Masculine Origin of Life

2 Tr. in *The Mysteries* (Papers from the Eranos Yearbooks, 2, 1955).

GEORGES NAGEL: The God Thoth according to the Egyptian Texts
MAX PULVER: Jesus' Round Dance and Crucifixion according to the Acts of St. John [2]
C. G. JUNG: The Spirit Mercurius
J. B. LANG: The Demiurge of the Priests' Codex (Gen. 1 to 2 : 4a) and His Significance for Gnosticism

X: 1943: Ancient Sun Cults and Light Symbolism in Gnosticism and Early Christianity

GEORGES NAGEL: The Cult of the Sun in Early Egypt
CHARLES VIROLLEAUD: The God Shamash in Ancient Mesopotamia
C. KERÉNYI: Father Helios
WALTER WILI: The Roman Sun-Gods and Mithras
PAUL SCHMITT: Sol Invictus: Reflections on Late Roman Religion and Politics
MAX PULVER: The Experience of Light in the Gospel of St. John, in the Corpus Hermeticum, in Gnosticism, and in the Eastern Church
LOUIS MASSIGNON: Astrological Infiltration in Islamic Religious Thought
HUGO RAHNER: The Christian Mystery of Sun and Moon

XI: 1944: The Mysteries

C. KERÉNYI: The Mysteries of the Kabeiroi (Appendix: The Castello of Tegna) [2]
WALTER WILI: The Orphic Mysteries and the Greek Spirit [2]
PAUL SCHMITT: The Ancient Mysteries in the Society of Their Time, Their Transformation and Most Recent Echoes [2]
GEORGES NAGEL: The "Mysteries" of Osiris in Ancient Egypt [2]
JEAN DE MENASCE: The Mysteries and the Religion of Iran [2]
FRITZ MEIER: The Mystery of the Ka'ba: Symbol and Reality in Islamic Mysticism [2]
WILHELM KOPPERS: On the Origin of the Mysteries in the Light of Ethnology and Indology
MAX PULVER: On the Scope of the Gnostic Mysteries
JULIUS BAUM: Symbolic Representations of the Eucharist [2]
HUGO RAHNER: The Christian Mystery and the Pagan Mysteries [2]

XII: 1945: Studies on the Problem of the Archetypal (For C. G. Jung on His Seventieth Birthday, July 26, 1945)

ANDREAS SPEISER: Plato's Theory of Ideas
C. KERÉNYI: Heros Iatros: On the Transformations and Symbols of the Genius of Medicine in Greece
WALTER WILI: Problems Connected with the Aristotelian Theory of the Soul
PAUL SCHMITT: The Archetypal in St. Augustine and Goethe

2 Tr. in *The Mysteries* (Papers from the Eranos Yearbooks, 2, 1955).

Hugo Rahner: The Flower That Heals the Soul: Moly and Mandragora in Ancient and Christian Symbolism
Louis Massignon: Archetypal Themes in Mussulmanic Oneirocriticism
John Layard: The Incest Taboo and the Virgin Archetype

XIII: 1945: The Spirit

C. Kerényi: Apollo Epiphanies [1]
Walter Wili: The History of the Spirit in Antiquity [1]
Andreas Speiser: Spirit and Mathematics
Max Pulver: The Experience of the Pneuma in Philo [1]
Paul Schmitt: Spirit and Soul
Karl Ludwig Schmidt: The Pneuma Hagion as Person and as Charisma
Hugo Rahner: Earth Spirit and Divine Spirit in Patristic Theology [1]
Louis Massignon: The Idea of Spirit in Islam
Fritz Meier: Spiritual Man in the Persian Poet 'Attar
Jean de Menasce: The Experience of the Spirit in Christian Mysticism
C. G. Jung: The Psychology of the Spirit [1] *

XIV: 1946: Spirit and Nature

Andreas Speiser: The Foundations of Mathematics from Plato to Fichte
C. Kerényi: The Goddess Nature
Karl Ludwig Schmidt: The Powers of Nature and Spirit in the Knowledge and Faith of St. Paul
Louis Massignon: Nature in Islamic Thought
Fritz Meier: The Problem of Nature in the Esoteric Monism of Islam [1]
Werner Kaegi: The Transformation of the Spirit in the Renaissance [1]
Friedrich Dessauer: Galileo and Newton: The Turning Point in Western Thought [1]
Paul Schmitt: Nature and Spirit in Goethe's Relation to the Natural Sciences
C. G. Jung: The Spirit of Psychology [1]
Erwin Schrödinger: The Spirit of Science [1]
Adolf Portmann: Biology and the Phenomenon of the Spiritual [1]

XV: 1947: Man

Adolf Portmann: The Problem of Origins
C. Kerényi: Primordial Man and Mystery
Friedrich Dessauer: Man and Cosmos
Karl Ludwig Schmidt: Man as the Image of God in the Old and the New Testament
Hugo Rahner: Origen's View of Man
Gilles Quispel: The Conception of Man in Valentinian Gnosis
Louis Massignon: The Perfect Man in Islam and Its Eschatological Originality

1 Tr. in *Spirit and Nature* (Papers from the Eranos Yearbooks, 1, 1954).
* Title changed in *Spirit and Nature* to "The Phenomenology of the Spirit in Fairy Tales."

VICTOR WHITE: Anthropologia rationalis: The Aristotelian-Thomist Conception of Man
LEO BAECK: Individuum ineffabile

XVI: 1948: Man

HUGO RAHNER: Man as Player
GILLES QUISPEL: Gnostic Man: The Doctrine of Basilides
GERARDUS VAN DER LEEUW: Man and Civilization: The Implications of the Term "Evolution of Man"
C. KERÉNYI: Man and Mask
JOHN LAYARD: The Making of Man in Malekula
C. G. JUNG: On the Self
ERICH NEUMANN: Mystical Man
HERMANN WEYL: Science as Symbolic Construction of Man
MARKUS FIERZ: On Physical Knowledge
ADOLF PORTMANN: Man as Student of Nature

XVII: 1949: Man and the Mythical World

GERARDUS VAN DER LEEUW: Primordial Time and Final Time [3]
C. KERÉNYI: The Orphic Cosmogony and the Origin of Orphism
E. O. JAMES: Myth and Ritual
HENRY CORBIN: The "Narrative of Initiation" and Hermeticism in Iran
ERICH NEUMANN: The Mythical World and the Individual
LOUIS BEIRNAERT: The Mythical Dimension in Christian Sacramentalism
GERSHOM G. SCHOLEM: Cabala and Myth
JULIUS BAUM: Representations of the Germanic Saga of Gods and Heroes in Nordic Art
PAUL RADIN: The Basic Myth of the North American Indians
ADOLF E. JENSEN: The Mythical World View of the Ancient Agricultural Peoples
ADOLF PORTMANN: Mythical Elements in Science

XVIII: 1950: From the World of the Archetypes (Special Volume for C. G. Jung on His Seventy-fifth Birthday, July 26, 1950)

HANS LEISEGANG: The God-Man as Archetype
HENRY CORBIN: Jābir ibn Hayyān's "Book of the Glorious"
FRITZ MEIER: The World of Archetypes in Ali Hamadani (d. 1385)
GILLES QUISPEL: Anima naturaliter christiana
GERARDUS VAN DER LEEUW: Immortality
KARL LUDWIG SCHMIDT: Jerusalem as Archetype and Image
PAUL RADIN: The Religious Experiences of an American Indian
PAUL SCHMITT: The Archetype in the Philosophy of Nicholas of Cusa
ERICH NEUMANN: On the Moon and the Matriarchal Consciousness
HANS BÄNZIGER: Faith as an Archetypal Attitude

3 Tr. in *Man and Time* (Papers from the Eranos Yearbooks, 3, 1957).

ADOLF PORTMANN: The Problem of Archetypes from the Biological Standpoint

XIX: 1950: Man and Rite

C. KERÉNYI: Dramatic Divine Presence in Greek Religion
LOUIS BEIRNAERT: The Symbolism of Ascension in Christian Liturgy and Mysticism
ERICH NEUMANN: On the Psychological Significance of Myth
GERSHOM G. SCHOLEM: Tradition and Creation in Cabalistic Ritual
HENRY CORBIN: Sabaean Ritual and Ismailian Exegesis of the Ritual
MIRCEA ELIADE: The Psychology and History of Religions: the Symbolism of the "Center"
PAUL RADIN: The Esoteric Rituals of the North American Indians
LOUIS MASSIGNON: The Living Rite
ADOLF PORTMANN: Animal Rites
RAFFAELE PETTAZZONI: The Babylonian Rite of Akitu and the Epic of Creation
F. J. J. BUYTENDIJK: On the Phenomenology of the Encounter

XX: 1951: Man and Time

ERICH NEUMANN: Art and Time [3]
HENRI-CHARLES PUECH: Gnosis and Time [3]
GILLES QUISPEL: Time and History in Patristic Christianity [3]
LOUIS MASSIGNON: Time in Islamic Thought [3]
HENRY CORBIN: Cyclical Time in Mazdaism and Ismailism [3]
MIRCEA ELIADE: Time and Eternity in Indian Thought [3]
LANCELOT LAW WHYTE: Time and the Mind-Body Problem: A Changed Scientific Conception of Progress
C. G. JUNG: On Synchronicity [3]
ERWIN R. GOODENOUGH: The Evaluation of Symbols Recurrent in Time, as Illustrated in Judaism
HELLMUT WILHELM: The Concept of Time in the Book of Changes [3]
HELMUTH PLESSNER: On the Relation of Time to Death [3]
MAX KNOLL: The Transformations of Science in Our Age [3]
ADOLF PORTMANN: Time in the Life of the Organism [3]

XXI: 1952: Man and Energy

MIRCEA ELIADE: Power and Sacrality in the History of Religions
GERSHOM G. SCHOLEM: On the Development of the Cabalistic Conception of the Shekhinah
GILLES QUISPEL: Man and Energy in Patristic Christianity
ERICH NEUMANN: The Psyche and the Transformation of the Planes of Reality
KARL LÖWITH: The Dynamics of History, and Historicism
HERBERT READ: The Dynamics of Art

3 Tr. in *Man and Time* (Papers from the Eranos Yearbooks, 3, 1957).

Martin D'Arcy: The Power of Caritas and the Holy Spirit
Adolf Portmann: The Significance of Images in the Living Transformation of Energy
Max Knoll: Quantum Conceptions of Energy in Physics and Psychology
Lancelot Law Whyte: A Scientific View of the "Creative Energy" of Man

XXII: 1953: Man and Earth

Erich Neumann: The Significance of the Earth Archetype for Modern Times
Mircea Eliade: Terra Mater and Cosmic Hierogamies
Gilles Quispel: Gnosis and Earth
Henry Corbin: Celestial Earth and the Body of the Resurrection according to Various Iranian Traditions: I. Mazdean Imago Terrae. II. Hurqalya's Mystical Earth (Shaikhism)
Gershom G. Scholem: The Conception of the Golem and Its Tellurian and Magical Contexts
Giuseppe Tucci: Earth as Conceived of in Indian and Tibetan Religion, with Special Regard to the Tantras
Daisetz Suzuki: The Role of Nature in Zen
Jean Daniélou: Earth and Paradise in Greek Mysticism and Theology
Ernst Benz: I. The Sacred Cave in Eastern Christianity. II. The Charismatic Type of the Russian Saints
Adolf Portmann: The Earth as the Home of Life

XXIII: 1954: Man and Transformation

Mircea Eliade: Mysteries and Spiritual Regeneration in Non-European Religions
Fritz Meier: The Transformation of Man in Mystical Islam
Henri Corbin: Divine Epiphany and Initiatic Birth in Shiite Gnosis
Erich Neumann: The Creative Principle in Psychic Transformation
Paul Tillich: New Being as the Central Concept of a Christian Theology
Daisetz Suzuki: The Awakening of a New Consciousness in Zen
Lancelot Law Whyte: The Growth of Ideas, Illustrated by Man's Changing Conception of Himself
Ernst Benz: Theogony and the Transformation of Man in Schelling
Jean Daniélou: The Transfiguration of Man in Early Byzantine Mysticism
Adolf Portmann: Metamorphosis in Animals

XXIV: 1955: Man and the Sympathy of All Things

Erich Neumann: The Experience of the One Reality and the Sympathy of Things
Gershom G. Scholem: Transmigration and the Sympathy of Souls in Jewish Mysticism
Louis Massignon: The Mohammedan Experience of Compassion, integrated with the Universal in connection with Fatima and Hallāj

Ernst Benz: Man and the Sympathy of All Things at the End of the Ages
Henry Corbin: Sympathy and Theopathy among the "Fedeli d'Amore" in Islam
Walter F. Otto: The Primordial Myth in the Light of the Sympathy of Man and the World
John Layard: Identification with the Sacrificial Animal
Chung-yuan Chang: Tao and the Sympathy of All Things
Max Knoll: Endogenous Rhythms and Biological Time
Adolf Portmann: The Organism: A Pre-established Relationship

XXV: 1956: Man and the Creative Principle

Erich Neumann: Creative Man and the "Great Experience"
Henry Corbin: Creative Imagination and Creative Prayer in Mystical Experience
Mircea Eliade: Mythology and Creativity
Gershom G. Scholem: Creatio ex Nihilo and God's Self-Immersion
Karl Reinhardt: Prometheus
Ernst Benz: The Holy Ghost as Creator in Joachim de Fiore
Herbert Read: Poetic Consciousness and the Creative Experience
Hellmut Wilhelm: The Creative Principle in the "Book of Changes"
Chung-yuan Chang: Creativity as Process in Taoism
Laurens van der Post: The Creative Pattern in Primitive Africa
Adolf Portmann: Levels of Organic Life

Index of Contributors

References are to volumes in the foregoing list. Places of residence at the time of publication are noted in parentheses.

Allberry, Charles R. C. (Cambridge), VII

Baeck, Leo (London), XV
Bänziger, Hans (Zurich), XVIII
Baum, Julius (Bern; 1949, Stuttgart), XI, XVII
Baynes, Charlotte A. (Oxford), V
Beirnaert, Louis (Paris), XVII, XIX
Benz, Ernst (Marburg), XXII–XXV
Bernoulli, Rudolf (Zurich), II, III
Buber, Martin (Heppenheim), II
Buonaiuti, Ernesto (Rome), I–VIII
Buytendijk, F. J. J. (Amsterdam), XIX

Cammerloher, C. M. von (Vienna), II
Chang, Chung-yuan (New York), XXIV, XXV
Collum, V. C. C. (London), VI
Corbin, Henry (Teheran), XVII–XX, XXII–XXV

Daniélou, Jean (Paris), XXII, XXIII
Danzel, Theodor-Wilhelm (Hamburg), V
d'Arcy, Martin (London), XXI
Dessauer, Friedrich (Fribourg), XIV, XV

Eisler, Robert (Unterach), III
Eliade, Mircea (Paris), XIX–XXIII, XXV

Fierz, Markus (Basel), XVI

Goodenough, Erwin R. (New Haven), XX

Hauer, J. W. (Tübingen), II
Heiler, Friedrich (Marburg), I, II
Heyer, G. R. (Munich), I–III, VI

James, E. O. (London), XVII
Jensen, Adolf (Frankfort on the Main), XVII
Jung, C. G. (Zurich), I–IX, XIII, XIV, XVI, XX

Kaegi, Werner (Basel), XIV
Kerényi, C. (Budapest; 1944, Ascona; 1945, Tegna; 1949, Ponte Brolla), VIII–XVII, XIX
Knoll, Max (Princeton), XX, XXI, XXIV
Koppers, Wilhelm (Vienna), XI

Lang, J. B. (Locarno; 1942, Lugano), III, IX
Layard, John (London; 1945, Oxford), V, XII, XVI, XXIV
Leeuw, Gerardus van der (Groningen), XVI–XVII
Leisegang, Hans (Berlin), VII, XVIII
Löwith, Karl (Heidelberg), XXI

Massignon, Louis (Paris), V–VII, X, XII–XIV, XIX, XX, XXIV
Masson-Oursel, Paul (Paris), IV, V
Meier, Fritz (Basel), XI, XIII, XIV, XVIII, XXIII
Menasce, Jean de (Fribourg), XI, XIII

Nagel, Georges (Geneva), IX–XI
Neumann, Erich (Tel Aviv), XVI–XXV

Otto, Walter F. (Königsberg; 1955, Tübingen), VII, XXIV

Pelliot, Paul (Paris), VII
Pettazzoni, Raffaele (Rome), XIX
Picard, Charles (Paris), VI
Plessner, Helmuth (Göttingen), XX
Portmann, Adolf (Basel), XIV–XXV
Post, Laurens van der (London), XXV
Przyluski, Jean (Paris), V, VI
Puech, Henri-Charles (Paris), IV, XX
Pulver, Max (Zurich), VIII–XI, XIII

Quispel, Gilles (Leiden; 1951, Utrecht), XV, XVI, XVIII, XX–XXII
Radin, Paul (Berkeley), XVII–XIX
Rahner, Hugo (Sion; 1945, Innsbruck), X–XIII, XV, XVI
Read, Herbert (London), XXI, XXV
Reinhardt, Karl (Frankfort on the Main), XXV
Rhys Davids, Mrs. (London), I–IV
Rousselle, Erwin (Frankfort on the Main), I–III

Schmidt, Karl Ludwig (Basel), XIII–XV, XVIII
Schmitt, Paul (Lucerne), X–XIV, XVIII
Scholem, Gershom G. (Jerusalem), XVII, XIX, XXI, XXII, XXIV, XXV
Schrödinger, Erwin (Dublin), XIV
Speiser, Andreas (Zurich; 1945, Basel), V, VIII, XII–XIV
Strauss-Kloebe, Sigrid (Munich), II
Suzuki, Daisetz (Enkakuji, Kamakura, Japan; 1954, New York), XXII, XXIII

Thurnwald, Richard (Berlin), VII
Tillich, Paul (New York), XXIII
Tucci, Giuseppe (Rome), XXII

Virolleaud, Charles (Paris), VI, VII, X
Vysheslawzeff, Boris (Paris), IV

Weyl, Hermann (Princeton), XVI
White, Victor (Oxford), XV
Whyte, Lancelot Law (London), XX, XXI, XXIII
Wilhelm, Hellmut (Seattle), XX, XXV
Wili, Walter (Bern), X–XIII

Yatiswarananda, Swami (Ramakrishna-Vivekenanda Mission), II

Zimmer, Heinrich (Heidelberg; 1939, Oxford), I, II, VI, VII

ABBREVIATIONS

ANCL	Ante-Nicene Christian Library. Edinburgh.
A.S.B.G.	Alan S. B. Glover (translator).
Baynes/Wilhelm	*The I Ching, or Book of Changes.* The Richard Wilhelm translation from German, translated into English by Cary F. Baynes. New York and London, 1950. 2 vols.
CSEL	*Corpus Scriptorum Ecclesiasticorum Latinorum.* Vienna, 1866–.
EJ	*Eranos-Jahrbuch.* Zurich.
GCS	*Die griechischen christlichen Schriftsteller,* ed. O. Stählin. Berlin, 1905–36. 4 vols.
Hastings, *ERE*	James Hastings, ed. *Encyclopaedia of Religion and Ethics.* Edinburgh and New York, 1908–27.
James, *ANT*	M. R. James, tr. *The Apocryphal New Testament.* Oxford, 1924.
LCL	Loeb Classical Library. Cambridge, Mass. (orig. New York) and London.
Migne, *PG* and *PL*	J. P. Migne, ed. *Patrologiae cursus completus.* *PG* = Greek Series. Paris, 1857–66. 166 vols. *PL* = Latin Series. Paris, 1844–64. 221 vols.
PEY	Papers from the Eranos Yearbooks (the present series).

INDEX

INDEX

Roman numerals refer to plates.

INDEX

INDEX

C

D

E

F

G

H

L

M

N

Q

R

T

U

V

X

Y